THE EXPLANAT
THE HOLY GOSPEL
ACCORDING TO LUKE

by Blessed Theophylact,
Archbishop of Ochrid and Bulgaria

Translated from the original Greek
by Fr. Christopher Stade

Volume 3 in the series:
**Blessed Theophylact's Explanation
of the New Testament**

Chrysostom Press
St. Herman of Alaska Brotherhood
2020

St. Herman of Alaska Brotherhood
P.O. Box 70
Platina, California, U.S.A.

website: www.sainthermanmonastery.com
email: stherman@stherman.com

Library of Congress Catalog Card No. 93-174571

Perfectbound: ISBN 0-9635183-5-6

1st printing 1997
2nd printing 2000
3rd printing 2004
4th printing 2007
5th printing 2016
6th printing 2020

Contents

Contents

Concerning Jesus, when He was led to the mountain
by the Jews, and passed through their midst.
Concerning the man with the demonic spirit.
Concerning Peter's mother-in-law.
Concerning those healed of various diseases.

Concerning the catch of fish.
Concerning the leper. Concerning the paralytic.
Concerning Levi the publican.
Concerning the Lord when He ate with publicans.
Why did John's disciples fast, and Christ's did not?

Concerning Christ's disciples who plucked the heads of grain
on the sabbath.
Concerning the man with the withered hand.
Concerning the choosing of the apostles.
Concerning the beatitudes. On loving one's enemies.
On not quarreling with one's neighbor.
On not judging one's neighbor.

Concerning the centurion.
Concerning the widow's son.
Concerning those sent by John.
Concerning the woman who anointed the Lord with myrrh.

Concerning the parable of the sower.
Concerning the mother, and brothers of the Lord, when they
wished to see Him.
Concerning the rebuking of the waters.
Concerning the legion of demons.
Concerning the daughter of the ruler of the synagogue.
Concerning the woman with an issue of blood.

Contents

Contents

Contents

Contents

Concerning Christ's arrest.
Concerning Jesus when He was led away to the high priest.

How the Saviour was led away to Pilate.
How He was mocked by Herod.
Concerning the women who bewailed Him.
Concerning the crucifixion of Christ.
Concerning the repentant thief.
Concerning the burial of Christ.

Concerning the women who looked at the tomb.
Concerning Peter who ran to the tomb.
Concerning Cleopas.
Concerning the appearance of Jesus.
Concerning the Ascension into heaven.

Introduction

The book in hand, *The Explanation of the Holy Gospel According to St. Luke,* is the third volume in our translation of the commentaries by Blessed Theophylact on the books of the New Testament. It follows in design the first two volumes, *The Explanation* of St. Matthew and *The Explanation* of St. Mark.

The translation has been made from the original Greek text of Migne, vol. 123 in the series *Patrologia Graeca.* The English text of the Gospel itself is for the most part that of the King James Version. We have revised that text in a few places to reflect patristic Orthodox interpretation and usage, and to avoid a few Elizabethan English expresions which are at the greatest risk of being unintelligible to the contemporary reader. Quotations from the Old Testament used by Bl. Theophylact in his *Explanation* are taken from Sir Lancelot Brenton's translation of the Septuagint,[1] except that quotations from the Psalms are taken from the *Psalter According to the Seventy.*[2] Square brackets within the text of the Explanation indicate a clarifying word or phrase added by the translator; text within parentheses is always Bl. Theophylact himself.

The author of this remarkable commentary is an eleventh century Byzantine churchman of great learning and piety, who served in Constantinople as a royal tutor, archdeacon, renowned preacher of the Gospel, and assistant to the Patriarch. About the year 1090 A.D. he obediently, though with reluctance, left behind this period of his life to travel to the distant city of Ochrid, the capital of the Bulgarian kingdom, to serve as Archbishop and chief hierarch of the Bulgarian Church. It was there, in the southwestern Balkans, that he wrote these commentaries, restating in simple and profound language that which has always and everywhere been taught by the fathers of the Church concerning the meaning of the Holy Gospel and Epistles. A fuller account of Bl. Theophylact's life, his writings, and his influence in both the East and the West, is to be found in the Introduction to the first volume of this series, *The Explanation* of St. Matthew's Gospel.

---

[1]*The Septuagint with Apocrypha: Greek and English,* Sir Lancelot C. L. Brenton, Samuel Bagster and Sons, London, 1851, reprinted, Zondervan Publishing House, Grand Rapids, Michigan, (1988).

[2]*The Psalter According to the Seventy,* Holy Transfiguration Monastery, Boston, Massachusetts, 1987.

The Life of the Evangelist Luke
According to Sophronius

Luke, a physician of Antioch, was not unacquainted with Greek culture, as is shown by his writings. He was a companion of the Apostle Paul and followed him in all his journeys to foreign lands. Luke wrote the Gospel to which Paul himself refers when he says, *And we have sent with him the brother, whose praise is in the Gospel throughout all the churches.*[3] And in his letter to the Colossians he says, *Luke, the beloved physician, greets you.*[4] And to Timothy he says, *Only Luke is with me.*[5] Luke wrote another excellent book entitled The Acts of the Apostles, a history which ends with Paul's two-year stay in Rome, that is, in the fourth year of Nero's reign. This leads us to believe that The Acts of the Apostles was written in Rome. The tale of the journey of Paul and Thecla, and every other fable, such as the baptism of the lion, should not be counted among the canonical Scriptures. For it is not possible that he who was inseparable from the Apostle should not have known of this act among all his other acts. Tertullian also mentions a certain elder in Asia at that time, a companion of the Apostle Paul, who, when it was proven in the presence of John that he was the author of this book, confessed that he had written it out of love for Paul. Some say that this is why Luke does not mention himself as the author. Whenever Paul says in his own Epistles, *according to my Gospel,*[6] it is clear that he means the Gospel written by Luke. But Luke learned the Gospel not only from the Apostle Paul, who was not with the Lord in the body at that time, but from the other apostles as well. He himself clearly states this at the beginning of his work, saying, *even as they were handed down to us by those who from the beginning were eyewitnesses.* Therefore he wrote the Gospel as he had heard it. But he wrote The Acts based on what he himself had experienced. Luke's relics were taken up and carried to Constantinople, together with the relics of the Apostle Andrew, in the twentieth year of the reign of Constantius.

---

[3] II Cor. 8:18

[4] Col. 4:14

[5] II Tim. 4:11

[6] Rom. 2:16, etc.

Life of the Evangelist Luke
from the *Synopsis* of the Martyr Dorotheus, Bishop of Tyre

Luke the Evangelist was a native of Antioch and a physician by profession. He wrote the Gospel by the command of the Apostle Peter, and The Acts of the Apostles by the command of the Apostle Paul. He travelled with the apostles, and especially with Paul, who mentions him in his Epistle, saying, *Luke, the beloved physician, greets you.*[7] He died in Ephesus and was buried there. His relics were later transferred to the city of Constantinople, together with those of the Apostles Andrew and Timothy, during the time of the Emperor Constantius, son of Constantine the Great.

---

[7] Col. 4:14

Preface by Blessed Theophylact

The divine Luke, an Antiochian and a physician, had a great knowledge of natural philosophy; but he was also much practiced in Hebrew learning. He lived in Jerusalem at the time when our Lord was teaching, so that some say that he himself became one of the seventy apostles, and together with Cleopas, met the Lord after He rose from the dead. After the Lord ascended, and Paul believed, Luke became a close companion and follower of Paul. He wrote his Gospel with great accuracy, as his preface makes clear. He wrote the Gospel fifteen years after the Lord's Ascension. He writes it to a certain Theophilus, a senator and perhaps a magistrate as well, calling him *most excellent.* Magistrates and governors are addressed in this fashion, as when Paul said to the governor Festus, *O most excellent Festus.*[8] Everyone who loves God and exercises dominion over his passions is a *Theophilus* and *most excellent,* and it is he who is truly worthy to hear the Gospel.

---

[8] Acts 26:25. The single Greek word *kratiste,* translated in Acts 26:25 by the KJV as *O most noble,* is the same word used in Luke 1:3 to address Theophilus, but rendered in this case by the KJV as *O most excellent.* It is the superlative form of an adjective derived from the noun *kratos,* meaning *might* or *dominion.* In the next line Bl. Theophylact makes a play on the meaning of this word, as well as on the meaning of the name Theophilus, *he who loves God.*

THE EXPLANATION

by

BLESSED THEOPHYLACT

of

THE HOLY GOSPEL

ACCORDING TO

ST. LUKE

ΙΞΣ   Ο   ΧΣ
ω̄   Ν

ГДЬ ВСЕДЕ   ЖИТЕЛЬ

PAINTED BY BISHOP ALYPY – CHICAGO, ILLINOIS 1983

CHAPTER ONE

The preface of St. Luke to his Gospel.
Concerning the parents of John the Baptist, and his birth.
Concerning the angel's salutation to Mary.
Concerning Mary's salutation to Elizabeth.

1-4. Forasmuch as many have attempted to set forth in order an account of those things which are confidently believed among us, even as they were handed down to us by those who from the beginning were eyewitnesses and ministers of the word, it seemed good to me also, having carefully searched out all these things from the beginning, to write them in order unto thee, most excellent Theophilus, that thou mightest better know the certainty of those things, wherein thou hast been instructed. Who were these *many* who *attempted to set forth in order an account*? The false apostles. For there were many who wrote so-called "gospels," for example, "The gospel according to the Egyptians," and "The gospel of the twelve." But these false apostles only attempted to set forth; they did not finish and perfect their narratives because they began without divine grace. Luke therefore says well that *many have attempted.* Only a few, such as Matthew and Mark, not only attempted to set forth, but finished and perfected their narrative. For they had the Holy Spirit, Which perfects. He speaks of *things which are confidently believed.* These things concerning Christ's life are not simply facts heard from another, but rather are received by tradition, in truth, with sure faith, and with all confidence. Tell us, Luke, how can these things be so confidently believed? Because *they were handed down to us by those who from the beginning were eyewitnesses and ministers of the word.* From this it is clear that Luke was not a disciple from the beginning, but at a later time. Others were disciples from the beginning, like those with Peter and the sons of Zebedee, and it is they who handed down to Luke those things which he himself had not seen or heard. What does it mean, *that thou mightest better know the certainty of those things, wherein thou hast been instructed?* This can be understood in two ways. The Evangelist is saying, "Formerly, O Theophilus, I instructed you by word of mouth; but now I pass on the Gospel to you in writing in order to fix those things in your memory so that you do not forget what was passed on to you by word of mouth." Another meaning is this: when

someone tells us something by word of mouth, we often suspect that
perhaps he is inaccurate. But if he then confirms it in writing, we believe,
since he would not have put it in writing unless he was convinced that he
was speaking the truth. So, in the same vein, the Evangelist is saying,
"For this reason have I written this Gospel for you, that you might have
greater assurance of those things in which you have been instructed by
word of mouth, believing me now all the more, because I am so
confident of what I taught by word of mouth that I now set them forth in
writing." Take note of the word *know*. Luke did not say, "that thou
mightest know [*gnōs*]," but *that thou mightest better know* [*epignōs*], that
is, receive even greater knowledge the second time, and have boldness
and certainty that I speak the truth.

**5. There was in the days of Herod, the king of Judea, a certain
priest named Zacharias, of the course of Abia: and his wife was of
the daughters of Aaron, and her name was Elizabeth.** He mentions
Herod the king, first of all, because he was following the form used by
the prophet, who began in this same manner, saying for instance, *There
was in the days of Jotham and Ahaz and Hezekiah.*[1] Moreover, because
he is about to speak about Christ, he mentions Herod to show that Christ
truly came during the time of Herod. For this Herod was king when the
line of the kings of Judah had failed, according to the prophecy of
Jacob,[2] and thus the coming of the Messiah is indicated. And something
more is accomplished by mentioning Herod. By fixing the time, he shows
the truth of the Gospel. He enables those who so desire to investigate for
themselves, and from the time given, to discover the truth of the Gospel.
He begins with Zacharias and the birth of John, and rightly so. For he is
about to speak of the birth of Christ, and since John was the Forerunner
of Christ, it is fitting that he recount the birth of John before the birth of
Christ. Nor is the birth of John without miracles. Since a Virgin was
about to give birth, the grace of God foreordained that an old woman
should give birth, not according to the law of nature, but still by a man.
What does this mean, *of the course of Abia*? Some understand it thus:
there were two priests who each served in turn, one named Abia, and the

---

[1] See Hos. 1:1.

[2] Gen. 49:10

other, Zacharias. After Abia had finished serving his course as priest, then Zacharias served. But it does not appear to have been this way. When Solomon finished building the temple, he also established *courses*,[3] that is, [assignments of those who would serve each] week.[4] For one week he appointed, perhaps, the sons of Kore, and for the next week, the sons of Asaph, and the next week, the sons of Abia, and so forth. Therefore, *Zacharias, of the course of Abia,* ought to be interpreted thus: Zacharias was of the week of service assigned to Abia.[5] Zacharias did not perform his priestly service after the week in which Abia served, for then Luke would have said that Zacharias was "after" the course of Abia; instead he says that Zacharias was *of the course of Abia,* showing that he belonged to Abia's division of priests appointed to serve for a week. Luke says, *his wife was of the daughters of Aaron,* wanting to show that John was descended on both sides from the priestly tribe, in accordance with the law, which commands that a man marry a wife of none other than his own tribe. *Elizabeth* means *God's rest,* and *Zacharias* means *the memory of the Lord.*

6. And they were both righteous in the sight of God. Many are *righteous,* not in the sight of God, but only in appearance, in the sight of men. But these were righteous before God. **Walking in all the commandments and judgments of the law blameless.** The *commandments* are, for example, *Thou shalt not commit adultery. Thou shalt not steal.* The *judgments* are, for example, *He that revileth his father or his mother shall surely die.*[6] For this is right and just. Know then that a *commandment* can also be called a *judgment,* because it makes man righteous, and because it is indeed the judgment of God.[7] On the day when God will judge us, He will hold the commandments like a written judgment [either

---

[3] *Ephēmeria, course,* means literally, [*service*] *for a day.*

[4] I Chron. 23:6 and 28:13.

[5] I Chron. 24:10

[6] Ex. 21:16

[7] The Greek word *entolē,* translated in the text as *commandment,* implies that which has been expressly ordered by the mouth of authority. By contrast, the Greek word *dikaiōma,* translated here as *judgement,* refers to that which has been judged to be right [*dikaios*] and therefore has the force of law.

for or against us]. For He says, *If I had not come and spoken unto them, they had not had sin.*[8] And again, *The word which I have spoken, the same shall judge him on the last day.*[9] Why does Luke add the word *blameless* to the text, *walking in all the commandments?* Listen: many walk in the law of God, but they do so in order to be seen by men. Such as these are not blameless. But Zacharias kept the commandments, and kept them blamelessly, not doing them to please men.

7. And they had no child, because Elizabeth was barren, and they were both now advanced in years. Righteous women, and the wives of righteous men, were often childless. You, O reader, should learn from this that the law did not command that one bear many offspring, but rather that one bear much spiritual fruit. Both of them were advanced, in body and also in spirit. They had matured and progressed in soul, making ascents in their hearts,[10] keeping their lives in the day, not in the night, as those who walk honestly in the light.[11]

8-10. And it came to pass, that while he executeth the priest's office before God in the order of his course, according to the custom of the priest's office, his lot was to burn incense when he went into the temple of the Lord. And the whole multitude of the people were praying outside at the time of incense. Only the pure serve as priests *before God,* Who turns His face away from those who are not pure. When was it his lot to burn incense? It was certainly at the time of Atonement, when the high priest alone entered the Holy of Holies. From this we learn that just as this high priest received offspring when he entered the Holy of Holies, so too the Lord Jesus, in truth the only and the great High Priest, when He entered the Holy of Holies, that is, when He ascended and entered into heaven in the flesh, received the fruit of His visitation among us in the flesh, namely, our adoption as sons and our salvation.

---

[8] Jn. 15:22

[9] Jn. 12:48

[10] See Ps. 83:6.

[11] See Rom. 13:13.

11. And there appeared unto him an angel of the Lord standing on the right side of the altar of incense. An angel does not appear to everyone, but only to the pure of heart, such as Zacharias. The Evangelist says, *the altar of incense,* because there was another altar, the altar of whole burnt offerings.

12-14. And when Zacharias saw him, he was troubled, and fear fell upon him. But the angel said unto him, Fear not, Zacharias: for thy prayer is heard; and thy wife Elizabeth shall bear thee a son, and thou shalt call his name John. And thou shalt have joy and gladness; and many shall rejoice at his birth. Zacharias was troubled, for the sight of something extraordinary is troubling even to the saints. But the angel dispels the fear. There is always this sign which distinguishes between visions that are from God and visions that are from demons: if the mind at first is troubled, but ends by being calm after the fear has been swiftly dispelled, indeed it is a divine vision. But if the fear and disquietude increase more and more, then the vision is demonic. What was the prayer of Zacharias which caused the angel to say, *thy prayer is heard, and thy wife Elizabeth shall bear thee a son?* Surely Zacharias was not praying for a son. Was he not praying for the sins of the people?[12] Some say, therefore, that on account of his prayer for the sins of the people, he would beget a son who would cry out, *Behold the Lamb of God, Which taketh away the sin of the world.*[13] Thus it is altogether fitting that the angel says to him, *thy prayer is heard,* meaning, ''thy prayer for the forgiveness of the sins of the people. Thou shalt beget a son through whom there will be forgiveness of sins.'' But others understand it this way: *''Thy prayer is heard,* O Zacharias, and God has forgiven the sins of the people.'' Then, as if Zacharias had asked, ''How can we know this is so?'' the angel says to him, ''I give thee this sign, that Elizabeth shall bear thee a son. By Elizabeth's childbearing thou shalt believe that the sins of the people have been forgiven.''

15-17. For he shall be great in the sight of the Lord, and shall drink neither wine nor strong drink; and he shall be filled with the

---

[12] See Heb. 9:7.

[13] Jn. 1:29

Holy Spirit, even from his mother's womb. And many of the children of Israel shall he turn to the Lord their God. And he shall go before Him in the spirit and power of Elijah, to turn the hearts of the fathers to the children, and the disobedient to the wisdom of the righteous; to prepare for the Lord a people made ready. The angel promises that John will be truly great, that is, great *in the sight of the Lord.* For there are many who are called great in the sight of men, but are not so in the sight of God. Such are the hypocrites. John was great in soul, unlike those easily offended ones who are little in soul. No one who is great is offended, but only those who are little in soul and have little faith. This is why the Lord says, *Whoso shall offend one of these little ones.*[14] Just as the parents of John were righteous in the sight of the Lord, so their child was great in the sight of the Lord. *Strong drink [sikera]* is any intoxicating drink that is not of the vine. While yet in his mother's womb he was filled with the Holy Spirit, when the mother of the Lord came to Elizabeth and *the babe leaped in her womb,* rejoicing at the Lord's coming. And he turned *the hearts of the fathers to the children,* meaning, he turned the hearts of the Hebrews to the apostles. *The fathers* were the Jews, and their *children* were the apostles. Therefore he turned the hearts of the Jews to the apostles, teaching them of Christ, and bearing witness to Him. By bearing witness to Christ, a teacher makes his own disciples ready for faith. John did turn the hearts of *many,* but not of all. But the Lord enlightened all. John went before Christ *in the spirit* of Elijah, meaning, just as grace was at work in Elijah, so too was grace at work in John. For Elijah is the forerunner of the second coming of Christ, while John is the Forerunner of the first coming. And John went before Him *in the power* of Elijah, for the advents of both Elijah and John have the same power, that is, they both lead together to Christ. In another sense John went *in the spirit and power of Elijah,* in that John too was a desert dweller, living without any excess, and he rebuked and reproved as did Elijah. And he turned the disobedient Jews *to the wisdom of the righteous,* that is, to the teaching of the apostles. For the wisdom of the apostles was the grace of the Spirit working in them and governing them. He *prepared for the Lord,* that is, for Christ, *a people made ready* to receive the preaching. For example, when a prophet

---

[14] Mt. 18:5

would come preaching, not all would believe, but only those who had made themselves ready to receive that preaching. It is like a man who enters a house by night. Not every one in the house welcomes him, but only those who are awake and have been expecting him and are prepared to welcome him. Likewise John prepared a people for the Lord, not from among the disobedient, but rather of those who had made themselves ready to welcome the Christ.

18-20. And Zacharias said unto the angel, Whereby shall I know this? For I am an old man, and my wife is far advanced in years. And the angel answering said unto him, I am Gabriel, who stands in the presence of God; and I am sent to speak unto thee, and to bring unto thee these good tidings. And, behold, thou shalt be in silence, and not able to speak, until the day that these things shall come to pass, because thou believest not my words, which shall be fulfilled in their season. Though Zacharias was righteous and holy, when he considered this awesome miracle of childbearing, he could not easily believe. This is why the angel reveals himself, saying, *"I am Gabriel, who stand in the presence of God,* not a deceiving demon but an angel of God. Since you do not believe, you shall be deaf and unable to speak."* It was fitting that Zacharias suffered these two things, the inability either to hear or to speak. For not giving heed, he was chastened with deafness; and for speaking back, he was chastened with muteness. But Zacharias also foreshadowed what would happen with the Jews. Although he was old and barren of fruit and did not believe, Zacharias begat a son greater than all the prophets. Likewise the assembly and the priesthood of the Jews had grown old, becoming fruitless, unbelieving, and disobedient; nevertheless this people gave birth in the flesh to God the Word, the Master of the prophets. And when Christ was born, those who before had been disobedient came to believe and to confess with a strong voice.

21-23. And the people waited for Zacharias, and marvelled that he tarried so long in the temple. And when he came out, he could not speak unto them: and they perceived that he had seen a vision in the temple: for he beckoned unto them, and remained speechless. And it came to pass, that, as soon as the days of his serving were accomplished, he departed to his own house. Do you see how the Jews were waiting expectantly until the high priest should come out of the temple? But we Christians, if we do not leave church almost as soon as we have entered it, think that we are suffering terribly. Zacharias beckoned to the people who perhaps were asking why he was silent, and he showed them with a gesture that he could not speak. See that he did not depart to his house until the days of his service were completed, but he remained in the temple. The *hill country,* [v. 39,] where Zacharias lived, was indeed some distance away from Jerusalem, but even if the priest had his house in Jerusalem, he was not permitted to leave the court of the temple during the time of his appointed service. But alas! how we neglect our service to God! The inability of Zacharias to speak and his wordless signals to the people foreshadow the way of life of those Jews who are without the Word. Having slain the Word, they have no word to give in answer for what they do and say, and if you ask them something concerning the prophecies of Christ, they are speechless and unable to give you either word or answer.

24-25. And after those days his wife Elizabeth conceived, and hid herself five months, saying, Thus hath the Lord dealt with me in the days wherein He looked on me, to take away my reproach among men. Elizabeth was chaste and modest, and she hid herself because she had conceived in her old age. She hid herself for five months, until Mary also had conceived. But when Mary too had conceived, and Elizabeth's babe had leaped in her womb, she no longer hid herself, but became more bold as the mother of such a child, which even before its birth had been honored with the rank of prophet.

26-30. And in the sixth month the angel Gabriel was sent from God unto a city of Galilee, named Nazareth, to a virgin betrothed to a man whose name was Joseph, of the house of David; and the virgin's name was Mary. And the angel came in unto her, and said, Rejoice, thou who art full of grace, the Lord is with thee. Blessed art thou among women. And when she saw him, she was troubled at his saying, and cast in her mind what manner of salutation this should be. And the angel said unto her, Fear not, Mary: for thou hast found favour with God. *The sixth month* means the sixth month after John's conception. The Evangelist says that the virgin was *betrothed to a man of the house of David,* to show that she too was descended from the tribe and lineage of David.[15] For it was the law that husband and wife should be of the same tribe and the same lineage. Because the Lord had once said to Eve, *In sorrow thou shalt bring forth children,*[16] that sorrow is now removed by the joy which the angel offers to the woman, saying to her, *Rejoice, thou who art full of grace.* Since Eve had been cursed, now Mary hears herself *blessed.* She considered in her mind what sort of salutation this might be: surely not an unseemly and provocative greeting as from a forward man to a young maiden? Or was it perhaps a divine salutation, since God was mentioned together with the greeting, *The Lord is with thee.* First the angel calms the fear in her heart, so that she might hear the divine decision when she was peaceful and untroubled. While she was troubled, she would not be able to hear and understand clearly the things that would take place. When the angel said to her, *Thou who art full of grace,* it is as if he were saying, "Thou hast found grace and favor in the sight of God, and thou art pleasing to God." This is not out of the ordinary, for there were many other women who had found favor with God. But what the angel says next has never before been heard:

31-33. And, behold, thou shalt conceive in thy womb, and bring forth a son, and shalt call His name JESUS. He shall be great, and shall be called the Son of the Most High: and the Lord God shall give unto Him the throne of His father David: and He shall reign over the house of Jacob for ever; and of His kingdom there shall be no end. *Behold, thou shalt conceive*—this is extraordinary, something of which no other virgin has been deemed worthy. The angel said, *in thy womb,* to show that the Lord actually took flesh from the very womb of the Virgin. It was right that He Who came for the salvation of our race was called *Jesus.* The name written in the Greek language, *Iēsous,* means *salvation from God.* Therefore, *Jesus,* being interpreted, is *Saviour,* for the word *Iaō* means *salvation. He shall be great, and shall be called the Son of the Most High.* John also was great, but he was not the Son of the Most High. But the Saviour was great in His teaching, and was the Son of the Most High, as shown by the authority with which He taught and the marvelous wonders which He worked. He Who appears as a man is

---

[15] See Vol. 1, *The Explanation* of St. Matthew, p. 17.

[16] Gen. 3:17

called the Son of the Most High; being of one hypostasis, the human son of the Virgin is in truth the Son of the Most High. Even before the ages the Word was the Son of the Most High, although He was not called or known as such. But when He became incarnate and appeared in the flesh, then He was called the Son of the Most High, Who has appeared and works wonders. When you hear *the throne of David,* do not understand this to mean a kingdom perceivable by the senses, but instead a divine kingship which He wields over all the nations through the divine proclamation of the Gospel. *The house of Jacob* means those of the Jews who believed; but indeed it also means those of the other nations who believed. In truth both the believing Jews and the believing Gentiles are *Jacob* [before he encountered God] and *Israel* [the same man after he saw God].[17] What does it mean, to sit on the throne of David? Listen: David was the smallest among his brothers,[18] and the Lord also was belittled and slandered as an eater and drinker and a son of a carpenter,[19] and was held in dishonor by His brothers, the sons of Joseph. *For neither did His brethren believe in Him,* the Gospel says.[20] David was persecuted by Saul for doing good,[21] and when the Lord worked wonders, He was slandered and stoned.[22] David conquered and reigned through meekness, and the Lord, through meekness, accepted the Cross and ruled as King. Do you see what it means, to sit on the throne of David? Just as David received a physical kingdom, so too the Lord receives a spiritual kingdom, which shall have no end. There shall be no end to the kingdom of Christ, that is, no end to the knowledge of God or to Christianity. For when we are persecuted, we shine with the grace of Christ.

34-35. Then said Mary unto the angel, How shall this be, seeing I know not a man? And the angel answered and said unto her, The Holy Spirit shall come upon thee, and the power of the Most High shall overshadow thee: therefore also that Holy Thing Which is

---

[17] Gen. 32:28-30.

[18] See Ps. [151]:1.

[19] Mt. 11:19, 13:55; Mk. 6:3.

[20] Jn. 7:5

[21] See I Kings 18-24.

[22] Jn. 10:31

begotten of thee shall be called the Son of God. It was not because the Virgin did not believe that she said, *How shall this be?* Rather, it was because she was wise and astute, and sought to understand the manner in which this would take place. For nothing like this had ever happened before, nor would it again. This is why the angel forgives her, and does not chastise her as he did Zacharias, but instead explains to her how it would come about. It was fitting that Zacharias was chastised, for he knew many examples of barren women who had given birth. But for the Virgin, there was no precedent. *The Holy Spirit,* he says, *shall come upon thee,* rendering thy womb fertile, and creating flesh for the Word Which is one in essence with the Father. *The power of the Most High,* that is, the Son of God, for Christ is the power of God,[23] *shall overshadow thee,* encompassing thee about from all sides. Just as the hen overshadows her chicks, taking them all in under her wings, so too the power of God completely encompassed the Virgin. This is what it means to *overshadow.* Someone else perhaps will say that just as a painter first shadows in the image and then completes it with color, likewise the Lord, in creating flesh for Himself and fashioning the icon of man, first drew the shadow of the image in the womb of the Virgin, incorporating flesh from the blood of the Ever Virgin, and then little by little gave it form. But this is unclear. Some say that when the Lord *overshadowed* the Virgin in her womb, immediately there was a completed infant. But others do not accept this. Listen to what the angel says: *Therefore also that Holy Thing Which is begotten of thee,*[24] in other words, that Holy Thing Which is growing within your womb in extraordinary manner, and does not at once exist in completed form. Here the mouth of Nestorius is sealed. For that man said that the Son of God did not take flesh by dwelling in the womb of the Virgin, but that a mere man was born of Mary, and only later was this man "accompanied" by God. Let Nestorius hear, therefore, that *that Holy Thing* Which is being begotten in the womb is the Son of God. That

---

[23] I Cor. 1:24

[24] *To gennōmenon,* here translated as *Which is begotten,* is the present passive participle of the verb *gennaō,* which means "to beget, to bear, to bring forth." The single Greek word encompasses the entire nine month process from conception to giving birth. The interpretation which Blessed Theophylact provides depends upon the force of the Greek present passive participle, which could be more literally expressed in English by the phrase "that Holy Thing Which is being begotten," or "Which is being brought forth."

which was carried in the womb and the Son of God are not two separate entities, but one and the same, the Son of the Virgin and the Son of God. See how the angel revealed the Holy Trinity by naming the Holy Spirit, the *Power* which is the Son, and the *Most High* which is the Father.

36-38. And, behold, thy kinswoman Elizabeth, she hath also conceived a son in her old age: and this is the sixth month with her who was called barren. For with God nothing shall be impossible. And Mary said, Behold the handmaid of the Lord; be it unto me according to thy word. And the angel departed from her. One might wonder how Elizabeth could be a relative of the Virgin since the Virgin was of the tribe of Judah, while Elizabeth was one *of the daughters of Aaron,* of the tribe of Levi. The law commanded that marriage take place within the same tribe, with the result that kinsfolk are of the same tribe as well. It might be said that there was a confusion of the tribes during the time of the Babylonian captivity. But a better explanation is this: Aaron married a woman named Elizabeth, who was the daughter of Aminidab who was of the tribe of Judah.[25] Do you see that from the beginning, through Aaron, the Theotokos was a kinswoman of Elizabeth? Since the wife of Aaron was of the tribe of Judah, as was the Theotokos, and Elizabeth was from the daughters of Aaron, Elizabeth is rightly said to be a kinswoman of the Theotokos. This is because Elizabeth's foremother, the wife of Aaron, was of the tribe of Judah. Consider also the parallel of this kinship: the wife of Aaron was Elizabeth, and her descendant, the wife of Zacharias, was also Elizabeth. But let us hear what the Virgin says. *Behold the handmaid of the Lord; be it unto me according to thy word.* I am a writer's tablet; let the Writer write upon it whatever He wishes. Let the Lord do as He wills. [From this we can see] that what she said earlier, *How shall this be?* was not spoken out of disbelief, but out of the desire to understand how it would occur. If she had not believed, she would not have said, *Behold the handmaid of the Lord; be it unto me according to thy word.* Learn that *Gabriel* means *man-God, Mary* means *mistress,* and *Nazareth* means *sanctification.* It is fitting that when God was about to become man, Gabriel, *man-God,* was sent. And the salutation of Mary occurred in a holy place, in Nazareth.

---

[25] Ex. 6:23

Where God is, there is nothing unholy.

39-42. And Mary arose in those days, and went into the hill country with haste, into a city of Judah; and entered into the house of Zacharias, and saluted Elizabeth. And it came to pass, that, when Elizabeth heard the salutation of Mary, the babe leaped in her womb; and Elizabeth was filled with the Holy Spirit: and she spake out with a loud voice, and said, Blessed art thou among women, and blessed is the fruit of thy womb. When the Virgin heard from the angel that Elizabeth had conceived, she ran to her, not only rejoicing at the good fortune of her relative, but also, being most wise, because she wanted to make completely sure that the one who had appeared to her had spoken the truth, and thus be free of any doubt concerning herself. Although she was certain, she was afraid that she might be in a state of delusion and prelest. It was not that she disbelieved, but that she wanted to understand the matter more clearly. Zacharias lived in *the hill country,* and this is why she ran there. John, having received a gift of grace far exceeding what others had received, leaps in the womb of his mother, thus showing that he is greater than the prophets. For they prophesied after they themselves were born, but he was deemed worthy of such grace that he prophesied while yet in his mother's womb. Look: the Virgin salutes Elizabeth, that is, greets her. But the voice of the Virgin is here the voice of God Who is taking on flesh within her. This is why the voice of salutation also gladdens the Forerunner in the womb, and causes him to prophesy. The words which Elizabeth speaks prophetically to Mary are not her own words, but are the words of the babe within her who speaks through the mouth of Elizabeth, just as the Son of God in the womb speaks through the mouth of Mary. For the babe leaped within the womb, and then Elizabeth was filled with the Holy Spirit. If the babe had not leaped, then Elizabeth would not have prophesied. In the same way it is said that prophets first undergo ecstasy and divine rapture, and then begin to prophesy, so too John first leaped, moved by this same excitation, and then prophesied through the mouth of his mother. What did he prophesy? *Blessed art thou among women.* And then, since many holy women have given birth to profane offspring, as when Rebecca bore Esau, he added, *and blessed is the fruit of thy womb.* But it can also be understood in another way. *Blessed art thou among women.* And then, as if someone had asked, "Why?" he gives the answer, "For *blessed is the* *fruit of thy womb,''* that is, the fruit of thy womb is God, and God alone is blessed, as David says, *Blessed is He that cometh.*[26] In Scripture, the conjunction "and" is commonly used instead of "for". For example, *Give us help from affliction, and vain is the salvation of man,''* meaning, "for vain is the salvation of men."[27] And again, *Behold, Thou wast angry and we have sinned,* instead of "for we have sinned."[28] He says that the Lord is the fruit of the womb of the Theotokos, because the conception is without a man. All other children are called the "fruit" of their fathers' [loins], but Christ is the fruit solely of the womb of the Theotokos. She conceived Him without the aid of any man.

43-45. And whence is this to me, that the mother of my Lord should come to me? For, lo, as soon as the voice of thy salutation sounded in mine ears, the babe leaped in my womb for joy. And blessed is she that believed that there shall be a performance of those things which were told her from the Lord. Just as John later tried, out of reverence, to prevent Christ from coming to him to be baptized, saying, *I am not worthy,*[29] so too now John utters the words, through the mouth of his mother, *Whence is this to me, that the mother of my Lord should come to me?* Before she had given birth to the Lord, he names the pregnant woman *the mother.* But with other pregnant women, before they have given birth they ought not to be called "mother", out of fear they might miscarry. With the Virgin, however, there was no such fear. Therefore, even before childbirth, O Mary, thou art *mother* and *blessed,* having believed that there shall be a fulfillment of those things which were spoken to thee from the Lord.

46-50. And Mary said, My soul doth magnify the Lord, and my spirit hath rejoiced in God my Saviour. For He hath regarded the low estate of His handmaiden: for, behold, from henceforth all

---

[26] Ps. 117:25

[27] Ps. 107:13. In the Septuagint the Greek word *kai,* with the literal meaning of 'and', is used. However, "for" appears in the English translation (of Holy Transfiguration Monastery) because the sense requires it, the very point here made by Bl. Theophylact.

[28] Is. 64:5

[29] Mt. 3:11; Mk. 1:7.

generations shall bless me. For the Mighty One hath done to me great things; and Holy is His Name. And His mercy is on them that fear Him from generation to generation. Now that she had certainty, the Virgin glorifies God, ascribing the miracle to Him and not to herself. God, she says, has looked down upon me who am lowly; it is not I who looked up to Him. It is God Who had mercy on me, not I who sought Him out. And from henceforth, not only Elizabeth, but *all generations* of believers *shall bless me.* Why shall they bless me? Because of my virtue? No, but rather because God *hath done to me great things.* She calls God *Mighty* so that no one would disbelieve these words, thinking that God had not the power to do these things. She says that His Name is *Holy,* showing that He Who is most pure was not stained in any way by having been conceived in the womb of a woman, but He remains Holy. His mercy is not only upon me, but upon all those who fear Him. But those unworthy ones who do not fear Him do not benefit from His mercy. By saying that the mercy of God is *from generation to generation,* she shows that those who fear Him receive God's mercy not only in this present generation, that is, in this present age, but also in the generation to come, I mean, in the age without end. Even in this life they receive His mercy a hundredfold, and in the next life, how much more? Notice that first the soul magnifies the Lord, and then the spirit rejoices. He magnifies God who lives in a manner worthy of God. But you, O reader, who are called a Christian, do not do the opposite and belittle the dignity of Christ and the name of Christian by doing what you should not do, but rather magnify Him with magnificent and heavenly deeds. And then your spirit will rejoice as well, that is, the gift of the spirit which you received to enable you to do magnificent deeds, will leap up and increase, and not wane and die out. Understand that Scripture, at a simple level, appears to identify *spirit* [*pneuma*] and *soul* [*psychē*] as one, but strictly speaking it differentiates between them.[30] Scripture calls that man *natural* [*psychikon*] [whose life is motivated by the soul, that is, the life force, and] who

---

[30] *Psychē* in Greek, *anima* in Latin, and *soul* in English, all denote the life force of man and of every living creature. The soul is that which "animates" the body. But man has both soul and spirit. The soul, being the "bridge" between the body and the spirit, may seem indistinguishable from the spirit, but it is not. Bl. Theophylact is here correcting this confusion. A pious and most illuminating discussion of the two separate entities, soul and spirit, is to be found in *The Law of God,* Archpriest Seraphim Slobodskoy, Holy Trinity Monastery, Jordanville, New York, 1993, pp. 100-103.

lives according to his physical nature, and is governed only by human thoughts as, for example, when he is hungry, or thirsty, or hates his enemy, and, in short, imagines nothing loftier that his own nature. But Scripture names that man *spiritual* [*pneumatikon*] who transcends the laws of his human nature, and thinks nothing that is merely human.[31] This is the difference in Scripture between the soul and the spirit. Perhaps physicians judge these things differently; our concern is Scripture. Let the physicians attend to their own work.

51-56. He hath showed strength with His arm; He hath scattered the proud in the imagination of their hearts. He hath put down the mighty from their seats, and exalted them of low degree. He hath filled the hungry with good things, and the rich He hath sent empty away. He hath holpen His servant Israel, in remembrance of His mercy; as He spake to our fathers, to Abraham, and to His seed for ever. And Mary abode with her about three months, and returned to her own house. The *arm* of the Father is the Son. Therefore God the Father, with His Son, hath showed strength and power over the order of nature. For when the Son took flesh, nature was overthrown, a Virgin gave birth, God became man, and man became God. And the Lord has *scattered the proud* demons, casting them out of the souls of men, sending some into the abyss and others into the swine. This can also be understood to refer to the unbelieving Jews, whom the Lord scattered into every land, where they are still scattered today. *He hath put down the mighty from their seats,* meaning, the demons who were tyrannizing mankind and using human souls as the seats upon which they rested. The Pharisees were also *mighty.* They plundered from the poor, and they occupied a seat, the chair of teaching, but they have been deposed. And God has exalted the lowly, meaning either those whom sin had brought low, or, the Gentiles. He has exalted them, granting them the gift of adoption as sons. And the Gentiles were also *the hungry,* for they had neither the Scriptures, the law, nor the commandments. He filled them with the good things of the Scriptures; but the unbelieving Jews, who were rich in the law and in the commandments, He has sent away from

---

[31] See, for example, I Cor. 2:14-15, where the Apostle Paul contrasts *the natural man* [*psychikos anthrōpos*] with *the spiritual man* [*pneumatikos anthrōpos*].

both the heavenly and the earthly Jerusalem, empty of every good thing. Though they think they have everything, lacking Christ they have nothing. He has helped His servant Israel, meaning the Israelites in both the physical and the spiritual sense. It is true in the physical sense, in that tens of thousands of the Israelites believed in Christ, and the promise that God spoke to Abraham was fulfilled, namely, that *in thy seed shall all the nations of the earth be blessed.*[32] But in the spiritual sense, everyone who sees God is Israel, for the name *Israel* means *seeing God.* The Lord has helped those who see God, leading them upwards to their heavenly inheritance. Mary remained with Elizabeth about three months, and then returned. When Elizabeth was about to give birth, the Virgin departed, because of the many women who would gather to assist at the birthing, and it did not befit a virgin to mingle with them. That the Virgin indeed returned to her own house when Elizabeth was about to give birth is clear from this: the angel came to Mary at the sixth month of the conception of the Forerunner. Mary abode with Elizabeth about three months. Behold, nine months.

57-64. Now the time was fulfilled that Elizabeth should give birth; and she brought forth a son. And her neighbours and kinsfolk heard how the Lord had showed great mercy upon her; and they rejoiced with her. And it came to pass, that on the eighth day they came to circumcise the child; and they called him Zacharias, after the name of his father. And his mother answered and said, Not so; but he shall be called John. And they said unto her, There is none of thy kindred that is called by this name. And they made signs to his father, how he would have him called. And he asked for a writing tablet, and wrote, saying, His name is John. And they marvelled all. And his mouth was opened immediately, and his tongue loosed, and he spake, blessing God. The Virgin abode with Elizabeth about three months, perhaps because she was overwhelmed with amazement at the great miracle, and needed to regain her calm by being with Elizabeth. But she departed when the time of the birth drew near. *Now the time was fulfilled that Elizabeth should give birth.* See that only at the birth of a righteous

---

[32] Gen. 22:18

man is it said that *the time was fulfilled* for him to be born.[33] This cannot be said of sinners. Their birth is, as it were, unfulfilled, empty, and without purpose; it would have been better for them had they never been born. Why was the name given after the circumcision? Because it was necessary first to receive God's seal, and then the human name. In another sense, circumcision symbolizes the casting off of fleshly things. Therefore he who has not first cast off, and circumcised, the flesh, is unworthy to be called the warrior of God, and to have his name enrolled in the book of heaven. Elizabeth spoke as a prophetess concerning the name, when she said, *His name is John.* Perhaps John gave himself this name, speaking prophetically through his mother. Not able to communicate the child's name by means of a gesture, Zacharias asked for a writing tablet. And when he agreed with his wife concerning the name of the child, they were all astonished. For there was no one of that name in their family, and so it could not be said that either parent had intended before this time to give him this name. *John* means *the grace of God.* And this is why John's father was immediately filled with grace as well, and prophesied first of Christ and then of the child.

65-75. And fear came on all that dwelt round about them: and all these sayings were noised abroad throughout all the hill country of Judea. And all they that heard them laid them up in their hearts, saying, What manner of child shall this be! And the hand of the Lord was with him. And his father Zacharias was filled with the Holy Spirit, and prophesied, saying, Blessed be the Lord God of Israel; for He hath visited and redeemed His people, and hath raised up an horn of salvation for us in the house of His servant David; as He spake by the mouth of His holy prophets of old: that we should be saved from our enemies, and from the hand of all that hate us; to perform mercy to our fathers, and to remember His holy covenant; the oath which He sware to our father Abraham: that He would grant unto us, that we, having been delivered without fear out of the hand of our enemies, might serve Him in holiness and righteousness in His sight all the days of our life. *Fear came on all* because of the extraordinary manner in which Zacharias suddenly began to speak. Just as the people

---

[33] See Lk. 2:6 regarding the Birth of Christ.

were astounded by his silence, so now they are astounded when he speaks, so that by means of these two miracles everyone would understand that the child which had been born was not an ordinary child. All these things took place by divine economy, so that he who was to bear witness concerning Christ would be believed by others, and so that everyone would be assured by the circumstances of John's birth that he was no ordinary man. Zacharias blesses God for having visited the Israelites, for He indeed came to the lost sheep of the house of Israel, but most of them did not wish to accept this gracious gift. Therefore He visited the true Israelites, those who did believe. *He hath raised up an horn of salvation,* that is, His saving power and kingship. The horned beast is strong on account of its horn and thus the horn is an emblem of power. It is also an emblem of kingship because kings are anointed with oil poured out from a horn. Christ, therefore, is both the power and the kingship of the Father, and it is Christ Who was raised up for us as our horn of salvation. He appeared to sleep, while He overlooked many sins and endured man's madness for idolatry. But in the latter times He put an end to His long-suffering and was roused from [what appeared to be] sleep. And He took flesh, and was raised up, and crushed all the demons who had such hatred for us. He was raised up in the house of David, that is, He was born in Bethlehem, which is the city of David, as the prophets said. For all the prophets spoke of the Incarnation. Micah even mentions the house of David, I mean, Bethlehem, when he says, *And thou, O Bethlehem, art by no means least. For from out of thee shall come a ruler.*[34] He has shown mercy, not only to those living, but also to our fathers. For the grace of Christ also reached back to those who had already died. He has given to us, the living, the hope of resurrection, and we will be raised from the dead. We are not the only ones who will be counted worthy of this grace, but also those who have died before us. All of our nature has obtained this great good. And in another way has He *performed mercy to our fathers.* He has fulfilled their hopes. All that they had longed for, they saw accomplished in Christ. Indeed, when the fathers see their children enjoying such good things, they rejoice, and by sharing in their children's joy, they accept God's mercy for themselves. What was the covenant, and what was the oath to Abraham, which He *remembered?*

---

[34] See Micah 5:2.

Surely it was *Blessing I will bless thee, and multiplying I will multiply thee.*[35] In truth Abraham has now been multiplied, in that, through faith, all the nations have been adopted as His sons. Just as Abraham believed, so too have all these others been made members of his household through faith. Christ has delivered us from our enemies, *without fear.* It often happens that rescues are made, but they are accompanied by fear and a great struggle, even warfare. But Christ was crucified for us, and we did not have to struggle at all. Therefore He delivered us *without fear,* that is, our rescue was without peril to us. And why did He deliver us? So that we could live a life of revelry and feasting? No, but that we might serve and worship Him, not one or two days, but all the days of our life. We must serve God, not only waiting upon Him bodily in worship and in service, but also, *in holiness and righteousness. Holiness* is what is right for us to render to God; *righteousness* is what is right for us to render to men. For example, if a man holds back in awe of holy things, and does not reach out to touch and profane divine things as if they were something common, and if he shows all possible honor for things that are precious and worthy of honor, such a man is holy. Likewise he who honors his parents is holy, for the parents are considered "the gods of the household." And if a man is not greedy, and is not an embezzler, nor a thief, nor an adulterer, nor a fornicator, such a man is righteous. Therefore one must serve God in holiness, that is, with piety towards divine things, and with righteousness, that is, with a praiseworthy life in regards to men. And one must serve God *in His sight,* not in the sight of men, as do the people pleasers and hypocrites.

76-80. And thou, child, shalt be called the prophet of the Most High: for thou shalt go before the face of the Lord to prepare His ways; to give knowledge of salvation unto His people by the remission of their sins, through the tender mercy of our God; by which the Dayspring from on high hath visited us, to give light to them that sit in darkness and in the shadow of death, to guide our feet into the way of peace. And the child grew, and waxed strong in spirit, and was in the deserts till the day of his showing unto Israel. It appears strange that Zacharias should speak to the child as he did; for indeed he

---

[35] See Gen. 22:17.

ought not to have discoursed to an infant who could not understand. But this was an infant who had been brought forth in a strange and wondrous manner, leaping and prophesying in the womb at the coming of Mary. And so it is not at all unbelievable that after his birth he understood the words spoken by his father. *"Thou shalt go before the face of the Lord,"* Zacharias says, "very soon leaving me behind." For Zacharias knew that he was soon to be deprived of his child, who was about to flee into the desert.[36] Why was John to *go before*? In order *to prepare the ways* of the Lord. *The ways* are the souls of those in whom the Lord makes His way. The Forerunner, therefore, prepared these souls so that the Lord might walk in them. How did he prepare them? By giving *knowledge of salvation unto His people. Salvation* is the Lord Jesus,[37] and the knowledge of this *salvation,* that is, the knowledge of Christ, was given by John to the people. For John bore witness to Jesus. Knowledge of Christ came by means of the remission of sins. The Lord would not otherwise have been recognized as God if He had not forgiven the sins of the people. For only God can forgive sins. He forgives us our sins through His *tender mercy,* not through any work of ours, for we have done nothing good. It is He Who *hath visited us from on high,* He Who is called the *Dayspring* because He is the Sun of righteousness. And He has appeared to us who were sitting *in darkness,* that is, in ignorance, and *in the shadow of death,* that is, in sin. There were two evils which held sway over human nature: ignorance of God, the evil to which the pagan Greeks were subject, and sin, the evil to which the Jews were subject, even though they knew God. Therefore God appeared to the human nature, to enlighten those sitting in darkness, that is, those living in ignorance and godlessness, and to enlighten those sitting in the shadow of death, that is, those living in sin. The shadow of death signifies sin for this reason, I believe: just as one's shadow is the companion of one's body, so too, sin is the companion of death. For example, Adam died, and sin was there as well. Not even Christ's death was unaccompanied by sin. When He died, it was for our sins. So it is fitting that sin is called

---

[36] A short time after the birth of Christ, three months later, when Herod was seeking to slay the innocents, Elizabeth and her son fled into the desert to hide, and Zacharias was slain. See *The Great Collection of the Lives of the Saints, Vol. I: September,* Chrysostom Press, House Springs, Missouri, 1994, pp. 101-102.

[37] The name *Jesus* means *salvation.*

the shadow of death, for sin always accompanies death. There is more to be said about this, and we have already mentioned it, I think, when we explained The Gospel According to St. Matthew.[38] Does it suffice for God merely to appear to those who are in darkness? No, it does not. But He must also *guide our feet into the way of peace,* that is, into the way of righteousness. Sin is enmity against God,[39] but righteousness is peace with God. *The way of peace,* therefore, is a life of righteousness, towards which our souls' "feet" have been guided by Christ Who is the Dayspring from on high. *The child grew* in physical stature, *and waxed strong in spirit.* For the spiritual gift grew together with his body. As the child grew in body, to the same degree did the energies of the Spirit show themselves in him, as he became strong enough to contain them. Why was he in the desert lands? So that he could live out of reach of the wickedness of the masses, and so that he could give his reproofs in boldness, fearing no one. If he had lived in the world, perhaps he would have been stained by friendships and the companionship of men. John was also in the desert, so that when it came time for him to proclaim Christ, he would be believed because he was a desert dweller, living a life beyond that of ordinary men. And he lived in the desert until it pleased God to reveal him to the people of Israel.

---

[38] See Vol. 1, *The Explanation* of St. Matthew, p. 41.

[39] See Rom. 8:7.

CHAPTER TWO

Concerning the enrollment.
Concerning Mary's birthgiving.
Concerning the shepherds. Concerning Simeon.
Concerning the Prophetess Anna. Concerning Jesus
when He was found in the midst of the teachers.

1-7. And it came to pass in those days, that there went out a decree from Caesar Augustus, that all the world should be enrolled. (And this enrollment was first made when Cyrenius was governor of Syria.) And all went to be enrolled, every one into his own city. And Joseph also went up from Galilee, out of the city of Nazareth, into Judea, unto the city of David, which is called Bethlehem; (because he was of the house and lineage of David:) to be enrolled with Mary his betrothed wife, being great with child. And so it was, that, while they were there, the days were fulfilled that she should give birth. And she brought forth her firstborn Son, and wrapped Him in swaddling clothes, and laid Him in a manger; because there was no room for them in the inn. An enrollment took place for this reason: so that, as every one went to their ancestral city, the Virgin too would go up to Bethlehem, her own ancestral city, and thus the Lord would be born in Bethlehem, and the prophecy fulfilled.[1] When the One God intended to bring to an end the worship of many gods, it was fitting that one king, Caesar, should rule, rather than many kings. And Christ also was enrolled with them all, for it was fitting that the Lord too should be enrolled with the whole world, to sanctify all those who were enrolled, and thus to abolish slavery.[2] Just as He abolished circumcision by Himself undergoing circumcision, so too He brought to an end the enslavement of our human nature when He Himself was enrolled as a slave. For we who are servants of the Lord are no longer the slaves of men, as the Apostle Paul says, *Be not ye the slaves of men.*[3] Even if we are slaves in the body, we are still freemen in the spirit, for there is no chain with which our

---

[1] See Micah 5:2.

[2] Rome did not exact tax from its citizens, but only from its enslaved tributaries.

[3] I Cor. 7:23

masters can drag us away into their impiety. The Evangelist rightly calls the Lord *the firstborn Son* of the Virgin, although she never gave birth to a second. *Firstborn* means "the first to be born," even if there is no second child. He was laid in a manger, that is, in a feeding trough, as if to teach us from the very beginning simplicity and frugality. But He was also laid in a manger to show us symbolically that He came to dwell in this world, the dwelling place of us who have become like the irrational beasts. Just as the trough is the usual and fitting place where irrational cattle are found, so too this fallen world appears familiar and suitable for us. The manger, then, is the world, and we are the irrational beasts. And it was for this very reason that the Lord came here, to deliver us from irrationality.

8-14. And there were in the same country shepherds abiding in the field, keeping watch over their flock by night. And, lo, the angel of the Lord came upon them, and the glory of the Lord shone round about them: and they were sore afraid. And the angel said unto them, Fear not: for, behold, I bring you good tidings of great joy, which shall be to all people. For unto you is born this day in the city of David a Saviour, which is Christ the Lord. And this shall be a sign unto you; ye shall find the Babe wrapped in swaddling clothes, lying in a manger. And suddenly there was with the angel a multitude of the heavenly host praising God, and saying, Glory to God in the highest, and on earth peace, and among men good will. *There were shepherds abiding in the field,* that is, living in the fields and taking shelter there as they tended their sheep. The angel appeared to these shepherds because of their simple and guileless ways. It is clear that they even imitated the way of life of the righteous. For Jacob, Moses, and David, the patriarchs of old, were likewise shepherds. The angel did not appear to the Pharisees and scribes in Jerusalem, for they were vessels of every kind of cunning. But since these shepherds were without guile, they were counted worthy of the vision of divine things. And God showed that immediately, from the beginning, He chose those who were more simple and made them heralds, for when they departed they proclaimed all that they had witnessed. The angel brought *good tidings of great joy, which shall be to all people,* meaning, in the first place, to the people of God, who included some, but not all, the Jews. For not all the Jews were the people of God. But the Incarnation of God also came to be the joy of the whole race of man. What does the hymn of the angels reveal? Above all, it shows the thanksgiving and joy of the heavenly hosts that God has done good things for us on earth. *Glory to God,* they say, for now there is peace on earth, where before human nature was hostile to God. Now there is such reconciliation that our human nature has been intertwined with God, and united to Him Who took human flesh. Do you see, then, the peace of God towards man? And *peace* may be understood in another way as well. The Son of God Himself is Peace. For He says, "I am Peace."[4] Know then that Peace Itself, the Son of God, has come on earth. And Good Will is among men, that is, God in His good pleasure has chosen to abide among us. Now He is well pleased with man, when, before, He was neither well disposed nor well pleased with man.

15-18. And it came to pass, as the angels were gone away from them into heaven, the shepherds said one to another, Let us now go even unto Bethlehem, and see this thing which is come to pass, which the Lord hath made known unto us. And they came with haste, and found Mary, and Joseph, and the Babe lying in a manger. And when they had seen it, they made known abroad the saying which was told them concerning this Child. And all they that heard it wondered at those things which were told them by the shepherds. These shepherds symbolize the spiritual shepherds, the hierarchs. For the hierarchs ought to guard their flock and play their shepherd's pipes, that is, sing of spiritual things and teach the people, so that the people will be deemed worthy of seeing and hearing divine things. *Bethlehem* means *house of bread.* And what else is the house of bread, if not the Church, in which the true Bread, Christ Himself, is found? Therefore, it is the work of reason-endowed shepherds to seek out Christ, the heavenly Bread, and when they have seen Him, they ought to proclaim Him to others, just as these shepherds saw the Babe and then spoke of Him to others.

19-20. But Mary kept all these things, and pondered them in her heart. And the shepherds returned, glorifying and praising God for all the things that they had heard and seen, as it was told unto them.

---

[4] See Lk. 24:36, *Jesus Himself stood in the midst of them, and saith unto them, Peace be unto you.* See also Eph. 2:14, *For He is our Peace.*

What are the *things* [*rēmata*] which Mary kept? Some say that *these things* are everything that the angel spoke to her and that the shepherds said.[5] These sayings she kept, and *pondered them* in her heart, meaning, she brought them together, comparing and considering them,[6] and discovered in them all one harmonious thought, that her Son is God. But it seems to me that *rēmata* here means the events themselves. So what the Evangelist is saying is this: *Mary kept all these things,* that is, all these events which I, the Evangelist, have told and thus made them *words* [i.e., *rēmata*]. For when an event is told, it becomes words. The shepherds returned, giving thanks to God for all things, for they were not envious and spiteful, as were the leaders of the Jews.

21-24. And when eight days were fulfilled for the circumcising of the Child, His name was called JESUS, which was so named by the angel before He was conceived in the womb. And when the days of their purification according to the law of Moses were fulfilled, they brought Him up to Jerusalem, to present Him to the Lord; (as it is written in the law of the Lord, Every male that openeth the womb shall be called holy to the Lord;) and to offer sacrifice according to that which is said in the law of the Lord, A pair of turtledoves, or two young pigeons. Commandments were given in the law, and anyone who transgressed those commandments was under condemnation. The Lord therefore is circumcised, so that by having fulfilled the law even in this, and by omitting nothing which the law commanded, He might remove the condemnation from us. Let them here be put to shame who say that the Lord only seemed to take flesh. How could He have been circumcised if He had taken flesh in appearance only? Furthermore, it is foolish to question where that portion of His flesh might be that was circumcised. We ought not to ask questions concerning those things on

---

[5] The Greek word translated in the KJV as *things* is *rēmata*, the plural of *rēma*, meaning literally *word, saying,* or *utterance*. But in the New Testament, this word, in imitation of its Hebrew equivalent, can also mean the events or *things* which are the subject matter of speech. The interpretation which Bl. Theophylact first reports (*some say*) is based on the literal Greek meaning of the word; the interpretation which he himself prefers makes reference to the underlying Hebrew idiom.

[6] The Greek word *symballō*, rendered in the KJV as *ponder*, has the literal meaning *throw together* or *bring together*.

which Scripture is silent, for those things are not for our benefit. But it could be said that when the portion of His flesh was cut away, it touched the earth and made it holy, as did the blood and water which flowed from His side. It may be that the Lord kept this portion of His flesh unharmed, and at the Resurrection He arose, taking back this portion, so that He would be perfect in every respect, even this. For we too at the general resurrection will receive back our bodies perfected. Take note that the Lord was not conceived at the very moment that the angel said, *Behold, thou shalt conceive a son.* Instead, the Lord was conceived afterwards, when He so wished. See what the Evangelist says here, *which was so named by the angel before He was conceived in the womb.* The very words themselves show that this is so. The angel did not say, ''Behold, thou art conceiving,'' but rather, *Behold, thou shalt conceive.* From this it is understood that the Lord was conceived at that hour, not indeed at the very moment in which the angel spoke, but perhaps when he had completed his words. But we do not say this as dogma. *And when the days of their purification were fulfilled according to the law of Moses.* The Evangelist spoke well when he said, *according to the law of Moses.* In truth the Virgin had no need to await the days of her purification, that is, the forty days after the time that she gave birth to a male child. For it says in the law, *Whatsoever woman shall have received seed and born a male child.*[7] But the Virgin did not receive seed, but gave birth by the Holy Spirit. Therefore there was no necessity for her to fulfill the law, yet she wanted to do so, and she went up to the temple. Why is it that the law says that if a woman shall receive seed and bear a male child she shall be unclean for seven days, but if she bears a female child, she shall be unclean twice seven days?[8] This is so, because if she bears a male child, she has brought another Adam into the world. But if she bears a female child, the law considered that she has given birth to a second Eve, the weak and deceived vessel which shattered when cracked, and who was the first of mankind to disobey, after whom we all follow. The law said, *Every male that openeth the womb shall be called holy to the Lord.* Only with Christ did this literally occur. He Himself opened the womb of the Virgin at His birth, while all other wombs which have borne a

---

[7] Levit. 12:2

[8] Levit. 12:2-5

child have been first opened by a man. The law commanded that a pair
of turtledoves be offered, to show that the child is the offspring of a
chaste union. For it is said that the turtledove is a chaste animal, so much
so that when one loses its mate, it does not mate a second time. But if
one does not have turtledoves, two young pigeons are to be offered, as
a prayer that the young boy, in his lifetime, would have many children,
for the pigeon is an animal that has many offspring.

**25-32. And, behold, there was a man in Jerusalem, whose name
was Simeon; and this man was righteous and devout, waiting for the
consolation of Israel: and the Holy Spirit was upon him. And it was
revealed unto him by the Holy Spirit, that he should not see death,
before he had seen the Lord's Christ. And he came by the Spirit into
the temple: and when the parents brought in the Child Jesus, to do
for Him after the custom of the law, then took he Him up in his
arms, and blessed God, and said, Now lettest Thou Thy servant
depart in peace, O Master, according to Thy word: for mine eyes
have seen Thy Salvation, which Thou hast prepared before the face
of all people, the light of revelation to the Gentiles, and the glory of
Thy people Israel.** Simeon was not a priest, but a God-fearing man, who
was waiting for the coming of the Messiah Who would bring consolation
to the Hebrews, delivering them from their slavery to sin, and thereby,
can we not say, even from their slavery to the Romans and to Herod. For
he who has believed in Christ is indeed a free man, honored by kings and
by all other men. Consider the apostles: were they not the slaves of the
Romans? But now the Roman emperors honor and venerate them.[9]
Behold how Christ became the consolation of the apostles, who were
Israelites. So then, Simeon, moved by the Holy Spirit, went up into the
temple at the same time that the Lord's mother took her Child. And
Simeon held the Child and confessed Him to be God. For by saying to
the Christ Child, *"Now lettest Thou Thy servant depart* [from this life],"
he is confessing that this Child is the Lord of life and death. See how the
saints consider the body to be like a tether. This is why Simeon says,
Now lettest Thou Thy servant depart, that is, loose me from this tether

---

[9] As the descendants and inheritors of the Roman Empire, the Byzantines (so named by modern
historians) called themselves *Romans,* not *Byzantines.*

and bond.[10] He says, *according to Thy word,* because of the divine
promise he had received that he would not die until he had seen the
Messiah. *In peace* means *at rest.* While a man is living, he is troubled,
as David says,[11] but when he dies, he is at peace. But you may also
understand *in peace* in another way, that is, he was in peace now that he
had received the object of his hope. Simeon is saying, "Before I saw the
Lord, I was not at peace in my thoughts, always expecting Him and
wondering when He would come. But now that I have seen Him, I am at
peace and have put aside such thoughts, so that I am indeed set free."
Thy salvation is the Incarnation of the Only begotten Son, which God has
prepared from before all ages. God has prepared this salvation *before the
face of all peoples,* so that He might save the world, and so that His
Incarnation might be revealed to all. This is why He became incarnate.
This salvation is both *the light of revelation to the Gentiles,* that is, the
enlightenment of the Gentiles who were in darkness, and also *the glory*
of the Israelites. Christ is indeed the glory of the true people of Israel, for
He arose like the sun from their midst, and those who are wise have Him
as their boast. Thus spoke Simeon. And it seems to me that even the
words of the prophet David apply to Simeon: *With length of days will I
satisfy him, and I will show him My salvation.*[12]

**33-35. And Joseph and His mother marvelled at those things which
were spoken of Him. And Simeon blessed them, and said unto Mary
His mother, Behold, this Child is set for the fall and resurrection of
many in Israel; and for a sign which shall be spoken against; yea, a
sword shall pierce through thy own soul also, that the thoughts of
many hearts may be revealed.** Simeon blesses them both, and then
turning from him who was supposedly the father, he addresses her who
was truly the mother, and says, *This Child is set for the fall and
resurrection of many in Israel,* for the fall of those who do not believe,
and for the resurrection of those who believe. Or, by another interpreta-

----

[10] The Greek verb, *apolyō,* translated here as *let depart,* has the literal meaning, *loose from.*
Therefore in the New Testament it has in some places the literal meaning, and in other places the
extended meaning, *to loose one from the requirement of staying here,* that is, *send away,* or *dismiss.*

[11] *My heart is troubled, my strength hath failed me.* Ps. 37:10, and many other references in the
Psalms.

[12] Ps. 90:16

tion, the Lord is set for the fall of evil things in our soul, and for the rising up of good things. Fornication falls, and chastity rises up. By yet another interpretation, "Christ is set for the fall," meaning, "He shall suffer and fall to death," and by this falling many shall be raised. To understand the text this way, place a comma after *fall* and then read: *This Child is set for the fall, and for the resurrection of many in Israel.*[13] *And for a sign which shall be spoken against.* The *sign* is the Cross, which until this very day is spoken against, that is, it is rejected by those who do not believe. The *sign* is also the Incarnation of the Lord, and it is a wondrous sign. For God became man, and a virgin became a mother. And this sign, Christ's Incarnation, is indeed spoken against and denied. Some say that the Lord's body was from heaven, while others say that He had a body in appearance only, and yet others speak other kinds of nonsense. *Yea, a sword shall pierce through thy own soul also,* O Virgin. In one respect, *sword* means the anguish that was to result from the Lord's Passion; in another respect, the *sword* means the doubt and temptation that the Virgin would experience, seeing the Lord crucified on the Cross. For she may have then thought, "He was born seedlessly, He worked miracles, He raised the dead—how can He now be crucified, spat upon, and killed?" *That the thoughts of many hearts may be revealed.* This means that the thoughts of many who fell into doubt would be uncovered and revealed, and having been rebuked, they would quickly find healing. The same will happen to you, O Virgin: your doubt concerning Christ will be uncovered and revealed, and then your faith in Him will be confirmed. In like manner, Peter's denial also was revealed, followed by the power of God Who received Peter back by repentance. The thoughts of many hearts were likewise revealed, when the betrayer appeared, and when those who loved the Lord appeared, such as Joseph of Arimathea when he went to Pilate, and the women disciples who waited at the foot of the Cross.

36-40. And there was one Anna, a prophetess, the daughter of Phanuel, of the tribe of Aser: she was of a great age, and had lived with a husband seven years from her virginity; and she was a widow

---

[13] It should be remembered that ancient Greek texts, such as that of the New Testament, were not punctuated at all, and the reader had to provide the divisions between words, phrases, and sentences. The punctuating of the text, as Bl. Theophylact is doing here, was part of the act of reading.

of about fourscore and four years, who departed not from the temple, but served God with fastings and prayers night and day. And she coming in at that same hour, gave thanks likewise unto the Lord, and spake of Him to all them that looked for redemption in Jerusalem. And when they had performed all things according to the law of the Lord, they returned into Galilee, to their own city Nazareth. And the Child grew, and waxed strong in spirit, filled with wisdom: and the grace of God was upon Him. The Evangelist continues with this account of Anna, and lists both her father and her tribe, so that we might be convinced that he is speaking the truth. He is summoning, as it were, many witnesses who knew her father and her tribe. She gave thanks to the Lord and taught many concerning the Lord, that He was the Saviour and consolation of us who were awaiting redemption. *After they had performed all things, they returned into Galilee, to their own city Nazareth.* Bethlehem was also their own city, it being the city of their fathers, but Nazareth was the city where they lived. Jesus grew in body, although He was able, straight from the womb, to have advanced to the stature of a man. But this would have appeared to have been a phantasy, and so for this reason He grew little by little. As He grew, the Wisdom of God the Word showed forth. He did not become wise by stages—far from it! Little by little He showed forth His innate Wisdom, in accordance with the stature of His body, and in this way it is said that He advanced and grew strong in Spirit. If He had showed forth all His wisdom while short in stature, He would have appeared to be a miraculous prodigy. But now He shows Himself to the degree appropriate to His age, fulfilling the divine plan of salvation. And He did not receive wisdom, (for how could that which is perfect from the beginning become more perfect?) but He exercised His wisdom little by little.

41-50. Now His parents went to Jerusalem every year at the feast of Pascha. And when He was twelve years old, they went up to Jerusalem after the custom of the feast. And when they had fulfilled the days, as they returned, the Child Jesus tarried behind in Jerusalem; and Joseph and His mother knew not of it. But they, supposing Him to have been in the company, went a day's journey; and they sought Him among their kinsfolk and acquaintance. And when they found Him not, they turned back again to Jerusalem, seeking Him. And it came to pass, that after three days they found

Him in the temple, sitting in the midst of the teachers, both hearing them, and asking them questions. And all that heard Him were astonished at His understanding and answers. And when they saw Him they were amazed: and His mother said unto Him, Son, why hast Thou thus dealt with us? Behold, Thy father and I have sought Thee sorrowing. And He said unto them, How is it that ye sought Me? Knew ye not that I must be about My Father's business? And they understood not the saying which He spake unto them. The Lord went up with His parents to Jerusalem, in order to show by all that He did that He was not opposed to God, nor was He against the commandments of the law. *When they had fulfilled the days,* that is, the seven days of Pascha, He remained behind in Jerusalem. He was conversing with the scribes and asking them questions from the law, and they were all astonished. Do you see in what sense [the Evangelist says below that] He *increased in wisdom?* By becoming known to many and astonishing them with His wisdom. For His *increase* in wisdom consisted of His increasing revelation of His wisdom to others. The Theotokos calls Joseph His *father* although she knew that he was not His father. She calls him *father* on account of the Jews, so that they would not think that the Lord was born of fornication. But in another sense she fittingly names Joseph *father* because he gave the Child fatherly care and help in upbringing. It is as if the Holy Spirit inspired her to honor Joseph with the title *father.* Why did they search for Jesus? Surely they did not think that He was lost, or had wandered away, in the manner of a child? Far be it from Mary, the most wise, to have such thoughts, for she had received a myriad of revelations concerning Him. Nor could Joseph harbor such thoughts, when it had been revealed to him that what had been conceived in her was of the Holy Spirit.[14] But they searched for Him, wondering if He was distancing Himself from them or had left them. When they found Him, see how He answers them. The Virgin calls Joseph His father and He replies, "He is not my true father, or I would have been in his house. God is My Father, and therefore I am in His house, that is, in His temple." But they did not understand what He said to them, for it was a mystery.

---

[14] Mt. 1:20

51-52. And He went down with them, and came to Nazareth, and was subject unto them: but His mother kept all these sayings in her heart. And Jesus increased in wisdom and stature, and in favour with God and man. He subjected Himself to His parents, giving an example even to us, that we should subject ourselves to our parents. The Virgin kept all these sayings in her heart. For both the Child's actions and His words were divine, and not those of a twelve year old, but of a mature man. See here how the Evangelist explains what it means that the Lord *increased in wisdom,* by adding, *and in stature,* showing that as the Lord increased in stature and age, He permitted more and more of His wisdom to manifest itself. And He found *favour with God and man,* that is, He did what was pleasing to God and what drew praise from men. First from God, and then from men. For we must first please God, and then men.

CHAPTER THREE

Concerning the preaching of John.
Concerning those who asked John what they should do.
Concerning Herod and John.
Concerning the Baptism of the Saviour.
Concerning the genealogy of Christ.

1-3. Now in the fifteenth year of the reign of Tiberias Caesar, Pontius Pilate being governor of Judea, and Herod being tetrarch of Galilee, and his brother Philip tetrarch of Iturea and of the region of Trachonitis, and Lysanias the tetrarch of Abilene, Annas and Caiaphas being the high priests, the word of God came unto John, the son of Zacharias, in the wilderness. And he came into all the country about Jordan, preaching the baptism of repentance unto the remission of sins. With good reason the Evangelist mentions both the year and the names of the rulers, to show that the rulers of the line of Judah had come to an end at the time of Christ, when Pilate, a foreigner, was governor, and the sons of Herod of Askalon[1] were tetrarchs. Thus it confirmed that the Messiah had come, in accordance with the prophecy of Jacob.[2] The Evangelist says, *The word of God came unto John,* so that you, O reader, might learn that John did not [in a self-willed manner] call himself to bear witness to Christ, but rather he was moved by the Holy Spirit. You should understand *the word* to mean either the Holy Spirit or the command of God. And it was *in the wilderness* that the word of God came to John. The prophecy of Isaiah was soon to be fulfilled that *more are the children of the desert,* meaning, of the Church of the Gentiles, *than of her that hath a husband,* that is, of the Jewish synagogue.[3] Hence it was fitting that the word and the command of God came to John in the wilderness. He preached to the people *the baptism of repentance,* that is, the baptism of the confession of sins. This baptism of John's worked

---

[1] An ancient Philistine city in Palestine on the Mediterranean coast, located between Joppa and Gaza. It was the center of worship of the pagan goddess Astarte, and was also the birthplace of Herod the Great.

[2] Gen. 49:10. See Vol. 1, *The Explanation* of St. Matthew, p. 18, footnote 14.

[3] See Is. 54:1.

together with the people *unto the remission of sins,* which was granted
through the baptism of Christ. For indeed the baptism of John did not
grant the remission of sins, but it led directly to the remission of sins,
that is, it prepared men to receive the baptism of Christ which gives
remission of sins.

**5-6. As it is written in the book of the words of Isaiah the prophet,
saying, The voice of one crying in the wilderness, Prepare ye the way
of the Lord, make His paths straight. Every valley shall be filled, and
every mountain and hill shall be brought low; and the crooked shall
be made straight, and the rough ways shall be made smooth; and all
flesh shall see the salvation of God.** The *way* is the life in Christ, for
which John commands all to prepare. For in a very short while the Lord
Himself would begin to preach. The *paths* are the commandments of the
law, along which many feet have already trod. John commands that these
paths be made straight, for the Pharisees had made them crooked and
perverted. The *way* can also be understood to mean the soul, and the
paths to mean one's thoughts and deeds. Therefore, we must prepare our
soul and also make straight, that is, rectify, our thoughts and deeds. Then
it is as if someone had raised the question, ''But how can we accomplish
this, when the way of virtue is so arduous, with many ravines and
obstacles which are from the evil powers and from the passions which
make their abode in us?'' And the answer is given, ''Nothing shall be
laborious, but instead all will be easy. For the valleys will be filled, that
is, our natural powers, which have been laid low and weakened in doing
good, shall be filled up with strength. And every mountain and hill,
meaning, the adverse powers, the demons, who have been lifted up
through pride, shall be brought low.'' In truth both the adverse powers
and the desires of the flesh, which had seemed part of the fabric of our
very nature, have been weakened. Everything has become smooth and
flat, and the crooked things have been made straight. For Christ has
destroyed the adverse powers,[4] which here are called *mountains and
hills,* and He has brought back to life our natural motivation to do good,
which the Evangelist describes as *valleys* that have been *filled.* It is for

---

[4] At Holy Baptism the priest says three times, making the sign of the Cross in the water of the
font into which the one prepared for baptism is about to enter, *Let all adverse powers be crushed by
the sign and image of the Cross.*

this reason that Christ took flesh, to restore our fallen nature to what it was before it fell. *And all flesh shall see the salvation of God.* No longer the Jews and their converts alone, but all flesh. For the Gospel has reached all the earth. Many other things could be said as well, but let this suffice, for the sake of clarity.

7-9. Then said he to the multitude that came forth to be baptized by him, O brood of vipers, who hath warned you to flee from the wrath to come? Bring forth therefore fruits worthy of repentance, and begin not to say within yourselves, We have Abraham as our father. For I say unto you, that God is able of these stones to raise up children unto Abraham. And now also the axe is laid unto the root of the trees: every tree therefore which bringeth not forth good fruit is hewn down, and cast into the fire. He calls the Jews a *brood of vipers* because they oppressed their own fathers and mothers. It is said that the viper eats its way out of its mother's womb, and thus is born. Likewise, the Jews had killed their prophets and teachers. *The wrath to come* means the eternal punishment. *Fruits worthy of repentance* are not only the avoidance of evil, but the steadfast application of oneself to do good. For the doing of good is indeed the fruit and the offspring of repentance. Do not begin to say among yourselves, ''We are well born,'' and so neglect virtue, being so confident in the lineage of your fathers. Even *of these stones* God is able to give children to the patriarch, just as He did before. For the womb of Sarah, which was as barren as a stone, by grace bore children. The *axe* is divine judgment, which cuts down those who are unworthy. Therefore, if you do not repent, you will be cut off from life. The axe is laid to the root of you, who are like the trees. Therefore, understand *root* to mean *life,* but it also means the kinship with Abraham. Those who are not worthy to be branches of Abraham, will be cut away from any kinship with Abraham, according to the Apostle.[5] The punishment is twofold: not only is the sinner who bears no fruit cut away from kinship with the righteous, but he is also cast into the fire.

10-18. And the multitude asked him, saying, What shall we do

---

[5] See Rom. 11:16-24.

then? He answereth and saith unto them, He that hath two coats, let him share with him that hath none; and he that hath food, let him do likewise. Then came also publicans to be baptized, and said unto him, Master, what shall we do? And he said unto them, Exact no more than that which is appointed you. And the soldiers likewise asked of him, saying, And what shall we do? And he said unto them, Extort from no man, neither accuse any falsely; and be content with your wages. And as the people were in expectation, and all men wondered in their hearts concerning John, whether he were the Christ, or not, John answered, saying unto them all, I indeed baptize you with water; but One mightier than I cometh, the thong of Whose sandals I am not worthy to unloose: He shall baptize you with the Holy Spirit and with fire: Whose winnowing fan is in His hand, and He will thoroughly cleanse His threshing floor, and will gather the wheat into His granary; but the chaff He will burn up with fire unquenchable. And with many other exhortations did he bring good tidings to the people. John admonished three kinds of people who came to him: the multitude, the publicans, and the soldiers. He exhorted the multitude to give alms, commanding the one who had two coats to share with him who had none. He advised the publicans, that is, the tax collectors, to exact no more than what was due. He admonished the soldiers not to extort from others, but to be satisfied with their wages, that is, the customarily generous sum paid by the emperor to his soldiers. See how he exhorts the multitude, because they are without guile, to do something good, to share with others, while the publicans and soldiers he admonishes to refrain from doing evil. For the publicans and soldiers did not yet have the capacity, and thus were not able, to do something good, and it sufficed for them not to do evil. Some understand in a spiritual sense the words, *He that hath two coats, let him share with him that hath none.* They say that the two coats are the spirit and the letter of Scripture. Here John is urging him who has both to give to him that is completely naked. For example, if someone understands Scripture in both senses, literal and spiritual, *let him share with him that hath none,* that is, let him teach another who is ignorant of Scripture, and at least share with him the literal meaning. John's virtue was so great that all the people were wondering if John himself could be the Messiah. But John rejects such a thought, saying, "So great is the difference between the Christ and me, that *I baptize with water* while *He shall baptize with the Holy Spirit and* *with fire.* And also, *I am not worthy to unloose the thong of His sandals.''* What do these things mean? That Christ would baptize with the Holy Spirit and with fire is absolutely clear. For Christ sent the Holy Spirit to the apostles, and the tongues of fire were seen upon them. *I am not worthy to unloose the thong of His sandals* has two meanings: the more obvious sense, that "I am not worthy to be considered the least of His servants," and the more hidden meaning, that the two sandals of the Lord represent His coming down from heaven to dwell among us on earth, and His descent from earth into hades. No one is able to explain the manner in which these two sojournings took place, not even if he were John the Forerunner. Who is able to say either how the Lord took flesh, or how He descended into Hades? *Whose winnowing fan is in His hand* means "Just because He will baptize you, do not think that you are not liable to condemnation. If, after baptism, you do not lead a blameless life, He will burn you with unquenchable fire." For indeed a man is like chaff, if he has a mind which has not born any good fruit and is only a heap of the husks and sweepings of worldly life. *And with many other exhortations did he bring good tidings to the people.* Good teaching is indeed exhortation and consolation,[6] and rightly is it also called *good tidings.*

19-22. But Herod the tetrarch, being reproved by him for Herodias his brother's wife, and for all the evils which Herod had done, added yet this above all, that he shut up John in prison. Now when all the people were baptized, it came to pass, that Jesus also being baptized, and praying, the heaven was opened, and the Holy Spirit descended in bodily form like a dove upon Him, and a voice came from heaven, which said, Thou art My beloved Son; in Thee I am well pleased. It is appropriate that the Evangelist inserted at this point an account of these matters concerning Herod, as if saying, "The multitude thought highly of John, but *Herod, being reproved by him, added yet this above all, that he*

---

[6] The Greek verb *parakalō,* translated in the text as *exhort,* has the literal meaning *call upon,* and in the New Testament especially, the extended meanings *exhort, beseech, console, comfort,* and *encourage.* Bl. Theophylact has this wide range of meanings in mind when he says that "good teaching is indeed *paraklēsis* [i.e., the noun form of *parakalō*]." Note that from this word we derive both the term Paraclete, the Comforter, and *paraklēsis,* the Greek name for a prayer service of supplication (in Russian, *moleben*).

shut John up in prison.'' It is as if the Evangelist were saying with some consternation as he related these events, that while the people had such high regard for John, Herod saw fit to do these evil things to him. Heaven is *opened,* to show us that heaven, which Adam had closed, is opened for all by baptism. And the Holy Spirit comes down upon Jesus so that we might learn from this that the Spirit comes upon us also when we are baptized. The Lord did not need the Spirit to descend upon Him. But He does all things for our sake, and He Himself becomes the first-fruits of all of us who later will receive the Spirit, becoming as it were the first-born of many brothers. The Holy Spirit descends in the form of a dove, to teach us that we must be meek and pure. And just as a dove announced to Noah that God's wrath had ceased, so too the Holy Spirit announces here that He has reconciled us to God by sweeping sin away in the flood waters of baptism. And the Son hears the voice coming from the Father, *Thou art My beloved Son,* showing that when we are baptized, sonship is also bestowed upon us by adoption. *In Thee I am well pleased* means "In Thee I have taken My rest.''

23-28. And Jesus Himself was about thirty years of age at the beginning, being (as was supposed) the son of Joseph, who was the son of Heli, the son of Matthat, the son of Levi, the son of Melchi, the son of Jannai, the son of Joseph, the son of Mattathias, the son of Amos, the son of Nahum, the son of Esli, the son of Naggai, the son of Maath, the son of Mattathias, the son of Semein, the son of Josech, the son of Judah, the son of Joannan, the son of Rhesa, the son of Zerubbabel, the son of Salathiel, the son of Neri, the son of Melchi, the son of Addi, the son of Cosam, the son of Elmadam, the son of Er, the son of Joshua, the son of Eliezer, the son of Jorim, the son of Matthat, the son of Levi, the son of Simeon, the son of Judah, the son of Joseph, the son of Jonam, the son of Eliakim, the son of Melea, the son of Menna, the son of Mattatha, the son of Nathan, the son of David, the son of Jesse, the son of Obed, the son of Boaz, the son of Salma, the son of Nahshon, the son of Amminadab, the son of Ram, the son of Hezron, the son of Pharez, the son of Judah, the son of Jacob, the son of Isaac, the son of Abraham, the son of Terah, the son of Nahor, the son of Serug, the son of Reu, the son of Peleg, the son of Eber, the son of Shelah, the son of Cainan, the son of Arphaxad, the son of Shem, the son of Noah, the son of Lamech, the

son of Methuselah, the son of Enoch, the son of Jared, the son of Mahalaleel, the son of Cainan, the son of Enos, the son of Seth, the son of Adam, the son of God. The Lord was baptized when He was thirty years old, because at this age one reaches full maturity, and a man's character is found to be either tried and true, or else unfit. Luke gives the genealogy of the Lord in reverse order to that of Matthew, in order to show that He Who now has been born in the flesh is from God. See how the genealogy ends with God, also teaching us that the Lord became incarnate for this very reason, that He might lead back to God all of His forefathers in the flesh and make them His sons. And I have yet another explanation to give: some could not believe that the birth of the Lord was without seed. The Evangelist therefore wants to show that once before a man came into being without seed, and so the Evangelist leads us back through the forefathers to Adam and then to God. It is as if he were saying to us, "If you do not believe that the second Adam was born without seed, ascend with me in mind to the first Adam and you will find that he too was begotten without seed by God. Therefore, do not doubt." Some have asked how it is that Matthew says that Joseph was the son of Jacob, while Luke says that he was the son of Heli. It is impossible, they say, that one man could be the son of two fathers. In answer to this question, we say that Jacob and Heli were brothers of the same mother, but each had a different father. When Heli died childless, Jacob took Heli's wife and begat a son from her. Thus it is said that Joseph was the son of Jacob by nature, but the son of Heli by law. Jacob begat Joseph physically and in actuality, and therefore is Joseph's physical father, while Heli is the father of Joseph only according to the law. For the law commanded that if a man die childless, his wife should be joined to his brother, and the child that thus was born would be considered the child of the dead man, even though by nature he was the child of the man who was living. Thus the Evangelists speak well, and do not contradict each other. Matthew records Joseph's physical father, while Luke records his father according to the law, that is, Heli, so that together the Evangelists might show that the Lord was born for this very reason, to sanctify both physical nature and the law.

CHAPTER FOUR

Concerning the Saviour's fasting and temptation.
Concerning Jesus, when He was led to the mountain
by the Jews, and passed through their midst.
Concerning the man with the demonic spirit.
Concerning Peter's mother-in-law.
Concerning those healed of various diseases.

1-12. And Jesus being full of the Holy Spirit returned from Jordan, and was led by the Spirit into the wilderness, being forty days tempted by the devil. And in those days He did eat nothing: and when they were ended, He afterward hungered. And the devil said unto Him, If Thou be the Son of God, command this stone that it be made bread. And Jesus answered him, saying, It is written, that man shall not live by bread alone, but by every word of God. And the devil, taking Him up onto a high mountain, showed unto Him all the kingdoms of the world in a moment of time, and the devil said unto Him, All this power will I give Thee, and the glory of them: for that is delivered unto me, and to whomsoever I will, I give it. If Thou therefore wilt worship me, all shall be Thine. And Jesus answered and said unto him, Get thee behind Me, Satan; for it is written, Thou shalt worship the Lord thy God, and Him only shalt thou serve. And he brought Him to Jerusalem, and set Him on a pinnacle of the temple, and said unto Him, If Thou be the Son of God, cast Thyself down from hence: for it is written, He shall give His angels charge over thee, to keep thee: and in their hands they shall bear thee up, lest at any time thou dash thy foot against a stone. And Jesus answering said unto Him, It is said, Thou shalt not tempt the Lord thy God. The Lord was baptized, that He might sanctify the waters for the sake of us who would enjoy this gift of grace. After He was baptized, He was led by the Spirit to a desert mountain. For it was the Holy Spirit Who was leading Him up for the contest with the devil. They go away into the desert, to give the devil an opportunity to attack Him, for it is especially when we are alone that the devil attacks us. He fasts for forty days, not exceeding the extent of Moses' and Elijah's fasting, so as not to give Satan immediate cause to suspect that the Lord was greater than Moses and Elijah, but instead to encourage Satan to attack, thinking that

He was only a man. The Lord also fasts for forty days so that we would not think that He took flesh in appearance only. He is tempted after His baptism, showing us that after our baptism temptations await us. He fasts to teach us that fasting is a great weapon in temptations, and that after our baptism we too should fast and stop gourmandizing. The enemy first assaults Him with the temptation of gluttony, as he did also to Adam. Then he tempted the Lord with the love of riches, showing Him all the kingdoms of the world. How did he show them? Some say that he suggested the kingdoms to Him in His thoughts; but I think that the devil did not suggest them to His thoughts but to His senses, making them to appear as a phantasm; but the Lord would not fantasize. Thirdly, the devil assaults Him with vainglory, *If Thou be the Son of God,* he says, *cast Thyself down from hence.* He flatters Him, while suggesting such nonsense, hoping that the Lord might be deceived by flattery, and would want to show that He was the Son of God by throwing Himself down. In this way the devil would discover who Christ really was. See how the Lord repels the devil with the words of Scripture, *Thou shalt not tempt the Lord thy God.* For a man ought not to throw himself into clear danger, testing to see if God will help him. Notice also what great benefit it is to know the Scriptures. Even the Lord Himself repelled Satan by means of the Scriptures. The words *man shall not live by bread alone* are from the books of Moses,[1] and were spoken in reference to the manna sent from heaven. For manna was not bread, yet it miraculously fed the people. And the words *Thou shalt worship the Lord thy God* and *Thou shalt not tempt the Lord thy God* are also from the books of Moses.[2]

13-15. And when the devil had ended every temptation, he departed from Him for a time. And Jesus returned in the power of the Spirit into Galilee: and there went out a fame of Him through all the region round about. And He taught in their synagogues, being glorified by all. Luke says that *every temptation* ended, even though the Lord was tempted by only three temptations, because these three, avarice, gluttony, and vainglory, are the chief temptations, the three heads of the serpent. He repelled gluttony by saying, *Man shall not live by bread*

---

[1] Deut. 8:3

[2] Deut. 6:13, 16

alone. The devil led Him first to this temptation, just as he had done to Adam. The devil would not have been able to trip up Adam by greed, for it was not possible for him greedily to desire more than his share, because he was alone [and everything was his]. Nor could Satan have tripped him up by anger, for in paradise there was nothing to cause anger. Nor could he have caused him to fall by envy. Therefore the devil tempted Adam through his stomach. The Lord repelled the temptation of the love of riches by not falling down in worship before Satan. He refused to bow down to the one who by means of a mirage revealed to His senses all the kingdoms. Some understand this to mean not actual kingdoms perceivable by the senses, but rather spiritual dominions ruled by one sin or another. For example, the devil showed Christ the kingdom of licentiousness, the kingdom of envy, and, in short, the kingdoms of each and every sin. It was as if the devil were saying to Christ, ''If You want to rule over all these passions, and if You have come for this very reason, to seize from me those who are in my grip, bow down and worship me, and receive all those who are under my tyranny.'' Indeed, the Lord does wish to reign as king, and He came for this very reason. However, He did not intend to become our king by committing sin or by avoiding struggle, but instead by entering into combat and defeating His opponent. Some have understood it this way; let the reader accept it as he prefers. The Lord also rejected the temptation of vainglory by speaking the word of Scripture. Deliver us also, O Lord, from these three heads of the dragon. *Jesus returned in the power of the Spirit.* It seems to me this means that Jesus returned full of divine rapture. You also, O reader, must attend to Scripture, for with Scripture the Lord defeated the tempter, and showed His own power, for it says that He returned *in the power of the Spirit.* And not without meaning are the words *he departed from Him for a time.* The devil attacks the Lord by means of two passions, pleasure and grief. He attacked the Lord with pleasure when he led Him up onto the mountain. Then the devil *departed from Him for a time,* that is, until the time of the Cross, when the devil attacked Him again, this time with grief.

16-21. And He came to Nazareth, where He had been brought up: and, as His custom was, He went into the synagogue on the sabbath day, and stood up for to read. And there was delivered unto Him the book of the prophet Isaiah. And when He had opened the book, He

found the place where it was written, The Spirit of the Lord is upon Me, on account of which He hath anointed Me: He hath sent Me to bring good tidings to the poor, to heal the broken-hearted, to proclaim deliverance to the captives, and recovering of sight to the blind, to set at liberty them that are bruised, to proclaim the acceptable year of the Lord. And He closed the book, and He gave it again to the attendant, and sat down. And the eyes of all them that were in the synagogue were fastened on Him. And He began to say unto them, This day is this Scripture fulfilled in your ears. The Lord wished to reveal Himself to the Israelites and to show that He was anointed by God the Father to save all those under heaven. Even the way in which He reveals Himself He arranged in a wondrous manner. Before anyone else, He first revealed Himself to the people of Nazareth, among whom He had been raised. Thus He teaches us that we should first work to teach and bring benefit to those of our own circle, before lavishing kindness on others. When He had been given the book, He opened it, not at random, but to the very passage He wanted to find. Do not think that He opened the book and by chance found this passage in which was written these things concerning Himself; rather, it happened as He willed. What was written there? *The Spirit of the Lord...hath anointed Me,* that is, has consecrated Me. The Spirit has established Me to bring good tidings to the poor, that is, to the Gentiles, who have neither the law nor the prophets, and who are therefore in great poverty indeed. *The broken-hearted* perhaps means those Israelites whose hearts were at first great and exalted, being the dwelling place of God; but later, after they turned to idolatry and committed many sins, their hearts were broken and crushed and ceased to be the dwelling place of God, and became instead a den of thieves. Therefore the Lord came to save even such as these, and to grant *deliverance to the captives* and *recovering of sight to the blind,* both Gentile and Jew. Both were prisoners of Satan, and both were blind. These things can also be understood to refer to the dead. For they too are *captives* and *bruised,* but they have been set free from the power of hades by the Resurrection of the Lord. And He *proclaimed the acceptable year.* What was *the acceptable year?* Perhaps it was the age to come, concerning which the Lord preached, saying, *In that day ye shall ask Me* *nothing.*[3] And again, ''The hour is coming when the dead shall rise again.''[4] That year is *acceptable,* that is, it is much desired and beloved by the righteous, and it is the time much awaited by all who labor here.[5] And the time when the Lord dwelt among us in the flesh is also *the acceptable year,* concerning which the Apostle Paul says, *Now is the accepted time; behold, now is the day of salvation.*[6] When Jesus had read these things, He said, *This day is this Scripture fulfilled in your ears,* openly presenting Himself to those who listened, revealing that He Himself was the One of Whom these things were written.

22-30. And all bore witness to Him, and marvelled at the words of grace which proceeded out of His mouth. And they said, Is not this Joseph's son? And He said unto them, Ye will surely say unto Me this proverb, Physician, heal thyself: whatsoever we have heard done in Capernaum, do also here in Thy country. And He said, Verily I say unto you, No prophet is accepted in his own country. But I tell you of a truth, many widows were in Israel in the days of Elijah, when the heaven was shut up three years and six months, when great famine was throughout all the land; but unto none of them was Elijah sent, save unto Sarepta, a city of Sidon, unto a woman that was a widow. And many lepers were in Israel in the time of Elisha the prophet; and none of them was cleansed, saving Naaman the Syrian. And all they in the synagogue, when they heard these things, were filled with wrath, and rose up, and thrust Him out of the city, and led Him unto the brow of the hill whereon their city was built, that they might cast Him down headlong. But He, passing through the midst of them, went His way. When the multitude heard the things spoken by Christ, they *marvelled at the words of grace.* They marvelled, and yet they mocked Him, saying, ''*Is not this the son* of a carpenter?'' But how could Joseph's occupation make the Lord less wondrous or less

---

[3] Jn. 16:23

[4] See Jn. 5:25, 28-29.

[5] The Greek word, translated here as *acceptable,* is *dektos,* which comes from the verb *dechomai, to accept with favor.* With a prefix added, the verb *prosdechomai* means *to expect, to await.* Bl. Theophylact uses this verb to help explain the meaning of *dektos.*

[6] II Cor. 6:2; see Is. 49:8.

worthy of respect? Do you not see the things He is doing? Do you not hear the things He is saying? Why then do you mock His father? It is indeed the truth to say of them, *Behold a foolish and senseless people, who have eyes and see not, and have ears and hear not.*[7] The Lord therefore says to them, "*Ye will surely say unto Me,* 'Do in Thy country the things which Thou didst in Capernaum,' (for this has the same meaning as *Physician, heal thyself,* a common saying among the Jews, spoken to physicians who were ill[8]). I say unto you, that I would have done many signs among you also, My countrymen. But I know that failing which is common to everyone, to overlook and ignore even the most extraordinary events when they are not rare in occurrence, but are so frequent and commonplace that everyone can easily enjoy them. It is always man's habit to think about and marvel at the strange and the exotic, and to ignore common everyday things. This is why no prophet is honored in his own country. But if the prophet were to come from somewhere else, they would marvel at him. So it was that the widows of Judea did not welcome Elijah, but only the widow of Sarepta, a foreigner. And Elisha cleansed the foreign leper who showed faith in him. But the lepers who were his fellow countrymen and were familiar with him had no faith in him, and so they were not cleansed. Likewise, I do not seem marvelous to you, My countrymen; instead, I am despised by you. Therefore I do not work miracles here. But to those in Capernaum I appear marvelous, and there I work miracles and I am accepted by them." When those in the synagogue heard these words, they were filled with anger when they ought to have marvelled, and they attempted to throw Him over a cliff. *But He, passing through the midst of them, went His way,* not to escape suffering, for He came to suffer for us, but to await the right moment. He had just now begun to preach, and so it was not right that He give Himself over to death so soon. But when He had taught sufficiently, then He allowed Himself to be put to death. From this it is clear that when He was crucified, it was not against His will. Instead He gave Himself over to death according to His own will. Understand that the *country* of the prophets is the synagogue of the Jews, in which the prophets suffer dishonor and are not accepted. But we who are

---

[7] Jer. 5:21

[8] In other words, "Attend first to what is close to you."

foreigners have accepted them. Like the widow who welcomed Elijah
when there was drought among the Jews, so too the Church of the
Gentiles accepted the prophetic word when there was spiritual famine in
Judea caused by those who would not hear the word of God. It was
concerning this "widow" that the prophet spoke, *More are the children
of the wilderness, than of her that has a husband.*[9] And again, *For the
barren has borne seven, and she that abounded in children has grown
feeble.*[10]

**31-37. And He came down to Capernaum, a city of Galilee, and
taught them on the sabbath days. And they were astonished at His
teaching, for His word was with authority. And in the synagogue
there was a man, who had a spirit of an unclean demon, and he cried
out with a loud voice, saying, Let us alone; what have we to do with
Thee, Thou Jesus of Nazareth? Art Thou come to destroy us? I know
Thee Who Thou art: the Holy One of God. And Jesus rebuked him,
saying, Hold thy peace, and come out of him. And when the demon
had thrown him into the middle, he came out of him, and hurt him
not. And they were all amazed, and spake among themselves, saying,
What a word is this! For with authority and power He commandeth
the unclean spirits, and they come out. And the fame of Him went
out into every place of the country round about.** Since teaching did not
bring the unbelieving to belief, the Lord proceeds to work miracles, like
a physician giving stronger medicine. Therefore the Lord works a miracle
in Capernaum, for there was much unbelief there and the people needed
much help to acquire faith. So, when He had taught them sufficiently, as
One with authority (for He did not say, "The Lord sayeth these things,"
as did the prophets, but "I say unto you," as befits the true Son of God),
He adds to His teaching this miracle, and heals the man possessed of a
demon. The demon first expresses hatred, so that his testimony might be
credible, and then he proceeds to give testimony of Christ, *I know Thee
Who Thou art: the Holy One of God.* First the demon accuses Him,
saying, *Art Thou come to destroy us?* Then he flatters the Lord, thinking
that the Lord would be softened by flattery and let him alone—so

---

[9] Is. 54:1

[10] I Kings (I Sam.) 2:5

irrational and foolish is evil. But the Lord, teaching us not to rely upon the testimonies or evidence provided by demons, says, *Hold thy peace, and come out of him.* He permits the demon to throw the man down so that those present would know that the man truly was demonized. And the words which he spoke were the words of the demon, although it was the tongue of the man which pronounced them. And indeed they all *spake among themselves,* marvelling at what had happened, saying, *What is this word,* that is, what is this command which He gave, *Hold thy peace, and come out of him?* Understand that even today there are many who have demons, that is, they perform the desires of the demons. For example, if someone is angry, he has the demon of anger. But if Jesus comes into the assembly, that is, into the mind of a man who has collected and rightly assembled his scattered thoughts, then Jesus will say to the wild demon of anger, *Hold thy peace.* And immediately *the demon* will *throw* the man *into the middle* and come out of him. Learn what this means, to *throw into the middle.* A man should not always be angry and bitter; that would be savagery. But neither should he always be without anger and feeling. Instead he should walk the middle path, and have anger only when anger is called for, that is, when confronting wickedness. When the evil spirit has thrown the man onto this middle path, then it comes out of him.

38-44. And He arose out of the synagogue, and entered into Simon's house. And Simon's mother-in-law was taken with a great fever; and they besought Him for her. And He stood over her, and rebuked the fever; and it left her: and immediately she arose and ministered unto them. Now when the sun was setting, all they that had any sick with various diseases brought them unto Him; and He laid His hands on every one of them, and healed them. And demons also came out of many, crying out, and saying, Thou art Christ the Son of God. And He rebuking them permitted them not to speak: for they knew that He was Christ. And when it was day, He departed and went into a desert place: and the multitude sought Him, and came unto Him, and kept Him that He should not depart from them. And He said unto them, I must bring the good tidings of the kingdom of God to other cities also: for this reason am I sent. And He preached in the synagogues of Galilee. The Master of all was given hospitality and fed by His disciples. And so now, having been given hospitality by Peter, the Lord heals his mother-in-law, teaching you, O reader, likewise to value the simple kindnesses shown to you by the lowly. The Lord does not simply heal her of her illness, but also gives her the vigor and strength to serve. And if we also welcome the Lord, He will quell our fever as well, the fever of anger and desire. He will raise us up to serve Him, that is, to do what is pleasing to Him. Consider also the faith of the multitude, how they brought their sick as the sun was setting, ignoring the lateness of the hour. For two reasons does the Lord not permit the demons to speak; first, because He has no need for the commendation of unclean spirits, for *praise is not seemly in the mouth of the sinner,*[11] and second, because He did not want to kindle the spite of the Jews by receiving praise from all sides. The multitude sought Him out even when He had gone away to a desert place and they *kept Him.* But He, being God, cannot be contained in one place. He says, *I must bring the good tidings of the kingdom of God to other cities also.* Neither should we be slothful, satisfied to remain in one place, but we should go about everywhere to bring benefit to others.

---

[11] Sirach (Ecclesiasticus) 15:9

CHAPTER FIVE

Concerning the catch of fish.
Concerning the leper. Concerning the paralytic.
Concerning Levi the publican.
Concerning the Lord when He ate with publicans.
Why did John's disciples fast, and Christ's did not?

1-11. And it came to pass, that, as the multitude pressed against Him to hear the word of God, He stood by the lake of Gennesaret, and saw two boats standing by the lake: but the fishermen were gone out of them, and were washing their nets. And He entered into one of the boats, which was Simon's, and prayed him that he would thrust out a little from the land. And He sat down, and taught the people out of the boat. Now when He had left speaking, He said unto Simon, Launch out into the deep, and let down your nets for a catch. And Simon answering said unto Him, Master, we have toiled all the night, and have taken nothing: nevertheless at Thy word I will let down the net. And when they had done this, they enclosed a great multitude of fishes, and their net broke. And they beckoned unto their partners, which were in the other boat, that they should come and help them. And they came, and filled both the boats, so that they began to sink. When Simon Peter saw it, he fell down at Jesus' knees, saying, Depart from me, for I am a sinful man, O Lord. For he was astonished, and all that were with him, at the catch of the fishes which they had taken; and so were also James, and John, the sons of Zebedee, who were partners with Simon. And Jesus said unto Simon, Fear not; from henceforth thou shalt catch men. And when they had brought their boats to land, they forsook all, and followed Him. The Lord flees glory, which all the more pursues Him. When the crowd pressed against Him, He entered the boat, so that from the boat He could teach those standing on the shore, and everyone would be in front of Him, rather than some coming towards Him from behind. And when He had finished teaching the people, He did not leave the owner of the boat without payment, but gave him a two-fold benefit: He bestowed on him an abundance of fish, and He made him His disciple. Marvel at how wisely the Lord arranges our salvation, drawing to Himself each one by means of the things that are his own and with which he is familiar. As

He had attracted the Magi with a star, so now He draws the fishermen by means of fish. See the gentleness of Christ, how He does not command, but requests that Peter put out from land. See also the obedience of Peter, how he welcomes into his boat a man whom he did not know, and obeys Him in everything. When the Lord tells him to launch out into the deep, Peter does not become exasperated and leave Him, nor does he reply, ''I have toiled the whole night and gained nothing, and now I should obey you and do it all again?'' Peter said nothing like this, but instead, *At Thy word I will let down the net.* Such was the warmth of his trust even before he had faith. And he caught so great a number of fish that he was not able to haul them in, and he beckoned to his companions in the other boat. He calls them with a signal, because his astonishment at the catch was so great that he could not even speak. Out of great reverence for Jesus, Peter begs Him not to remain in the boat, and calls himself a sinner who is not worthy to be with Him. You may also understand these things in a spiritual sense. The boat is the synagogue of the Jews. Peter represents the teachers of the law. For the teachers of the law also toiled the whole night before Christ came (the time before Christ's sojourning on earth was indeed *night*) and took in nothing. But when Christ came, and it became day, the teachers of the law were replaced by the apostles who, at His word, that is, at His command, *let down the net* of the Gospel in which they caught so great a number of men that the apostles could not haul in the catch by themselves. And so they beckon to their partners and companions and together they pull in the net. These are the pastors and teachers of the Church in every generation who teach and interpret the words of the apostles, laboring with the apostles to catch mankind. Consider also the words, *Let down the net.* The net is the Gospel; like the fisherman's net, which is a lowly and commonplace thing, the Gospel is composed of humble, everyday words which reach down and condescend to the simplicity of the people. This is why it is said that the net is *let down.* And if any one should say that letting down the net also indicates the depth of meaning of the Gospel, neither would he be off the mark. Therefore the words of the prophet have also been fulfilled, *Behold, I will send many fishermen, saith the Lord, and they shall fish for them; and afterward I will send many hunters, and they shall hunt for them.*[1] The

---

[1] Jer. 16:16

fishermen are the holy apostles, and the hunters are the leaders and teachers of the Church in each generation.

12-16. And it came to pass, when He was in one of the cities, behold a man full of leprosy: who, seeing Jesus, fell on his face, and besought Him, saying, Lord, if Thou wilt, Thou canst make me clean. And He put forth His hand, and touched him, saying, I will: be thou clean. And immediately the leprosy departed from him. And He charged him to tell no man: but go, and show thyself to the priest, and offer for thy cleansing, according as Moses commanded, for a testimony unto them. But so much the more went there word of Him abroad: and great multitudes came together to hear, and to be healed by Him of their infirmities. And He withdrew Himself into the wilderness, and prayed. The leper is worthy of admiration, having such a divine understanding concerning the Lord when he said, *If Thou wilt, Thou canst make me clean.* This shows that the leper thought of Christ as God. He did not approach Jesus as a physician, (for the hands of a physician cannot heal leprosy,) but as God. God alone can heal such ailments as these. Not without reason did the Lord touch the leper. According to the law, one who touched a leper became unclean himself, and so the Lord wanted to show that He has no need to observe such small points of the law, since He Himself is Lord of the law. He also wanted to show that no one who is pure can be stained by what appears to be unclean: it is only sin, the leprosy of souls, which stains. This is why He touched the leper. But, at the same time, He touched the leper to show that His holy flesh has divine power and is purifying and life-creating, being the flesh of God the Word. He commands the leper to speak to no one, teaching us not to seek words of praise from those whom we have helped. The Lord said to the leper, *Go, and show thyself to the priest, and offer* the gift *for a testimony unto them.* For it was the law that the priest should examine those who had leprosy to determine if they had been cleansed or not. If after seven days the former leper were still clean, he could remain inside the city, but if not, he was cast out. The Lord therefore says this to him, *Go, and show thyself to the priest, and offer* the gift. What was the gift? Two birds. And what does this mean, *for a testimony unto them*? It means, "as a reproof and an accusation against them. When they accuse Me of transgressing the law, they shall be reproved by this fact, that I did not transgress the law, but

commanded you to offer the gift which Moses commanded.'' It is not out
of place to explain how these two birds were offered to God. Only one
of the birds was slaughtered and its blood was received in a new vessel
made of clay. Then both wings of the other bird were dipped in the
blood, and it was released, living. These things depict the life of Christ.
The two birds are the two natures of Christ, the divine and the human,
one of which was slain, namely, His human nature, while the other was
released, alive. The divine nature remained unsuffering, but it was
anointed with the blood of the suffering nature, taking upon itself that
suffering. And the blood of the Lord was received in a new earthen
vessel which is, I say, the new people from among the Gentiles who
received the New Testament. See that it is after a man has been cleansed
of leprosy that he is worthy to offer this gift, that is, to [offer the]
sacrifice [of] Christ[2] and to celebrate the Divine Liturgy. As long as his
soul is leprous and unclean, he would not be deemed worthy to offer such
gifts as these, namely, the Body and Blood of the Lord, which have been
united to the divine nature. Take note as well how ineffably greater the
Lord is than Moses. Moses was unable to heal at once his sister when she
had leprosy, even though he prayed fervently.[3] But by His word alone
the Lord cleansed the leper. Comprehend also the humility of the Lord,
how, when the multitude was clamoring to touch Him, He preferred to
pray alone in the wilderness. In everything He did He taught us by His
own example to turn away from celebrity and to pray in solitude.

**17-26. And it came to pass on a certain day, as He was teaching,
that there were Pharisees and teachers of the law sitting by, who
were come out of every town of Galilee, and Judea, and Jerusalem:
and the power of the Lord was present to heal them. And, behold,
men brought on a bed a man who was paralyzed; and they sought
means to bring him in, and to lay him before Him. And when they**

---

[2] Bl. Theophylact actually says, ...*he is worthy to offer this gift, that is, to sacrifice Christ...*
(emphases added). Because of Scholastic errors and misconceptions of the Western middle ages, some
may find it difficult to hear in English that the priest, in the celebration of the Divine Liturgy,
"sacrifices Christ." For a lucid explanation of the true meaning of *sacrifice,* namely, that it is an
offering and not retributive punishment, see *The Dogma of Redemption,* Metropolitan Antony
Khrapovitski, Monastery Press, Montreal, 1979, pp. 42-45.

[3] Numbers 12:13-15

could not find by what way they might bring him in because of the multitude, they went upon the housetop, and let him down through the tiling with his bed, into the middle before Jesus. And when He saw their faith, He said unto him, Man, thy sins are forgiven thee. And the scribes and the Pharisees began to reason, saying, Who is this who speaketh blasphemies? Who can forgive sins, but God alone? But perceiving their thoughts, Jesus answering said unto them, What reason ye in your hearts? Which is easier, to say, Thy sins be forgiven thee; or to say, Rise up and walk? But that ye may know that the Son of Man hath authority upon earth to forgive sins, (He said unto the paralytic,) I say unto thee, Arise, and take up thy bed, and go into thine house. And immediately he rose up before them, and took up that whereon he lay, and departed to his own house, glorifying God. And they were all amazed, and they glorified God, and were filled with fear, saying, We have seen wondrous things today. With His enemies gathered there together, it was fitting that the Lord perform some new wonder. Therefore He heals a man who had an ailment which was difficult to cure, so that by healing such a disease He could also treat the fury of the Pharisees, which was likewise difficult to cure. First He heals the ailment of the soul, saying, *Thy sins are forgiven thee,* thus teaching us that many illnesses are caused by sins. Then He also heals the ailment of the body, when He sees the faith of those who brought the paralytic. For the Lord often saves one man on account of the faith of another. The Pharisees say, *Who is this who speaketh blasphemies? Who can forgive sins but God alone?* By saying this, they pass a sentence of death upon Him, for the law commanded that one who uttered blasphemy against God was liable to death. The Lord then proves to them, by means of yet another miracle, that indeed He is God and is not making empty boasts. He reveals their thoughts, thus making it abundantly clear that He is God. For God alone knows the hearts of men. The Lord then says, ''Which appears easier to you, to forgive sins, or to heal the body? Of course by your reckoning it appears easier to forgive sins, because that is something invisible, which cannot be verified, although in fact it is more difficult. To heal the body appears more difficult to you, because it is visible, although in truth it is easier than to forgive sins. But I am able to do both. And by healing the body, which to you seems more difficult, I shall confirm that I have also healed the soul, which, although it is difficult, appears easy to you because it is invisible." See that sins are forgiven on earth. While we are on the earth we are able to blot out our sins by repentance. But after we have left the earth, we ourselves can no longer do this: the door has been shut. We have said more concerning this passage in *The Explanation* of the other Gospels.[4]

27-32. And after these things He went forth, and saw a publican, named Levi, sitting collecting tax: and He said unto him, Follow Me. And he left all, and rose up, and followed Him. And Levi made Him a great feast in his own house: and there was a great company of publicans and of others that sat down with them. But their scribes and Pharisees murmured against His disciples, saying, Why do ye eat and drink with publicans and sinners? And Jesus answering said unto them, They that are whole need not a physician; but they that are sick. I came not to call the righteous, but sinners to repentance. Matthew openly proclaims his own name, saying in his Gospel, Jesus *saw a man, named Matthew, sitting collecting tax.*[5] But Luke and Mark, out of deference to the Evangelist, give his other name, Levi. Marvel at God's love for man, how He snatches a tool out of the very hand of the evil one. The publican is a tool of the devil and a wicked beast, as those who have experience with these merciless tax collectors know full well. For the publicans were those who paid a sum of money [to the emperor] in return for a license to collect all the taxes they could extract from the people in a given tax district, and to pocket the profit so gained, to the condemnation of their own souls. But the Lord used every means to gain, not only Matthew himself, but also the other publicans with whom He ate. The Lord deemed it right to eat even with these publicans, so that He might draw them to Himself. When the Pharisees accuse Him, see the answer they are given: *"I came not,"* the Lord says, *"to call the righteous,* that is, those of you who count yourselves righteous. Instead I came to call sinners, not that they continue in their sin, but that they might repent." And, in another sense, the Lord is saying, "I have not come to call the righteous, for I have found none, because all men are

---

[4] See Vol. 1, *The Explanation* of St. Matthew, pp. 76-77; Vol. 2, *The Explanation* of St. Mark, pp. 25-26; and the forthcoming Vol. 4, *The Explanation* of St. John, for Jn. 5:1-9.

[5] Mat. 9:9

sinners. Had it been possible to find any righteous men without sin, there would have been no need for Me to come.'' The publican [in his dealings with the ruler] also represents everyone who is enslaved to the ruler of this world, and who pays what is demanded by the flesh. The glutton gives food as tribute to his belly, the fornicator gives his fornication, and likewise each sinner gives his sin as tribute to the flesh. But when the Lord, that is, the Word of the Gospel, sees the sinner sitting down at the tax booth, that is, not up and about pursuing more and more evil, but taking his rest from wickedness, then the Gospel Word will raise that sinner up from evil to follow Jesus, and that man will invite the Lord into the house of his soul. But like the Pharisees, the proud demons, who have set themselves apart from God, grumble and complain that God communes with sinners. For *Pharisee* means *one who is set apart.*

33-39. And they said unto Him, Why do the disciples of John fast often, and make prayers, and likewise the disciples of the Pharisees; but Thine eat and drink? And He said unto them, Can ye make the sons of the bridal chamber fast, while the bridegroom is with them? But the days will come, when the bridegroom shall be taken away from them, and then shall they fast in those days. And He spake also a parable unto them: no man putteth a piece of a new garment upon an old; if so, then both the new maketh a rent, and the piece that was taken out of the new agreeth not with the old. And no man putteth new wine into old wineskins; else the new wine will burst the wineskins, and be spilled, and the wineskins shall perish. But new wine must be put into new wineskins; and both are preserved. No man also having drunk old wine straightway desireth new; for he saith, The old is better. We have spoken concerning these things in *The Explanation* of St. Matthew.[6] But we shall speak again now, briefly. The Lord calls the apostles the *sons of the bridal chamber.* For the coming of the Lord is likened to a marriage in which the Lord betroths Himself to the Church and takes her as His Bride. Therefore the apostles ought not to fast now. The disciples of John, on the other hand, ought to fast, because their teacher accomplished virtue through toil and hard labor.

---

[6] Vol. 1, *The Explanation* of St. Matthew, p. 79.

"*For John came,*" the Lord says, "*neither eating nor drinking.*[7] But the disciples who are with Me, God the Word, do not need the benefit of fasting now, for they are guarded by Me and receive grace directly. When I have ascended, and they have been sent forth to preach, then they will fast and pray, because they will undergo great struggles. Furthermore, because they are now weak and have not yet been made new by the Holy Spirit, they are like old wineskins and old cloth. They ought not to be overburdened and strained by a more austere way of life, for the same reason that an old garment ought not to be patched with a piece of new cloth." As I have just said, you may understand the old wineskins to mean the apostles while they were still weak. But you may also understand the old wineskins to mean the Pharisees, as if the Lord were saying to the Pharisees, "My teaching is new wine. But you, who are old wineskins, are not able to receive this new teaching. And because you are drinking the old wine, that is, the old tradition, you do not want My new wine, and you say that the old wine, that is, the Old Testament, is better."

---

[7] Mt. 11:18

CHAPTER SIX

*Concerning Christ's disciples who plucked
the heads of grain on the sabbath.
Concerning the man with the withered hand.
Concerning the choosing of the apostles.
Concerning the beatitudes. On loving one's enemies.
On not quarreling with one's neighbor.
On not judging one's neighbor.*

1-5. And it came to pass on the second sabbath after the first, that He went through the grain fields; and His disciples plucked the heads of grain, and did eat, rubbing them in their hands. And certain of the Pharisees said unto them, Why do ye that which is not lawful to do on the sabbath days? And Jesus answering them said, Have ye not read so much as this, what David did, when he himself hungered, and they which were with him; how he went into the house of God, and did take and eat the loaves of oblation, and gave also to them that were with him; which it is not lawful to eat but for the priests alone? And He said unto them, the Son of Man is Lord also of the sabbath. The Jews called every feast a *sabbath* because *sabbath* means *rest.* Therefore, when a feast day fell on a Friday, as it often would, they would call that Friday *sabbath* because of the feast. In that case they would call the following day, which was the actual sabbath day, *the second sabbath after the first,*[1] because it came second in time, preceded by the "first sabbath" which was the feast day. It happened to be just such an occasion on this day, and so the Evangelist calls it *the second sabbath after the first.* When the Pharisees accused the disciples of working on the sabbath by plucking and rubbing the heads of grain in their hands, and eating, the Lord offers as evidence in their defense the example of David, who ate the loaves of oblation when he became hungry. For when he was fleeing from Saul, David approached Abiathar the high priest, and tricked him by saying that the king had sent him on some urgent mission. And, since he was hungry, David took the loaves of oblation from the priest, that is, he took those twelve loaves which

---

[1] *deuteroprōton*

were set forth on the holy table each day, six on the right side and six on
the left. David also took the sword of Goliath.[2] The Lord relates this
incident to the Pharisees in order to shame them by David's own actions.
"If you hold David in honor," He is saying, "how can you condemn My
disciples? Moreover, I Myself, the Son of Man, am Lord of the sabbath,
since I am Creator, Maker, Master, and Lawgiver, and I have the
authority to relax the laws of the sabbath." No one else can be called the
Son of Man except Christ, the Son of God, Who for man's sake saw fit
to become and to be called, paradoxically, the Son of Man. For you or
me to be called a son of man is nothing strange, but it is only Christ,
Who became man in a manner beyond understanding, who can be rightly
called *the Son of Man.*

**6-11. And it came to pass also on another sabbath, that He entered
into the synagogue and taught: and there was a man whose right
hand was withered. And the scribes and Pharisees were watching
Him, whether He would heal on the sabbath day; that they might
find an accusation against Him. But He knew their thoughts, and said
to the man who had the withered hand, Rise up, and stand forth in
the middle. And he arose and stood forth. Then said Jesus unto them,
I will ask you one thing; Is it lawful on the sabbath days to do good,
or to do evil? to save life, or to destroy it? And looking round about
upon them all, He said unto the man, Stretch forth thy hand. And He
did so: and his hand was restored whole as the other. And they were
filled with madness; and conversed one with another what they might
do to Jesus.** We have already spoken concerning this miracle in *The
Explanation* of St. Matthew's Gospel.[3] Now we also say that a man who
does no works of virtue is the man whose hand is withered. The hand is
that member of the body which performs work, and if a man's hand is
withered, he can do no work. Therefore whoever wants his withered hand
made whole, it will be made whole on the day of rest. What I mean is
this: a man cannot do any deed of virtue unless he rests from doing evil.
First turn away from evil, and then do good.[4] Therefore, when you have

---

[2] I Kings (I Samuel) 21:1-9

[3] Vol. 1, *The Explanation* of St. Matthew, pp. 101-102.

[4] See Ps. 33:14.

kept a sabbath day of rest, that is, when you have ceased from doing works of evil, then stretch out your hand to do works of virtue, and your hand shall be restored. It was fitting that the Evangelist said that the man's hand was *restored.* For there was a time when human nature had the power to do good, and when the *hand,* that is, the strength to act, was whole. But when human nature lost this power, Christ by grace recovered it, and restored it to its former good estate.

12-19. And it came to pass in those days, that He went out onto a mountain to pray, and continued all night in prayer to God. And when it was day, He called unto Him His disciples: and of them He chose twelve, whom also He named apostles; Simon, (whom He also named Peter,) and Andrew his brother, James and John, Philip and Bartholomew, Matthew and Thomas, James the son of Alphaeus, and Simon called the Zealot, and Judas the brother of James, and Judas Iscariot, who also became the traitor. And He came down with them, and stood in the plain, and the company of His disciples, and a great multitude of people out of all Judea and Jerusalem, and from the sea coast of Tyre and Sidon, who came to hear Him, and to be healed of their diseases; and they that were vexed with unclean spirits: and they were healed. And the whole multitude sought to touch Him: for there went power out of Him, and healed them all. In everything He did, the Lord teaches us to do likewise. See how He went up onto a mountain when He intended to pray. We also ought to pray in solitude, free from distractions, and not when we are in the midst of other people. And we should also *continue all night* in prayer, and not stop immediately after starting. After prayer He chose the disciples, teaching us that when we intend to ordain someone for spiritual ministry, we should first pray before choosing the candidate and be guided by God, beseeching Him to reveal to us the one suited for this task. Having chosen the twelve, He descended from the mountain to heal those who came to Him from the cities, and to bring benefit to them in both soul and body. Listen to what the Evangelist says: they *came to hear Him*—this is the healing of the soul—and *to be healed of their diseases*—this is the healing of the body. *For there went power out of Him, and healed them all.* The prophets and the other saints did not have power which went out from them, for they were not themselves the source of power and of mighty deeds. But the Lord had power which went out from Him, for He is the

source of power. The prophets and the saints only received power from
above.

**20-26. And He lifted up His eyes on His disciples, and said, Blessed
be ye poor: for yours is the kingdom of God. Blessed are ye that
hunger now: for ye shall be filled. Blessed are ye that weep now: for
ye shall laugh. Blessed are ye, when men shall hate you, and when
they shall separate you from their company, and shall reproach you,
and reject your name as evil, for the Son of Man's sake. Rejoice ye
in that day, and leap for joy: for, behold, your reward is great in
heaven: for in the like manner did their fathers unto the prophets.
But woe unto you that are rich! for ye have received your consolation. Woe unto you that are full! for ye shall hunger. Woe unto you
that laugh now! for ye shall mourn and weep. Woe unto you, when
all men shall speak well of you! for so did their fathers to the false
prophets.** These words of the Lord are directed to the disciples. After
ordaining them, the Lord uses these beatitudes and teachings to guide
them into a more spiritual life. He first blesses the poor, whom you may
understand to mean either those who are humble or those who live
without greed for money. Simply put, all the beatitudes teach us
lowliness, humility, self-effacement, and self-reproach. And accordingly
Woe! awaits those who are rich and prosperous now, in this life, those
who the Lord says *have received* their *consolation,* meaning that in this
life they have enjoyed revelry, laughter, feasting, and the praise of men.
Let us tremble, brothers, to hear that *Woe!* awaits those who are praised
by men. First we ought to live such a life that will draw down upon us
the praise of God, and then others will indeed speak well of us.

**27-36. But I say unto you which hear, Love your enemies, do good
to them which hate you, bless them that curse you, and pray for them
which despitefully use you. And unto him that smiteth thee on the
one cheek offer also the other; and him that taketh away thy cloak
forbid not to take thy tunic also. Give to every man that asketh of
thee; and of him that taketh away thy goods ask them not again. And
as ye would that men should do to you, do ye also to them likewise.
For if ye love them which love you, what thank have ye? For sinners
also love those that love them. And if ye do good to them which do
good to you, what thank have ye? For sinners also do even the same.**

And if ye lend to them of whom ye hope to receive, what thank have ye? For sinners also lend to sinners, to receive as much again. But love ye your enemies, and do good, and lend, hoping for nothing again; and your reward shall be great, and ye shall be the sons of the Most High; for He is kind unto the unthankful and to the evil. Be ye therefore merciful, as your Father also is merciful. The apostles were about to be sent out to preach and many persecutors and plotters awaited them. If the apostles were fearful and dismayed by persecution, they might want to protect themselves from their persecutors by keeping silent and not teaching. If that happened, the radiant sun of the Gospel would be extinguished. In anticipation of this, the Lord exhorts the apostles not to give way to defensive measures against their enemies, but instead bravely to endure all things, even insults and murderous plots. This is what He Himself did on the Cross, saying, *Father, forgive them, for they know not what they do.*[5] To prove to the apostles that this commandment to love one's enemies is possible to keep, He then says, "What you want to be done to you, do the same to others; and be to others that kind of person you want others to be to you." If you want your enemies to be hard, unfeeling, and angry towards you, then be the same yourself to them. But if you want them to be kind and compassionate towards you, and not to remember wrongs, do not think that it is impossible for you yourself to be the same towards them. Do you see this natural law which is written in our hearts? That is why the Lord also said, *In those days I will surely put My laws into their mind, and write them on their hearts.*[6] Then He adds another compelling reason to keep this commandment: if you love those who love you, you are like the sinners and the Gentiles; but if you love those who do evil to you, you are like God, *Who is kind unto the unthankful and to the evil.* Which do you desire, to be like sinners, or to be like God? Do you see the divine teaching? First He persuaded you by means of the natural law: what you want to be done to you, do to others. Then He persuades you with the result and the reward—He promises that you will become like God.

37-40. Judge not, and ye shall not be judged; condemn not, and ye

---

[5] Lk. 23:34

[6] Jer. 38:33

shall not be condemned; forgive, and ye shall be forgiven; give, and it shall be given unto you: a good measure, pressed down, and shaken together, and running over, shall they give into your bosom. For with the same measure by which ye measure it shall be measured to you again. And He spake a parable unto them, Can the blind lead the blind? Shall they not both fall into the ditch? The disciple is not above his teacher: but every one that has learned perfectly shall be as his teacher. The Lord cuts out a most grievous sickness which is rooted in our souls: looking down on others. Consider a man who does not examine himself, but only scrutinizes his neighbor, hoping to find fault there. It is very clear that such a man is so busy looking down on others that he is oblivious of himself. Because he never sees himself as a sinner, he is quick to accuse others of sinning. Therefore if you do not want to be condemned yourself, do not condemn others. Tell me, why do you condemn someone else? Is it because he has transgressed God's laws? But do you think that you yourself do not transgress God's law? Never mind all your other sins; by this alone, judging others, you yourself transgress the law. For God has given you this commandment, that you not judge your brother. Since you are a transgressor yourself, you should not judge another to be a transgressor; a judge ought to be above crime. Therefore *forgive, and ye shall be forgiven; give, and it shall be given unto you: a good measure, pressed down, and shaken together, and running over, shall they give into your bosom.* Not sparingly, but generously, does the Lord measure out to you again. In measuring some flour, you press it down, and shake it, and make it a heaping measure, if you do not wish to measure stintingly. In just the same way the Lord will give you a large heaping measure that runs over. But a listener who pays close attention might ask, "How can the Lord say, *By the same measure with which ye measure, it shall be measured to you again,* and at the same time say, *A measure...running over shall they give into your bosom*? If it runs over, how can it be the same measure?" We answer that He did not say, "In an equal amount shall it be measured to you again," but instead He said, *by the same measure.* If the Lord had said, "In an equal amount," then His words would have been troublesome and contradictory. Since He actually said, *by the same measure,* there is no contradiction. To give something according to the same measure is not the same as giving something in equal amount. The Lord, therefore, is saying this: if you do good to others, you will receive good by that same measure. The measure *running over* means that when you have done good on one occasion, you will receive good ten thousand fold. It is the same with judging others. He who judges another and then comes to be judged himself, receives by the same measure as he gave. Because he receives greater condemnation for having judged his fellow man, his measure also is *running over*. Having spoken these words in which He forbids us to judge others, the Lord then gives us a parable, that is, an example. ''Tell Me,'' He says, ''a man who judges another when he himself has the same sins, is he not like a blind man leading the blind? If you judge another to be a sinner and yet you fall to the same sins yourself, are you not both blind? You think that you are guiding him towards the good by judging him, but you are not guiding him at all. How can he be guided to the good by you, when you yourself are in error? *The disciple is not above his teacher,* that is, the student cannot know more than his teacher. Therefore, if you fancy yourself as someone else's teacher and guide even though you are yourself in error, then the one who is taught and guided by you will certainly err as well. For the student who has learned perfectly everything taught to him by his teacher shall be just like his teacher.'' The Lord said these things concerning how we ought not to condemn those who fall short of our standards and appear to sin. Then he speaks more on the same subject.

41-45. And why beholdest thou the speck that is in thy brother's eye, but perceivest not the beam that is in thine own eye? Or how canst thou say to thy brother, Brother, let me pull out the speck that is in thine eye, when thou thyself beholdest not the beam that is in thine own eye? Thou hypocrite, pull out first the beam from thine own eye, and then shalt thou see clearly to pull out the speck that is in thy brother's eye. For a good tree bringeth not forth bad fruit; neither doth a bad tree bring forth good fruit. For every tree is known by its own fruit. For from thorns men do not gather figs, nor from a bramble bush gather they grapes. A good man out of the good treasure of his heart bringeth forth that which is good; and an evil man out of the evil treasure of his heart bringeth forth that which is evil: for out of the abundance of the heart his mouth speaketh. Why, He asks, do you look at the speck, that is, the small sin of your brother, while not perceiving the timber, that is, your own great sin? The Lord here directs His words to all, but especially to teachers and rulers who punish the smallest sins of those who are under them, while their own much larger sins go unpunished. Therefore the Lord also calls them hypocrites, because they appear in one light, righteous punishers of the sins of others, when in fact they are something quite different, even greater sinners themselves. Then the Lord confirms His words with an example. Just as it is impossible, He says, for a good tree to produce bad fruit, or for a bad tree to produce good fruit, neither could a man be evil who tries to recall others to their senses, to correct them, and to lead them to the good. If he were evil, he would not labor to make others better. The heart of each man is a treasury; if it contains good things, then the man himself is good, and he speaks good things. But if the heart is full of evil, then the man is evil, and he speaks evil things. You may also understand all these things to refer to the Pharisees. Addressing them the Lord is saying, *Pull out first the beam from thine own eye, and then...pull out the speck from thy brother's eye. As the Lord says in another place, they strain at the gnat and swallow the camel.*[7] Then He asks the Pharisees, "How can you who are corrupt bring forth good fruit? Your speech is corrupt, and your life as well, because what you say spills out of what is in your hearts. How then will you correct others? Will you punish the sins of others when you yourselves commit even greater sins?"

46-49. And why call ye Me, Lord, Lord, and do not the things which I say? Whosoever cometh to Me, and heareth My sayings, and doeth them, I will show you to whom he is like. He is like a man who built a house, and dug deep, and laid the foundation on a rock. And when the flood arose, the stream beat vehemently upon that house, and could not shake it: for it was founded upon a rock. But he that heareth, and doeth not, is like a man that built a house upon the ground without a foundation, against which the stream did beat vehemently, and immediately it fell; and great was the ruin of that house. This too is necessary for us to hear, because we confess the Lord with our lips but deny Him with our deeds. If I am your Lord and Master, He says, then you ought to do what servants do. The work of servants is to do what their master commands. Then He tells us how it

---

[7] Mt. 23:24

profits a man not only to hear His words, but also to do them. Such a one is like a man who built a house upon the rock. The rock is Christ, as the Apostle testifies.[8] And that man digs deep who does not receive the words of Scripture in a superficial manner, but searches out their depth with the aid of the Spirit. Such a man also lays his foundation upon the Rock. And when the flood of persecution or temptation arises, the tempter, whether demon or man, will beat against that house like a stream, and will not be able to shake it. He who tempts another is likened to a flooding river, and rightly so. Just as the rain falling from above causes the river to swell and overflow its banks, likewise Satan who fell from heaven causes a man to swell up and try his brother's faith. The house falls when its builders do not do the words of the Lord, and great is the ruin of that house. It is those who hear, but do not do, what the Lord says, whose fall is *great*. For the sin of the man who heard but did not do what the Lord said is more grievous than the sin of the man who never heard the Lord at all.

---

[8] I Cor. 10:4

CHAPTER SEVEN

Concerning the centurion.
Concerning the widow's son.
Concerning those sent by John.
Concerning the woman who anointed the Lord with myrrh.

1-10. Now when He had ended all His sayings in the audience of the people, He entered into Capernaum. And a certain centurion's servant, who was dear unto him, was sick, and ready to die. And when he heard of Jesus, he sent unto Him the elders of the Jews, beseeching Him that He would come and heal his servant. And when they came to Jesus, they besought Him urgently, saying, He for whom Thou shouldest do this is worthy: for he loveth our nation, and he hath built us a synagogue. Then Jesus went with them. And when He was now not far from the house, the centurion sent friends to Him, saying unto Him, Lord, trouble not Thyself: for I am not worthy that Thou shouldest enter under my roof. Wherefore neither thought I myself worthy to come unto Thee: but say the word, and my servant shall be healed. For I also am a man set under authority, having under me soldiers, and I say unto one, Go, and he goeth; and to another, come, and he cometh; and to my servant, Do this, and he doeth it. When Jesus heard these things, He marvelled at him. And He turned about, and said unto the people that followed Him, I say unto you, I have not found so great faith, no, not in Israel. And they that were sent, returning to the house, found the servant whole that had been sick. This is the same centurion mentioned in Matthew.[1] And if Matthew does not say that the centurion sent the Jews to make his request and supplication to Jesus, what of it? It is likely that first the centurion sent the Jews, and then he came himself: therefore Luke says what Matthew omitted. And perhaps the Jews out of envy did not want the centurion to come to the feet of Jesus. For this brought renown to Jesus when, in the end, the urgency of his request compelled the centurion himself to approach Jesus. Again, someone might wonder why Matthew says that the centurion himself, with his own voice, declined to

---

[1] Mt. 8:5-13

have Jesus come to his house, but Luke says here that he sent others to beg Jesus not to come. In answer it can be said that it is not strange that he first sent others, and then he himself came to speak these words, begging Him not to come. Truly wondrous is the faith of this man who calls himself unworthy to be visited by Jesus. This is why the Lord says, *"I have not found so great faith, no, not* even among the people of Israel."* The centurion was a Gentile, probably a Roman. The centurion also represents every mind which in wickedness stands out above a hundred others, and busies himself in the world with a hundred and one things. Such a mind has a servant who has fallen sick, by which I mean the nonreasoning faculties of the soul, namely, the abilities to stir to action and to desire.[2] These faculties had been assigned by God to serve the mind [but now are ailing and cannot do so]. This mind calls upon Jesus, sending to Him as mediators the *Jews,* that is, thoughts and words of confession. For *Jew* [from *Judah*] means *confession.* Are not the words *I am not worthy that Thou shouldest come under my roof* words of confession and humility? And when the mind has faith in Jesus, it will quickly receive back whole and sound its servant, the emotions.

11-16. And it came to pass the day after, that He went into a city called Nain; and many of His disciples went with Him, and much people. Now when He came nigh to the gate of the city, behold, there was a dead man carried out, the only son of his mother, and she was a widow: and much people of the city was with her. And when the Lord saw her, He had compassion on her, and said unto her, Weep not. And He came and touched the bier: and they that bare him stood still. And He said, Young man, I say unto thee, Arise. And he that was dead sat up, and began to speak. And He delivered him to his mother. And there came a fear on all: and they glorified God, saying, that a great prophet is risen up among us; and, that God hath visited His people. Because the Lord, while not even present, had healed the centurion's servant, He now performs another even more remarkable miracle. He does this so that no one could say, "What is remarkable about the healing of the centurion's servant? Perhaps the servant would not have died in any case." This is why the Lord now raises up the dead

---

[2] On the three faculties of the soul, see Vol. 1, *The Explanation* of St. Matthew, p. 116.

man as he was being carried out for burial. He does not perform the miracle by His word alone, but He also touches the bier, teaching us that His very Body is life. Because God the Word Who gives life to all things Himself became flesh, therefore His flesh itself is likewise life-creating, and takes away death and corruption. The dead man sat up and began to speak, so that some would not think that his rising was only an apparition. Sitting up and speaking are definite proof of resurrection from the dead; for how can a lifeless body sit up and speak? You may also understand the widow to mean the soul which has suffered the loss of its husband, the Word of God Which sows the good seed. And the son of such a widow is the mind which is dead and is being carried outside the city, that is, outside the heavenly Jerusalem which is the land of the living. The Lord then takes pity, and touches the bier. The bier which carries the dead mind is the body. And indeed the body is like a tomb, as the ancient Greeks said, calling the body [sōma] a burial mound [sēma], which means a tomb. Having touched the body, the Lord then raises the mind, restoring its youth and vigor. And after the young man, meaning the mind, has sat up, raised from the tomb of sin, he will begin to speak, that is, to teach others. For while he is in the grip of sin, he cannot speak or teach: who would believe him?

17-30. And this report of Him went forth throughout all Judea, and throughout all the region round about. And the disciples of John declared unto him all these things. And John calling unto him two of his disciples sent them to Jesus, saying, Art Thou He that cometh, or do we look for another? When the men were come unto Him, they said, John the Baptist hath sent us unto Thee, saying, Art Thou He that cometh, or do we look for another? And in that same hour He cured many of their infirmities and plagues, and of evil spirits; and unto many that were blind He gave sight. Then Jesus answering said unto them, Go your way, and tell John what things ye have seen and heard; how that the blind see, the lame walk, the lepers are cleansed, the deaf hear, the dead are raised, the poor have the good tidings. And blessed is he, whosoever shall not be offended in Me. And when the messengers of John were departed, He began to speak unto the people concerning John, What went ye out into the wilderness for to see? A reed shaken with the wind? But what went ye out for to see? A man clothed in soft raiment? Behold, they which are gorgeously

apparelled, and live delicately, are in kings' courts. But what went ye
out for to see? A prophet? Yea, I say unto you, and much more than
a prophet. This is he, of whom it is written, Behold, I send My angel
before Thy face, who shall prepare Thy way before Thee. For I say
unto you, Among those that are born of women there is not a greater
prophet than John the Baptist: but he that is younger in the kingdom
of God is greater than he. And all the people that heard Him, and
the publicans, justified God, being baptized with the baptism of John.
But the Pharisees and lawyers rejected the counsel of God against
themselves, being not baptized by him.** News of the miracle that Jesus
did in Nain spread throughout all Judea and the surrounding region, and
it was also heard by John's disciples. They were smitten with envy at the
praise given to the Lord, because they did not yet have full understanding. Therefore John wanted to show them Christ's greatness, and the
distance between himself and Christ, and so he arranged what followed.
He gave his disciples no information concerning Christ, but instead
pretended that he himself did not know Who Christ was. He sent two of
his disciples, so that they would see the miracles and thus come to
believe, from the very deeds which He did, that the distance was
enormous between Jesus the Master and John the servant. Do not think
that John was in fact ignorant of Who Christ was, and for this reason he
sent disciples to ask. How could he not know Christ when, before his
own birth, he had leapt in his mother's womb as he recognized Christ,
and when in the Jordan he had borne witness to Him as the Son of God?
Therefore he sends his disciples, telling them to ask Jesus, *Art Thou He
that cometh?* Do you see how John is leading his disciples step by step
to the belief that Jesus is God? For the Scriptures say that the prophets
were *sent,* just like John himself, of whom the Evangelist says, *There was
a man sent from God.*[3] But the Lord is *He that cometh.* He came on His
own authority, not as another's messenger. Therefore John's disciples ask,
''Art Thou He Who is expected to come into the world?'' Some say *He
that cometh* also means *He that cometh* into Hades [where the righteous
who died before Christ awaited Him]. What then does the Lord do?
Knowing the purpose for which John sent the disciples, that they should
see the things which Jesus did, and through these things believe, He says

---

[3] Jn. 1:6

to them, *Tell John what things ye have seen.* Then He lists the miraculous deeds, which had been foretold by the prophets. *The blind see, the lame walk, the poor have the good tidings*—these things were foretold by Isaiah.[4] Then the Lord says, *Blessed is he, whosoever shall not be offended in Me,* as if He were saying to them, "And you yourselves are blessed, if you are not offended by Me." For it is likely that many were offended that John, who before had spoken such great words of testimony concerning Jesus as the Christ, should now be sending disciples to ask if Jesus were *He that cometh.* This is why Christ says to the multitudes, "Do not think that way about John. He is not a reed which bends this way and that, one moment bearing testimony of Me, and the next ignorant of Who I am. If he were, why would you have gone out into the desert to see him? Have luxuries dulled his mind, you wonder? No, his clothing shows that he is far removed from delicacies. And if he did live luxuriously, he would live in a palace. Do you not consider him to be a prophet? *Yea, I say unto you, and much more than a prophet.*" The other prophets only foretold the coming of Christ, but John also saw Christ, and revealed Him to others, saying, *Behold, the Lamb of God.* And the other prophets first left their mothers' womb and then prophesied, but John, even before he had left the womb, recognized the Lord and leapt for joy. Then the Lord introduces the testimony of the prophet Malachi, saying, *This is he, of whom it is written, Behold, I send My angel before Thy face.*[5] John was an angel, on account of his angelic and almost immaterial way of life, and also because he announced the Saviour's visitation among men. The Lord says, "Verily I say unto you, there has not been raised up among those born of women one greater than John," thus exalting the Forerunner above all men. Then, as if in answer to the question, "Is he greater than Thee also, O Christ?" He adds these words, "But I, Who am younger than John, am greater than he in the kingdom of heaven. Now I am thought to be younger and lesser than he in age, lineage, and glory, but in the kingdom of the heavens, that is, in divine and spiritual things, I am greater than he." Thereupon all the people that had heard the preaching of John *justified God,* that is, they honored God because they had received His prophet. But the Pharisees dishonored God

---

[4] Is. 29:18-19; 35:6; 61:1.

[5] Mal. 3:1

by not receiving John. Some have interpreted as follows the words *among those born of women*: the Lord spoke well to exclude himself from *those born of women*. For He was born of a virgin, not of a woman, that is, one who is married.[6] The words *he that is younger in the kingdom of God* have also been interpreted to mean "he who is younger in the life in Christ, is greater than he who was righteous in the law."[7] For example, John was blameless in the righteousness of the law. But if there is one who has just been baptized, and who has not yet done anything evil or good, though he is the youngest and the least in the kingdom of the heavens, that is, in living the life of the Gospel, even so, this one is greater than he, who though righteous in the law, is still unbaptized. And by another interpretation: although John lived as one who was all but immaterial and without flesh, yet he was still in the flesh. Therefore he who is the least in the resurrection, for the kingdom of heaven means the resurrection, is greater than John. In the resurrection we will be completely incorruptible, and we will no longer live according to the flesh. And he who is the least in the resurrection is greater than he who now is righteous, but still bears corruptible flesh.

31-35. And the Lord said, Whereunto then shall I liken the men of this generation? And to what are they like? They are like unto children sitting in the marketplace, and calling one to another, and saying, We have piped unto you, and ye have not danced; we have mourned to you, and ye have not wept. For John the Baptist came neither eating bread nor drinking wine; and ye say, He hath a demon. The Son of Man is come eating and drinking; and ye say, Behold a glutton and a drinker of wine, a friend of publicans and sinners. But Wisdom is justified by all her children. There was a certain game the Jewish children would play. They would divide into two groups, and, as if imitating life, those in one group would mourn and wail, and those in the other group would play dancing tunes on flutes. Those piping would not join together with the mourners, and those mourning would not join together with the pipers. The Lord here is

---

[6] The Greek word for *woman* (*gynē*, nominative, *gynaika*, accusative) implies married status. Even in modern Greek, it remains today the general word for *wife*.

[7] See Vol. 1, *The Explanation* of St. Matthew, p. 95, ftnt. 5, for an account of the different patristic interpretations of this passage.

ridiculing the Pharisees for doing something similar. When John was living a life of mourning, teaching them repentance, they would not mourn with him or imitate him. But when Jesus showed them a more gracious and pleasing life, neither would they believe or join with Him. They rejected both, neither mourning with John as he mourned, nor piping with Jesus as He piped in a more carefree manner. And therefore the *Wisdom* of God *is justified,* that is, honored, not by the Pharisees but by her children, those who have accepted the words of both John and Jesus.

36-43. And one of the Pharisees asked Him to eat with him. And He went into the Pharisees's house, and took His place at table. And, behold, a woman in the city, who was a sinner, when she knew that Jesus sat at table in the Pharisee's house, brought an alabaster box of myrrh, and stood at His feet behind him weeping, and began to wash His feet with tears, and did wipe them with the hairs of her head, and kissed His feet, and anointed them with the myrrh. Now when the Pharisee who had bidden Him saw it, he spake within himself, saying, This man, if He were a prophet, would have known who and what manner of woman this is that toucheth Him: for she is a sinner. And Jesus answering said unto him, Simon, I have something to say unto thee. And he saith, Master, say on. There was a certain creditor which had two debtors: the one owed five hundred pence, and the other fifty. And when they had nothing to pay, he freely forgave them both. Tell Me therefore, which of them will love him more? Simon answered and said, I suppose that he, to whom he forgave more. And He said unto him, Thou hast rightly judged. It would appear that this Pharisee who invited Jesus was not straightforward in his intentions, but was instead full of guile and hypocrisy. When he says, *This man, if He were a prophet,* he shows that he did not believe. Although the Lord knew that the man was not straightforward, He nevertheless enters his house and sits at table with him, thus teaching us to act in a simple and guileless manner towards those who are deceitful with us. Many have asked how many women there were who anointed the Lord with myrrh. Some say that there were two, the woman mentioned by John, who was the sister of Lazarus, and the woman mentioned by Matthew and Mark,[8] and now here by Luke. But I am persuaded by those who say that these were actually three different women, and three different episodes: first, the woman mentioned by John, six days before the Pascha, who was the sister of Lazarus; second, the woman mentioned by Matthew and Mark, two days before the Pascha; and third, the woman mentioned here by Luke towards the middle of the Gospel. She anointed the Lord; and there is nothing strange that she did this before it was time for the Lord's Passion, and then the other two anointed Him again, close to the time of the Passion, perhaps imitating this woman. Even though the man who invited the Lord to his house in Matthew's account is named Simon, as well as the man here in Luke's account, is it so strange that the names are the same? The man in Matthew was a leper, but not the man here in Luke. And the man in Matthew, after being healed of his leprosy, invites Christ to his house as a token of his gratitude, but this man in Luke is neither a leper, nor speaks words of gratitude. And that man in Matthew said nothing, while this man complains and is bitter towards both Jesus and the woman: the woman, because she was a sinner, and Jesus, because He showed compassion. O, what senselessness! In his irrational spite, this man shows himself to be indeed a Pharisee. And so the Lord questions him by means of a parable, comparing two debtors, and thus suggesting to him that he too is a debtor. Even if he appears to owe less than some others, he is a debtor all the same. The same is true for you, O reader. You may owe less than the sinful woman, but you are no more able to repay your debt than she, because in your pride you refuse to confess your indebtedness. And when both are forgiven, who will love more? Certainly that debtor who was forgiven more. By saying these things, the Lord shuts the mouth of that arrogant man.

44-50. And He turned to the woman, and said unto Simon, Seest thou this woman? I entered into thine house, thou gavest Me no water for My feet: but she hath washed My feet with tears, and wiped them with the hairs of her head. Thou gavest Me no kiss: but this woman since the time I came in hath not ceased to kiss My feet. My head with oil thou didst not anoint: but this woman hath

---

[8] Jn. 12:1-8, Mt. 26:6-13, Mk. 14:1-9.

anointed My feet with myrrh. Wherefore I say unto thee, Her sins, which are many, are forgiven; for she loved much: but to whom little is forgiven, the same loveth little. And He said unto her, Thy sins are forgiven. And they that sat at table with Him began to say within themselves, Who is this that even forgiveth sins? And He said to the woman, Thy faith hath saved thee; go in peace. The Lord shows that Simon is both arrogant and foolish. He is arrogant because he condemns the sins of a fellow human, though he himself is just as human. And he is foolish because he does not understand that the deeds of the woman are signs of her faith and love, which he ought to have welcomed rather than scorned. The Lord therefore rebukes him for senselessly condemning her for doing what he himself had failed to do. Simon had not shown even the most rudimentary hospitality. Giving examples, the Lord says, "Though you did not even give Me water to wash My feet, she has poured out her tears on them. You did not greet Me by kissing My face, but she has covered My feet with kisses. You did not anoint Me with oil, but she has anointed Me with costly myrrh. Therefore, because you said that I did not discern that this woman was a sinner and hence cannot be a prophet, behold, I rebuke the thoughts in your heart. Understand that if I know your thoughts which are hidden, how could I not know that which is public knowledge? Therefore, *her sins are forgiven because she loved much,* meaning, "because she showed great faith." *They that sat at table with* Jesus also grumbled and complained, not even considering the possibility that the words which the Lord had addressed to Simon applied to them as well. But the Lord quiets their murmuring. Because He wanted to show them that it is each man's faith which saves him, He did not say, "O woman, I save thee," lest He increase their spite, but instead He says, *Thy faith hath saved thee.* He says this, as I have explained, first, to curb their spite, and, secondly, once they understood that it is faith which saves, to bring them also to believe. *Go in peace* means "Go in righteousness." Righteousness is peace with God, while sin is hostility towards God. See that when Jesus has forgiven her her sins, He does not stop there, but adds to this the commandment to do good. For you ought to understand, *Go in peace,* to mean, "Go and do those things which will put you at peace with God."

CHAPTER EIGHT

Concerning the parable of the sower.
Concerning the mother, and brothers of the Lord,
when they wished to see Him.
Concerning the rebuking of the waters.
Concerning the legion of demons.
Concerning the daughter of the ruler of the synagogue.
Concerning the woman with an issue of blood.

1-3. And it came to pass afterward, that He went throughout every city and village, preaching and bringing the good tidings of the kingdom of God. And the twelve were with Him, and certain women, who had been healed of evil spirits and infirmities, Mary called Magdalene, out of whom went seven demons, and Joanna the wife of Chuza, Herod's steward, and Susanna, and many others, who ministered unto Him from their own substance. Having come down from heaven to be a model and example for us in all things, here He teaches us not to be slothful in teaching, but to go and preach in every place. Everything He did was for our instruction. Therefore *He went throughout every city and village.* And He was accompanied by the twelve disciples; they did not teach or preach, but instead were being taught by Him, learning from what He did as well as from what He said. The Lord preached, not about the good things of earth, but about the kingdom of heaven. Who better to preach the things of above than He Who came down from above? This is why none of the prophets preached the kingdom of heaven. How could they have preached things which they had not seen? For this reason the Forerunner also said, *He that is of the earth...speaketh of the earth. But He that cometh from heaven...what He hath seen...that He testifieth.*[1] There were also women who followed Jesus; this teaches us that the female sex is not hindered by weakness from following Christ. See how these women, despite their great wealth, gave up everything and instead chose poverty with Christ and for Christ. To understand that they indeed were wealthy, listen to the words of the Gospel: *they ministered unto Him from their own substance,* not with the

---

[1] See Jn. 3:31-32.

money of others, or with money gained by wrongdoing, as is often the case. Many have understood the words *out of whom went seven demons* to mean ''out of whom went many demons.'' For in Scripture the number seven often means *many*. One might also say that just as there are seven spirits of virtue, so also there are seven spirits of wickedness. There is, for example, the spirit of the fear of God, and its opposite, the spirit of irreverence, which does not fear God. There is the spirit of understanding, and its opposite, the spirit of incomprehension, and so on. Therefore, unless these seven spirits of wickedness are cast out of the soul, one cannot follow Christ. First Satan must be cast out; only then can Christ dwell within.

4-10. And when many people were gathered together, and were come to Him out of every city, He spake by a parable: a sower went out to sow his seed. And as he sowed, some fell along the way; and it was trodden down, and the winged creatures of the air devoured it. And some fell upon a rock; and as soon as it was sprung up, it withered away, because it lacked moisture. And some fell among thorns; and the thorns sprang up with it, and choked it. And other fell on good ground, and sprang up, and bare fruit an hundredfold. And when He had said these things, He cried, He that hath ears to hear, let him hear. And His disciples asked Him, saying, What might this parable be? And He said, Unto you it is given to know the mysteries of the kingdom of God: but to others in parables; that seeing they might not see, and hearing they might not understand. What David said of old, speaking prophetically in the person of Christ, has now come to pass: *I will open My mouth in parables.*[2] The Lord speaks in parables for many reasons: to make His listeners more attentive and to stir up their minds to seek the meaning of what is said. For we are apt to be curious about sayings that are obscure in meaning and to disregard sayings that are clear. He also speaks in parables so that those who are unworthy may not understand what is said concerning spiritual mysteries. And there are many other reasons why He speaks in parables. A *sower,* therefore, *went out,* that is, the Son of God went forth from the Father's bosom, from the hidden fastness of the Father, and became

---

[2] Ps. 77:2

manifest to all. Who went out? He Who is ever sowing. The Son of God never ceases to sow in our souls. Not only by His teaching, but by all of creation and by the events of our daily lives, He plants good seed in our souls. He *went out,* not to slay trespassers or to burn off the stubble, but to sow. For there are many reasons why a farmer might go forth, besides to plant. He went out to sow His own seed: the word of teaching was His own, and not another's. The prophets had spoken, not their own words, but the words of the Holy Spirit. This is why they said, *Thus saith the Lord.* But Christ had His own seed to sow. When He taught, He did not say, "Thus saith the Lord," but, "I say unto you." *As He sowed,* that is, as He taught, *some* seed *fell* along the road. He did not say that the sower threw the seed along the road, but instead that *some fell* there. Christ the Sower sows and teaches, and His word falls upon his listeners everywhere, and it is they who show themselves to be like a road, or a rock, or thorns, or good soil. When the disciples ask about the parable, the Lord says, *Unto you it is given to know the mysteries of the kingdom of God,* that is, unto you who desire to learn, *for everyone that asketh, receiveth.*[3] To the others who are not worthy of the mysteries, He speaks obscurely. They think that they see, but they do not; they hear, but they do not understand. And this is to their benefit. The Lord hides these things from them so that they will not fall under greater condemnation for understanding the mysteries and then disregarding them. He who understands, and then disregards, deserves a more severe punishment.

11-15. Now the parable is this: The seed is the word of God. Those along the way are they that hear; then cometh the devil, and taketh away the word out of their hearts, lest they should believe and be saved. They on the rock are they, which, when they hear, receive the word with joy; and these have no root, who for a while believe, and in time of temptation fall away. And that which fell among thorns are they, which, when they have heard, go forth, and are choked with cares of riches and of pleasures of this life, and bring no fruit to perfection. But that on the good ground are they, which in an honest and good heart, having heard the word, keep it, and bring forth fruit with patient endurance. Here are described three types of those who are

---

[3] Mt. 7:8

not saved. First, there are *those along the way,* who do not receive and accept the word at all. Just as a pathway, which is well trodden and compacted, cannot receive the seed because it is hard, so also those who are hardened in their hearts do not accept the word at all. Though they hear the word, they give it no heed. Next there are those on the rock who hear the word, and then do not endure temptations because of human weakness, and deny the faith. The third kind are those who hear the word and then are choked by the cares of life. Three parts, therefore, perish, and only one part is saved. Few are saved; most perish. See that it is not said of those who are choked, that they are choked by riches, but rather by the *cares of riches.* It is not wealth that harms, but the cares and worries about wealth which fill the mind. Indeed many have received great benefit from their wealth, when they poured it out to feed the poor. Consider the preciseness of the Evangelist, when he says of those who are saved, that when they have heard the word, *they keep it,* in contrast to those who are along the pathway, who do not keep the word; instead, the devil takes the word from them. And *they bring forth fruit,* in contrast to those who are choked by the thorns, and who bring no fruit to maturity. In truth those whose fruit never ripens bear no fruit at all. And those who bring forth fruit *with patient endurance* stand in contrast to those who are on the rock, who receive the word but then do not endure the onslaught of temptations and show that they cannot withstand the test. See how the Evangelist says three things concerning those who are saved, that they keep the word, that they bring forth fruit, and that they do so with patient endurance. By these three statements he distinguishes the saved from those who perish: those who are along the pathway who do not keep the word; those who are among thorns who bring no fruit to perfection; and those who are on the rock who do not patiently endure the assault of temptations.

16-18. No man, when he hath lighted a lamp, covereth it with a vessel, or putteth it under a bed; but he setteth it on a lamp stand, that they which enter in may see the light. For nothing is secret, that shall not be made manifest; neither any thing hid, that shall not be known and come to light. Take heed therefore how ye hear: for whosoever hath, to him shall be given; and whosoever hath not, from him shall be taken even that which he seemeth to have. Here begins another teaching. The Lord addresses these words to the disciples, urging

them on to a strict way of life and teaching them to be strugglers in
virtue, because they will be seen by all. He who teaches and preaches is
indeed seen by all, for all examine him to see if he is good or not, and
nothing about him remains hidden. Therefore, O disciples, if you have
diligence and zeal, you will be given greater grace from God. But he who
has neither diligence nor zeal, by his negligence will extinguish and lose
even that grace which he seems to have from God.

**19-21. Then came to Him His mother and His brethren, and they
could not reach Him because of the multitude. And it was told Him
by certain which said, Thy mother and Thy brethren stand outside,
desiring to see Thee. And He answered and said unto them, My
mother and My brethren are those who hear the word of God, and
do it.** Here it is apparent that Christ was not in the company of His
relatives according to the flesh. He had left them to devote Himself to
spiritual teaching. But now His relatives come to Him. Thus we learn that
anyone who is entrusted with serving God must put God's service before
all else, and must even set his parents to one side if they are about to
impede him from doing God's work with thoughtless and pointless
requests. This is what the Lord does now. When some speak to Him
concerning His relatives, He does not restrict His kindred to the few
related to him according to the flesh, and does not consider only the sons
of Joseph worthy to be called His brothers. He has come to save the
whole world and to make all men His brothers, and therefore He says, *My
mother and My brethren are those who hear the word of God...* But
merely to hear the word of God saves no one and is instead a condemnation, and so He adds, *and do it.* After hearing, one must do. The word of
God means His own teaching, for all that He spoke was of His Father. He
was not, as some thought, God's adversary, speaking words that were not
of God. Some have also understood this passage to mean that while
Christ was teaching and gaining renown through His teaching, some
became envious and tried to ridicule Him by saying, "Behold, *Thy
mother and Thy brethren stand outside, desiring to see Thee.*" His
mother appeared to be poor and humble, and His brothers insignificant,
the sons of a carpenter. And so, by calling attention to His mother and
brothers, they sought to demean Him as someone of lowly origin. But the
Lord, knowing their thoughts, replies, "Lowliness of birth does not
offend Me; rather, even if someone is lowly, let him heed the word of

God and I will make him My kinsman.''

22-25. Now it came to pass on a certain day, that He went into a boat with His disciples: and He said unto them, Let us go over unto the other side of the lake. And they launched forth. But as they sailed He fell asleep: and there came down a storm of wind on the lake; and they were filling with water, and were in jeopardy. And they came to Him, and awoke Him, saying, Master, Master, we perish. Then He arose, and rebuked the wind and the raging of the water: and they ceased, and there was a calm. And He said unto them, Where is your faith? And they being afraid marvelled, saying one to another, What manner of man is this! For He commandeth even the winds and water, and they obey Him. The Lord is training the disciples and testing their faith to see if they are unshaken by temptations, and for this reason He deliberately permits Himself to be overcome by sleep. Thus, when His disciples are overcome by fear, He can rebuke their weakness. For the disciples do not show perfect faith, but faith mixed with unbelief. They show belief in His power when they say, *Save us,*[4] but they show little faith when they say, *we perish.* If they had perfect faith, they would have been assured that it was impossible for them to perish while in the company of Him Who can do all things. *Then He arose, and rebuked the wind.* He had allowed the disciples to become alarmed so that His power would be all the more apparent. For it is our human nature that the greater the peril from which we have been rescued, the more clearly we remember and the more gratitude we feel towards the one who rescued us. See how, in a spiritual sense, this event is a type and prefigurement of what happened later to the disciples. The lake is Judea, upon which descended a fierce storm of rage against Christ, when the leaders of the Jews, in their fury, crucified the Lord. The disciples again were terrified, and they all left Him and fled. But the Lord awoke from sleep, that is, He arose from the dead, and again there was calm among the disciples when He appeared to them and said, *Peace be unto you.* Thus we may also understand these things in this spiritual sense. When the disciples said, *What manner of man is this?* they were not asking a question to which they did not know the answer. Rather, they exclaimed it in wonderment

---

[4] Mt. 8:25: *And His disciples came to Him, and awoke Him, saying, Save us: we perish.*

and astonishment, as if saying, "How great He is in nature, and how great is His authority and power by which He does these things!"

26-33. And they arrived at the country of the Gadarenes, which is across from Galilee. And when He went forth to land, there met Him out of the city a certain man, possessed by demons for a long time, who wore no clothes, neither abode in any house, but in the tombs. When he saw Jesus, he cried out, and fell down before Him, and with a loud voice said, What have I to do with Thee, Jesus, Son of God most high? I beseech Thee, torment me not. (For He had commanded the unclean spirit to come out of the man. For oftentimes it had caught him: and he was kept bound with chains and in fetters; and he broke the bands, and was driven by the demon into the wilderness.) And Jesus asked him, saying, What is thy name? And he said, Legion: because many demons were entered into him. And he besought Him that He would not command them to go out into the abyss. And there was there an herd of many swine feeding on the mountain: and they besought Him that He would suffer them to enter into them. And He suffered them. Then went the demons out of the man, and entered into the swine: and the herd ran violently down a steep place into the lake, and were drowned. See how the demon is torn between two wicked passions: impudence and fear. When he says, *What have I to do with Thee?* he shows the impudence of a shameless slave; when he says, *I beseech Thee,* he shows his fear. He was dwelling among the tombs because he wanted to instill in men the false suspicion that the souls of those who have died become demons. The demons ask not to be cast into the abyss, but that they be permitted to remain a while longer upon the earth. The Lord permits them to remain upon the earth in order that they might fight and contend with men and thus make men tested veterans. For if man had no adversaries, there would be no struggles and contests; and if there were no contests, there would be no crowns of victory. There is a more spiritual sense which you should learn as well: the man who has *demons* within him and wears no garment and makes his home outside the *house,* is anyone who does evil and demonic deeds, and who has stripped himself of his baptismal robe, and who dwells outside the Church. Such a man is not worthy to enter into the Church, but instead he lives in the tombs of dead and rotting deeds, for example, in brothels and in the chambers of publicans and graft. These indeed are tombs of iniquity.[5]

34-39. When they that fed them saw what was done, they fled, and went and told it in the city and in the country. Then they went out to see what was done; and came to Jesus, and found the man, out of whom the demons were departed, sitting at the feet of Jesus, clothed, and in his right mind: and they were afraid. They also which saw it told them by what means he that was possessed of the demons was healed. Then the whole multitude of the country of the Gadarenes round about besought Him to depart from them; for they were taken with great fear: and He went up into the boat, and returned back again. Now the man out of whom the demons were departed besought Him that he might be with Him: but Jesus sent him away, saying, Return to thine own house, and tell what great things God hath done unto thee. And he went his way, and proclaimed throughout the whole city what great things Jesus had done unto him. When those who had been feeding the swine fled into the city, it became an opportunity for salvation for the Gadarenes, but they did not understand. They ought to have marvelled at the Saviour's power and to have believed in Him. The Evangelist says that they *besought Him to depart from them,* instead of calling upon Him in supplication. They did this out of fear that they would suffer another loss like that of the swine. But the man who had been healed shows indisputable proof of his healing. That he had been healed in his mind is shown by the fact that he now both recognizes Jesus and begs His permission to be with Him. For he was afraid, it would seem, that the demons would again easily assault him when he was separated from Jesus. But the Lord shows him that even if he is not with Jesus, the Lord's grace can shelter him from demonic attack. The Lord says to him, *Return to thine own house, and tell what great things God hath done unto thee.* By not saying, ''what great things I have done unto thee,'' the Lord gives us an example of humility and teaches us that we should attribute all our accomplishments to God. And even though the Lord had commanded him to tell what things God had done for him, he told instead what things Jesus had done for him, so great was his

---

[5] In the Roman Empire and in Bl. Theophylact's own time the tax collectors were symbols of iniquity because they were free to amass vast personal fortunes through extortion and unbridled greed.

gratitude. Therefore when you do something good for someone, do not desire it to become public knowledge; but he who is the beneficiary of that good deed ought to be moved by gratitude to tell it to others, even though you do not want him to do so.

40-44. And it came to pass, that, when Jesus was returned, the multitude gladly received Him: for they were all waiting for Him. And, behold, there came a man named Jairus, and he was ruler of the synagogue: and he fell down at Jesus' feet, and besought Him that He would come into his house: for he had one only daughter, about twelve years of age, and she lay a dying. But as he went, the multitude thronged Him. And a woman having an issue of blood twelve years, who had spent all her living upon physicians, and could not be healed by any, came behind Him, and touched the border of His garment: and immediately her issue of blood stanched. Jesus returned from the country of the Gadarenes, and the multitude was waiting for Him, eager for both His teaching and His miracles. Then He was approached by a certain *ruler of the synagogue,* a man who was neither poor nor insignificant, but the foremost of society. The Evangelist even gives the man's name, so that the miracle might become the more renowned through this confirmable evidence of its truth. In his great need this man falls down before Jesus, although even without the urgency of this need, he ought to have fallen down and acknowledged Jesus as God. Nevertheless, affliction can compel a man to turn to what is better, as David says when he speaks of the horse or mule which has no understanding, *whose jaws thou must afflict with bit and bridle when they come not nigh unto thee.*[6] But as Jesus went along the way to the house of Jairus, a woman approached Him who showed exceedingly great faith. She approached and touched the border of His garment with the firm faith that if she could only touch His clothing, she would be made whole. And immediately the flow of blood stopped. Like a man who brings his eye close to a bright light, or brings a dry stick close to fire, and they immediately react, so also the woman brought her faith close to Him Who has power to heal, and immediately she obtained healing. She gave

---

[6] Ps. 31:9. The translation here of this particular verse differs somewhat from that of the Psalter published by Holy Transfiguration Monastery, which we usually cite. See the Introduction, p. 1, of the present volume.

no thought to anything else, neither the many years of her illness, nor the failure of her doctors. She only believed and was made whole. Understand that first she touched Jesus noetically, and only then did she touch Him bodily.

45-48. And Jesus said, Who touched Me? When all denied, Peter and they that were with Him said, Master, the multitude throng Thee and press Thee, and sayest Thou, Who touched Me? And Jesus said, Somebody hath touched Me: for I perceive that power is gone out of Me. And when the woman saw that she was not hid, she came trembling, and falling down before Him, she declared unto Him before all the people for what cause she had touched Him, and how she was healed immediately. And He said unto her, Daughter, take courage: thy faith hath made thee whole; go in peace. The Lord desires to show the woman's faith to all the people so that they might become imitators of her, and also so that Jairus might have good hope for his daughter. Therefore He makes manifest what had happened in secret and asks who it was that touched Him. Peter, being bold, scolds the Lord for His question, saying, "So many people throng Thee, and yet *sayest Thou, Who touched Me?*" But he did not understand what the Lord was asking. The Lord was inquiring, "Who touched Me with faith?" and not simply, "Whose hand touched Me?" Just as one man has ears with which he hears, while another has ears but does not hear, so also one man touches with faith, while another draws near but his heart is far away. The Lord knows that it was the woman, but He asks the question, as I have said, in order to reveal her faith and to give hope to the ruler of the synagogue. He asks, and thus draws attention to the woman. *For I perceive that power is gone out of Me,* He says, and rightly so. The prophets did not have power that went out from them; instead, they worked miracles by the grace of God. But Jesus is the source of every good thing and the source of all power, and He indeed has power that goes out from Him. The Lord grants the woman a double healing: He first heals her sickness and then He dispels the fear from her trembling soul by saying, *Daughter, take courage.*

49-56. While He yet spake, there cometh one from the ruler of the synagogue's house, saying to Him, Thy daughter is dead; trouble not the Master. But when Jesus heard it, He answered him, saying, Fear

not: only believe, and she shall be made whole. And when He came into the house, He permitted no man to go in, save Peter, and James, and John, and the father and the mother of the maiden. And all wept, and bewailed her: but He said, Weep not; she is not dead, but sleepeth. And they laughed Him to scorn, knowing that she was dead. And He put them all out, and took her by the hand, and called, saying, Maid, arise. And her spirit came again, and she arose straightway: and He commanded to give her food. And her parents were astonished: but He charged them that they tell no man what was done. When Jesus heard a man say to the ruler of the synagogue, *trouble not the Master,* He did not wait for the ruler of the synagogue to say something to Him, but instead speaks first, so that the ruler of the synagogue could not say, "I have no need for You; the evil deed has already happened; behold she has died, the one whom we expected You to heal," or any such words as these. For he did not believe, and was a Jew. Christ, therefore, speaks first and says, *"Fear not; only believe. Consider the woman who had the issue of blood. Imitate her and you will not miss the mark."* He permits only Peter, John, and James to enter because they were the Lord's favorites and chief of the apostles, and because they were able to keep silent concerning the miracle. The Lord did not want to reveal Himself to many before it was time, perhaps because of the spite of the Jews. Thus He hid most of His deeds so that the Jews would not become inflamed with envy and thus liable to judgment. We also ought to do the same; when someone becomes envious of us, we should not reveal our accomplishments to him, so as not to wound him and cause him to be even more envious and cast him into sin. Instead we should strive to escape his attention. The Lord said, *she is not dead, but sleepeth,* calling death *sleep* because He was about to raise her from the dead as if from sleep. Those who heard Him *laughed Him to scorn,* so that the miracle would be all the more miraculous. In order that later they would not be able to say that she was not dead, but had been asleep, the Lord arranged by divine economy that He should first be mocked when He said that she was not dead but asleep. Thus He shut the mouths of those who wanted to slander Him, for it was so clear that she was dead that they even mocked Him when He said that she was not dead. He put them all outside, perhaps to teach us not to crave glory and not to do anything for show, and also to teach that when someone is about to work a miracle, he ought not to be in the midst of many people, but alone and undistracted. Then the Lord brought back the spirit of the young girl. He did not put another soul into her but made the same soul which had slipped away return to her body again. He commanded that she be given something to eat, to provide even greater assurance and confirmation that she had risen from the dead. These things may also be understood in this manner: the woman with the issue of blood represents every soul which pours forth bloody and murderous sin. For each and every sin is the murderer and slayer of the soul. When this soul, therefore, touches the clothing of Jesus, when it touches, that is, His Incarnation, believing that the Son of God took on human flesh, then the soul is healed. And this is possible even if someone should be a *ruler of the synagogue,* that is, if someone has a mind which rules over the many things it has collected in its greed.[7] Then the daughter of that mind, its thought, is sick. But let that mind only call upon Jesus and believe, and his thought will be made whole.

---

[7] The word *synagogue* [*synagōgē*] is derived from the verb *synagō* which means *to bring together,* whether it be people in an assembly or things in a collection. Bl. Theophylact here plays on both senses of the word.

CHAPTER NINE

On the commissioning of the twelve.
Concerning Herod when he heard of Jesus.
Concerning the five loaves and two fishes.
Concerning the Lord's question.
Concerning the Transfiguration of Christ.
Concerning the man who was lunatic.
Concerning the discussion as to who was the greatest.
Concerning the man who was prevented
by the disciples from driving out demons.
On not asking punishment for those
who do not receive the apostles.
Concerning the man who was not permitted to follow Christ.

1-6. Then He called His twelve disciples together, and gave them power and authority over all demons, and to cure diseases. And He sent them to preach the kingdom of God, and to heal the sick. And He said unto them, Take nothing for your journey, neither staff, nor satchel, neither bread, neither money; neither have two tunics apiece. And whatsoever house ye enter into, there abide, and thence depart. And whosoever will not receive you, when ye go out of that city, shake off the very dust from your feet for a testimony against them. And they departed, and went through the towns, preaching the Gospel, and healing every where.[1] Even here is revealed the surpassing greatness of the divinity of Jesus. Not only did He Himself work miracles, but He granted the same power to His disciples as well. Indeed it is the mark not of man but of God to grant such gifts to one's friends. Jesus did not just give them authority over evil spirits, but He also commanded them to preach the Gospel. These whom He entrusted with the teaching He commanded both to preach and to work miracles: the miracles to confirm the preaching and the preaching to confirm the miracles. There have been many who have worked miracles by the power of the demons, but their preaching was not sound, from which it is clear

---

[1] See also Mt. 10:1-15 in Vol. 1, *The Explanation* of St. Matthew, pp. 83-85, and Mk. 6:6-13 in Vol. 2, *The Explanation* of St. Mark, pp. 50-52.

that their miracles were not from God. He sends out the twelve without possessions, wanting them to carry neither bread nor any of the other things which we commonly take with us on a journey. He also commands them not to go about from place to place, but to remain in whatever house they enter lest they appear to be inconstant and fickle. And if any do not welcome them, He tells the twelve to shake off the dust from their feet as *a testimony against them,* that is, as a reproof and condemnation, showing that the apostles had undertaken a great journey for their sakes, but those townsmen had received no benefit at all. Some have understood the commandment that the apostles should carry neither satchel, nor staff, nor have two tunics apiece, to mean "Do not store up treasures." For the satchel, in which many things are collected, is a symbol of storing up treasures. "Carry no staff" means "be not prone to anger or violence," and *neither have two tunics apiece* means "be not of two minds nor subject to many moods and dispositions."

7-9. Now Herod the tetrarch heard of all that was done by Him, and he was perplexed, because it was said by some, that John was risen from the dead; and by some, that Elijah had appeared; and by others, that one of the old prophets was risen again. And Herod said, John have I beheaded; but who is this, of whom I hear such things? And he desired to see Him. This is Herod the Younger, the son of Herod the Great who slew the infants. Herod the Great was king; this Herod was only a tetrarch.[2] He was perplexed as to who Jesus was. *"John,"* he says, *"have I beheaded;* if John is risen from the dead, surely I will recognize him when I see him." Therefore Herod wanted to see Jesus. See that the Jews thought, erroneously, that the resurrection of the dead was a resurrection into a life of the flesh, with food and drink. But resurrection is not unto food and drink and not unto the life of the flesh, but instead unto a life such as that of the angels of God.

10-17. And the apostles, when they were returned, told Him all that they had done. And He took them, and went aside privately into a desert place belonging to the city called Bethsaida. And the people,

---

[2] To distinguish further the several Herods, see Vol.1, *The Explanation* of St. Matthew, p. 23, footnote 2.

when they knew it, followed Him: and He received them, and spake unto them of the kingdom of God, and healed them that had need of healing. And when the day began to wear away, then came the twelve, and said unto Him, Send the multitude away, that they may go into the towns and country round about, and lodge, and get provisions: for we are here in a desert place. But He said unto them, Give ye them to eat. And they said, We have no more than five loaves and two fishes, unless we should go and buy food for all this people. For they were about five thousand men. And He said to His disciples, Make them sit down by fifties in a company. And they did so, and made them all sit down. Then He took the five loaves and the two fishes, and looking up to heaven, He blessed them, and brake, and gave to the disciples to set before the multitude. And they did eat, and were all filled: and there was taken up of fragments that remained to them twelve baskets. When Jesus was about to perform the miracle of the loaves, He departed into *a desert place* so that no one could say that there was a city nearby from which loaves were brought. He received the multitude, both teaching and healing them, so that you, O reader, might learn that our Christian philosophy consists of both word and deed. Thus we ought not to speak without doing, nor do without speaking the word. As night approached, the disciples took pity on the multitude, for even then they had started to become loving shepherds of the people. And so they said to Jesus, "*Send* them *away,*" that is, "heal their weaknesses quickly and fulfill their requests." But the Lord says to His disciples, *Give ye them to eat.* He said this, not in ignorance of their lack of means, but in order to induce them to tell how many loaves they had, and thus to show the greatness of the miracle by their own confession which established what a small number of loaves they had. His command, *Make them sit down by fifties in a company,* teaches us that when we give hospitality to someone we also should invite him to sit down and should show him every respect and attention. He looks up to heaven to teach us to give thanks to God when we are about to eat. He gives the food to the disciples to hand out to the multitude, so that the miracle would be indelible in the memory of the disciples whenever they recalled the loaves which had passed through their own hands. There were twelve baskets of pieces remaining so that we might learn how much hospitality is able to accomplish, and that whatever we have is multiplied when we offer it to those in need. More has been said of these things in *The Explanation* of St. Matthew.[3]

18-22. And it came to pass, as He was alone praying, His disciples were with Him: and He asked them, saying, Whom say the people that I am? They answering said, John the Baptist; but some say, Elijah; and others say, that one of the old prophets is risen again. He said unto them, But ye, whom say ye that I am? Peter answering said, The Christ of God. And He admonished them, and commanded them to tell no man that thing; saying, The Son of Man must suffer many things, and be rejected by the elders and chief priests and scribes, and be slain, and be raised the third day. When the Lord questions the disciples, He does not immediately ask them what they think, but first He asks what is the opinion of the people, and then their own opinion. He does this so that by revealing the erroneous opinion of the multitude, He might lead the disciples to the true understanding, which is indeed what took place. When the disciples had answered, "Some say that Thou art John, and others say Elijah," the Lord asks, "*But ye?*" that is, "Ye who differ from all the others, ye who are the elect and chosen, *whom say ye that I am?*" Peter leaps to the fore and speaking for all the disciples confesses that Jesus is the One Who was proclaimed of old, the Christ, the Anointed of God. Peter did not say "a christ, an anointed one of God," but instead with the definite article, *the Christ of God,* to show that Jesus is the very Christ. For there were many who were anointed, but the Christ of God—there is only One.

23-27. And He said to them all, If any man will come after Me, let him deny himself, and take up his cross daily, and follow Me. For whosoever desireth to save his life shall lose it: but whosoever will lose his life for My sake, the same shall save it. For what is a man advantaged, if he gain the whole world, and lose or forfeit himself? For whosoever shall be ashamed of Me and of My words, of him shall the Son of Man be ashamed, when He shall come in His own glory, and in His Father's, and of the holy angels. But I tell you of a truth, there be some standing here, who shall not taste of death, till

---

[3] See Vol. 1, *The Explanation* of St. Matthew, pp. 123-125, and also Vol. 2, *The Explanation* of St. Mark, pp. 54-56.

they see the kingdom of God. Having already said of Himself that *the Son of Man must suffer many things,* here He adds a universal teaching that applies to all: "It is not only I Who must undergo death. Everyone who desires to follow Me must deny himself, that is, have nothing in common with the flesh, and condemn himself." The cross here means the most shameful of deaths, for there was no death that was more inglorious than that of crucifixion. The Lord shows that anyone who wants to be His disciple must die [every day], not with glory, but rather as a condemned murderer dies, with reproaches and shame. But the Lord adds the words, *and let him follow Me,* that is, let him practice every virtue, since there are many brigands and evil doers who have been ingloriously executed for their crimes. *For whosoever desireth to save his life shall lose it;* that is, whoever wants to live according to this world will undergo the death of his soul. He who is ashamed of Christ is the man who says, "How can I believe in a God Who was crucified and mocked?" And he who is ashamed of Christ's words is the man who laughs at the simplicity of the Gospel. Of such a man will the Lord be ashamed when He comes in His glory, that is, at the second coming. What He means is this: "Like a master of the house who has an evil servant, and is ashamed to call him his own servant, I too will be ashamed to call that man My servant who has denied Me." Having said above, *Whosoever will lose his life for My sake, the same shall save it,* now He shows the great things of which such a man will be counted worthy, saying, *There be some standing here, who shall not taste of death, till they see the kingdom of God,* that is, until they see the glory which the righteous will share. He said this concerning the Transfiguration. For the Transfiguration was a type and foreshadowing of the heavenly glory to come. Just as Jesus on Mt. Tabor flashed like lightning with glory beyond our understanding, in the same way will the righteous shine in heaven. *There be some,* the Lord says, meaning John, Peter, and James, "who will not die until after they have seen what glory will belong to those who confess Me." And they saw this at the time of the Transfiguration.

28-36. And it came to pass about eight days after these sayings, He took Peter and John and James, and went up into a mountain to pray. And as He prayed, the appearance of His countenance was altered, and His raiment was lightning white. And, behold, there talked with Him two men, who were Moses and Elijah, who appeared

in glory, and spake of His departing which He would accomplish at Jerusalem. But Peter and they that were with Him were heavy with sleep: and when they awoke, they saw His glory, and the two men that stood with Him. And it came to pass, as they departed from Him, Peter said unto Jesus, Master, it is good for us to be here: and let us make three tabernacles; one for Thee, and one for Moses, and one for Elijah: not knowing what he said. While he thus spake, there came a cloud, and overshadowed them: and they feared as they entered into the cloud. And there came a voice out of the cloud, saying, This is My beloved Son: hear Him. And when the voice was past, Jesus was found alone. And they kept it close, and told no man in those days any of those things which they had seen. While Matthew says that six days had passed after these sayings and then Jesus went up onto the mountain,[4] Luke says that eight days had passed. Luke includes both the day on which those sayings were spoken and the day on which the Transfiguration took place, but Matthew counts only the intervening days. He took with Him only three disciples: Peter, because he loved the Lord, John, because he was beloved by the Lord, and James, because he also had fervent zeal for the Lord, and also because he was a man of discretion who could keep news of this event to himself and not make it common knowledge. *The Lord went up into a mountain to pray,* to show that when we pray we must be alone, and we must ascend in spirit and not incline ourselves to anything earthly. And as Jesus prayed, *the appearance of His countenance was altered,* but He was not changed in nature. He remained what He was, except that the appearance of His face was brighter than before. And the same thing happened with His clothing. It was only the appearance of His clothing that blazed with light; the substance of the clothing was unchanged and only the surface appearance was different. Moses and Elijah stood with Him as He prayed, to show that Christ was not an opponent of the prophets and the law. If He had been, neither Moses the lawgiver nor Elijah the most zealous of the prophets would have endured to stand with Him in escort. They were speaking of the *departing,* that is, His death, *which He would accomplish in Jerusalem.* While Christ prayed, Peter was *heavy with sleep.* He was weak and did what was human, becoming a slave of sleep. But when he

---

[4] Mt. 17:1

awakes, he sees the glory, and the two men. Then, as if happy to live there because of the splendor and the vision of the prophets, he says, *It is good for us to be here.* For he thought that the end of the world, and Jesus' kingdom, had come. But he did not know what he was saying. It was not yet the end, nor was the day of the kingdom at hand, nor the time of the enjoyment of those good things in which the saints will share. At the same time, Peter said these things because he feared Christ's crucifixion. He had heard the Lord say that it was necessary for Him to be slain and to be raised on the third day, and so Peter now says these words as if meaning, "Let us not go down from the mountain, but remain here, to avoid the Cross and the Passion. If the Jews come after us, we have as our helper Elijah who called down fire and destroyed the captains of fifty,[5] and we have Moses who vanquished so many heathens." He said these things *not knowing what he said.* He thought that the Cross was something exceedingly harsh and an evil to be avoided. But the Lord thirsted to be crucified, for there was no other way by which man could be saved. When Peter says, *Let us make three tabernacles,* the Lord at once forms from cloud a tabernacle not made by hands, and enters into it together with the prophets, to show that He is in nowise less than the Father. As in the Old Testament a cloud was said to contain the Lord, and Moses entered into it and thus received the law, likewise a cloud now receives Christ, but this is not a dark cloud.[6] The shadow of the law and the darkness of obscurity has passed, and now it is a cloud of light. Truth has come and the grace of the Lord shines forth, and there is no longer any darkness. And there is also a voice from the cloud, just as of old the voice of God was heard from the cloud. *Jesus was found alone* lest anyone think that the words, *This is My beloved Son,* were spoken concerning Moses or Elijah. But there is this meaning as well, that the law and the prophets were manifest for a time, as were Moses and Elijah here, and then they passed away and *Jesus was found alone.* For the Gospel now holds sway and the things of the law have passed away. The apostles were silent and declared nothing of what they had seen. Before the Cross, it was not right to say anything about Jesus that befitted His divinity. For if men heard such words and then saw Christ crucified, what

---

[5] IV Kings (II Kings) 1:10

[6] Ex. 19:16

would they conclude? Would they not think that He was only a deluded visionary? This is why the apostles, before the Cross, did not proclaim any of the Lord's works that were extraordinary and divine. Concerning this passage, we have given an edifying account in *The Explanation* of St. Matthew.[7]

37-43. And it came to pass, that on the next day, when they were come down from the mountain, a great multitude met Him. And, behold, a man from the multitude cried out, saying, Master, I beseech Thee, look upon my son: for he is mine only child. And, lo, a spirit taketh him, and he suddenly crieth out; and it teareth him so that he foameth, and bruising him hardly departeth from him. And I besought Thy disciples to cast him out; and they could not. And Jesus answering said, O faithless and perverse generation, how long shall I be with you, and endure you? Bring thy son hither. And as he was yet a coming, the demon threw him down, and tore him. And Jesus rebuked the unclean spirit, and healed the child, and gave him back again to his father. This man was exceedingly faithless. And for this reason the demon did not depart from his child, the unbelief overcoming the power of the apostles. Even now the man brazenly displays his unbelief, approaching the Lord in the presence of all to accuse His disciples. But the Lord shows him that his unbelief caused the child not to be healed, and He in turn rebukes him in the presence of all, and not only him, but all the others with him as well. When He says, *O faithless generation,* He includes all the Jews. The word *perverse* indicates that their wickedness is neither from the beginning nor by their nature. By nature they were upright, for the seed of Abraham and Isaac was holy. But they had been turned and twisted by evil. The Lord's words, *How long shall I be with you, and endure you?* show that He hungered for death and that He wished to be freed from them quickly. He is saying, therefore, "How long shall I endure your unbelief?" Then, to show that He has the power to vanquish the unbelief of the Jews, He says, *Bring thy son hither.* And He healed the boy *and gave him back to his father.* Prior to this the demonized child was not his father's, but belonged to the

---

[7] Vol. 1, *The Explanation* of St. Matthew, pp. 145-148. See also Vol. 2, *The Explanation* of St. Mark, pp. 72-74.

evil spirit which possessed him. The Lord gives him back to his father, who had lost the boy and has now found him.

43-45. And they were all amazed at the mighty power of God. But while they wondered every one at all things which Jesus did, He said unto His disciples, Let these sayings sink down into your ears: for the Son of Man shall be delivered into the hands of men. But they understood not this saying, and it was hid from them, that they should not perceive it. And they feared to ask Him of that saying. All the others marvelled at everything which Jesus did, not just at this one miracle. But He turned from the others and addressed His disciples, saying, ''Let all these things *sink down into your ears,* both the miracles and My words which accompany the miracles. Why? Because I am about to be handed over for crucifixion; think on all these things, so that when you see Me hanging on the Cross you will not imagine that I am suffering because I am powerless to do otherwise. I Who have the power to work these wonders have the power to escape the Cross.'' *But they understood not this saying, and it was hid from them.* Why was this? So that they would not grieve beforehand and be shaken by fear. Just as a father out of compassion for his young children might hide from them some grievous sorrow, in the same way God condescends to the weakness of the disciples and veils their understanding of what was said concerning the Cross. Behold the reverence of the disciples, how they revered Christ so much that they dared not to ask Him, indeed they *feared to ask.* [Reverence for God and the fear of God are alike:] the fear of God is reverence intensified, while reverence is fear that has been quieted.

46-50. Then there arose a dispute among them, which of them should be greatest. And Jesus, perceiving the thought of their heart, took a child, and set him by Him, and said unto them, Whosoever shall receive this child in My name receiveth Me: and whosoever shall receive Me receiveth Him that sent Me: for he that is least among you all, the same shall be great. And John answered and said, Master, we saw one casting out demons in Thy name; and we forbad him, because he followeth not with us. And Jesus said unto him, Forbid him not: for he that is not against us is for us. The passion of vainglory overtook the apostles. It seems to me that this passion arose among them because they could not heal the demon-possessed child. It is likely that they were quarreling over this failure, each one saying, "It was not because of my weakness but because of your, or someone else's, weakness that the child was not healed." And this kindled an argument between them as to who was the greatest. But the Lord Who sees the heart of each man intervenes before this passion could increase, and He hastens to cut it out by the roots. For the passions are easily defeated when they have just sprung up, but they are difficult to root out once they have grown to any height. How does the Lord cut away this evil? He takes a child, the Evangelist says, and shows him to the disciples, teaching them that we ought to cultivate in ourselves the same kind of disposition that children have by virtue of their tender age. Young children have no knowledge and experience of evil; they are simple and uncomplicated; they are not troubled by thoughts of vainglory and rank. *Whosoever shall receive* such a *child in My name receiveth Me.* What He means is this: "You think that if you appear to be haughty and important you will make a pleasing impression on the crowd, and greater numbers will welcome you. But I say to you, that I rejoice in simplicity, and simplicity is therefore such an essential mark of My disciples that whosoever receives the most simple and guileless man as My disciple (for this is what *in My name* means), receives Me. He who receives an arrogant man, receives no disciple of Mine and does not receive Me." *John answered and said, Master, we saw one casting out demons in Thy name, and we forbad him.* Is there a connection between these words of John and what the Lord had just said? Indeed there is, and a profound one. Because the Lord had just said, *He that is least among you, the same shall be great,* John was afraid that they had done evil by forbidding the man in a domineering and arrogant manner. To forbid someone to do something shows that the one who forbids thinks he is greater, not lesser, than the one who is forbidden. John therefore was afraid that he had acted arrogantly by forbidding the man. Why had the disciples forbidden the man? Not out of envy, but instead because they had judged him to be unworthy to work miracles. For the man had not received together with them the gift of working miracles, nor had the Lord sent him out as He had the disciples, nor was he even a follower of Jesus. What then does the Lord say? "Let him do what he is doing. He also is trampling down the power of Satan, and since he does not hinder us from preaching, he is not working with the devil, and therefore he is on our side. Whoever is not against God is for God, just as whoever is not gathering with God is with the devil.''[8] Marvel with me, O reader, at the power of the name of Christ. See how divine grace is at work even in those who are unworthy and not His disciples, when only Christ's name is spoken. Therefore if a priest is unworthy, nevertheless God's grace is still active, sanctifying all, even though the priest is impure.

51-56. And it came to pass, when the days were fulfilled that He should be taken up, He steadfastly set His face to go to Jerusalem, and sent messengers before His face: and they went, and entered into a village of the Samaritans, to make ready for Him. And they did not receive Him, because His face was set to go to Jerusalem. And when His disciples James and John saw this, they said, Lord, wilt Thou that we command fire to come down from heaven, and consume them, even as Elijah did? But He turned, and rebuked them, and said, Ye know not what manner of spirit ye are of. For the Son of Man is not come to destroy men's lives, but to save them. And they went to another village. What does this mean, *It came to pass, when the days were fulfilled that He should be taken up?* It means that the time was at hand for Him to endure for our sake the saving Passion and to be taken up into heaven and to be enthroned with God the Father. Therefore, since the time was at hand for His Passion and His Ascension from this world, He determined to go about no longer from place to place, but to go up to Jerusalem. *He steadfastly set His face* means that having made His decision and fixed His will upon it, He resolutely determined to depart for Jerusalem. He sends out *messengers before His face* to prepare His reception, knowing that He would not be received by the Samaritans. Still He sends them out, so that the Samaritans would have no excuse to say later, ''We would have received Him if He had sent someone ahead of His arrival.'' At the same time, He does this to benefit His own disciples, so that when they later see Him being insulted and abused on the Cross, they will not be scandalized. Now He wants them to learn by seeing how He patiently endures the rejection of the Samaritans, and how He rebukes, not the Samaritans, but His own disciples who were urging Him to strike back. Thus, later, when they see Him crucified, the

---

[8] See also Vol. 1, *The Explanation* of St. Matthew, p. 105, and Vol. 2, *The Explanation* of St. Mark, p. 79, as well as the explanation in this volume of Lk. 11:23 on p. 129.

disciples would understand that He endures this, not as one powerless, but as the One Who is patient and long-suffering. He brings benefit to the disciples, teaching them by His own example to be long-suffering. The disciples had in mind Elijah who had burned up with fire the two captains of fifty with their fifties,[9] and were urging the Lord to act against those Samaritans who had insulted Him. They did this because they were not yet perfected in virtue. To show them that His law is on a higher plane than Elijah's conduct, the Lord rebukes them and turns them away from such an intention, teaching them instead to endure insults meekly. What does this mean, *And they did not receive Him, because His face was set to go to Jerusalem?* Does this mean that the reason why the Samaritans did not receive Jesus was because [they saw that] He Himself had decided to depart for Jerusalem? No, for if we understand it in this manner, those who did not receive Him are without blame. Instead we can say that the Evangelist here means that the Samaritans did not receive Him, and that neither did the Lord enter Samaria. Then it is as if someone had asked, "Why did He not enter Samaria despite their unwillingness to receive Him? Surely not because He was weak? Did He not have the power to enter Samaria no matter what the Samaritans might desire?" The Evangelist then answers these questions by saying, *because His face was set to go to Jerusalem.* In other words, it was not out of weakness, but because He Himself had decided to depart for Jerusalem and not to enter Samaria. If this were not so, He would have entered the village whether the Samaritans desired it or not.

57-62. And it came to pass that as they went in the way, a certain man said unto Him, Lord, I will follow Thee whithersoever Thou goest. And Jesus said unto him, Foxes have holes, and birds of the air have nests; but the Son of Man hath not where to lay His head. And He said unto another, Follow Me. But he said, Lord, suffer me first to go and bury my father. Jesus said unto him, Let the dead bury their dead: but go thou and preach the kingdom of God. And another also said, Lord, I will follow Thee; but let me first go bid them farewell, which are at home at my house. And Jesus said unto him, No man, having put his hand to the plough, and looking back, is fit

---

[9] IV Kings (II Kings) 1:9-12

for the kingdom of God. This man who approached Jesus and asked if he might follow Him did so with an evil intention. Because he had seen a great multitude of people pursuing the Lord, he thought that the Lord was collecting money from them, and he imagined that if he became a follower of the Lord he too could collect money. This is why the Lord turns him away, as if saying to him words like these: "You plan to collect money by following Me, thinking that My life is something which it is not. I practice and teach such poverty that I have no house, though even the animals have their dwelling places." And so He turns him away. But another man, who is likewise unworthy, the Lord permits to follow Him. And when this man asks permission to go and bury his father, the Lord does not allow this, saying, *Let the dead bury their dead,* implying that the father was not a believer and therefore unworthy of the care of his son who believed. He is saying, "Let your dead relatives, that is, those who do not believe, take care of your unbelieving father in his old age until death." To *bury* means here to bestow care on him even to the grave. Even in common parlance we say, "So and so buried his father," which means not only that he placed him in the ground when he died, but that he also did every other good thing for him that was necessary, caring for him until his end and his burial. Therefore, *let the dead bury their dead,* that is, let those who are unbelievers take care of your unbelieving father, but because you have believed, you must preach the Gospel as My disciple. The Lord said this not to forbid us from caring for our parents, but to teach us that we ought to place piety above the demands of unbelieving parents. We must allow no obstacle to our doing of good, and we must scorn nature itself when it stands in the way. Therefore, the Lord does not permit even this man whom He has deemed worthy to become His follower to first bid farewell to those in his house. Such a man shows that he has ties to the world, and does not have the disposition of the apostles who immediately followed Jesus when they heard Him call, and who gave no thought to anything else, not even to bid farewell to members of their household. For it often happens that while a man is saying farewell to his relatives, some of them try to prevent him from following a godly life. Therefore it is best when one desires to do good to accomplish it at once without any delay. For *no man, having put his hand to the* spiritual *plow, and looking back* to the world, *is fit for the kingdom of God.* You may understand the foxes and the birds of the air to mean the crafty demons. For the Apostle Paul says, *According to the* *prince of the power of the air.*[10] The Lord therefore is saying to the man, ''The demons have their lair in you, and this is why I, the Son of Man, have no place to lay My head, that is, I see no place in your heart, which is full of demons, for faith in Me.'' The *head* of Christ is faith in Christ. When a man believes that Jesus is God, then Christ takes His rest and dwells in him. The sinner is dead, and the sinner buries his dead, that is, he buries his evil thoughts and does not confess them. But the Lord prevents such a man who wants to follow Him from burying his evil thoughts and hiding them. For the Lord desires that he reveal them by confessing them.

---

[10] Eph. 2:2

CHAPTER TEN

Concerning the appointment of the seventy apostles.
Concerning the questioning by the lawyer.
Concerning the man who fell among thieves.
Concerning Martha and her sister Mary.

1-3. After these things the Lord appointed an other seventy also, and sent them two and two before His face into every city and place, whither He himself would come. Therefore said He unto them, The harvest truly is great, but the labourers are few: pray ye therefore the Lord of the harvest, that He would send forth labourers into His harvest. Go your ways: behold, I send you forth as lambs among wolves. It is written in the Book of Exodus that the sons of Israel *came to Elim, and there were there twelve fountains of water and the trunks of seventy palms.*[1] This event occurred not only as historical fact, but also as a type and foreshadowing of what now in truth has come to pass. *Elim* interpreted means *ascent,* signifying that as we ascend in spiritual growth towards perfect understanding, not remaining behind within the letter of the law, as have the Jews, but soaring upwards to the Christian Gospel, we will find the *twelve fountains,* meaning the twelve chief apostles who are well-springs of the most sweet water of teachings. And we will also find the seventy palm trees, that is, the seventy apostles. They are called *palms* and not *fountains* because the seventy were nourished and taught by the twelve. Although the Lord chose both the twelve and the seventy, the seventy were subordinate to the twelve, and later became the disciples and followers of the twelve. These *palms,* therefore, were nourished by the *fountains,* that is, by the apostles. And the seventy have in turn provided us with fruit which is sweet yet tempered with astringency. Such are the teachings of the saints: not always sweet and to our taste, and not always astringent and stinging, they instead possess both qualities. The teaching is indeed seasoned with salt, but it is also full of grace, for as the Apostle Paul cries out, *Let your speech be always with grace, seasoned with salt.*[2] The Lord appoints the seventy disciples because of

---

[1] Ex. 15:27

[2] Col. 4:6

the great number of those in need of teaching. Just as fields that are heavy with crops require many harvesters, so also are those who will believe great in number, indeed beyond count, and in need of many teachers. He sends them out two by two because the goal is more certain to be achieved when there are two to help each other.[3] They go *before His face* because they were to teach as did John the Forerunner: *Prepare ye the way of the Lord.*[4] Notice how He says, *Pray ye therefore the Lord of the harvest, that He would send forth labourers,* and then He Himself sends them out by His own command. Christ is truly the Lord of the harvest, that is, the Lord of those who believe, because He is true God. He also forewarns them of persecutions, saying that they will be like lambs in the midst of wolves, preparing them so that persecutions will not come upon them unexpectedly and shake them by their sudden onslaught.

4-9. Carry neither purse, nor satchel, nor sandals: and salute no man along the way. And into whatsoever house ye enter, first say, Peace be to this house. And if a son of peace be there, your peace shall rest upon it: if not, it shall return to you again. And in the same house remain, eating and drinking such things as they give: for the labourer is worthy of his hire. Go not from house to house. And into whatsoever city ye enter, and they receive you, eat such things as are set before you: and heal the sick that are therein, and say unto them, The kingdom of God is come nigh unto you. Since He was about to send them to preach the Gospel, He says to them, *"Carry neither purse, nor any other belongings; it suffices for you to think only about the word of preaching. If you carry a purse, it is obvious that you will be concerned with it and neglect the word."* But also, *"Since you will be fed and cared for by those whom you teach, what need have you of a purse, or a satchel for provisions, or sandals? Those who are taught by you will provide all that you need."* He adds this command to them, *Salute no man along the way,* so that they do not become preoccupied with greetings and civilities, and thus be hindered from preaching. For it is likely that the one who is greeted will extend a greeting in return, and perhaps a more lengthy conversation, so common among travellers, will

---

[3] See Vol. 2, *The Explanation* of St. Mark, p. 50.

[4] Mt. 3:3

ensue. Then, as if a close friendship had already been made, excessive civilities will be extended, and thus little by little the apostle will be ensnared by social ties and will neglect the word. For this reason the Lord forbids them to salute anyone along the way, but it is different when they enter a house. Then He tells them to say, *Peace be to this house,* meaning that they should salute those who are in that household. He shows that the words, *Peace be to this house,* are not only a greeting, but also a blessing. For He says, ''If the master of the house is worthy, he will be blessed, but if he is a violent man who rejects peace, fighting and opposing the word and your teaching, the blessing will not remain on him but will return to you.'' The Lord directs them not to go from house to house, lest they appear to be greedy and scandalize many and grieve those who welcomed them first. And He tells them, ''Eat what they offer you even if it is little and simple, and ask for nothing more. As wages you will have your food and keep; do not expect to be fed and then, in addition, to receive a wage, but consider your food to be your wage.'' See how He makes the disciples secure, although they possess nothing, and how He directs them to heal the sick in all the cities so that by working miracles they will draw men to their teachings. For He says, *And say unto them, The kingdom of God is come nigh unto you.* If you first heal and then teach, your word will be swift and lively, and all will believe that the kingdom of God is upon them. They could not have been healed if it were not divine power which had accomplished these things. Moreover, when the disciples heal those who are sick in soul, then the kingdom of God has come upon them as well. For the kingdom of God is far from that man who has a diseased soul in which sin still rules as king.

10-12. But into whatsoever city ye enter, and they receive you not, go your ways out into the broad streets of the same, and say, Even the very dust of your city, which cleaveth on us, we do wipe off against you: notwithstanding be ye sure of this, that the kingdom of God is come nigh unto you. But I say unto you, that it shall be more tolerable in that day for Sodom, than for that city. When they do not receive you, He says, go out and bear witness to them, ''There is nothing in common between us and you, and we have nothing from your city. Even the dust of your city which clings to us we shake off and wipe off and cast it back to you. Nevertheless be sure of this: the kingdom of God

has come nigh unto you as well.'' Here someone will ask, ''Why does
the Lord say that the kingdom of heaven has come nigh to those who
have not received the apostles as well as to those who have?'' It can be
said in answer that there is nothing contradictory in this. For those who
accepted the apostles, the kingdom of God drew nigh with benefaction,
but for those who did not accept the apostles, it drew nigh with condemnation. Imagine some public assembly at which there are present many
condemned criminals as well as those who are far from condemnation,
such as honorable senators, generals, and noblemen. Then a herald
proclaims to one and all, both the condemned and the esteemed, ''The
king draws nigh unto you!'' Does this not mean that the king draws nigh
to some with punishment and to others with honors and benefaction? So
it is here. *''It shall be more tolerable for Sodom,''* the Lord says, ''than
for that city which does not welcome you.'' Why? Because no apostles
were sent to Sodom. Therefore those who do not receive the apostles are
worse than the Sodomites. Notice that the city which does not receive the
apostles has *broad streets.*[5] For *broad is the way that leadeth to destruction.*[6] Whoever does not accept the divine and apostolic word is on the
broad way to destruction.

**13-16. Woe unto thee, Chorazin! Woe unto thee, Bethsaida! For if
the mighty works had been done in Tyre and Sidon, which have been
done in you, they would a great while ago have repented, sitting in
sackcloth and ashes. But it shall be more tolerable for Tyre and
Sidon at the judgment, than for you. And thou, Capernaum, which
art exalted to heaven, shall be thrust down to hades. He that heareth
you heareth Me; and he that despiseth you despiseth Me; and he that
despiseth Me despiseth Him that sent Me.** Tyre and Sidon were pagan
cities; Bethsaida and Chorazin were cities of Judah. The Lord is saying,
therefore, that at the judgment it will be more tolerable for the pagans
than for you who saw these miracles and did not believe. For if the
pagans had seen them, they would have believed. ''But *thou, Capernaum,
which art exalted to heaven* and made glorious by the many miracles that
have taken place in thee, *shall be thrust down to hades* and condemned

---

[5] *Plateias,* from the adjective *platys,* meaning *broad* or *wide.*

[6] Mt. 7:13

for this very reason, that even after so many miracles, thou didst not believe.'' And then, so that those who were sent to preach could not say, ''Why do You send us out to preach if some cities will not accept us?'' He says, ''Do not be sad. He who despises you despises both Me and My Father. Therefore their insult does not rest upon you, but is laid against God. Let this be a consolation for you, that they are insulting not you but God. Likewise neither should you boast or think highly of yourselves when some heed your words. This is not your doing; it is My doing and the work of grace.''

17-20. And the seventy returned again with joy, saying, Lord, even the demons are subject unto us through Thy name. And He said unto them, I beheld Satan as lightning fall from heaven. Behold, I give unto you power to tread on serpents and scorpions, and over all the power of the enemy: and nothing shall by any means hurt you. Notwithstanding, in this rejoice not, that the spirits are subject unto you; but rather rejoice, because your names are written in heaven. Earlier it was said that the seventy had been sent forth. Now the Evangelist says that they returned rejoicing that they had not only driven out all manner of diseases but that they had also put to flight the worst evil of all, the demons. See that the apostles do not think highly of themselves, for they say, ''In Thy name the demons are subject unto us. It is by Thy grace, not by our own strength.'' The Lord says to them, ''Do not marvel that the demons are subject to you. For their prince in olden times fell from heaven and he has no power. Though his fall was not seen by men, it was seen by Me, Who can see the unseen. He fell like lightning, because he, the archangel Lucifer, the Light-Bearer, was light, though he became darkness. Therefore if he has fallen from heaven, what will his servants, the demons, not suffer?'' Some also say that *fall from heaven* means *fall from glory.* Because the seventy had told the Lord that the demons were subject to them, He says to them, ''I also knew this. For I saw Satan fall from the heavens, that is, from the glory and honor which he had.'' Before Christ came in the flesh, Lucifer had been honored by pagans as a god. But now he has fallen from heaven, that is, he is no longer honored as god, nor thought to be in heaven. ''Therefore, *behold I give unto you power* to trample down his mighty works.'' *Serpents and scorpions* are the ranks of demons which crawl below. Those demons which strike openly and visibly are *serpents;* and those demons which strike invisibly are *scorpions.* For example, the demons of fornication and murder are *serpents* which incite a man to sin openly and obviously. But the demon which induces a man on the pretext of health to frequent the bath houses and to be massaged with oils, and other such foolishness which leads to fornication, such a demon would be called a *scorpion.* For its sting is not visible, but instead in secret it urges a man to groom and pamper his flesh in order to cast him into a great fall. But thanks be to the Lord Who has given us power to trample upon such serpents and scorpions. To teach the disciples not to have haughty thoughts about themselves, the Lord says to them, ''But do not rejoice because the spirits are subject unto you, for it is someone else who receives the benefit from this, namely, those who are granted healing. Instead, rejoice that your names are written in the heavens, not in ink, but in the memory of God and in grace.'' From above this great angel fell downwards, but now men, who are below, are written above. True joy is to have our names written above and to be remembered by God.

21. In that hour Jesus rejoiced in spirit, and said, I thank Thee, O Father, Lord of heaven and earth, that Thou hast hid these things from the wise and clever, and hast revealed them unto babes: yea, Father; for so it seemed good in Thy sight. Just as a good father rejoices when he sees some accomplishment of his children, so too the Saviour rejoices that the apostles have been deemed worthy of such good things. Therefore He thanks the Father that He has hidden these mysteries from the *wise,* that is, from the experts such as the Pharisees and the Scribes who interpreted the law, and from the *clever,* that is, the students of those Scribes. The teacher is the expert, and the student who is clever learns what is taught. For example, Gamaliel was such an expert teacher and Paul was just such a clever student.[7] The Lord calls His own disciples *babes* because they were not students of the law, but for the most part had been chosen from the crowd and from among fishermen. The disciples might also be called babes because they were guileless. On the other hand, those who were reputed to be wise and learned in these matters, were not guileless. Therefore God has hidden the mysteries from

---

[7] See Acts 22:3.

those who think they are wise and learned but are in fact merely expert and ciever. If they indeed had wisdom and understanding, God would have revealed the mysteries to them. *Yea, Father, I thank Thee; for so it seemed good in Thy sight.* This means, ''I thank Thee that it was always Thy pleasure and good will, and that so it has pleased Thee to do.''

22-24. And He turned unto His disciples, and said, All is delivered to Me by My Father: and no man knoweth Who the Son is, but the Father; and Who the Father is, but the Son, and he to whom the Son desireth to reveal Him. And He turned unto His disciples, and said privately, Blessed are the eyes which see the things that ye see. For I tell you, that many prophets and kings have desired to see those things which ye see, and have not seen them; and to hear those things which ye hear, and have not heard them. *All is delivered* to the Son by the Father in that all is to be subject to the Son. There are two ways in which God rules over all. First, He rules over all, independently of their own will. And second, He rules over those who willingly subject themselves to Him. Hence I can say: God is my Master, independently of my will, inasmuch as He is my Creator. But He is also my Master whenever I, as a grateful servant, fulfill His will by working to keep the commandments. Formerly human nature was a servant subject to God, even though it did not desire to be, and even though it served Satan. But when Christ waged war against the demons on our behalf, and rescued us from the tyranny of the devil, He made us laborers and doers of the commandments, and from that time on we became His grateful servants, both by nature and by our own will. The first condition of servitude was by nature only, but the second was by our own will as well. This is what the Lord means when He says, *All is delivered to Me by My Father,* that is, ''All is to be subject to Me and falls under My rule.'' It is similar to what He said elsewhere, *All authority has been given unto Me in heaven and on earth.*[8] Christ can say this because in His triumph over sin He has established peace between all in heaven and on earth. And in another sense, all, that is, all the acts of the divine economy, God's plan for our salvation, are delivered to the Son by the Father. Since it was neither the Father nor the Spirit Who became incarnate, suffered, and arose for our

---

[8] Mt. 28:18

sakes, but the Son Who enacted all these things and became the Author of our salvation, therefore He says that *all is delivered to* Him. It is as if He were saying, "My Father has entrusted the whole of the divine plan of salvation to Me, that I take flesh, suffer, and rise so as to save the human nature that had been driven out of paradise. For no one knows the Son except the Father, and no one knows Who the Father is except the Son." Because He had said, *All is delivered to Me,* it is as if He were now answering a question that could be asked, "Why are all things delivered to You, and not to another, such as an angel or an archangel?" He answers, "They are delivered to Me because I am of the same nature and essence as the Father. Just as no one knows the Father, so too no one knows Me except the Father alone. Therefore it is right that all things are delivered to Me because I have the same nature as the Father and I am beyond all knowledge just as the Father is beyond all knowledge." And the Father Himself, He says, is known only by the Son, and by that man to whom the Son has willed to reveal Him. See that the Son does not know the Father by means of revelation. Created beings know the Father by revelation, for they receive knowledge as a gift from God. But the Son is not created, [and therefore has no need of revelation to know the Father]. The Lord then turns to His disciples and blesses them, and He blesses all those who with faith see Him in the flesh walking about and working wonders. The prophets and kings of old desired to see the Lord in the flesh and to hear Him, but they did not obtain this desire. In another sense, because He said above that the Father is known by him to whom the Son has revealed Him, He blesses the disciples for having received this revelation. For He revealed the Father to them through Himself: *He that hath seen* Christ *hath seen the Father.*[9] Before the divine Plan of our salvation took flesh, none of the holy ones received this gift. They did not see the Lord in the flesh, He through Whom the Father is known, and therefore they did not see [and know] the Father as the apostles did.

25-28. And, behold, a certain lawyer stood up, and tempted Him, saying, Master, what shall I do to inherit eternal life? He said unto him, What is written in the law? How readest thou? And he

---

[9] Jn. 14:9

answering said, Thou shalt love the Lord thy God with all thy heart, and with all thy soul, and with all thy strength, and with all thy mind; and thy neighbour as thyself. And He said unto him, Thou hast answered right: this do, and thou shalt live. This lawyer was not only arrogant and proud but also deceitful, as is shown by what follows. He comes to put the Lord to the test, and he imagined that he would trip the Lord by the answer which He gave. But the Lord leads him to the very law of which the lawyer boasted such great knowledge. See how precisely the law commands us to love God. Man is more perfect than all other created things, being in some respect like all created things, but in addition having something exceptional. For example, there is a part of man that is like stone, for he has hair and nails which are unfeeling, like a stone. And he is also in part like a plant, in that he grows and is nourished and engenders his own kind, just as plants do. He is in part like the irrational animals, in that he has emotions, and becomes angry, and desires. But unlike all other animals, he is also in part like God, in that he has a mind. Therefore the law teaches that man must give each and every part of himself entirely to God, and must expend all the forces of his life in loving God. When the law says, *with all thy heart,* it speaks of that force of human life that is purely physical and organic, a force likewise present in plant life. When the law says, *with all thy soul,* it speaks of that force of human life which feels, a force likewise present in animals. When the law says, *with all thy mind,* it speaks of that power which is unique to man, the intellect. *With all thy strength* means that we must use all these powers to pull [our stubborn selves to God]. We must harness even the organic, plant-like force of our soul to the love of Christ. How? With strength, and not faintheartedly. And we must also subject, with strength, the power of all our senses to the love of Christ. And the power of our rational soul, this too we must subject with all our strength to the love of Christ. So then, we must give all of ourselves to God, and we must subject our biological powers, our sensory powers, and our intellectual powers to the love of God. *And thy neighbour as thyself.* The law was not yet able to teach perfection on account of the spiritual immaturity of its listeners. Therefore the law urged a man only to love his neighbor as himself. But Christ taught man to love one's neighbor more than oneself. For He says, *Greater love hath no man than this, that* *a man lay down his life for his friends.*[10] Therefore He says to the lawyer, *Thou hast answered right.* Since you are still subject to the law, you have answered correctly, for your thoughts are in accordance with the old law.

29-37. But he, wanting to show himself to be righteous, said unto Jesus, And who is my neighbour? And Jesus answering said, A certain man was going down from Jerusalem to Jericho, and fell among thieves, who stripped him of his raiment, and wounded him, and departed, leaving him half dead. And as it happened there came down a certain priest that way: and when he saw him, he passed by on the other side. And likewise a Levite, when he was at the place, came and looked on him, and passed by on the other side. But a certain Samaritan journeyed and came to him: and when he saw him, he had compassion on him, and went to him, and bound up his wounds, pouring on oil and wine, and set him on his own beast, and brought him to an inn, and took care of him. And on the morrow when he departed, he took out two pence, and gave them to the innkeeper, and said unto him, Take care of him; and whatsoever thou spendest more, when I come again, I will repay thee. Which now of these three, thinkest thou, was neighbour unto him that fell among the thieves? And he said, He that showed mercy on him. Then said Jesus unto him, Go, and do thou likewise. After the Saviour praised him, the lawyer's pride and arrogance knew no bounds. That is why he said, *And who is my neighbour?* that is, "Who is close to me?"[11] He imagined himself to be righteous and thought that there was no one like him and that no one could come close to him in virtue. He imagined that a righteous man could have as "neighbor" only another righteous man. Therefore *wanting to show himself to be righteous* and superior to all men, he says haughtily, *And who is my neighbour?* But the Saviour as Maker of all, knowing that all men are one creation, defines *neighbour* not according to deeds or merits, but according to human nature. "Do not think," He says, "that just because you are righteous, no one is like you.

---

[10] Jn. 15:13

[11] The Greek word for *neighbour, plēsios,* has the literal meaning "one who is close." The question *Who is my neighbour?* in Greek sounds very much like "Who is close to me?" The English word "neighbor" and its German cognate "Nachbar" likewise refer to "one who is nigh," or near.

All mankind shares the same nature and thus all men are your neighbors. Therefore, you too must be a neighbor to them and be near to all, not by location, but by the disposition of your heart and by your care for others. Therefore I present to you a Samaritan to be an example, to show you that no matter how different or foreign he may have seemed, he was the neighbor of the one in need of mercy. You also must show yourself to be a neighbor by your compassion, and even unasked you must go to the help of others.'' Thus we learn from this parable to be always ready to show mercy and to make haste to be near those in need of our help. But this parable also teaches us the goodness of God towards man. It was our human nature that *was going down from Jerusalem,* that is, was descending from tranquillity and peace, for *Jerusalem* means *vision of peace.* Where was man descending? To Jericho, a place sunk down low and suffocating with heat, that is, to a life of passions. See that He did not say, "went down," but, *was going down.* For fallen human nature is always inclined downwards, not just once of old, but continuously going down towards passionate life. And man *fell among thieves,* that is, among demons. For if a man did not come down from that high place where the spiritual mind rules, he would not fall among demons who strip the man, depriving him of his raiment of virtue, and then inflict the wounds of sin. They strip us of every good thought and of God's protection, and when we are thus naked, they lay on the stripes of sin. They leave human nature *half dead,* that is, with a mortal body and an immortal soul. And human nature was left only half dead in the further sense that man did not lie completely in despair, but hoped to find salvation in Christ. Human nature had not yet been slain outright; though death had entered the world through Adam's transgression, death was soon to be abolished by the righteousness of Christ. The priest and the Levite signify the law and the prophets, who desired to make human nature righteous, but were unable to do so. *For it is not possible,* says Paul, *that the blood of bulls and goats should take away sin.*[12] The law and the prophets took pity on man and sought to heal him. But they were defeated by the severity of the wounds of sin, and they passed into the past. This is what it means that they *passed by.* The law came and stood over the fallen man, but since it could not heal him, it turned away in revulsion and went *on the*

---

[12] Heb. 10:4

other side. See that the words *as it happened* also have a certain spiritual meaning. For indeed the law was not given for the express purpose [of healing the wounds of sin, for Christ, not the law, was to be the healing of Adam's wound]. Instead, the law was given [as a stopgap measure] on account of human weakness which could not immediately receive the mystery of Christ. This is why He says that it was *as it happened,* or, as we say, "by chance," and not intentionally, that the priest, signifying the law, came to heal the man. But our Lord and God, Who *for our sake was made a curse*[13] and was called a Samaritan,[14] *journeyed* to us, that is, His journey had as its very purpose and goal our healing. He did not just catch a glimpse of us as He happened to pass by: He actually came to us and lived together with us and spoke to us. Therefore He at once bound up our wounds. He no longer permitted wickedness to operate in us freely and at will, but He bound and restrained our sinfulness and *poured on oil and wine. Oil* is the word of teaching which exhorts us to virtue by the promise of good things; *wine* is the word of teaching leading us towards virtue by the fear of punishment. For example, when you hear the Lord say, *Come unto Me and I will give you rest,*[15] this is the oil of gladness and rest. And it is the same when He says, *Come ye and inherit the kingdom prepared for you.*[16] But when He says, "Depart into darkness,"[17] this is the wine of sharp teaching which stings as it cleanses our wounds. You may also understand it this way: *oil* represents Christ's human actions and *wine* represents His divine actions, for I may say that the Lord acted at times as a man and at times as God. When He ate and drank and relaxed, not displaying the austerity and asceticism of John the Forerunner, this is the oil. But His extraordinary fasting, His walking on the water, and all His mighty deeds of divine power, these are the wine. We can compare Christ's divinity to wine, which no one could tolerate if it were poured onto a wound, unless it were tempered with oil, that is, accompanied by His humanity. Therefore, since Christ has saved us both by His divinity and by His humanity, this is why it is said that oil and

---

[13] Gal. 3:13

[14] Jn. 8:48

[15] Mt. 11:28

[16] Mt. 25:34

[17] See Mt. 25:30.

wine were poured out. And at every baptism those who are baptized are delivered from wounds of the soul when they are chrismated with the oil of myrrh and then immediately commune of the divine Blood. The Lord lifted up our wounded nature upon His own *beast* of burden, namely, upon His own Body. For He made us members of Himself and communicants of His own Body; and when we were lying down, wounded, He raised us up to His own dignity, making us one Body with Himself. The *inn* is the Church, which receives all.[18] But the law did not receive all. For the law says, *the Ammanite and the Moabite shall not enter into the Church of God.*[19] But now, from every tribe and people, God accepts those who fear Him and who desire to believe and to become a member of Christ's Body, the Church. God receives all, even sinners and publicans. See the preciseness of His expression, how He says that the Samaritan *brought him to an inn, and took care of him.* Before he brought him to the inn, he had only bound his wounds. What then am I saying? That when the Church had been established, becoming the inn which receives all, and was increased by the faith of nearly all peoples, then there were the gifts of the Holy Spirit, and the grace of God was spread far and wide. You may learn this from the Acts of the Apostles. The *innkeeper* is a type and symbol of every apostle, teacher, and archpastor, to whom the Lord gave *two pence,* representing the two Testaments, Old and New. Just as both coins bear the image of the one king, so do both Testaments bear the words of the same God. When the Lord ascended into the heavens He left these two coins in the hands of the apostles, and in the hands of the bishops and teachers of every generation. And He said to them, *And whatsoever thou spendest more* of thine own, *I will repay thee.* Indeed the apostles spent much more of their own: with great labors they sowed the word of teaching everywhere. And those teachers in each generation who have explained the Old and the New Testaments have also spent much of their own, for which they will be rewarded when the Lord returns at the second coming. Then may each of them say to Him, "Lord, Thou gavest me two pence; behold, another two pence have I spent of mine own." And to him the Lord will answer, "Well done, thou good servant."

---

[18] *Pan-docheion, inn,* has the literal meaning "that which receives all."

[19] Deut. 23:3

38-42. Now it came to pass, as they went, that He entered into a certain village: and a certain woman named Martha received Him into her house. And she had a sister called Mary, who also sat at Jesus' feet, and listened to His word. But Martha was cumbered about much serving, and came to Him, and said, Lord, dost Thou not care that my sister hath left me to serve alone? Bid her therefore that she help me. And Jesus answered and said unto her, Martha, Martha, thou art careful and troubled about many things: but one thing is needful: and Mary hath chosen that good part, which shall not be taken away from her. Hospitality, which Martha displays, is a great virtue which ought not to be scorned; but it is even greater to give heed to spiritual words. By means of the first, the body is nourished; by means of the second, the soul is brought to life. The Lord says, "I have not come, Martha, to fill the belly with all sorts of foods, but instead I have come to bring benefit to souls." See the Lord's way of thought: He did not say anything to Martha until she had first given Him a reason to rebuke her. Only when she tried to draw her sister away from listening, did the Lord use the occasion to rebuke her. To practice hospitality is honorable, until that point is reached when it causes turmoil and draws us away from the things that are more important. When hospitality begins to hinder us from doing the things that are more important, then listening to divine words is preferable. To say it more precisely, it is not hospitality which the Lord forbids, but extravagance and upset, that is, distractions and turmoil. Simple hospitality He praises. "Why, Martha," He asks, "art thou full of cares and troubled about many things?" meaning, "Why are you distracted and disturbed? We need only to eat one kind of food, whatever is at hand, not a great variety." But some have understood *one thing is needful* to refer, not to food, but to the importance of listening to the teaching. By what He says to Martha, the Lord is teaching the apostles that when they enter into anyone's house, they should not seek an elaborate welcome, but should be content with a simple reception, desiring nothing more than that their hosts pay close attention to the teaching. Understand that Martha represents active virtue, while Mary represents divine vision. Action entails distractions and disturbances, but divine vision, having become the ruler of the passions (for *Maria* means *mistress,* she who rules), devotes itself entirely to the contemplation of the divine words and judgments. Give heed also to these words of the Gospel: Mary *sat at Jesus' feet and listened to His words.* The feet are understood as symbols of active virtue, representing movement and step-by-step progression. And sitting is a symbol of steadfastness and constancy. Therefore, whoever sits at the feet of Jesus, that is, whoever steadfastly follows and imitates Jesus, is established in all active virtue. Then such a man will also come to the listening of the divine words, that is, he will attain to divine vision. Mary first sat, and by doing this she was then able to listen to Jesus' words. Therefore, you also, O reader, if you have the strength, ascend to the rank of Mary: become the mistress of your passions, and attain to divine vision. But if you do not have the strength, be Martha, and devote yourself to active virtue, and by this means welcome Christ. See also the words, *Mary hath chosen that good part which shall not be taken away from her.* Activity has a part that will be taken away from it, namely, the cares and distractions that accompany it. For as a man progresses and attains to divine vision, he is freed from distractions and troubles, and so it can be said that something is taken away from him. But he who is engaged in divine vision shall never be deprived of *that good part,* the vision of God. What else is there to attain, once he has reached this pinnacle, that is, once he sees God, which means that he is deified? He who is found worthy to see God, becomes God.[20] For something is comprehended only by that which is like unto to it.

---

[20] *O gar Theon blepein axiōtheis, Theos ginetai.*

CHAPTER ELEVEN

Concerning prayer.
Concerning the man possessed of a mute demon.
Concerning the woman of the company
who lifted up her voice.
Concerning those who asked for a sign.
Concerning the Pharisee who invited Jesus.
Concerning the woe of the lawyers.

1-4. And it came to pass, that, as He was praying in a certain place, when He ceased, one of His disciples said unto Him, Lord, teach us to pray, as John also taught his disciples. And He said unto them, When ye pray, say, Our Father Who art in the heavens, hallowed be Thy name. Thy kingdom come. Thy will be done, on earth as it is in heaven. Give us day by day our daily bread. And forgive us our sins, for we also forgive every one that is indebted to us. And lead us not into temptation; but deliver us from the evil one. This disciple of Christ is jealous of John's disciples, which is why he wants to be taught how to pray. The Lord teaches and does not reject the demand of the disciple. He says, *Our Father Who art in the heavens.* See the power of prayer. It immediately leads you upwards. And it encourages you, since you have called God, *Father*, not to fall far short of the likeness between you and your heavenly Father, but to strive to make yourself like your Father. The Lord did not say, "My Father," but, *Our Father*, so as to urge us to have brotherly love and to oblige us to love all men as our very own brothers. He says, *Who art in the heavens*, not to limit God to that place, but to lead the listener upwards to the heavens and away from earthly things. *Hallowed be Thy name* means "Glorified be Thy name," that is, "Make our lives be to Thy glory." Just as God's name is blasphemed by the wicked, so too is it glorified by those who lead a good life. *Thy kingdom come.* The sinner begs that the kingdom of God not come, because he fears the judgments and punishments that will accompany it. By contrast, the righteous man prays that the kingdom of God will come quickly, so that he might be delivered from temptations and find rest. "And may Thy will be done, just as in heaven by the angels, likewise by us men on earth." For every deed of every angel is done according to God's will. He teaches us to seek only our *daily bread*, that is, that bread which is required for our being and for the sustenance of our life, and not to ask for more than we need. That we enter not into temptations means that we not leap into temptations by our own will. We should not ask God to throw us into temptations; we should instead beseech Him to do just the opposite. But when temptations come upon us, then we should withstand them with courage. We may say, here, that there are two kinds of temptations. The first kind are voluntary temptations, such as drunkenness, murder, adultery, and the other passions. We willingly entangle ourselves in these kind of temptations. The other kind of temptations are involuntary, such as those which tyrants and violent men inflict upon us. From voluntary temptations, that is, from the passions, we must therefore flee, and pray that they not come, and say, "*Lead us not* into them," that is, "Do not permit us to fall into temptation, namely, voluntary passion. But deliver us from the evil one." For it is the evil one who leads us into both involuntary and voluntary temptations. Therefore when you are tempted against your will by a man, do not think that the man is the cause of your temptation; it is not he, but instead the evil one who persuades the man to rage against you.

5-8. And He said unto them, Which of you shall have a friend, and shall go unto him at midnight, and say unto him, Friend, lend me three loaves; for a friend of mine in his journey is come to me, and I have nothing to set before him? And he from within shall answer and say, Trouble me not: the door has already been shut, and my children are with me in bed; I cannot rise and give thee. I say unto you, Though he will not rise and give him because he is his friend, yet because of his importunity he will rise and give him as many as he needeth. The Lord gives a parable and an example, teaching us to pray tirelessly. What does the parable mean? *Midnight* is the end of life, when a man often comes to a consciousness of good and runs to God, Who is the *Friend* Who loves all mankind and *Who desireth that all men be saved.*[1] Therefore at the end of their life many approach God as their friend and say to Him, "Give me three loaves," that is, "Give me faith in the Holy Trinity. *For a friend is come,* namely, the angel who will

---

[1] I Tim. 2:4

receive my soul.'' The *friend* is also every angel, as the Lord Himself says, *There is joy in the presence of the angels of God* at the salvation of any man.[2] The children resting on the bed are those who have repented and become like children and have been counted worthy to rest with the Lord. The man's *importunity* is his patient and persistent prayer. The parable may also be understood in another way: *Midnight* is the central part, the peak, of temptation. For every temptation is night, and the blackest part of temptation is midnight. Therefore when one is in the middle of temptations, he approaches God, our Friend, and says to Him, *Lend me three loaves,* that is, ''Grant me salvation of body, soul, and spirit.'' From temptations comes his fear that all three may be endangered. Who is the *friend in his journey* who comes to him? Is it not the Lord, Who tests us during our temptations and Who hungers for our salvation? But the man who has fallen into temptations *has nothing to set* before the Lord. He has grown too weak to withstand the temptations on his own and to serve God. *The door has already been shut* means that it is necessary for us to be prepared before the temptations come. But if we are unprepared when temptations come, the door is shut, that is, there is no time left to prepare and we are in great peril, unless God should come to our aid. The *children* signify, as was said before, those who have become sons of God by means of their virtue, and who now recline and rest in God.

9-13. And I say unto you, Ask, and it shall be given you; seek, and ye shall find; knock, and it shall be opened unto you. For every one that asketh receiveth; and he that seeketh findeth; and to him that knocketh it shall be opened. If a son shall ask bread of any of you that is a father, will he give him a stone? Or if he ask a fish, will he for a fish, give him a serpent? Or if he shall ask an egg, will he offer him a scorpion? If ye then, being evil, know how to give good gifts unto your children, how much more shall your heavenly Father give the Holy Spirit to them that ask Him? See the preciseness of the words. He did not say, ''Ask once, and it shall be given you,'' but

---

[2] See Lk. 15:10.

instead, *Ask,* that is, keep asking.[3] *For everyone that asketh receiveth.*[4] Does the one who asks for something that is not good for him also receive? Indeed not. First of all, a request for something that is not good cannot be called a request directed towards God. He who prays to God should ask for the things which God gives. If he asks for something that is not good for him, he is not making his request to God, for God gives us only what is good for us. Listen, then, how the Lord teaches us to ask for what we ought to ask. The son, He says, asks for a loaf of bread, a fish, and an egg. Just as these things are food for man, so also our requests should be for those things which are good and profitable for us. Understand that the man who asks for bread signifies every one who asks that faith in the Trinity, and Orthodox dogmas, be revealed unto him. For these things are as bread which *strengtheneth man's heart.*[5] He who asks for a fish is he who is in the sea of life, seeking help from God so that he not drown in the midst of temptations but be preserved, just as the fish are preserved from death in the sea. He who asks for an egg is he who asks for that which is born of a virtuous soul. For the virtuous soul can indeed be likened to a bird because it takes wing and is carried aloft by the breath of the Holy Spirit, and flies upwards from the earth.

14-20. And He was casting out a demon, and it was dumb. And it came to pass, when the demon was gone out, the dumb man spake; and the people marvelled. But some of them said, He casteth out demons through Beelzebub the prince of the demons. And others, tempting Him, sought of Him a sign from heaven. But He, knowing their thoughts, said unto them, Every kingdom divided against itself is brought to desolation; and a house divided against a house falleth. If Satan also be divided against himself, how shall his kingdom stand? Because ye say that I cast out demons through Beelzebub. And if I by Beelzebub cast out demons, by whom do your sons cast them out? Therefore shall they be your judges. But if I with the finger of God cast out demons, no doubt the kingdom of God is come

---

[3] All the commands in this text of the Gospel, *ask, seek,* and *knock,* are in the present imperative in the Greek, signifying continuous, ongoing action. They are not in the aorist imperative, which would imply a single, completed action.

[4] Mt. 7:8

[5] Ps. 103:17

upon you. Usually someone is called *dumb* when he cannot speak. Someone might also be called *dumb* if he cannot hear, and generally, the two go together.[6] This is particularly true of those who were born deaf. In that case, by necessity neither can they speak. For we speak what we have learned through hearing. If one cannot hear, it is likely that he also cannot speak, unless he suffered the loss of hearing later in life, in which case nothing prevents him from speaking. This man, then, was brought to the Lord, mute in both tongue and ear. He is a symbol of our human nature which was possessed by demons and could not endure to hear the words of God and, therefore, by necessity was unable to speak them. But the Lord came and drove out the demons, our demonic deeds full of passion, and caused us to speak and to proclaim the Truth. For we must not only hear the words of God but also tell them to others. Therefore, we who are full of demonic deeds, who think to teach others and who desire to be called "Master" by other men, let us hear: only when the demon is gone can there be true speech, that is, teaching. While the activity of the demon is within us, even though we appear to be speaking, we are not. The Pharisees slander the miracle and insult the Lord as a sorcerer. They say that He has as His friend the prince of the demons, and that it is by his help that the Lord casts out demons. In reply the Lord says to them, "How is it possible for one demon to cast out another? This would result in the destruction of their kingdom. For the demons think that possessing a man provides them both a throne and a kingdom. Therefore, if the prince of demons casts them out, it is clear that he is destroying himself. Every kingdom divided into rebelling factions must destroy itself, and a house divided will fall. *House* you should understand to mean either the structure of the house, or those living within the house. For a house stands only as long as it preserves the integrity of its walls. When the walls are separated from each other, the house will fall. And while the members of the household are at peace with one another, they stand together. But when they rise up against each other, the household falls. Let us suppose that I in fact cast out demons by Beelzebub: by whom do your sons, that is, the apostles, cast them out? Is it not clear that they do so in My name? How then can you say that I

---

[6] The Greek word *kōphos*, translated here as *dumb*, signifies the inability to speak, or the inability to hear, or both.

cast out demons by Beelzebub and that I have need of his power, when your sons, the apostles, cast out demons in My name? Therefore, the apostles themselves condemn you. For if the apostles cast out demons in My name, it is obvious that I have no need of another's power. I cast them out *with the finger of God,* that is, by the Holy Spirit, and not by an evil spirit.'' He calls the Holy Spirit *the finger of God,* to teach us that just as the finger has the same essence as the whole body, so also the Holy Spirit has the same essence as the Father and the Son. Perhaps He also names the Holy Spirit *the finger of God* because the Son is called the hand of God. The seven energies of the Holy Spirit rest in the Son [as if they were the fingers of a hand]; but He does not derive His energy from them for He is of one essence with the Spirit. To heal is one of the gifts and the energies of the Holy Spirit. This is why it is said that He casts out demons *by the finger of God,* that is, by the grace of the Holy Spirit. Just as the finger is a part of the hand, so too the energy of healing is only a part of what Jesus had, namely, all the energies of the Holy Spirit. ''Therefore if I cast out demons by divine energy,'' He says, ''*the kingdom of God is come upon you.*'' This means that the kingdom of the devil has been destroyed, and God Who drives out the demons now rules as king. Listen to what He says next:

21-26. When a strong man armed keepeth his palace, his goods are in peace: but when a stronger than he shall come upon him, and overcome him, he taketh from him all his weapons wherein he trusted, and divideth his spoils. He that is not with Me is against Me: and he that gathereth not with Me scattereth. When the unclean spirit is gone out of a man, he walketh through dry places, seeking rest; and finding none, he saith, I will return unto my house whence I came out. And when he cometh, he findeth it swept and adorned. Then goeth he, and taketh to him seven other spirits more wicked than himself; and they enter in, and dwell there: and the last state of that man is worse than the first. There was, the Lord says, before My coming *a strong man,* Satan, who guarded his palace, that is, who captured our human nature and held it with an unshakable grip. But I came, Who am stronger than he, and overcame the world and the full panoply of Satan's *weapons wherein he trusted,* that is, all the forms of sin. For sin is the weaponry of the devil, and, brandishing these weapons, he made bold and overpowered man. All this weaponry of his have I shattered, I Whom he found to be sinless, and from that time he has grown weak. And his spoils, namely, mankind whom he held as booty, I have snatched from Him and divided up, giving each one to an angel to be that man's faithful guardian, so that an angel might have him instead of the demon who before had tyrannized him. Furthermore, what communion do I have with Beelzebub? It is My work to gather together the children of God who have been scattered; it is his work to scatter those who have been gathered together. How then can you have such thoughts about Me, that I keep company with Satan? Instead, such thoughts have occurred to you by the inspiration of the demons. Once before you had an unclean spirit dwelling in you, when you worshipped the idols and slew the prophets. Then it appeared that this unclean spirit had gone out of you, but now it has returned into its own house, into your souls, together with seven, meaning, many, other foul spirits. In Scripture *seven* means *many*. Now this unclean spirit has made your last condition worse than it was before. Before when you worshipped idols and killed the prophets you did not yet insult the Son of God Who appeared clearly in the flesh for your sakes. But what hope of salvation is there for you, now that the Son of God has taken flesh and has worked wonders for you, and you show the same ingratitude and violence? The *dry places* are the souls of those who are not dank and overgrown swamps, but instead are dry and carefully tended, and hence the spirit of uncleanness finds no rest in them. In souls such as these the evil one has no place to dwell, and so he has returned to these Jews, and their last condition has become worse than their former state. No longer are there any prophets among them, for they have killed the Word. No longer do they have any chrism, for they have crucified the very Christ.[7] Before, they had all this, even though they worshipped idols. But now they have sinned against the Son of God and have lost all.

27-32. And it came to pass, as He spake these things, a certain woman of the company lifted up her voice, and said unto Him, Blessed is the womb that bare Thee, and the paps which Thou hast

---

[7] Without chrism, a special holy oil, the Israelites could not anoint their kings and prophets. When Christ, the Anointed One, came and was slain by the Jews, the "chrism" of the Old Testament came to an end, in fulfillment of the prophecy: *Chrism shall be destroyed.* (Daniel 9:26) See Bl. Theophylact's explanation of Luke 16:27-31 on p. 218 of this volume.

sucked. But He said, Yea, indeed blessed are they that hear the word of God, and keep it. And when the people were gathered thick together, He began to say, This is an evil generation: they seek a sign; and there shall no sign be given it, but the sign of Jonah the prophet. For as Jonah was a sign unto the Ninevites, so shall also the Son of Man be to this generation. The queen of the south shall rise up in the judgment with the men of this generation, and condemn them: for she came from the utmost parts of the earth to hear the wisdom of Solomon; and, behold, a greater than Solomon is here. The men of Ninevah shall rise up in the judgment with this generation, and shall condemn it: for they repented at the preaching of Jonah; and, behold, a greater than Jonah is here. The Pharisees and the scribes slandered the miracles, but the simple and guileless woman praised them. Where are those who say that the Lord appeared on earth in imagination only? Behold, even the breasts which He suckled as an infant bear witness. He blesses those who keep the word of God, not excluding His mother from that blessing—far from it![8]—but showing that even she would have received no benefit from giving birth to Him and suckling Him if she did not also possess every virtue. He also addresses these words to the occasion. Since these tormentors, who would not heed His words, were accusing those who did listen to Christ, He does just the opposite and blesses those who listen to Him. And perhaps He also says this for the benefit of the mute man who had been healed, so that he too would hear and keep His word, lest his new found power of hearing be to his condemnation. *When the people were gathered thick together,* the Lord began to reprove those who were ungrateful. For some of them were seeking from Him a sign from heaven. They were saying, "The miracles He is working are from earth, and He works them through Beelzebub, the ruler of this world who has power on earth. But Jesus is not able to work signs from heaven because He is not the Son of the heavenly Father." Because of those who were saying such things, the Lord gives this rebuke and says, "A sign shall be given to you which will show that I am the true Son of the heavenly Father." What sign is this? The sign of Jonah,

---

[8] The Greek word *menounge*, translated above in the text of verse 28 as *yea, indeed,* but rendered inaccurately in the KJV as "yea, rather," is the same word which occurs in Phil. 3:8, where the KJV gives *Yea, doubtless,* and in Rom. 10:18, where the KJV gives *Yes verily.* The force of *menounge* is that it corrects the previous statement, not by negating it, but by amplifying it.

which is the Resurrection. Just as Jonah spent three days in the belly of the whale, so too will I spend three days in the belly of the whale, the great beast, hades, and then I will rise. But the men of Ninevah believed Jonah when he preached after he came to life again, as it were, from the belly of the whale, but this generation will not believe Me even though I rise from the dead. Therefore this generation will be condemned because they did not imitate the Ninevites, although *behold, a greater than Jonah is here*. There is a vast difference between us, both in rank, and in what we preach. I am the Master; he was a servant. I preach the kingdom of heaven; he preached salvation only from their city's destruction. My words are accompanied by miracles; he worked no miracles. In the same manner, *the queen of the south* will judge this generation, *for she came from the utmost ends of the earth to hear the wisdom of Solomon.* You may also understand the queen of the south to mean every soul which holds and stands firm in what is good. For in Scripture the north is called the place of the adversary—from whence comes cold, numbness, and death. But the south is praised as having a warm and life-giving breath and spirit, thawing what is frozen. Therefore the bride in the Song of Solomon drives out the north wind, saying, *Awake, O north wind; and come, O south.*"[9] And again the prophet says, *The Lord will destroy him who is from the north,*[10] namely, Satan. Therefore the soul which rules over the south, that is, which governs the good portion and the spiritual life which belongs to it, derives its authority to do this from its practice of the virtues. And that soul comes *to hear the wisdom,* that is, to ascend to divine vision. For the wisdom of Solomon, the peaceful king,[11] is the vision of our Lord and God, into which there is no other way to enter except by leading a good life and governing oneself by the practice of virtue.

33-36. No man, when he hath lighted a lamp, putteth it in a secret place, neither under a bushel, but on a lampstand, that they which are coming in may see the light. The lamp of the body is the eye: therefore when thine eye is single, thy whole body also is full of light;

---

[9] Song of Solomon 4:16

[10] See Joel 2:20.

[11] *Solomon* means *peace.*

but when thine eye is evil, thy body also is full of darkness. Watch therefore that the light which is in thee be not darkness. For if all thy whole body be light, having no part dark, then shall all be full of light, as when the bright shining of the lamp doth give thee light. Because the malicious Jews saw Christ's miracles and slandered them with their evil mind, the Lord spoke these words to them: "Man has received from God by grace and as a gift a lamp which is the mind, by which we see, just as if a light had been given to us. But some have blocked the mind's ability to discern, and have darkened it by malice, and thus do not see the miracles and the benefactions of God. Yet we received the gift of the mind for this very reason, that we might put it on the lampstand so that others might see the light as well." I think the Lord is saying this: "You have knowledge, O Pharisee, which is the lamp. You ought to have used this lamp of knowledge to see these miracles for what they truly are, and then to make the miracles shiningly visible for others to see that they are the works of the Son of God, and not of Beelzebub. If you had done so, those who *are coming in*, that is, the beginners and the inexperienced, might see the light. He who is wise has already come in; he who is learning is still coming in. But you, O Pharisees, did not wish to do this. Instead, the eye of your soul, your mind, which once was single and whole, you have made squinted and dark." The condition of the eye of the body determines the condition of the body: if the eye has light, the body will be in the light, but if the eye does not have light, the body will be in the dark. So it is with the condition of the soul and the mind: if the "eye" and the "light" which the soul received from God is found to be darkened by malice, or love of money, or love of anything material, the soul itself is blinded.

37-41. And as He spake, a certain Pharisee besought Him to dine with him; and He went in, and sat down at table. And when the Pharisee saw it, he marvelled that He had not first washed before dinner. And the Lord said unto him, Now do ye Pharisees make clean the outside of the cup and the platter; but your inward part is full of ravening and wickedness. Ye fools, did not He that made that which is without also make that which is within? But give alms of such things as ye have within, and, behold, all things are clean unto you. The Lord knew the foulness of the Pharisees, but He ate dinner with them for this very reason, that they were wicked and in need of correction. He eats with them in order to use the opportunity to better their way of life. So it is now that He ridicules their foolish custom of ritually cleansing themselves before eating, teaching that one must cleanse the soul with good deeds. Washing with water cleanses only the body, not the soul. But they foolishly believed that immersing and washing the body would, at the same time, cleanse the soul. The Lord uses the apt example of the cup. Because they were at that moment eating dinner, the Lord mentions the cup and the platter, using objects that were lying before their very eyes to prove His point. He urges the Pharisee to understand that just as no benefit is derived from a cup which is clean on the outside but covered with filth on the inside, neither does it benefit the body to have been immersed and washed while the soul is full of every uncleanliness such as ravenous extortion and wickedness. By mentioning extortion and wickedness, the Lord refers to the two chief passions which held sway among the Jews: avarice and spite and the effects of spite. Washing the body brings no benefit when the soul is in such a condition. "O fools, did not He Who made the body, on which you lavish such attention, also make the soul? You ought therefore to cleanse the soul as well." Then He teaches them how to clean what is inside—by almsgiving. See how He heals their two passions of extortion and spite by prescribing almsgiving. For he who truly shows mercy and gives alms will neither extort from, nor show spite to him to whom he has given alms. Since the Lord had chastised them for these two passions, now He uproots these passions with a single medicine, almsgiving, which is the first door to love. And it is love which makes us Godlike. Where love is, how can there be greed and spite? *Give alms of such things as ye have within,* meaning, give of those possessions which belong to your heart. See that the Lord did not say, "Give as alms anything that is yours;" instead He said with exactness, "Give of that which is within." For the wealth of the avaricious man enters into his heart and sits there enthroned. Hence David says, *If riches flow in, set not your hearts thereon,*[12] meaning, do not chain or nail the two together.

42-51. But woe unto you, Pharisees! For ye tithe mint and rue and all manner of herbs, and pass over judgment and the love of God:

---

[12] Ps. 61:10

these ought ye to have done, yet not to leave the other undone. Woe unto you, Pharisees! For ye love the uppermost seats in the synagogues, and greetings in the markets. Woe unto you, scribes and Pharisees, hypocrites! For ye are as graves which appear not such, and the men that walk over them are not aware of them. Then answered one of the lawyers, and said unto Him, Master, thus saying Thou reproachest us also. And He said, Woe unto you also, ye lawyers! For ye laden men with burdens grievous to be borne, and ye yourselves touch not the burdens with one of your fingers. Woe unto you! For ye build the sepulchres of the prophets, and your fathers killed them. Truly ye bear witness that ye approve the deeds of your fathers: for they indeed killed them, and ye build their tombs. Therefore also said the Wisdom of God, I will send them prophets and apostles, and some of them they shall slay and persecute: that the blood of all the prophets, which was shed from the foundation of the world, may be required of this generation; from the blood of Abel unto the blood of Zacharias, who perished between the altar and the temple: verily I say unto you, it shall be required of this generation.

The Pharisees would make a tithe of the most insignificant items, supposedly to avoid transgressing the law. And if someone were to accuse them of concerning themselves with trivia, they would defend themselves by citing the law which commands the people to give to the priest as an offering tithes of everything.[13] The Lord therefore is saying, "Just as you do not neglect these small matters, so you ought also to concern yourself with judgment and the love of God." Because they were unjust, ruining orphans and widows, He says, "You ought to have judgment," meaning, you ought to judge fairly. And because they were scorners of God, carelessly performing holy deeds, He commands them to have love of God, for he who loves God does not perform with scorn the deeds of God. Perhaps, it seems to me, since there are two types of love, love of God and love of neighbor, He is suggesting these two loves when He speaks of *judgment* and *the love of God.* On the one hand, *judgment* indicates love for one's neighbor. To judge one's neighbor fairly and not to tyrannize him comes from having love towards him. On the other hand, when a man is completely turned towards God, then he

---

[13] See Levit. 27:30-32 and Deut. 14:22, 23, 28.

has *love of God.* When a man loves his neighbor, not for some worldly reason, or because of a shameful passion, but according to God, it can be said that this is that *love of God* which God has commanded and which He accepts. The Pharisees wanted every one to honor them and to address them as teachers when they saw them in the markets. "You are like tombs," He tells them, "which teem with corruption, but on the outside they shine with marble; and when men see them, they do not realize what they are standing on. If they did, they would be disgusted by the loathesomeness of what is inside." The lawyer foolishly brings censure down upon himself. The lawyers were different from the Pharisees. The Pharisees thought of themselves as ascetics who were set apart from all the others. But the lawyers were scribes and teachers who answered other men's questions about the law. The lawyers loaded men down *with burdens grievous to be borne* by commanding the people to observe those particulars of the law which were difficult to keep, while they themselves did not touch those burdens with one of their fingers, that is, they themselves did nothing of what they commanded others to do. When the teacher himself does the things which he teaches others to do, he has lightened the load by his own example, and thus he gives encouragement and consolation to his students. But when he does nothing of what he teaches, then the burdens indeed seem heavy to the students, when they see that even their teacher cannot do them. The Lord shows that these Jews are descendants and inheritors of the wickedness of Cain by saying that all the blood shed from Abel to Zacharias shall be required of this generation. He says, "For you slew your own brothers, the prophets, just as Cain slew his brother Abel." Therefore some have quite fittingly likened Cain to the people who slew the prophets, and have likened Lamech to those who slew Christ. Cain's punishment was less than Lamech's, for it is written: *Vengeance has been exacted seven times on Cain's behalf,* but *on Lamech's behalf seventy times seven,*[14] that is, they who slew Christ were scattered into a captivity from which they did not return. Who then was this Zacharias, whom they slew between the altar and the temple? Some say that he was the Zacharias of the Old Testament, the son of Joade, who was stoned, as can be learned in the Book

---

[14] Gen. 4:24

of Kings.[15] Others say that he was the father of the Forerunner, who placed the Theotokos among the virgins after she had given birth to Christ, and had her stand in the place in the temple where the virgins stood. This place was between the temple and the outer altar of bronze. This is why they slew him. Some expected and waited for the Christ to come and be their king. But these Jews did not want to be ruled by a king and so they slew this holy man, Zacharias, who confirmed that the Virgin had given birth and that the Christ had been born Who would be their King. But they rejected Him because they did not want to live under a king.

52-54. Woe unto you, lawyers! For ye have taken away the key of knowledge: ye entered not in yourselves, and them that were entering in ye hindered. And as He said these things unto them, the scribes and the Pharisees began to be sorely vexed, and to besiege Him with many questions: lying in wait for Him, and seeking to catch something out of His mouth, that they might accuse Him. The teaching and the guidance given by means of the law the Lord called *the key of knowledge,* because it led to Christ. The law was indeed a guide leading to Christ. The lawyers seemed to be interpreting the law, but were in fact maliciously holding back the key of knowledge, and were not opening the doors of the law by which both they and the people could enter in to Christ. The law is a door leading to Christ, but this door is shut unless someone clarifies that which is obscure in the law and opens the door. For Christ Himself said, *Had ye believed Moses, ye would have believed in Me.*[16] And again, *Search the Scriptures...it is they which testify of Me, and ye will not come unto Me.*[17] To give only one example, a lamb was slain by the Jews, they anointed their doorways, they ate the meat, and this was their means of victory over the destroyer. But these things also revealed the whole mystery of Christ Who was slain as a blameless and unblemished Lamb. Just as the lintel and two side posts of their doorways were anointed with the blood of the lamb, so also the three powers of our soul were anointed and marked with Christ. The three powers of the soul

---

[15] IV Kings 13 and II Chron. 24:21.

[16] Jn. 5:46

[17] Jn. 5:39-40

are its ability to be stirred to action, its ability to desire, and, uppermost, its ability to reason. And we have eaten the Flesh of the Son of Man and have defeated that one who destroys the powers of our soul. In similar fashion, the greater part of the law pointed to Christ. But the law was closed, like a door, by the obscurity of the letter of the law. Whoever was entrusted with teaching the law held the key of knowledge. If he so desired, he could open the door and go in himself and become a guide for others. But the lawyers did not do this; instead they took away the key of knowledge, that is, they hid it and removed it from sight. And as the key, that is, the explanation of the law, had been taken from their midst, the door remained shut. You may also understand *the key of knowledge* to mean faith. Through faith comes knowledge of the truth. Therefore the prophet Isaiah says, *If ye believe not, neither will ye understand.*[18] The lawyers, then, took away the key of knowledge, namely, faith, and they hid it, barring others from believing in Christ, the Saviour of all. For Christ was working miracles, and because of the miracles the people believed and were on the point of understanding that He was God. But the lawyers began to say that He performed these miracles in the name of Beelzebub. Do you see how they took away the key of knowledge by not permitting the people to believe in the Lord, through Whom knowledge would come to them? Christ was teaching them the will of God in the synagogues, but they were saying, "He has a demon, He is mad. Why do you listen to Him?" In truth they took away the key of knowledge, and did not go in themselves, and hindered others from going in, namely, those who were capable of receiving divine knowledge. While the Lord was still saying these things, they began, as it were, to attest to the truth of what He was saying. They ought to have acknowledged their own failings and weakness, but instead they tried to show themselves more expert than He. They began to *besiege Him*, that is, to ply Him with so many questions that they thought He would be at a loss what to answer. Being many in number, they piled on Him question upon question on all different topics. Then, because it was not possible for Him to answer them all at once, He gave the impression to those mindless men that He was at a loss for an answer. In this way these accursed ones played games of sophistry against Christ. Because many were asking

---

[18] Is. 7:9

questions of one, they seemed to have shut His mouth and to render Him at a loss for words, as if He were not able to answer them. But this was indeed the case, for how can one person answer many people who are asking all different questions at once? *They besieged Him* may also be understood to mean that they set a trap for Him, trying to catch Him by His words. For when a man is caught in the words which he speaks, it can be said that he was caught by his own mouth, and therefore condemned. This meaning is shown by what follows. For *they were seeking,* the Evangelist says, *to catch something out of His mouth.* Where a little before he says that they *besieged Him with many questions,* now he says that they were trying *to catch something out of His mouth.* They were asking Him questions, first about the law, so that they could rebuke Him as a blasphemer who accused Moses, for this is what they thought, and then about Caesar, so that they could denounce Him as a fomenter of sedition and a usurper. And, in short, they asked Him whatever question came to their evil and malicious minds.

CHAPTER TWELVE

Concerning the leaven of the Pharisees.
Concerning the man who wanted to divide the inheritance.
Concerning the man whose ground brought forth plentifully.
Concerning disdain for the things of the world.
On fleeing from the love of money.
Concerning the watchful servant.
On not disputing with thy brother.

1-3. In the meantime, when there were gathered together an innumerable multitude of people, insomuch that they trode one upon another, He began to say unto His disciples first of all, Beware ye of the leaven of the Pharisees, which is hypocrisy. For there is nothing covered, that shall not be revealed; neither hid, that shall not be known. Therefore whatsoever ye have spoken in darkness shall be heard in the light; and that which ye have spoken in the ear in private chambers shall be proclaimed upon the housetops. The Pharisees were striving to trap Jesus in His speech, in an effort to separate the multitude from Him. But just the opposite occurred. The multitude approached Him all the more, gathering in the tens of thousands, with the result that they even stepped on one other as they struggled to get closer to Him. Such is the strength of truth, and such, always, is the feebleness of deceit. Jesus saw the deceit of the Pharisees, who pretended to ask questions but in fact were setting a trap for Him, and He spoke to His disciples concerning the hypocrisy of the Pharisees, always chastising them and revealing the hypocrisy which filled their hearts. He calls hypocrisy *leaven* because it is sour, the product of old corruption, and it changes and corrupts, together with itself, the minds of other men in whom it is mixed. For there is nothing which deforms conduct as much as does hypocrisy. Therefore those who are disciples of Christ must flee hypocrisy. Since Christ is Truth, He is clearly the adversary of falsehood. All hypocrisy and play-acting are full of falsehood, whether done by an actor on stage or by a man who in his life pretends to be what he is not.[1] The Pharisees imagine that by acting out a part they will keep hidden what they really are and will appear to be good and upright. But *there is nothing covered, that shall not be revealed.* Every word and thought will be laid bare at the last judgment, and even in this life much that is hidden comes to light. Therefore whatever you have spoken secretly in darkness or in private will be shouted in the light and from the rooftops. While appearing to say these things to the disciples, the Lord in fact is addressing the Pharisees, hinting at their plots against Him. It is as if He were saying to the Pharisees, although appearing to speak to the disciples, "Whatever you have thought *in darkness*, O Pharisees, that is, within your darkened hearts, desiring to set a trap for Me, will be heard and made known in the light. For I am the Light, and you cannot hide from Me, and everything which your darkened hearts have plotted will be made known by Me, the Light. And I have heard every word of what you have plotted with others secretly *in the ear*, as clearly as if it had been shouted from the high rooftops." You may also understand that the light signifies the Gospel, and the high rooftops signify the lofty souls of the apostles. For what the Pharisees were secretly plotting to do was later proclaimed and heard in the light of the Gospel, with the great Proclaimer standing on the rooftops, that is, the Holy Spirit speaking through the mouths of the apostles.

4-7. And I say unto you My friends, Be not afraid of them that kill the body, and after that have no more that they can do. But I will forewarn you Whom ye should fear: Fear Him, which after He hath killed hath power to cast into gehenna; yea, I say unto you, Fear Him. Are not five sparrows sold for two farthings, and not one of them is forgotten before God? But even the very hairs of your head are all numbered. Fear not therefore; ye are of more value than many sparrows. When the Lord had separated His disciples from the hypocrisy of the Pharisees, He then openly chastised the Pharisees by saying, *Whatsoever ye have spoken in the darkness shall be heard in the light.* But now He converses with His friends concerning more perfect

---

[1] The Greek word *ypokrisia* has the primary sense of an actor playing a part on stage and then, metaphorically, of being a "hypocrite". Here Bl. Theophylact comments upon the falseness inherent in any type of dissembling, whether on stage or in life.

things. He first plucked out the thorns and now He sows the good seed. He says, *I say unto you, My friends.* For what He said before had not been addressed to His disciples, but to the Pharisees. His sayings now are not suitable for everyone to hear; instead, they are directed to those who love Him with all their soul and who are able to say, *Who shall separate us from the love of God?*[2] To those who love Him, then, He addresses this admonition: "*Be not afraid of them that kill the body,* and can do no further harm. For the harm which occurs when they kill the body is a small matter; will not the body suffer the same thing, when it dies, even if they do not kill it? But fear Him Who can punish not only the body but the soul as well, subjecting the immortal part of man to everlasting punishments and fire." By taking away their fear of other men Christ imparts bravery to His friends in order to prepare them for the contest[3] and for martyrdom. Men, He says, can direct their rage only against the perishable body, and the very last step of their plotting against us is the death of our flesh. But when God punishes, the suffering is not only that of the flesh, but the wretched soul undergoes torment as well. Notice here that death comes to sinners as a punishment, both in this life to those who are punished by death and in the next life to those who are cast into gehenna. By examining His words closely, you will understand something else as well. See that He did not say, "Fear Him, which after He hath killed, casteth into gehenna," but rather, *hath power to cast into gehenna.* For not all sinners who die are cast into gehenna: God has power to do this, but also to forgive. I say this because of the offering of prosphora loaves[4] and the giving of alms on behalf of the dead. These things have

---

[2] See Rom. 8:35.

[3] Literally, "He anoints His friends unto bravery." In the ancient world the athlete anointed himself with oil as preparation for the contest.

[4] Before the Divine Liturgy, the faithful prepare and offer small loaves of leavened bread for the altar. These loaves are called *prosphora*, meaning, literally, *offerings*. From these loaves the priest prepares the host on the diskos (paten) to be consecrated during the Liturgy. Part of this preparation consists of removing small particles from these loaves and placing them on the diskos, while reading aloud the names of the living and dead for whom that prosphora is offered. Thus, later, at the consecration of the Holy Gifts, those particles of commemoration become part of the mystical Body of Christ, and the fervent prayer of the whole Church is lifted up before the throne of God on behalf of all those commemorated in that Liturgy, both the living and the dead. By this God-pleasing means, as well as by giving alms in memory of the dead, the Church militant implores God to have mercy and to forgive those Christian souls who have died and are in hades. This prayer of the Church is effectual in "moving God to show mercy," but it does not do so in an automatic and mechanical

no small effect even on those who have died in grievous sins. God does not always cast into gehenna such a sinner after he has died, but He has the power to do so. Therefore let us not be negligent, but zealous with our alms and intercessions to incline to mercy Him Who has the power to cast into gehenna, even though He does not always use it. For He also has the power to forgive. Because some may think that if a man dies for Truth's sake it means that God has abandoned him, the Lord says, "Do not you, My disciples, think like this. You will not die as though abandoned by Me. If God does not forget even sparrows being sold, how much more so will I not forget the death of you, who are My friends, as if I had taken no forethought for you? On the contrary, I have such great concern for your well-being that I know every detail of each one of you, so that, for example, I know even the number of hairs of your head. Therefore if I permit you to enter into temptation, I will certainly provide you with the strength to endure it. It often is the case that when I see one who is weak, I do not allow him to fall into temptation. For I take care of all, and I know everything, and I have numbered every detail. And so I order and arrange[5] the life of every man according to his strength and according to what is appropriate and beneficial for him." If you observe closely, you will find that in Scripture all manful virtue is numbered by God, whatever has reached maturity and is worthy of being counted by God.[6] The *head* of each believer signifies a manner of life befitting Christ. The hairs of this head, which are somewhat deadened when compared to the flesh, signify those deeds of the body which are dead to the passions and it is these deeds which God numbers and remembers. For God looks down and sees these deeds of ours which are worthy of being counted. Some also understand the five sparrows to signify the five senses, which are redeemed for two farthings, that is, for the price of the New and the Old Covenants, and thus they are not forgotten by God. The

---

fashion: God's grace and justice are always a mystery beyond human comprehension. The distinction between hades and gehenna must also be clearly understood: the souls of sinners are in hades after the departure from the body, until the last judgment. After the last (and final) judgment, the souls of unrepentant sinners, whose hearts are hardened in hatred of God, will join Satan and all his demons in the everlasting torments of gehenna.

[5] *oikonomō*

[6] See, for example, Numbers 26. As God looked down upon (*episkepsis*) the tribes of Israel, He numbered only those men who had reached maturity.

Lord remembers those whose five senses have been tamed and led to the Word, making the senses no longer useless for spiritual nourishment.

8-12. Also I say unto you, Whosoever shall confess in Me before men, in him shall the Son of Man also confess before the angels of God; but he that denieth Me before men shall be denied before the angels of God. And whosoever shall speak a word against the Son of Man, it shall be forgiven him; but unto him that blasphemeth against the Holy Spirit it shall not be forgiven. And when they bring you unto the synagogues, and unto magistrates, and powers, take ye no anxious thought how or what thing ye shall answer, or what ye shall say: for the Holy Spirit shall teach you in the same hour what ye ought to say. Because they will soon undergo the contest of martyrdom, He now sets before them the prize of the contest. Having said, *Be not afraid of them that kill the body,* He then added, *Even the hairs of your head are numbered.* But perhaps someone might say, "Give me some reward for my bearing witness of You, for what benefit is it to me if the hairs of my head are numbered or not?" The Lord therefore says, "Do you want a reward? Listen: Whosoever shall confess in Me, I shall also confess in him before God." He means, "Whosoever shall confess while in My strength and while I work in synergy with him, I also shall confess in him, that is, in him who works in synergy with Me. First of all we need God, for without Him we can do nothing. But at the same time, [for there to be this salvific collaboration,] God needs us. For if God does not find us working worthy deeds, He cannot work with us; if He did so, [that is, arbitrarily choosing some and not others,] He would be *a respecter of persons.*[7] Therefore, we confess in Him, that is, in Him Who works with us, and He confesses in us, that is, in us who work with Him. If we do not give Him cause to do so, He will not confess on our behalf. But he who denies, does not deny with God's help, and therefore the Lord did not say, "He that denieth in Me," but simply, *He that denieth Me.* Also, it may be that because every saint dwells in Christ, and Christ in him, this is why the Lord said, *Whosoever shall confess in Me,* meaning "Whosoever shall confess, dwelling in Me, I also shall confess, dwelling in him." *And whosoever shall speak a word against the Son of*

---

[7] Acts 10:34

Man, it shall be forgiven him. This means, "Because I eat and drink in the company of publicans and harlots, and thus appear to be merely the son of man, he who blasphemes against Me shall be forgiven, whether he repents or not." This is not imputed as sin to a man who does not believe. What did he see that would cause him to believe? Indeed, what did he see that did not deserve his censure? He saw [what he thought was] a man going about with harlots, and therefore he blasphemes Him. Hence it is not imputed to him as sin. It is understandable that he would think to himself, "How can this man, who goes about with harlots, be the Son of God?" He will blaspheme, therefore, and call Him a deceiver for living in such a manner and making himself out to be the Son of God. But when someone blasphemes *against the Holy Spirit*, he is not forgiven. What the Lord means is this: when someone sees signs from God, great and extraordinary deeds, and does not believe but instead slanders them, attributing the activity of the Holy Spirit to Beelzebub, then he blasphemes against the Holy Spirit, saying that these signs were done by an evil, not a divine, spirit. Such a blasphemer is not forgiven and will be guilty, unless he repents. To him who blasphemes against the Son of Man it is not imputed as sin, and therefore he is forgiven, even if he does not repent. But for him who sees the works of the divine Spirit and blasphemes, there will be no forgiveness without repentance. Furthermore, this will be considered the greatest of all sins. Then the Lord speaks of *when they bring you unto the synagogues, and unto magistrates, and powers.* Our weakness is twofold: we flee from witnessing for Christ, that is, from martyrdom, either out of fear of punishment or because we are simple people, unable to give a reasoned defense of our faith. The Lord already healed our fear when He said, *Be not afraid of them that kill the body;* now he heals our simpleness. Because few had believed from among those who were wise according to the flesh and the standards of the world, while many of the simple and the unlearned had believed, He says, "Do not fear, you who are simple, ordinary folk; and take no anxious thought how you shall answer when you are questioned by the tyrant, or what you shall say. There will be another way in which you will speak in public. *For the Holy Spirit shall teach you in the same hour what ye ought to say.* So what need is there to worry, if you will be guided by the Holy Spirit at that moment as to what to say?" Thus He prepares and urges us on to martyrdom, removing both the fear of bodily weakness and the fear of being simple.

13-15. And one of the multitude said unto Him, Master, speak to my brother, that he divide the inheritance with me. And He said unto him, Man, who made Me a judge or a divider over you? And He said unto them, Take heed, and guard yourselves against greed: for a man's life consisteth not in the abundance of his possessions. Teaching us how to disregard the things of this life, and that we ought not to be distracted by earthly things, the Lord dismisses the man who asked Him to divide the family inheritance. This is why He also said, *Who made Me a judge or a divider over you?* The man had neglected to ask for things that were useful or beneficial for the salvation of his soul, instead requesting that the Lord portion out earthly and temporal things. Because he is disruptive and does not want to learn the important things being taught, the Lord sends him away. But He does so meekly, and not with harsh rebukes. By this action He teaches all His listeners, then and now, to disregard every temporal and earthly thing, and not to argue with their brothers but instead to yield to them even when they are covetous and greedy. *And of him that taketh away thy goods ask them not again,*[8] but instead seek those things which are useful and necessary for the salvation of your soul. This is why He added, *Take heed, and guard yourselves against greed,* urging us to flee from it as if it were a pit of demons. To whom did the Lord address the words *Take heed, and guard yourselves against greed*? To both brothers. Since their dispute was over an inheritance, it is altogether likely that each one was acting unfairly to the other, and this is why the Lord spoke to them about avarice. Greed is a great evil. Paul calls it *idolatry,*[9] something fit only for those who do not know God. This is indeed the truth, since *the idols of the heathen are of silver and gold.*[10] Those who honor silver and gold are like those who worship idols. For the avaricious man and the idolater alike think about and worship the same substance. We must flee, therefore, from abundance. Why? Because *a man's life consisteth not in the abundance of his possessions,* that is, the length of his life is not increased by possessions. For he who owns many things will not thereby live longer, nor is long life a consequence of great wealth. The Lord says this to refute the

---

[8] Lk. 6:30

[9] Col. 3:5

[10] Ps. 113:12

reasonings of those who love wealth. Lovers of wealth reason that they are concerned about wealth because they love life and they gather wealth from all quarters because they want to live a long time. The Lord therefore says, "O wretched and miserable man, will you live a long time because you have much? Why do you torment and afflict yourself for the sake of a retirement that is quite uncertain? It is uncertain whether you will reach that old age for which you are laying up treasures, but, on the other hand, it is certain that you squander your life now in acquiring possessions."

16-21. And He spake a parable unto them, saying, The ground of a certain rich man brought forth plentifully, and he thought within himself, saying, What shall I do, because I have no room where to gather my crops? And he said, This will I do: I will pull down my barns, and build greater; and there will I gather all my fruits and my goods. And I will say to my soul, Soul, thou hast much goods laid up for many years; take thine ease, eat, drink, and be merry. But God said unto him, Thou fool, this night they shall require thy soul of thee: then whose shall those things be, which thou hast prepared? So is he that layeth up treasure for himself, and is not rich toward God. The Lord had said that the life of a man is not lengthened by an abundance of possessions, and now He offers this parable in confirmation of this truth. See how He describes for us the insatiable thoughts of the foolish rich man. God did His part and showed His mercy; for all the ground of the rich man brought forth plentifully, not just one of his fields. But the rich man himself bore so little fruit from the mercy shown him that even before he had gathered the crops, he imagined them already locked up for himself. See also the pleasures of the rich man: *What shall I do?* Does not the pauper say the same thing as well, "What shall I do? I have nothing to eat or to put on." Think, if you will, about the words of the rich man. *What shall I do, because I have no room where to gather my crops?* At the very least, he could take a good rest. If both the pauper says, "What shall I do because I have not?" and the rich man says, "What shall I do because I have not?" then what do we gain by gathering more and more? We do not gain any rest, and it is clear from all the cares that come from our further efforts that we are piling up for ourselves only a great multitude of sins. Yet the foolish man says, *I will pull down my barns, and build greater.* And if your land yields even more bountifully in the future, will you pull these down and build again? But what need is there to pull down and build? You have available to you as storehouses the stomachs of the poor which can hold much, and are indestructible and imperishable. They are in fact heavenly and divine storehouses, for he who feeds the pauper, feeds God. See something else that is foolish: *my fruits and my goods.* The rich man did not consider that he had received these things from God. If he had, he would have treated these things as would a steward of God. But he imagined that these things were the fruits of his own labors, which is why he usurped them for himself, calling them *my fruits and my goods.* "I am the sole owner," he thinks, "and there is no one else entitled to a share. These things are not God's, but mine, and therefore I alone will enjoy them. I will not now take God in as a partner to enjoy my profit." Because he spoke foolishly, let us see what happened. *Soul, thou hast much goods laid up for many years.* He determines that he will have a long life, as if length of years was something else he could obtain by working his land. But a long life is not a crop you can grow, and it is not another of your belongings. *"Eat, drink, and be merry.* Three cheers for the good things of my soul!" But to eat and drink are the good things only of an irrational soul. Because this man has an irrational soul, it is fitting that he plans to reward himself with these things. But the good things of a rational soul are to understand, to reason, and to be glad in the law of God and in good thoughts. Do eating and drinking not suffice for you, O fool, but you must also order up for your soul that which accompanies these things, namely, shameful and base pleasure? Euphemistically did the Lord employ the words *be merry,* indicating by them the most wanton passions which are the consequence of too much of food and drink. *But God said unto him, Thou fool, this night they shall require thy soul of thee.* The words *God said unto him* do not mean that God conversed with the rich man, although the parable puts it in this form. Instead, the thoughts that came into the man's mind are what God spoke. *Thou fool.* He calls him a fool because everything he wanted was foolish, as we have shown. And every man like him is foolish and acts in vain, for, as David says, *In vain doth every man disquiet himself.*[11] Why? Because he stores up things without knowing for whom he gathers them. How can

---

[11] Ps. 38:14

he not be called a fool who does not know that the length of a man's life rests with God alone and that no man can set the limits of his own life? Notice also the words *they will require.* Like some stern imperial officers demanding tribute, the fearsome angels will ask for your soul, and you will not want to give it because you love this life and claim the things of this life as your own. But they do not demand the soul of a righteous man, because he himself commits his soul into the hands of the God and Father of spirits, and he does so with joy and gladness, not in the least bit grieved that he is handing over his soul to God. For him the body is a light burden, easily shed. But the sinner has made his soul fleshy, something in substance like the body and like the earth, rendering it difficult to separate from the body. This is why the soul must be demanded of him, the same way that harsh tax collectors treat debtors who refuse to pay what is due. See that the Lord did not say, "I *shall require thy soul of thee,"* but, *they shall require.* For the souls of the righteous are already in the hands of God. Truly it is at night when the soul of such a sinner is demanded of him. It is night for this sinner who is darkened by the love of wealth, and into whom the light of divine knowledge cannot penetrate, and death overtakes him. Thus he who lays up treasure for himself is called foolish: he never stops drawing up plans and dies in the midst of them. But if he had been laying up treasure for the poor and for God, it would not have been so. Let us strive, therefore, to be *rich toward God,* that is, to trust in God, to have Him as our wealth and the treasury of wealth, and not to speak of *my goods* but "the good things of God." If they are God's, then let us not deprive God of His own goods. This is what it means to be *rich toward God*: to trust that even if I empty myself and give everything away, I will not lack the necessities. God is my treasury of good things, and I open and take from that treasury what I need.

22-26. And He said unto His disciples, Therefore I say unto you, Take no anxious thought for the soul, what ye shall eat; neither for the body, what ye shall put on. The soul is more than food, and the body is more than raiment. Consider the ravens: for thy neither sow nor reap; which neither have storehouse nor barn; and God feedeth them: how much more are ye better than the fowls? And which of you by anxious thoughts can add to his stature one cubit? If ye then be not able to do that thing which is least, why take ye anxious

thought for the rest? Little by little the Lord directs His teaching towards that which is more perfect. See the order of His teaching: first He taught that we should guard ourselves against avarice and then He added the parable concerning wealth, in which He showed that the man who desires more is foolish. Then, advancing in thought, He tells us not to worry about the necessities of life. Just as the devil began with little things and then made us fall into greater and greater sins (which is why Job called him *the ant-lion*[12]) so the Lord undoes the work of the devil by doing here just the opposite, first putting to flight the great sins and then showing their origin in little things. Having taught us to guard ourselves from greed, He now proceeds to cut away the root of greed, which is worry. Hence He says, *"Therefore, on account of this greed, I say unto you."* Because it is a foolish man who marks out for himself a long life, and being thus deceived grasps for more things in this life, as did the rich man of the parable, *"on account of this I say unto you, Take no anxious thought for the soul, what ye shall eat."*[13] The soul does not eat, for it is spiritual, but it is clear that the soul cannot endure to remain joined to the body unless we eat, and this is why He spoke as He did. Moreover, when the body sinks into death, it is no longer fed. Since only a body still joined to its soul is fed, it is fitting that He spoke of feeding the soul. Is He not also speaking of that part of the soul which nourishes?[14] *"Take no anxious thought, therefore, concerning the nourishing part of the irrational soul, what ye shall eat; neither for the body, what ye shall put on."* Then He adds the reason: Will not He Who gives what is greater, the living soul itself, also give what is lesser, food for it to

---

[12] Job 4:11

[13] *mē merimnate tē psychē ymōn.* The Greek word *psychē* is variously translated in the New Testament as *soul* or *life*. Here the KJV renders it "life" while three verses earlier the same word is rendered "soul". But in fact in Scripture and in the writings of the Church fathers it means both at the same time. This is because "the soul was given by God as the life-giving principle in order to govern the body... The soul is the *life force* of man and of every living being... The soul of man is the link between the body and spirit, being, as it were, a bridge from the body to the spirit." Archpriest Seraphim Slobodskoy, *The Law of God*, Holy Trinity Monastery, Jordanville, New York, 1993, p. 101. We have consistently translated *psychē* as *soul* throughout this passage so as not to break the unity of thought of the Gospel or its patristic explanation.

[14] In many places in his Explanation, Blessed Theophylact refers to the patristic analysis of the soul by which the various "powers" or faculties of the soul are identified. One of these faculties is the power of nourishment and growth, which is sometimes likened to the power at work in plant life. See, for example, pp. 116 and 136-137 of this volume.

live? Will not He Who gives the body also give clothing for it? Then, to make us ashamed by the example of crows, He brings forward the birds. He might have raised the example of the holy prophets Elijah and Moses who were fed miraculously, but instead He mentions birds to arouse greater shame in us. Then He adds yet another reason why we should not worry. "Tell Me, what do you gain by your anxiety? Can you increase your height by the slightest amount? Indeed not; on the contrary, you destroy the flesh, for anxiety consumes. Therefore, if you are unable to add even the least thing, why should you have anxious thoughts about the rest?" It is clear, then, that it is God Who grants increase, and likewise He will give the other things as well.

27-31. Consider the lilies how they grow: they toil not, they spin not; and yet I say unto you, that Solomon in all his glory was not arrayed like one of these. If then God so clothe the grass, which is today in the field, and tomorrow is cast into the oven, how much more will He clothe you, O ye of little faith? And seek not ye what ye shall eat, or what ye shall drink, neither be ye agitated. For all these things do the nations of the world seek after: and your Father knoweth that ye have need of these things. But rather seek ye the kingdom of God; and all these things shall be added unto you. He adds the example of the lilies to shame us all the more. God clothes the lilies with such beauty that even Solomon in all his glory was not able to adorn himself as one of them. God does this despite the fact that there is no need for the lilies to be clothed in beauty. How much more will He clothe you, His honored creation, especially since there is a need for your bodies to be clothed? "What then?" someone may ask, "Do you command that we not cultivate the ground?" The Lord did not say, "Till not the ground," but, *"Take no anxious thought.* I do not forbid you to work; I forbid you to worry, which is the same as to hope in yourselves." He who works hoping in God passes his days without worry. It is clear that the Lord is cutting away from us this worry which leads away from God, for He says, *Seek not ye what ye shall eat, or what ye shall drink, neither be ye agitated. Agitation* means nothing other than the perturbed and unstable turning of the mind when it remembers one thing one moment and then leaps to something else the next, always imagining something greater and greater. Is this not the agitation of an anxious mind? Because this anxious agitation leads us away from God, the Lord

forbids it, saying, *All these things do the nations of the world seek after.*
Worry is not satisfied with the necessities of life, but, as I have said, it
always seeks something greater, swirling in agitation. For example, I
might say, "We are out of bread, we should think about getting some."
But we do not stop there, but begin to worry about finding some fine
white bread; and what about wine, a vintage with a good bouquet? And
something else to go with the bread and wine, some roasted partridge or
pheasant. Do you see the anxious thought and the agitated mind?
Therefore the Lord cuts off this kind of thought from us. These things do
the heathen seek. Then He adds another reason for us not to worry, that
our heavenly Father knows what we need—but this reason contains
within it many reasons, not just one. God is your Father, the Lord says,
and if He is your Father, how will He not give? He knows, and does not
ignore, your true needs, as distinguished from the things which are in
excess of your needs. Therefore, since He is your Father, and since you
are in need, and He knows that you are in need, how can He not give?
But seek ye first the kingdom of God, and put away all worry concerning
your daily life, for this worry cuts you off from the kingdom of God.
When you do this, all these things will be added unto you.[15] Do you see
that if you seek after the small things, you do what is not pleasing to
God, for you scorn His great gift. If you seek the great things, you will
receive them, and you will have the small things as well. For if He sees
that you are busy working for Him in His kingdom, He will of course
provide for your needs. Do we not do the same in our own households
when we take especially good care of those who have given themselves
over entirely to serve us, and we provide for them since they do not
provide for themselves? How much more will the Lord do this? The Lord
therefore cuts away from us anxious thought about our daily life, in order
to persuade us to seek His kingdom. For this is impossible to do when we
are filled with worry.

**32-34. Fear not, little flock; for it is your Father's good pleasure
to give you the kingdom. Sell that ye have, and give alms; make for
yourselves purses which grow not old, a treasure in the heavens that
faileth not, where no thief approacheth, neither moth destroyeth. For**

---

[15] See Mt. 6:33.

where your treasure is, there will your heart be also. To all those who want to become His disciples, the Lord gives the name *little flock,* either because in this world the saints are small and insignificant on account of their voluntary poverty and lack of possessions, or because they are fewer in number than the host of the angels, who are beyond count and beyond compare more excellent than we. That the angels exceed us in number is clear from the Lord's parable concerning the shepherd who rejoices more in the one which was lost and then found, than in the ninety and nine which were not lost.[16] The Lord showed in that parable that just as the one is to the ninety-nine, so too is the human race when compared to the angelic host. *Fear not, little flock,* He says, meaning, Do not doubt that God will provide for you, even if you take no anxious thought for yourselves. Why? Because *it is your Father's good pleasure to give you the kingdom.* Since He is giving you the kingdom, how much more so will He give the things you need on earth? Therefore, have faith that if you willingly follow a life of poverty, you will not lack a Provider. Sell your possessions, give alms, and thereby lay up for yourselves an unfailing treasure. Then the Lord convinces us with irrefutable arguments. Here, He says, there are moths which destroy, but it is not so in heaven. Is it not foolish to store up treasure in a place where there is decay? But moths cannot destroy gold, and so He adds, *where no thief approacheth.* Though gold cannot be eaten by moths, it can be stolen by thieves. Even so, not every one suffers loss at the hands of thieves, and therefore He adds the most invincible argument of all: *For where your treasure is, there will your heart be also.* Let us suppose, He says, that no moth destroys nor thief approaches. Nevertheless, does not a far worse loss occur when your heart is fastened to treasure which you have buried deep in the ground? Then that divine thing, your soul, is buried alive in the earth. Does this not deserve the greatest punishment? In fact, if one thinks about it, does not this very deed constitute, in and of itself, the greatest punishment? *Where your treasure is, there will your heart be also.* If your treasure is buried in the earth, then your heart will be buried in the earth. If your treasure is in heaven, there on high will your heart be. Therefore, who would not want to be lifted up on high rather than remain below the earth? Who would not prefer to be an angel, instead of a mole crawling

---

[16] Mt. 18:12-14. See Vol. 1, *The Explanation* of St. Matthew, pp. 155-156.

through tunnels?

35-40. Let your loins be girded about, and your lamps burning; and ye yourselves like unto men that wait for their lord, when he will return from the wedding; that when he cometh and knocketh, they may open unto him immediately. Blessed are those servants, whom the lord when he cometh shall find watching: verily I say unto you, that he shall gird himself, and make them to recline at table, and will come forth and serve them. And if he shall come in the second watch, or come in the third watch, and find them so, blessed are those servants. And this know, that if the householder had known what hour the thief would come, he would have watched, and not have suffered his house to be broken in. Be ye therefore ready also: for the Son of Man cometh at an hour when ye think not. The Lord has first freed His disciple of all that is superfluous, and has stripped him of all anxious thought and agitation concerning physical life, thus making him light and free. Now He makes that disciple His servant. A man who wants to serve must be unencumbered and free of impediment, which is why the Lord says, *Let your loins be girded,*[17] which means, always be ready to do the work of your Master. And have *your lamps burning,* which means, do not live in darkness, without discernment, but let the light of the Logos always show you what you should and should not do. The night is this world. Those who have girded their loins are those who are engaged in active virtue. This is how laborers at work appear. And they must also have their lamps lit. For the gift of discernment must accompany action so that the man who is active in virtue can not only know what to do, but also be able to see so that he can do it. For there are many who have set about to do good, but have done it poorly. They girded their loins for action but did not have their lamps lit, that is, they lacked discernment because they did not have the light of the Logos within them, and thus fell into arrogance or some other foolish pitfall. You should understand this as well, that we first gird our loins and then see that our lamps are lit. First comes active virtue, and then comes divine vision, which is the enlightenment of the mind. The lamp

---

[17] i.e. hitch up your tunic with a belt so that you are able to work without interference from your loose garment.

represents our mind, which we can say is *burning* when it has the light of God shining in it. Let us strive, therefore, to practice virtue, that we may have our two lamps burning, the Word within always illuminating the soul, and the spoken word shining forth from the mouth.[18] The one is a lamp shining within us, and the other is a lamp of speech and teaching shining outwardly for others. And let us be like men waiting for their lord to return from the wedding. Who is this lord, if not Jesus Christ? He took human nature as His bride and united her to Himself, wedding her and cleaving to her, becoming One Flesh. Indeed, He did not make just one wedding, but many.[19] For every day the Lord in heaven is wedded to the souls of the saints which the Apostle Paul, or those who come after Paul, present to Him as pure virgins.[20] The Lord returns from the weddings in heaven, that is, He returns universally, once and for all, at the end of the world when He will come from heaven in the glory of the Father. He also returns at every hour when He comes unseen and unexpectedly at the end of each man's life. Blessed is he, therefore, whom the Lord shall find with loins girded and with lamp lit, that is, ready to serve God by fulfilling the commandments of Christ concerning action, and with his mind illuminated by the lamp of the Word and of discernment. Such a man not only does good, but does it well. He receives nothing less than divine vision, as if he had been given a lamp. It is by girding our loins that the burning lamp of divine vision is given to us, or rather, the two lamps, the one inner and the other of speech. To such a servant, therefore, the Lord Himself comes as Servant. *He shall gird himself,* He says, *and make them to recline at table, and will come forth and serve them.* God girds and binds Himself in that He does not let flow all His abundance of good things on us at once, but restrains that outpouring. For who can contain all of God, as great as He is? This is made clear by the Seraphim who must cover themselves because of the exceeding brightness of the divine light.[21] He makes His good servants

---

[18] Compare the words of the Troparion of St. John Chrysostom: "Grace shining forth from thy mouth like a beacon hath illumined the universe."

[19] The Greek word for *wedding, tōn gamōn,* in verse 36 is in the plural form, perhaps referring literally to the many days of feasting that were, and in some places still are, the custom.

[20] St. Paul writes, *For I have espoused you to one Husband, that I may present you as a chaste virgin to Christ.* (II Cor. 11:2)

[21] Is. 6:2

to *recline,* granting them complete rèst. Just as one who reclines rests his whole body, so also at the second coming will the saints find complete rest. Here in this life they find no ease for the body, but there, when their spiritual and divine bodies will have inherited incorruption together with their souls, they will enjoy complete rest, and God will be for them *all in all.*[22] He will serve the worthy and reward them in equal measure: just as they served Him, He Himself will serve them and set before them a bountiful table, bestowing on them the delight of spiritual gifts. *The second* and *third watch* you may understand to mean the different periods of our life. For example, I might say that a man who is awake at the second and third watch seems to be the most vigilant, for it is during these hours of the night that the first and deepest period of sleep occurs. Likewise, you may understand that in the various circumstances of our life there are particular times at which, if we are found to be awake and vigilant, we are blessed. Has someone stolen your goods? Have your children died? Have you been slandered? If at these times you do not fall, but your God and Master finds you awake, and you have not been moved to do something that is outside the path of His commandments, then you are blessed indeed. For He has found you awake at the second and third watches, that is, at times of terrible tribulations, which induce in a lax soul a deathlike slumber and a fall. Therefore we must be awake and vigilant, for we are like a householder from whom, if he is awake, the thief cannot steal his goods. But if he is asleep, the thief will take everything and be gone. Some have understand *the thief* here to mean the devil, as the house is the soul and the householder is the man. But it seems that this interpretation is not consistent with the sequence of thought. Here the coming of Christ is likened to a thief because it is unexpected; as one of the apostles says, *But the day of the Lord will come as a thief in the night.*[23] And here, in the passage at hand, see how the Lord explains for us who is the thief. He says, *"Be ye therefore watchful, for the Son of Man cometh at an hour when ye think not."* Some say that those who are awake at the first watch represent those who are the most diligent of all; those who are awake at the second hour are those who are somewhat less diligent, and those who are awake at the

---

[22] See I Cor. 15:28.

[23] II Peter 3:10

third watch are those who are still less diligent. Others have explained the watches as the different ages of a man's life. In the first watch we are youths, in the second watch we are men, and in the third watch we are old men. Blessed is he, at whatever age he may be, who is found awake and diligent in doing good.

41-44. Then Peter said unto Him, Lord, speakest Thou this parable unto us, or even to all? And the Lord said, Who then is that faithful and wise steward, whom his lord shall make ruler over his household, to give them their portion of food in due season? Blessed is that servant, whom his lord when he cometh shall find so doing. Of a truth I say unto you, that he will make him ruler over all that he hath. Peter was kindled with brotherly love towards all who were listening, as if he were already caring for the Church, and so he asked if the Lord had addressed the parable to everyone. But the Lord did not give a plain answer to his question. Instead He showed in a hidden manner that the previous parable was for everyone and that it applied to all believers. But now, He says, listen to this parable which I address just to you, the apostles and all who are entrusted with the teaching and the protection of the faithful. *Who is the faithful and wise steward?* The previous parable applies to many, but this one speaks of those into whose hands the care of the faithful is given. He begins this parable in the form of a question, asking, ''Will anyone be found who has both faith and wisdom? Such men are few and far between.'' If the steward of the master's holdings is faithful, but lacks wisdom, the property is ruined because he is not able to administer it as he should. When it is necessary to provide for the household, he does not, and the greater part is ruined. On the other hand, if the steward is a wise and able administrator, but is not faithful, he is no better than a thief, and the cleverer he is, the more disastrous the result. So it is with the things of God: both faithfulness and wisdom are required. I myself know many who appear zealous in virtue and are God-fearing and faithful, but because they are not able to manage wisely the affairs of the Church, they cause damage not only to property but to souls as well. For example, when someone has had a spiritual fall, if the pastor is not wise but only has faith, that is, he has virtue without discernment, the one who has fallen may be harmed, either from too severe a punishment or from untimely mildness, and instead of being healed he will be crushed. Therefore, whoever can be found that is both faithful and wise, he shall be made *ruler over the household* of the Lord, that is, over all His servants. And he will give each one his *portion of food in due season,* whether that be the word of teaching by which souls are nourished, or the example of good deeds and instruction on how to live. If he is found doing these things, such a man is blessed, and the Lord *will make him ruler over all that He hath.* Having found him worthy of a higher rank, the Lord will make him ruler not only over His servants, but over *all,* so that both the things of earth and the things in heaven obey him. Such wise and faithful stewards were Joshua son of Nun and Elijah; the one commanded the sun[24] and the other the clouds in the sky.[25] And in general all the saints, as friends of God, make use of what belongs to God, their Friend. For friends hold in common their possessions. Also, everyone who practices active virtue in a quiet life is steward and manager of the servile passions, anger and desire. He gives to each its food in due season: for anger, he gives hatred for those who hate the Lord and consuming zeal against the enemies of God; as food for desire, he provides what is necessary for the maintenance of the flesh and acknowledges God as the Provider. Therefore everyone who does this is blessed, and indeed will obtain even the vision of God, and will be made ruler over all that the Lord has. For he whose mind has attained to the vision of God is worthy to see and to oversee not only particular things in time, but also that which exists universally, namely, the eternal things.

45-46. But if that servant say in his heart, My lord delayeth his coming; and shall begin to beat the menservants and maidens, and to eat and drink, and to be drunken; the lord of that servant will come in a day when he looketh not for him, and at an hour when he is not aware, and will separate him, and will appoint him his portion with the unbelievers. Woe to those unworthy servants who have received from God the gift of spiritual authority, and who then corrupt that responsibility entrusted to them by drinking and becoming drunk. You may understand this literally, for even such things as these occur among the wicked pastors of the church when they drink up the money in the poor box. You may also understand *drunkenness* to mean a mind in

---

[24] i.e. to lengthen the day. See Joshua 10:12-14.

[25] i.e. to cause it to rain. See III Kings (I Kings) 18.

frenzy, engaged in teaching perverted dogmas or in squandering wealth. Such pastors *beat the menservants and maidens,* meaning, they cause scandal to the weaker brethren of the Church and strike blows to their conscience. When a weak man, small in soul, sees me, a hierarch, living wickedly, his conscience is struck and he receives a blow to his heart. He stumbles and falls and is enfeebled all the more. All these things occur when that wicked servant says, *My Lord delayeth His coming.* They are caused by laziness, and by forgetfulness of the hour of the end. For if we remembered that the Lord will come, and that the end and the consummation of our life is at the very gates, we would sin less. See what is the punishment: *He will separate him,*[26] the Lord says, meaning that He will deprive him of the gift of spiritual instruction. Lest anyone imagine that the gift of grace he had once received preserves him from harsh punishment, He says, "How can this grace help him when he will be found stripped of it?" To be *separated* means to be deprived of his former gift. The wretched man will be found at that time to be flesh and not spirit. [When the Lord returns,] either He finds us walking in the Spirit, or we will be ranked with the unbelievers. For, as the Apostle Paul says, *Ye are not in the flesh, but in the Spirit, if so be that the Spirit of God dwell in you.*[27] He who does not walk in the Spirit, but is in the flesh and is found to have no share in spiritual life, will be ranked with the unbelievers, that is, he will be condemned along with the world which did not believe, and he will receive no benefit from the faith which he seemed to have. For true faith was not in him. If true faith had been in him, he would have been a faithful servant. But his drunkenness, and the ruin brought by him upon his Master's belongings, show that he lacked that true faithfulness which is required of stewards. It is right that his portion be placed with that of the unbelievers. For once deprived of grace and made bare, he is seen to be stunted and incomplete.

47-48. And that servant, who knew his lord's will, and prepared not himself, neither did according to his will, shall be beaten with many stripes. But he that knew not, and did commit things worthy of stripes, shall be beaten with few stripes. For unto whomsoever

---

[26] *dichotomēsei auton*

[27] Rom. 8:9

much is given, of him shall be much required: and to whom men have committed much, of him they will ask the more. Here the Lord reveals to us something even more frightening. Such a man who is stripped of grace not only is not saved from punishment by his former gift, but his high rank in and of itself will become the cause of even greater condemnation. For the greater the knowledge he had when he sinned, the greater the punishment he brings upon himself. The Lord makes this clear in the words which follow. *Unto whom much is given,* He says, *of him shall be much required: and to whom men have committed much, of him they will ask the more.* In these words He refers to the greater punishment to which the teachers are liable. To them some things are *given* outright while other things are *committed,* that is, deposited with them to be called for at a later date. For example, the gift of working wonders and healing the sick is given to them outright; but the gift of the Word and the teaching is only committed and deposited with them. The Lord says of those who have been *given* much, that only as much, and not more, will be required. On the other hand, the Lord says of those to whom much has been *committed* and deposited, that even more will be required. For the gift of the Word must indeed be worked and cultivated like a piece of farm land that has been let out. That is why more is demanded of the teacher; he must not be idle, but instead must increase the talent of the Word. You should understand *to whom men have committed much* to mean "to whom men have lent much." For in this passage He is calling the loan a "deposit". Also, some have raised the question, "Let us grant that the man who knew the will of his master and did not do it merited his punishment. But why was there punishment for the man who did not know the master's will?" He too was punished because he was able to learn the will of the master, but did not want to do so. Because of his laziness, he was the cause of his own ignorance, and he deserves punishment for this very reason, that of his own will he did not learn. Brothers, let us tremble with fear. If even he who knows nothing deserves to be beaten, what excuse will deliver those who are brimming with knowledge, especially those who are teachers? Their condemnation will be even more severe.

49-50. I am come to send fire upon the earth; and what is My desire but that it were already kindled? But I have a baptism to be baptized with; and how anguished am I till it be accomplished? *Fire* means the proclamation of the Gospel, for the Word is fire which consumes every materialistic and coarse thought and destroys idols made of whatever substance. *Fire* also means zeal for the good which is kindled in each one of us. And it may be said that this zeal, which comes from the Word of God, is not at all different from the preaching. It is indeed with this fire that the Lord desires to kindle our hearts, for we must have fiery zeal for the good. *What is My desire but that it were already kindled?* means "How greatly do I desire that it be already kindled!" For the Lord is eager and zealous that this fire be kindled, as the Apostle Paul says, *Be fervent in spirit,* that is, be burning hot.[28] And again, *I am jealous over you with godly jealousy,* that is, I burn with vigilant concern over your welfare.[29] *Baptism* means the Lord's death, for this fire could not have been kindled until after His death,[30] and from then on the preaching and the fiery zeal increased. This is why He mentions His death, calling it *baptism.* With an intense desire for His death, He says, *How anguished am I,* meaning "How much do My thoughts about this press upon Me, and how fiercely am I in anguish *until it be accomplished?* I thirst for that death which is the salvation of all." The Lord came to cast fire, not only upon all the earth over which the Word and the faith has spread, but also into the "earth" of every soul which is thorn-ridden and fruitless. Such a field is first scorched by the divine Word as if by fire, and then it is ready to receive the divine seed and to bring forth spiritual fruit. For when a soul is touched invisibly by divine grace, it seems to burn with desire for God, in such a manner as it is impossible to describe, but undoubtedly in the same manner as Cleopas and his companion who were invisibly aflame with the fire of God's grace. For they said, *Did not our heart burn within us?*[31] If anyone has experienced this burning desire, he will understand what we are saying. There are many who have experienced this many times while reading the Divine Scriptures or the Lives of the holy fathers, or while

---

[28] *Tō pneumati zeontes.* Rom. 12:11.

[29] *Zēlō ymas theou zēlō.* II Cor. 11:2. The Greek word *zēlō* here and the word *zeontes (zeō)* in the previous footnote both denote heat from fire. Note that *jealous* and *zealous* have the identical etymology, namely, *zēlō.*

[30] See Jn. 16:7.

[31] Lk. 24:32

listening to exhortations and teachings. The soul is kindled towards the good: with some, the soul remains ablaze until the very end, while others soon grow cold again.

51-53. Suppose ye that I am come to give peace on earth? I tell you, Nay; but rather division. For from henceforth there shall be five in one house divided, three against two, and two against three. The father shall be divided against the son, and the son against the father; the mother against the daughter, and the daughter against the mother; the mother-in-law against her daughter-in-law, and the daughter-in-law against her mother-in-law. Christ indeed is our peace, but He says, "I have not come to give peace." Thus He seems to speak in riddles. We say, therefore, that not every peace is good and beyond reproach; there is a peace which is dangerous and drives us away from the love of God, for example, when we make peace and establish harmony by destroying truth. This is not the peace Christ came to give. Indeed, concerning what is true and good, He wants us to be at odds with each other rather than appease one another by compromise of the good. This of course has happened in persecution. For in one house the pagan father was at odds with his believing son, and the mother with her daughter, and so forth. Why did he say, *There shall be five in one house divided,* and then enumerated six individuals?[32] We say, therefore, that two of the figures are counted as one person. For the daughter and the daughter-in-law are the same person: in regards to her mother, she is called daughter, and in regards to her mother-in-law, she is called daughter-in-law. Therefore, three, that is, the father, mother, and mother-in-law, shall be divided against two, that is, the son and daughter. The daughter, as we have said, is only one person differently related to her mother and mother-in-law, and of course she is not two different people. You may also understand that the father, mother, and mother-in-law, represent in a general sense everything that is old, while son and daughter represent everything that is new. The Lord, therefore, wants His new commandments and teachings to do battle with all our old habits and beliefs. Also, it may be understand in this way: the father is the mind as a whole, and the son is mere logic, and there was a division, one against

---

[32] viz. father, son, mother, daughter, mother-in-law, and daughter-in-law.

the other, in a single household, that is, in a man. For example, to put it more clearly, the mind of St. Dionysius the Areopagite was enlightened and straightway, without any weighing of proofs, he accepted the preaching of the Gospel.[33] But such a mind which accepts the faith must grapple with logic which demands proofs and insists that the confined path of rational argument be followed. Do you see the division between this father and this son when they battle each other on account of Christ and the Gospel? And the mother and the mother-in-law you may call the intellect, and the daughter and the daughter-in-law, the senses. Between them there is a battle on account of Christ, the intellect ranged against the senses. The intellect urges the senses to prefer the imperishable to what is perishable, and the unseen to the seen, and it rallies many proofs to its side. But sometimes the senses must wage war against the intellect, when the senses are guided towards belief by miracles and visible signs. The senses then are not persuaded by the reasonings of the intellect, nor do they desire to follow the proofs of Greek philosophy which compel those who listen to such sophistry to disbelieve that God became man, or that the Virgin gave birth. Such are the babblings of a pagan logic enslaved to fallen nature. Indeed, when miracles are seen, the senses are more powerful than any logical proof to bring a man to the knowledge of God. Therefore, know that not every peace and harmony are good. There are times when strife and dissent are of God. Let there be no friendship with those who are evil, and even if father or mother should be found to be adversaries of Christ, strive with them as enemies of truth.

54-59. And He said also to the people, When ye see a cloud rise out of the west, straightway ye say, There cometh a storm; and so it is. And when ye see the south wind blow, ye say, There will be heat; and it cometh to pass. Ye hypocrites, ye know how to discern the face of the sky and of the earth; but how is it that ye do not discern this season? And why do ye not of your own selves judge what is right? When thou goest with thine adversary to the ruler, as thou art on the way, endeavour that thou be released from any claim by him; lest he drag thee to the judge, and the judge deliver thee to the officer, and

---

[33] St. Dionysius the Areopagite was a learned Athenian converted by St. Paul's preaching (see Acts 17:34). He is commemorated on October 3. See *The Great Collection of the Lives of the Saints, Volume 2: October,* Chrysostom Press, House Springs, Missouri, 1995, pp. 64-72.

the officer cast thee into prison. I tell thee, thou shalt not depart thence, till thou hast paid the very last mite. Because He had spoken about the preaching of the Gospel, and had named it *fire* and sword, it is likely that His listeners were troubled, not comprehending what had been said. Therefore He says to them, "Just as you understand by certain signs the approaching conditions of the weather, so you ought to understand My coming by what I say and by what I do. For both My words and My deeds show that there is a conflict between us. You are publicans and thieves, and so I have nowhere to lay My head. Just as you can tell from a cloud that a storm is coming, and from a south wind that there will be burning heat, so also ought you to examine the season of My coming and to know from the signs that I have not come to bring peace, but rather, storm and turbulence. For I Myself am that cloud risen out of the west, that is, I have sprung forth from human nature which until now was sunk low in the west and in the dark gloom of sin. And I have come to cast fire and to make heat: I am the south wind, blowing warmth and fervor, the opposite of the coldness of the north. For I appeared in Bethlehem, which lies to the south." By saying these things, He also teaches them about that peace which is praiseworthy. First He showed them the praiseworthy strife. Now He shows them the blameless peace, and says, "When your adversary takes you to court, while still on the way exert every effort," for this is the meaning of *endeavour*, "and think of any means whatsoever by which you may be released and acquitted by him." By another interpretation, *endeavour* means, even if you have nothing, borrow what you need and repay your adversary what belongs to him, together with the profit you have gained from it, so that you may be saved from him. Otherwise he will drag you to the judge, and the judge will hand you over to the officer, that is, to the enforcer, who will throw you into prison until you have paid back the very last penny. The Lord says these things in order to frighten the dull-witted into making peace. For He knows that the fear of loss and the fear of punishment grip those who are earthly-minded, and this is why He speaks as He does. These things may also be understood to mean the devil, for indeed he is our *adversary.* Therefore, while we are still *on the way,* that is, in this life, let us endeavor to be diligent in virtue, so that at the judgment to come the devil will be obliged to admit that we have nothing that belongs to him and thus he will be barred from bringing any claim against us. For the works of the devil which we have done in this life will deliver us into the hands of the judge, and the judge will hand us over to the enforcer, that is, to the power of punishment and affliction. Then we will be punished until we have paid the penalty for the least sins, and have fulfilled the measure of punishment. But since the measure of punishment is never fulfilled, we will be punished forever. For if we will be in prison until we have paid the very last penny, we will never be able to pay it back. From this it is clear that the punishment will be eternal.

CHAPTER THIRTEEN

Concerning the Galileans and those at Siloam.
Concerning the fig tree which beareth no fruit.
Concerning the woman with a spirit of infirmity.
Concerning the parable of the grain of mustard seed,
and the parable of the leaven.
Concerning the man who asked if the saved be few.
Concerning those who spoke to Jesus about Herod.

1-5. There were present at that time some that told Him of the Galileans, whose blood Pilate had mingled with their sacrifices. And Jesus answering said unto them, Suppose ye that these Galileans were sinners above all the Galileans, because they suffered such things? I tell you, Nay: but, except ye repent, ye shall all likewise perish. Or those eighteen, upon whom the tower in Siloam fell, and slew them, think ye that they were sinners above all men that dwelt in Jerusalem? I tell you, Nay: but, except ye repent, ye shall all likewise perish. There was a man named Judas of Galilee, whom this same Evangelist mentions in the Acts of the Apostles.[1] He was a self-proclaimed student of the law who had led astray many other Galileans with his teachings. He taught his followers that they should call no man "Lord," neither speaking the word with their mouth, nor showing any master honor or affection, not even the king. As a result, many of these Galileans were cruelly tortured for not calling Caesar their lord. These men had also been teaching others not to offer any sacrifices except those commanded by Moses, and thus they were interfering with the sacrifices made on behalf of Caesar and the Roman people. It is likely, therefore, that Pilate became infuriated with them and gave orders that they be slain alongside those very sacrifices offered on behalf of the Roman people to which they objected, so that their own blood was mixed with the blood of the sacrifices. Certain men related these events to the Saviour as if the Galileans had acted in defense of piety, and they wanted to find out whether it pleased Him. For some thought that these Galileans were sinners and had rightly suffered this punishment, in that they had caused

---

[1] Acts 5:37

a revolt and had aroused Pilate to hate the Jews. This was because their rebellion of not calling Caesar "Lord" had spread among all the Jews. The Saviour does not deny that they were sinners, but He says that those who suffered this punishment were no more sinful than others who had not so suffered. "Unless you too repent," He says, "and stop stirring up rebellion and civil strife, and unless you strive to serve God with your deeds, you will suffer worse things than this. You should not strive to bring renown upon yourselves by inciting civil strife under the pretext of religious zeal." The tower which fell at Siloam was a sign of what would later happen to the people. By means of the few who were killed on that occasion, the Lord instructed many that they would suffer worse things. What happened to the tower prefigured what would happen to the whole city, and the eighteen who died foreshadowed all the people: the whole race of those who remained stubborn in their unbelief was destroyed when the city of Jerusalem fell at the hands of Titus. Let this also be a warning to us in regards to the events which befall us every day. Because some fall into great dangers and temptations, while we remain untouched, let this not cause us to be negligent, imagining that we have not experienced such troubles because we are so righteous. On the contrary, we are instructed that those others are being chastised so that we may correct our own lives, lest we suffer something worse.

6-9. He spake also this parable: A certain man had a fig tree planted in his vineyard; and he came and sought fruit thereon, and found none. Then said he unto the worker in his vineyard, Behold, these three years I come seeking fruit on this fig tree, and find none: cut it down; why doth it uselessly occupy the ground? And he answering said unto him, Lord, let it alone this year also, till I shall dig about it, and put on dung to see whether it bear fruit. And if not, then after that thou shalt cut it down. This parable follows in perfect sequence. Because the Lord had just said, *Except ye repent, ye shall perish,* He aptly adds this parable. The *fig tree* is the generation of the Jews producing no fruit but only bitter leaves. It stood in God's vineyard, that is, in the Judaic life under the law. The master of the house, Christ, came seeking from that tree the fruit of faith and good deeds, and found none. Three times He came: first through Moses, then through the prophets, and finally He came Himself. At last, those who did not repent He cut away from the love of God, for they could no longer be called the nation of God, a holy people. In their place were put the Gentiles who were able to bring forth fruit. The fig tree may also be interpreted to mean all of human nature. The master of the house is God the Father; the worker in the vineyard is the Son of God, Who came among us to tend painstakingly the vineyard in which we are planted. Christ does not permit this fruitless fig tree to be cut down, but says, *"Let it alone this year also.* Neither the law nor the prophets have improved these people, and they have not yielded any fruit of repentance. Yet I Myself will water them with My teachings and with My Passion, to see whether they will bear the fruit of obedience. *And if not, then after that, Thou shalt cut it down,* and remove these people from the portion of the righteous." Three times has God sought from our nature the fruit of obedience, and it was not given: once, when we transgressed the commandment in paradise; again, when they made a calf at the time of the lawgiving, *and they changed His glory into the likeness of a calf that eateth grass;*[2] and the third time, when the Saviour and Lord was rejected by those who said, *We have no king but Caesar.*[3] It can also be said that each one of us is a fig tree planted in God's vineyard, that is, in the Church, or simply, in this world. God comes seeking fruit of each fig tree. If He finds you without fruit He commands that you be cut out from this life. But the worker in the vineyard makes an entreaty that you be spared. Who is this worker in the vineyard? It is either your guardian angel, or you yourself. For each man tends his own vine. It often happens that when we become gravely ill or we are beset by some grievous danger, we say, "Spare us, O Lord, this year also, and we shall repent." To *dig about the tree and put on dung* means to repent. The soul, therefore, is dug around when the compacted soil of earthly cares around it is broken up and loosened. And manure is put on it, signifying the warmth of that way of life which is held in dishonor and despised by all. For when a man rejects worldly glory and humbles himself ingloriously for the sake of the salvation of his soul, it is as if he has put dung on his soul so that it may bring forth fruit. If we bear fruit, well and good; but if not, the Lord no longer permits us to remain in His vineyard, but cuts us off from this world so that we do not uselessly occupy the ground. For when someone sees a

---

[2] Ps. 105:21

[3] Jn. 19:15

sinner live for many years, he is harmed and becomes worse himself. Thus, not only is the sinner himself found to be fruitless, but he also hinders others from bearing fruit. But if he is cut off from this life, perhaps other sinners will see him cut off, and will come to their senses and repent and bear fruit. It is said that the master of the house comes to the fig tree *these three years*, signifying that the Lord comes to us through the three laws we have been given: the natural law, the Mosaic law, and the spiritual law. We ought to have borne fruit after receiving the instruction of the natural law, for nature itself teaches us what we ought to do. But when God found that the natural law had been of no avail in us, He gave us the Mosaic law to assist the natural law. When this too was found to have been of no avail on account of our laziness, He gave us the spiritual law. Therefore, when these three laws have not corrected the soul of a man, nor has he benefited from a longer life or further forbearance, then he is allowed no more postponements. God is not deceived time and again by a plea for the extension of the period of grace. But can you not also understand the *three years* to mean the three ages in a man's span of life? Childhood, which is considered to last until the age of eighteen; adulthood; and old age, when one begins to turn gray. When we do not bear fruit in old age, that is, in the third year, and yet we are permitted to live a little longer so that we may put on dung, that is, to undertake the life in Christ that is without honor in this world, if even then we prove false, the Lord will no longer spare us. He will cut us away so that we do not uselessly occupy the earth and harm others. This explanation seems to me to fit more closely the purpose of the text.

10-17. And He was teaching in one of the synagogues on the sabbath. And, behold, there was a woman who had a spirit of infirmity eighteen years, and was bent over, and could in no wise straighten herself. And when Jesus saw her, He called her to Him, and said unto her, Woman, thou art loosed from thine infirmity. And He laid His hands on her: and immediately she was made straight, and glorified God. And the ruler of the synagogue answered with indignation, because Jesus had healed on the sabbath day, and said unto the people, There are six days in which men ought to work: in them therefore come and be healed, and not on the sabbath day. The Lord then answered him, and said, Thou hypocrite, doth not each one of you on the sabbath loose his ox or his ass from the stall, and

lead it away to watering? And ought not this woman, being a daughter of Abraham, whom Satan hath bound, lo, these eighteen years, be loosed from this bond on the sabbath day? And when He had said these things, all His adversaries were ashamed: and all the people rejoiced for all the glorious things that were done by Him. The woman suffered from this affliction as a result of demonic assault, as the Lord Himself says, *This woman...whom Satan hath bound, lo, these eighteen years.* Perhaps God had departed from her on account of certain sins, and as a result Satan was punishing her. For Satan is in part the cause of all the hardships which afflict our bodies, when God on high permits him. From the very beginning it was Satan who brought about our fall by which we lost the incorruptibility in which we had been created; it was Satan who caused us to be bound to diseased bodies prone to suffering, symbolized by the garments of dead skins in which Adam and Eve were wrapped.[4] But now the Lord, with the majestic voice of the Godhead, full of power, drives out the infirmity of this woman. He places His hands on her, so that we might learn that His holy flesh imparted both the power and the energy of the Logos. For His flesh was His own, and not that of some other human person alongside Him, separate from Him in hypostasis, as the impious Nestorius thinks.[5] So great is the goodness of the Lord, Who in this manner took mercy on His own creation. But Satan, who had bound the woman in the first place, was vexed at her deliverance because he desired her continued affliction, and so he bound the ruler of the synagogue with spite, and through the mouth of this man, Satan reviled the miracle. This is how he always attacks the good. Therefore the Lord uses the apt example of irrational animals to rebuke the man who was indignant that a healing had taken place on the sabbath. And thus not only this man, but all the other

---

[4] Gen. 3:22

[5] The heretic Nestorius, who was Patriarch of Constantinople from 428 to 431 A.D., taught that the co-unoriginate Logos was not conceived and did not take flesh in the Virgin's womb, but instead was united to Christ the man at some later time. This implied that the two natures of Christ, the divine and the human, were not united in one hypostasis, that is, in one person, but in two, and therefore were not truly united. If this were so, Christ would not have accomplished the salvation of the human race. As a result Nestorius called the Virgin Mary *Christokos*, that is, the Birthgiver of Christ, but refused to call her the *Theotokos*, the Birthgiver of God. This false teaching was condemned as heresy at the Third Ecumenical Council held in Ephesus in the year 431, and from that time Nestorius and all who follow his teaching have been outside the Church.

adversaries of Jesus as well, were put to shame by Christ's words. For it was insane to hinder the healing of a man on the sabbath using as a pretext the commandment that the sabbath be a day of rest. So it was, that even while the people were rejoicing at the Lord's deeds, His adversaries were put to shame by His words. For these adversaries, rather than joining in the jubilation which followed His work of healing, instead burned with rage that He had healed at all. But the multitude, because they derived benefit from His signs, rejoiced and took pleasure in this healing. You must also understand these miracles to refer to the inner man. The soul is bent over in infirmity whenever it inclines to earthly thoughts alone and imagines nothing that is heavenly and divine. It can truly be said that this soul has been infirm for eighteen years. For when a man is feeble in keeping the commandments of the divine law, which are ten in number, and is weak in his hope of the eighth age, the age to come, it can be said that he has been bent over for ten and eight years.[6] Is not that man indeed *bent over* who is attached to the earth, and who always sins in disregard of the commandments, and who does not look for the age to come? But the Lord heals such a soul on the sabbath in the assembly of the synagogue. For when a man assembles together within himself thoughts of confession (Judah means "confession") and keeps the sabbath, that is, he rests from doing evil, then Jesus heals him, not only by word when He says to him, *Thou art loosed from thine infirmity,* but also by deed. For when He has placed His hands on us, He requires that we accept the energy from His divine hands to do in collaboration with Him the works of virtue. We must not be satisfied to receive only that healing which comes by word and by instruction.

18-22. Then said He, Unto what is the kingdom of God like? And unto what shall I liken it? It is like a grain of mustard seed, which a man took, and cast into his garden; and it grew, and became a great tree; and the winged creatures of heaven lodged in the branches of it. And again He said, Whereunto shall I liken the kingdom of heaven? It is like leaven, which a woman took and hid in three measures of flour, till the whole was leavened. And He went through

---

[6] The Greek text of the Gospel expresses the number of years in this fashion: *etē deka kai oktō,* ten and eight years.

the cities and villages, teaching, and journeying toward Jerusalem. He
compares the kingdom of God to a grain of mustard seed. The kingdom
of God is the Word and the preaching, for it is by means of the preaching
of the Gospel that Christ rules over the souls of men. And just as the
mustard seed appears insignificant even though it has great power, so too
the Word of the Gospel is disdained by many because it appears foolish
to them. Yet when a man takes the seed of the Gospel and casts it into
his garden, that is, into his own soul, it makes a great tree with branches
in which lodge the winged creatures of heaven, that is, those men who
wish to soar upwards to the heavens. For those who surpass earthly things
find rest in the branches of the preaching, that is, in the far-reaching
thoughts of the Gospel. If I may give an example, Paul took the mustard
seed, which was the small amount of instruction which Ananias gave
him,[7] and Paul planted this seed in the rich soil of his garden. And the
seed produced branches, many in number, which are his good teachings
and his Epistles, in which lodged not only the men of his times who were
lofty and keen in mind and wisdom, such as the Corinthians, and
Dionysius, Hierotheus, and many others, but also men of succeeding
generations. The grain of mustard seed may also be understood to signify
the Lord Himself, Who appeared to be lowly, the impoverished son of a
carpenter. But when He fell into the heart of the earth at His death, and
was buried in the garden, He put forth beautiful branches, the apostles.
And these *branches* gave shelter and a place of rest to all those who
before had been buffeted about by every spirit of deception. For example,
the pagan intellectuals are not at all different from such birds, in that their
reasonings flit about in every direction, [not being grounded in Truth,]
and hence they are easily deceived. Do you see how all those who are
deceived are like the birds of the air? Again He likens the divine Word
to leaven which a woman, signifying human nature, took and hid in three
measures of flour, that is, in the body, in the soul, and in the spirit, in
order to sanctify them completely, as the blessed Paul says,[8] so that all
parts of a man might become a unified whole, leavened throughout by the
Holy Spirit. You may also understand the woman to be the soul, and the
three measures the three parts of the soul, namely, the abilities to reason,

---

[7] Acts 9:10-19

[8] See I Thess. 5:23.

to be stirred to action, and to desire. Therefore if a man should hide the Word of God in these three parts, he will make the whole thing spiritual, so that the reasoning part of the soul does not err in doctrines, and so that irrationality does not sway those parts of the soul which desire and stir to action. Then the soul is leavened and made like the Word of God. Jesus *went through the cities and villages, teaching.* Unlike those who wish to deceive the simple and the unlearned, He did not go only to the small places, such as the villages, and avoid the cities; and unlike the vainglorious He did not go to the cities only and avoid the villages. But as the Master of all, and indeed like a father who cares for all his children, He went to every place. And surely He did not go only to those cities outside Jerusalem in which there were no learned students of the law, and avoided Jerusalem itself, out of fear of being rebuked by its lawyers or because He suspected death at their hands? Such a view cannot be maintained, since, on the contrary, the Evangelist says that the Lord journeyed towards Jerusalem as well; for the physician is compelled to go where there are the greatest number of sick.

23-30. Then said one unto Him, Lord, are there few that be saved? And He said unto them, Strive to enter in at the narrow gate: for many, I say unto you, will seek to enter in, and shall not be able. When once the Master of the house is risen up, and hath shut the door, and ye begin to stand without, and to knock at the door, saying, Lord, Lord, open unto us; and He shall answer and say unto you, I know you not whence ye are: then shall ye begin to say, We have eaten and drunk in Thy presence, and Thou hast taught in our streets. But He shall say, I tell you, I know you not whence ye are; depart from Me, all ye workers of iniquity. There shall be weeping and gnashing of teeth, when ye shall see Abraham, and Isaac, and Jacob, and all the prophets, in the kingdom of God and you your-selves thrust out. And they shall come from the east, and from the west, and from the north, and from the south, and shall sit down in the kingdom of God. And, behold, there are last which shall be first, and there are first which shall be last. Few are saved because there is not enough room for many to pass through the narrow gate. The *Master of the house* is the Lord Who calls together all mankind to the feast and to the enjoyment of His unending good things. All who are zealous strive until the very hour of the dinner to enter in, but those who are slothful arrive after the hour of the dinner and are shut out. What is the hour of the dinner, if not this present life? Indeed it is while we are still in this life that we must make spiritual preparation for the feast, before *the Master of the house is risen up,* that is, risen up and come forth to judge, *and hath shut the door,* which means, closed the pathway of virtue. For further progress on that path cannot be made after we leave this life. It is only while we are in this life that we can walk the way of virtue. After their death, those who lived negligently in this life at last begin to knock at the door, only now, because of their useless repentance, seeking to find the path of virtue, calling out for it with mere words like so much pounding and banging, but devoid of any deeds. Justly has the Master of the house already closed the door and He pretends not to know them. Rightly so, for these belong to the devil, while the Lord knows only those who belong to Him. The words, *We have eaten and drunk in Thy presence, and Thou hast taught in our streets,* refer, in the first place, to the Israelites, for Christ came in the flesh from out of their midst and ate and drank with them. But these words may also be understood in a more spiritual sense to refer to those who performed the worship prescribed by the law and offered to God blood sacrifices, and partook and were gladdened, and who listened to the reading of the divine books in the synagogues. Indeed it was the Lord Who was teaching them through the prophets. The prophets did not set forth their own words, but pronounced the words of God, which is why they said, *Thus saith the Lord.* But the worship through blood sacrifice was not sufficient to the Jews for righteousness, because they did not accept that faith which makes even the impious righteous. And do these words not also apply to us Christians who live a careless life? For we also eat the divine Body and drink the Blood of Christ in His presence each time we approach the Mystical Table. And does the Lord not teach us in the streets, that is, have we not, while we were among the crowd, heard Him teach publicly? But it is of no benefit to us if we only hear the divine law and not do it. Indeed, unless we keep God's law, the fact that we heard it is grounds for even greater torments for us, just as our partaking of the Divine Mysteries unworthily is to our condemnation. Observe that it is those whom the Lord taught in the streets, that is, who only received the Lord's teachings in public, who are rejected. But if we receive His teaching, not just in public, but also within the closeness of our contrite and compunctionate heart, then we will not be rejected. The words, *There shall be weeping*

...when ye shall see Abraham, Isaac, and Jacob, refer both to the Israelites to whom He spoke these things, and also to the unbelievers of every age. For the Jews were vexed above all else by hearing that others from among the Gentiles would find rest with Abraham and the fathers while they themselves would be thrust out. But these words also apply to us who do not do those things which follow from our faith. We too boast in the law of Christ, but reject it by transgressing against it. We think we are *first* because from infancy we have put on Christ and have been taught the Word, but we shall become *last* when perhaps greater honor is given to those Gentiles who have believed towards the close of their life and have lived even for a short time in a manner pleasing to God.

31-33. The same day there came certain of the Pharisees, saying unto Him, Get Thee out, and depart hence: for Herod will kill Thee. And He said unto them, Go ye, and tell this fox, Behold I cast out demons, and I do cures today and tomorrow, and the third day I am finished. Nevertheless, today and tomorrow, and the following day I must depart: for it cannot be that a prophet perish outside of Jerusalem. Consumed with spite, the accursed Pharisees try to frighten the Lord and to present Herod as a perilous threat to Him. They did not want to see Him working miracles, because they feared that He would attract the people by doing such a great number of signs and then would win them over to Himself by the power of the word which He taught. Therefore they allege that Herod is threatening Him and pretend to be concerned for the Saviour. But He knows their hearts and answers them in a meek but also a veiled manner, as is His custom, saying, *Tell this fox.* He appears to be naming Herod a fox, but in fact, if one looks closely, He is calling the Pharisees the fox. He did not say "that fox," but *this fox,* deliberately using a phrase that could be understood in more than one way. By speaking of a fox in the singular He gave them reason to believe that He was referring to Herod, but by using the word *this* to point to what was close at hand, He implied that the cunning Pharisees themselves were *this fox.* For indeed the Pharisees showed themselves to be as wily and devious as a fox. See how He responds to their malice. Because they were full of spite at His healings and attempted to shake Him with fear of Herod, He said something which He knew would displease them. *Behold,* He says, *I cast out demons and I do cures.* As I have said before, they were attempting to drive Him away for this very reason, to prevent Him from using miracles to catch many in the net of faith in Him. The phrase *today and tomorrow* signifies a number of days. Likewise, when we say in common speech, "Such and such is going to happen today and tomorrow,"[9] we mean that the event will happen some time soon, but not necessarily within two days. In the same way, when the Lord said, *I do cures today and tomorrow, and the third day I am finished,* He did not mean that in exactly three days He would be finished, but instead that His death would occur soon. "But I must continue here today and tomorrow," that is, for some length of time, "working miracles, and then on the following day I journey to Jerusalem. For I have foreordained that I will undergo My Passion in that place." It is in Galilee, where Herod was the ruler,[10] that the Pharisees say to the Lord, *Get Thee out, for Herod will kill Thee.* But the Lord shows them that no matter how many plots Herod may devise, he will not succeed in killing Christ in Galilee. For His Passion was foreordained to occur in Jerusalem, not in Galilee. To make the words of the Gospel even clearer to you, do not think that Christ is saying, "I must journey today and tomorrow." Instead, pause after the words "today and tomorrow" and then say, "and the day following journey."[11] We often do the same ourselves when we are counting off days and say, for example, "Sunday, Monday—and Tuesday I leave." We do not mean by this that we are going to leave on Monday and leave on Tuesday. Rather, we are counting off the first two days to emphasize the third day on which the event will take place. So too the Lord is here counting off the days, as it were,

---

[9] This is a common expression of Bl. Theophylact's time which is not directly translatable into English. A rough equivalent would be "any day now."

[10] Herod Antipas, son of King Herod the Great, was Tetrarch of Galilee and Perea.

[11] Here Bl. Theophylact is explaining to the Greek reader of his day how to interpret the word order of the Greek text of the Gospel: *Plēn dei me sēmeron kai aurion kai tē erchomenē poreuesthai.* A word for word translation would be: "But it is necessary for Me today and tomorrow and the following [day] to journey." Bl. Theophylact is in fact instructing the reader not only to pause after the word "tomorrow", but to read the words "and the day following to journey" as a single phrase. The twentieth century reader must always bear in mind that ancient Greek texts provided no punctuation and no spaces between words and sentences. Thus the reader of these ancient texts must continuously make choices as to where these punctuation breaks occur, according to his sense and interpretation of the flow of letters before his eyes. It goes without saying that the Christian reader of the sacred Christian texts understands them with the mind of the Church. On the other hand, a reader who reads Scripture according to his private opinion does not understand Scripture. He merely sees in it what he wants to see.

saying, "Today, tomorrow, and then the third day I must journey to Jerusalem. For it is in that place that My end has been foreordained." As I have already said, the Lord does not mean that His life is going to end in three days, but rather, after not too many more days, indeed not a long way off in the future. It is as if He were addressing those who were filled with spite against Him: "Why do you trouble yourselves about My death? Behold, it will take place soon enough." When you hear that *it cannot be that a prophet perish outside of Jerusalem,* do not imagine that some force now compels the Jews to do these things because the Lord said this. Instead, understand that the Lord said this as a consequence of the Pharisees' own murderous disposition. For example, if you see a bloodthirsty robber lying in wait along a certain stretch of road, you would say, "It is not possible that this road, along which the killer lies in wait to prey upon wayfarers, will be unstained by blood." The prediction follows from the highwayman's deeds, and not the other way around. So it is with those robbers lying in wait in Jerusalem, I mean, the Pharisees and the scribes. It cannot be that the Master of the prophets should perish in any other place than where there are robbers. For these robbers had grown accustomed to shedding the blood of the servants, and now they will slay the Master.

34-35. O Jerusalem, Jerusalem, which killest the prophets, and stonest them that are sent unto thee; how often would I have gathered thy children together, as a hen doth gather her brood under her wings, and ye would not! Behold, your house is left unto you desolate: and verily I say unto you, Ye shall not see Me, until the time come when ye shall say, Blessed is He that cometh in the name of the Lord. The repetition of the name Jerusalem shows the deep love which the Lord has for them. Like a lover scorned by his beloved, the Lord cries out to the adulterous synagogue. He shows the depth of His love for mankind when He says that He wanted so many times to gather them to Himself, but He also indicates their insane defiance by saying, *and ye would not!* "So be it," He says, "I leave you. So much do I hate your wickedness that I do not even call the temple My house but *your house.* As long as you attempted to live a life of virtue, it was also My temple. But you have defiled even the temple, and with minds full of greed you have made it a marketplace and a den of thieves by your extortionate prices and haggling. What difference is there between what you do when you cheat your own brother and take his goods, and what robbers do who tie up the hands and feet of wayfarers and seize everything they have? Therefore, since you have made the temple a den of thieves by the kind of business you have practiced in the house of prayer, it is no longer My house, but your house." Do not understand *house* to refer only to the temple, but also to the whole generation of the Jews as well. For Scripture also calls the tribe itself a *house*. For example, *O house of Levi, bless ye the Lord.*[12] Therefore this passage may also be understood to mean, "I have left not only your house but your nation," as He says elsewhere through the prophet, *I have forsaken My house, I have left Mine heritage.*[13] There *house* means the Israelites. He shows that from the beginning it has been He Himself Who sustains them and vanquishes their enemies. His words, *Ye shall not see Me, until ye shall say, Blessed is He that cometh in the name of the Lord,* refer to His second coming. At that time they will confess, whether they want to or not, that He is the Saviour and Lord, but then their confession will be of no benefit to them. But how can this be? Did they not see Him again after He said these things? Yes, of course. Therefore, when He says, "Ye shall not see Me from now on," He was not referring to that very hour, but to the time following His crucifixion. It is as if He had said, "After you have crucified Me, you shall no longer see Me until I come again."

---

[12] Ps. 134:19. The entire verse reads: *O house of Israel, bless ye the Lord. O house of Aaron, bless ye the Lord. O house of Levi, bless ye the Lord.*

[13] Jer. 12:7

CHAPTER FOURTEEN

Concerning the man who suffered from dropsy.
On not desiring the places of honour.
On inviting the poor, instead of friends, to the supper.
Concerning those who were invited to the supper.
Concerning the parable of the building of the tower.

1-6. And it came to pass, as He went into the house of one of the chief Pharisees to eat bread on the sabbath, that they watched Him. And, behold, there was a certain man before Him who suffered from dropsy. And Jesus answering spake unto the lawyers and Pharisees, saying, Is it lawful to heal on the sabbath? And they were silent. And He took him, and healed him, and let him go; and answered them, saying, Which of you shall have an ass or an ox fallen into a pit, and will not straightway pull him out on the sabbath? And they could not answer Him again to these things. Even though the Lord knew the perverse disposition of the Pharisees, He still went into their homes. He did this because He desired to bring benefit to souls. The Pharisees could be helped either by the word of His teaching or by His working of signs, if only they were willing. Therefore when the man with dropsy came into their midst, it was the Lord's desire to benefit the sick in need of healing, and He did not turn from this purpose out of fear that the Pharisees might be scandalized. And whenever the occasion arises to bring great benefit to others, neither should we worry about those foolish ones who may be scandalized. The Lord rebukes the mindlessness of those who are about to accuse Him, and says, *"Is it lawful to heal on the sabbath, or not?"* Is He not openly ridiculing them as foolish? If God Himself has blessed the sabbath, why do these foolish men prevent the doing of good on the sabbath, and thus render the sabbath cursed? For a day on which no good work is permitted cannot be blessed. But the Pharisees understood where His question was leading them, and were silent. Then Jesus does what is His to do, and heals the man by His touch. He shames the Pharisees as well, by saying to them what amounts to this: "If the law prohibits showing mercy on the sabbath, why do you help your child when he falls into danger on the sabbath? But why mention your child? You do not even ignore your ox when you see it in danger on the sabbath. Therefore is it not foolishness to find fault with the healing of a man with dropsy on the sabbath?'' The man with dropsy, swollen with water, represents every man who is grievously afflicted in soul because his way of life is watery and irresolute, soft, and full of pleasures. He is in need of Christ. But even he will be healed, if only he comes before Christ, as did the man with dropsy. For he who always remembers that he is in the presence of God, and that God sees him, will sin very little.

7-11. And He told a parable to those who had been invited, when He observed how they chose out the places of honour, saying unto them, When thou art invited by any man to a wedding, sit not down in the place of honour; lest a more honourable man than thou be invited by him, and he that invited both thee and him come and say to thee, Give this man place; and thou begin with shame to take the lowest place. But when thou art invited, go and sit down in the lowest place; that when he that invited thee cometh, he may say unto thee, Friend, go up higher: then shalt thou have glory in the presence of them that sit at table with thee. For whosoever exalteth himself shall be abased; and he that humbleth himself shall be exalted. Do you see the kind of supper Christ gives? His suppers are for the benefit of the soul, not for the filling up of the stomach. Behold, when He had healed the man with dropsy He taught the Pharisees that it is right to do good on the sabbath. Then when He saw them clamoring for the seats of honor, He heals this passion as well. This is a passion which does not spring from something trivial but, on the contrary, has its origin in something grievous and difficult to escape, namely, vainglory. And let no one think that Christ's teaching on this is a small matter, unworthy of the majesty of God. Indeed, would you call a physician compassionate who promised to heal gout in the feet, and other serious illnesses, but refused to treat a broken finger or a toothache? But then again, how can the passion of vainglory, which constantly assaults those who desire the places of honor, be considered minor? It was imperative, therefore, that Christ, Who is the Teacher of humility and its very Origin and Perfection, should cut off every shoot from the wicked root of vainglory. Consider this as well. If the Lord had been speaking about this on an occasion other than supper time, and if He had interrupted His other teachings to make this point, there might be reason to dismiss His teaching on this matter as something trivial. But now it was supper time, and before His very eyes the Saviour sees these miserable men vexed by the passion to be first, and so His exhortation was necessary and timely. See how the Lord saves a man from utter reproach and gives him greater respect. Think what a complete disgrace it would be if you took a seat that did not befit your rank, and then a more distinguished person came, and the host said, ''Give up your seat to this man,'' and this happened repeatedly, and you descended lower and lower, while others went higher. On the other hand, how deserving of praise would that man be, who was indeed worthy of the first seat at the table, but who took a low seat at the beginning. Then everyone would rise and give way to him and seat him in the place of honor. Does it indeed seem to you a small matter, this exhortation of the Lord which underscores the greatest of all the virtues, humility? The Lord establishes humility within the souls of those who listen, and leads them to act with decorum, as Paul, the disciple of Christ, said later, *Let all things be done decently and in order.*[1] How is this accomplished? Let no one pursue his own advantage, but let each one seek the advantage of others. Do you see that the disciple Paul is saying the same thing as his Teacher? How shall we understand the words, *Whosoever exalteth himself shall be abased*? How can this be? There are many in this life who exalt themselves and seem to enjoy honor. But to enjoy great honor in the world is, in fact, to be abased, for such a man in the eyes of God is wretched and abased. Besides this, a man who enjoys worldly honor never in fact receives it from everyone, nor does he receive it until the very end of his life. For while some may honor him, there are always others who mock him, often the same ones who gave him honor. Hence, this declaration of truth holds true. *Whosoever exalteth himself* unworthily, usurping honor for himself, *shall be abased,* both by God at the Last Judgment, and even by all men in this life. Because of his fallen nature no man is worthy to be exalted. Therefore let no one exalt himself, lest at the end he be brought low.

12-15. Then said He also to him that invited Him, When thou makest a dinner or a supper, call not thy friends, nor thy brethren, neither thy kinsmen, nor thy rich neighbours; lest they also invite thee in return, and a recompence be made thee. But when thou makest a feast, invite the poor, the maimed, the lame, the blind: and thou shalt be blessed; for they cannot recompense thee: for thou shalt

---

[1] I Cor. 14:40

be recompensed at the resurrection of the righteous. And when one of them that sat at table with Him heard these things, he said unto Him, Blessed is he that shall eat bread in the kingdom of God. Those at the dinner fall into two groups: the hosts and the guests. First the Lord gave an exhortation to the guests, and by guiding them to the saving virtue of humility, He set before them, as it were, a tasty dish that is never depleted. But also to the host who had invited Him, the Lord shows generous hospitality in return, feasting him with His exhortation not to give dinners in order to win the favor of men and for the sake of getting something quickly in return. Those of small soul invite their friends or their relatives expecting the favor to be returned at once, and if it is not, they are grieved. Those of great soul wait to receive their reward in the future from Him Who is truly rich. In saying these things the Lord does not bar us from honoring our friends with hospitality; instead He teaches us not to show kindness for a price. When a certain man there at the dinner heard the Lord say these things, he thought that God will reward with hospitality and will make feasts for the righteous with material food, and said, *Blessed is he that shall eat bread in the kingdom of God.* This man, being still a natural man and not spiritual, was not able to understand the things that are beyond the senses, and as a natural man was governed by human reasonings.[2] Such a natural man believes in nothing that is beyond physical nature, and understands everything in terms of physical nature. There are three conditions of man: the carnal [*sarkikē*] state, the natural state [*psychikē*], and the spiritual [*pneumatikē*] state. The carnal state is when a man takes pleasure and rejoices by maltreating others. Such is the condition of those who are greedy for more [at another man's expense]. The natural state is when a man desires neither to hurt nor to be hurt. In this state a man lives according to nature. For nature itself teaches us to desire neither to hurt nor to be hurt. The spiritual state is when a man is willing even to be harmed and to be ill-treated for the sake of the good. The first state, then, is against nature, the second state is according to nature, and the third state is above nature. Every one,

---

[2] See I Cor. 2:14: *But the natural man* [psychikos anthropos] *receiveth not the things of the Spirit of God.* And Jude 18-19: *Who walk after their own ungodly lusts. These be they who separate themselves, sensual* [psychikoi], *having not the Spirit.* The adjective *psychikos* [*natural, sensual*] refers to that lower part of the soul [*psychē*] pertaining to the mere animal, or animate, life of the senses and appetites.

therefore, who thinks only human thoughts, and is unable to understand anything that is beyond nature, is said to be a natural man, and he is governed not by the spirit alone, but by his animal soul as well. But when a man is led by the Holy Spirit, it is no longer he himself that lives, but Christ living in him.[3] This is a spiritual man, who surpasses nature. But the man here in the Gospel who thought that the saints would receive material rewards of a kind knowable by the senses, was a natural and sensual man, unable to understand anything beyond nature.

16-20. Then said He unto him, A certain man made a great supper, and called many, and sent his servant at supper time to say to them that were called, Come; for all things are now ready. And they all with one accord began to make excuse. The first said unto him, I have bought a piece of ground, and I must needs go and see it: I pray thee have me excused. And another said, I have bought five yoke of oxen, and I go to prove them: I pray thee have me excused. And another said, I have married a wife, and therefore I cannot come. Because the man who sat at table with Him had said, *Blessed is he that shall eat bread in the kingdom of God,* the Lord teaches him at some length what it means to feast with God, and tells this parable. By *a certain man* the Lord means His Father, the Lover of man. Whenever Scripture alludes to God's power to punish, He is called a panther, a leopard, or a bear.[4] But whenever it alludes to God's love for man, He is presented as a man, as is the case here. Since the parable treats of God's extreme love for man and the divine economy of the Incarnation which He worked in us, making us sharers of the Flesh of His Son, the parable calls God *a man* and this divine economy *a great supper*. It is a *supper* because the Lord came in the last days, as it were at the evening of this age. And this supper is *great* because great indeed, we confess, is the mystery of our salvation.[5] *And he sent his servant at supper time.* Who is this servant? The Son of God, Who assumed the form a servant and became man, and as a man is said to have been sent forth. Notice how He did not say "a servant," but instead, using the definite article,

---

[3] See Gal. 2:20

[4] Hos. 13:7-8

[5] See I Tim. 3:16.

the servant [of his].[6] Christ is the One and only Servant Who in His human nature was perfectly obedient and pleasing to God. For Christ is pleasing to the Father not only as Son and God, but also as Man. He is the only Sinless One Who carried out all the counsels and command- ments of the Father and fulfilled all righteousness, and in this sense is said to serve God the Father. He alone can be called the true Servant of God. He was sent *at supper time,* that is, at the appointed and proper time. For there was no other time more opportune for our salvation than the reign of Caesar Augustus, when iniquity had reached its peak and it was critical that it be cleansed. Just as physicians allow a festering and malignant boil to burst and release all its foul pus, and only then apply the medication, so too it was necessary that sin first display all its forms, and then the Great Physician applied His medicine. For this very reason the Lord waited for the devil to fill the full measure of iniquity, and then the Son of God took flesh and healed every form of iniquity by every aspect of His holy life. Therefore He was sent at that hour, that is, at that comely and opportune season of which David says, *Gird Thy sword upon Thy thigh, O Mighty One, in Thy comeliness.*[7] Certainly the *sword* here signifies the Word of God,[8] while the words *upon Thy thigh* indicate His Nativity in the flesh which was *in comeliness,* that is, when the time was right and seemly. He was sent to speak to those who had been called. Who are those *that were called?* Perhaps this refers to all men. For God has called all to the knowledge of Him, by means of the order and harmony of visible creation, and by means of the natural law. But those *that were called* are also, more specifically, the children of Israel, who were called through the law and the prophets. In the first place, then, the Lord was sent to the sheep of the house of Israel.[9] The Lord was saying to all the Jews, *Come, for all things are now ready,* when He proclaimed

---

[6] The definite article is present in the Greek text, *ton doulon autou* [*the servant of him*], but not in the English translation, *his servant,* because in English the possessive pronoun coming before the noun replaces any articles.

[7] Ps. 44:3. The Greek word *ōraiotētos,* rendered here as *comeliness,* derives from the adjective *ōraios,* which in turn derives from the noun *ōra,* which means "hour". This Greek word for "beautiful," *ōraios,* has a broad range of meanings including "coming at the right season [*ōra*], seasonable, timely, ripe, at the bloom of youth, beautiful."

[8] See Heb. 4:12.

[9] Mt. 15:24

the good tidings that *the kingdom of heaven is at hand,*[10] *and among you.*[11] *And they all with one accord began to make excuse,* that is, as if at a signal. For all the leaders of the Jews refused to have Jesus as their King, and thus were found unworthy of the supper, one because of his love of wealth, and another because of his love of pleasure. The man who bought a piece of ground and the man who bought the five yoke of oxen signify those who love wealth, while the man who married a wife signifies those who love pleasure. Furthermore, the man who bought a piece of ground signifies the man who cannot accept the mystery of faith because he is governed by the wisdom of this world. The piece of ground represents the world and, in general, nature, and the man who must *go and see his piece of ground* is he who sees only nature, and cannot accept what is beyond nature. Therefore the Pharisee, for example, "sees his piece of ground," that is, he looks only at the laws of nature and cannot accept that a Virgin gave birth to God, because that is beyond nature. Because they are examining this "piece of ground," that is, nature, none of those who boast in external wisdom have recognized Jesus Who made nature new. The man who bought five yoke of oxen, and tested them, also represents a man who loves the material world. He has yoked the five senses of the soul to the five senses of the body and has made the soul into flesh. For this reason he is concerned only with the earth and does not desire to commune of the rational Supper, for as Wisdom says, *How can he get wisdom that holdeth the plough?*[12] He who stays behind because of a wife is a lover of pleasure who has devoted himself to the flesh, the mate of the soul. By cleaving to the flesh he cannot please God. You may also understand these things literally. We also fall away from God because of fields, because of yokes of oxen, because of marriages, when we become so attached to them that they consume our whole life and we are carried away even to the point of shedding blood over them. Then there is no divine thought or word that we can practice, or even comprehend.

21-24. So that servant came, and declared to his lord these things.

---

[10] Mt. 4:17

[11] Lk. 17:21

[12] Ecclesiasticus (Wisdom of Sirach), 38:25

Then the master of the house being angry said to his servant, Go out quickly into the streets and lanes of the city, and bring in hither the poor, and the maimed, and the halt, and the blind. And the servant said, Lord, it is done as thou hast commanded, and yet there is room. And the lord said unto the servant, Go out into the highways and hedges, and compel them to come in, that my house may be filled. For I say unto you, That none of those men which were called shall taste of my supper. The rulers of the Jews were rejected, and not one of them believed in Christ. And they even boasted of their malice, saying, *Have any of the rulers believed on Him?*[13] Therefore these students of the law and scribes, as the prophet says, became foolish and fell from grace. But the simple from among the Jews are likened to the halt, the blind, and the maimed. It is the foolish of this world, the lowly, who were called. For the multitude marvelled at the words of grace which proceeded from the mouth of Jesus, and they rejoiced in His teaching. But after these had come to Him from the sons of Israel, that is, from the chosen whom God foreordained for His glory, such as Peter, and the sons of Zebedee, and the tens of thousands of those Jews who believed, then God's goodness was poured out also upon the Gentiles. For those who are in *the highways and hedges* mean the Gentiles. The Israelites were within the city, inasmuch as they had received the lawgiving and inherited a civil and moral way of life. But the Gentiles were strangers to the Covenants and the lawgiving of Christ was foreign to them. They were not fellow citizens of the saints, and did not travel the one true path, but instead followed many highways of lawlessness and coarseness, and were to be found in the hedges, that is, in sins. For sin is a great hedge and middle wall which separates us from God. By *highways* He signifies the Gentiles' coarse way of life, which led them to so many false beliefs. By *hedges* He signifies their life of sins. The master does not command his servant simply to call all those in the highways and hedges, but to *compel them to come in,* although each man is free whether to believe or not. But He uses the word *compel* to teach us that it is a sign of God's great power that the Gentiles, who were in such ignorance, came to believe. If the power of the preaching and the might of the word of truth had not been so great, how could men who were crazed with idol worship

---

[13]Jn. 7:48

and practiced unspeakable things have been persuaded all at once to know the true God, and to perfect a spiritual life? He called this "compulsion" to show the miraculousness of their change. One might say that the pagan Greeks did not want to leave their idols and their rich feasting, yet they were compelled to flee from them by the truth of the Gospel. Also, the power of the miracles He worked was a strong force that induced them to be converted to faith in Christ. Every day this Supper is prepared and we are all invited to the kingdom which God prepared for man even before the foundation of the world. But we are not worthy of this Supper: some of us because of useless philosophical musings, others because of love of material things, and yet others because of pleasures of the flesh. But God in His love for man freely bestows this kingdom upon other sinners, upon the blind who have no spiritual vision to perceive the will of God; or if they can perceive it, upon those who are crippled and unable to take a step to do the will of God. And in short He grants the kingdom of heaven to all the poor who have fallen away from the glory above, and even to the maimed who cannot show forth in themselves a blameless life. To invite these sinners to the supper, who are wandering astray in the streets and broad avenues of sin, the Father sends His Son Who became a Servant according to the flesh, and Who came not to call the righteous, but sinners. All these He feasts liberally, instead of the clever, the rich, and those who indulge the flesh. By the judgments known to Him alone He sends diseases and dangers upon many, causing them, even against their will, to renounce this life. Thus He leads them to His Supper, "compelling" them by means of the dangers. There are many examples of this. Understood in a simpler way, this parable also teaches us to show favor to the poor and the crippled rather than to the rich, just as He exhorted us to do a short while before.[14] It is for this reason that He tells this parable, to confirm that we must give hospitality to the poor. And we may also learn from this that we should be so eager and generous in welcoming our brethren that, even when they are reluctant, we should compel them to partake of our good things. This is also good advice for teachers: teach what is necessary, even when the students are unwilling.

---

[14] In verses 13-14.

25-27. And there went great multitudes with Him: and He turned, and said unto them, If any man come to Me, and hate not his father, and mother, and wife, and children, and brethren, and sisters, yea, and his own life also, he cannot be My disciple. And whosoever doth not bear his cross, and come after Me, cannot be My disciple. Because many of those who went with Jesus were lukewarm and did not follow Him with zeal and obedience, He teaches them how His disciple ought to be. He describes and depicts His true disciple, explaining that he must *hate* not only those to whom he is united outwardly by the bonds of love or kinship, but he must "hate" even his own life. See to it that you are not seized and carried away by this saying, interpreting it literally and without understanding. The Lover of man does not teach hatred for man, nor does He counsel us to take our own lives. But He desires His true disciple to *hate* his own kin when they prevent him from giving reverence to God and when he is hindered from doing good by his relationship to them. If they do not hinder us in these things, then He teaches us to honor them until our last breath. How does He teach us this? By that great teaching—His own deeds. He was obedient to Joseph, even though Joseph was not truly His father, but was only regarded as such. And He showed such care for His mother on every occasion that He did not neglect to care for her even while He was hanging on the Cross, but entrusted her to His beloved disciple.[15] How then could He Who taught such things by His own deeds set forth a different teaching with His words? As I have said, He commands us to *hate* our own relatives only when they hinder us from obeying God. When they stand in the way of what is so beneficial to us, they are not then to be considered parents, family, or friends. What we are saying becomes clear from the words that follow, the commandment that we "hate" our own life. Certainly this is not a command that we kill ourselves, but that we renounce those desires of the soul that separate us from God. And if martyrdom is imminent, we should take no thought for our life, but only for the profit to be gained in the age to come. That this is what He means, and not that we should simply kill ourselves, He Himself again makes clear when the devil was tempting Him to cast Himself down from the temple, and He rejected that temptation. Nor did He give Himself

---

[15] Jn. 19:26-27

over to the Jews when they were seeking to slay Him, but instead departed and passed through the midst of them, and hid Himself from those who would take His life. Therefore, if any man is hindered from giving reverence to God by one of his own family, such a man loves that family tie and gives it higher place than his duty to please God. And often, when martyrdom is before him, a man may be carried away by his love of this life to deny Christ. Such a man is not able to be Christ's disciple.

28-30. For which of you, intending to build a tower, sitteth not down first, and counteth the cost, whether he have sufficient to finish it? Lest, after he hath laid the foundation, and is not able to finish it, all that behold it begin to mock him, saying, This man began to build, and was not able to finish. By this parable of the tower the Lord teaches us that once we have chosen to follow Him we should always guard this resolution we have made. We should not lay down the foundation, that is, begin to follow Christ, without being ready with sufficient zeal to finish the task. Such were those of whom John the Evangelist said, *From that time many of His disciples went back, and walked no more with Him.*[16] And every man who decides to practice virtue, but does not first take as his helper the knowledge of God, will make a beginning that is imperfect and irrational. Thus his building will be imperfect and flawed and he will not be able to complete his tower of lofty knowledge. Then he is mocked by those who look at him, both men and demons. In another sense, you may understand *the foundation* to mean the word of teaching. For the word of teaching, which lays down the principle of self-control, is like a foundation which is laid in the soul of the disciple. We must then build an edifice of deeds upon this foundation, the word of teaching, so that when the virtue of self-control which was first laid down has been brought to completion in us, it may become our strong tower of defence against the enemy. That the Word is the foundation and our deeds are the building, the Apostle Paul clearly teaches when he says, *I have laid the foundation, which is Jesus Christ, and another buildeth thereon.*[17] And immediately he lists the various

---

[16] Jn. 6:66

[17] See I Cor. 3:10-11.

constructions, that is, the works of either good or evil deeds.[18] Let us tremble with fear lest we are mocked by the demons of whom the prophet said, *Mockers shall have dominion over them,*[19] that is, have dominion over those who have been rejected by God.

31-33. Or what king, going to make war against another king, sitteth not down first, and consulteth whether he be able with ten thousand to meet him that cometh against him with twenty thousand? If not, while the other is yet a great way off, he sendeth an embassy and desireth conditions of peace. So likewise, whosoever he be of you that forsaketh not all that he hath, he cannot be My disciple. Salt is good: but if the salt has lost its savour, wherewith shall it be seasoned? It is fit neither as earth, nor as dung; men cast it out. He that hath ears to hear, let him hear. With this parable He teaches us again not to be of two minds and not to be attached both to God and to the flesh. If we intend to make war against the evil powers, we must treat them as enemies and indeed array ourselves against them in battle. One king is sin, which reigns over our mortal bodies when we permit it; and the king who goes to make war against sin is the mind which God created to govern us as a king. Therefore, if a man intends to stand against sin, let him make war against sin wholeheartedly. The army of sin is fierce and terrible and seems greater and more numerous than our own force. For the warriors of sin are the demons, and they appear to advance with twenty thousand against our ten thousand. Being bodiless, they appear to have greater might when compared to us who are in the flesh. But although they appear stronger, we are able to stand against them. As it is written, *In God we shall work mighty deeds;*[20] and *the Lord is my light and my Saviour; whom then shall I fear? Though a host should array itself against me, my heart shall not be afraid.*[21] For indeed God Who became flesh for our sake has given us strength to trample on all the power of the enemy.[22] Therefore, although we are in

---

[18] See I Cor. 3:11-15.

[19] Is. 3:4

[20] Ps. 59:14

[21] Ps. 26:1,3

[22] See Lk. 10:19.

the flesh, our weaponry is not of the flesh; and although we seem to have only ten thousand because we are in the body, while the army of demons numbers twenty thousand because of their bodiless nature, still we ought to say, "O Lord my God, Thou art my strength,"[23] and never make peace with sin, that is, never be enslaved to the passions. Instead, we should resist them and show a hatred towards them that gives no quarter, and we should not desire to have any attachment to the things of the world, but should forsake them all. For a man cannot be a disciple of Christ unless he forsakes all the passions and refuses to make peace with anything in the world which harms the soul. And the disciple of Christ ought to be like salt, that is, first he ought to be good himself and have no part in wickedness, and then he ought to transmit that goodness to others. Such is the nature of salt: it remains itself unspoiled and unharmed, and by transmitting its nature to other things, it preserves them from spoiling as well. But if salt loses its own nature, it becomes totally useless, and *it is neither fit as earth, nor as dung.* What the Lord means is this: I want every Christian to be useful and full of savor, not just those who have been entrusted with the gift of teaching, as were the apostles, teachers, and pastors. I also require that the layman be useful and beneficial to his neighbor. But if he who intends to benefit others is himself unfit and has departed from the condition which is proper to a Christian, he shall be able neither to receive nor to give any benefit. *It is fit neither as earth, nor as dung,* the Lord says. By *earth* He implies that which receives benefit [when it is fertilized with manure] and by *dung* He implies that which gives benefit to the earth. Therefore, when a man is unable either to receive or to give benefit, he is altogether worthless and fit only to be cast out. Because this saying was obscure and allegorical, the Lord urges His listeners not to understand in a simple manner His words concerning salt. He urges them by saying, *He that hath ears to hear, let him hear,* that is, "He that hath understanding, let him understand." *Ears* refer, in this place, to the faculty of the soul's senses, the aptitude to understand. Therefore, each one of us who believes is like salt, and we have received this quality of salt from the divine words and from the grace which comes from above. To be assured that grace is salt, listen to the words of the Apostle Paul: *Let your speech be with grace,*

---

[23] See Ps. 139:7.

seasoned by salt.[24] When speech is without grace, it can be said to be without salt. Therefore, if we despise the savor of the divine words, and do not accept it for ourselves and let it salt us, then indeed we have become insipid and stupid. Our salt has then lost its savor, lacking the quality of grace which comes from above.

---

[24] Col. 4:6

CHAPTER FIFTEEN

Concerning the parable of the hundred sheep.
Concerning the parable of the prodigal son.

1-10. Then drew near unto Him all the publicans and sinners for to hear Him. And the Pharisees and scribes murmured, saying, this man receiveth sinners, and eateth with them. And He spake this parable unto them, saying, What man of you, having an hundred sheep, if he lose one of them, doth not leave the ninety and nine in the wilderness, and go after that which is lost, until he find it? And when he hath found it, he layeth it on his shoulders, rejoicing. And when he cometh home, he calleth together his friends and neighbours, saying unto them, Rejoice with me; for I have found my sheep which was lost. I say unto you, that likewise joy shall be in heaven over one sinner that repenteth, more than over ninety and nine righteous persons, which need no repentance. Or what woman having ten coins, if she lose one coin, doth not light a lamp, and sweep the house, and seek diligently till she find it? And when she hath found it, she calleth her friends and her neighbours together, saying, Rejoice with me; for I have found the coin which I had lost. Likewise, I say unto you, there is joy in the presence of the angels of God over one sinner that repenteth. The Lord was doing the very thing for which He became incarnate, drawing to Himself sinners and publicans, as a physician draws the sick. But the Pharisees, who were the real sinners, repaid His love for mankind with grumbling. They considered the publicans to be contemptible, even as they themselves were devouring what little the widows and orphans had. How did the Lord respond? He treated those who slandered His love for mankind with the same love that He showed to the publicans. He did not reject the Pharisees out of hand as incurable grumblers, but meekly tended to them, telling them the parable of the sheep to persuade them by what is clear and obvious, and to curb their vexation at His great outpouring of goodness. If there is such great joy at finding one irrational sheep, not made in the image of God, after it has gone astray, how much joy must there be over rational man, who was created in the image of God? The parable clearly says that the ninety and nine sheep are the righteous, and the one sheep is the sinner who has fallen away. But some say that the hundred sheep are the whole rational creation, and that the one rational sheep which went astray is man. The Good Shepherd sought it out, leaving the ninety and nine in the *wilderness,* that is, in heaven. For the wilderness, removed from worldly tumult and steeped in stillness and peace, signifies heaven. When the Lord found this erring sheep, He placed it upon His shoulders. For He Himself bore our infirmities and our sins, and He took upon Himself our burdens which to Him were light. He paid off all that we owed, and easily and without toil carried us off safely to His own home, that is, to heaven. And *He calleth together His friends and neighbors,* who signify the angels, whom we have also called *sheep* when considered from a different aspect. Inasmuch as all created nature is animal-like and brutish in comparison to God, in this sense the angelic powers may be called *sheep.* Yet inasmuch as the hosts of the angelic powers are rational, intellectual beings, closer to God than any other created thing, in this sense they may also be understood as the *friends and neighbours* of God. You may understand the *woman* to signify the Wisdom and Power of God the Father, that is, His Son, Who lost the one coin, man, from among the rational creatures created in the image of God, and Who lights a lamp, His own flesh, to look for him. Just as a lamp, which is an earthly object, enlightens things that are in darkness by means of the light which it receives, so also the flesh of the Lord, which is earthly and like our own flesh, shone with the light of Divinity which assumed it. Indeed the house was swept, that is, the whole world was cleansed of sin. For it is Christ Who taketh away the sin of the world. And the coin was found, bearing the image of the King, and there is joy for Him Who found it, Christ, and for the heavenly powers who are His *friends* and *neighbors.* The angels are His *friends,* because they do His will; and they are His *neighbors* because they are bodiless. But I wonder if His *friends* are not perhaps all the heavenly powers, and His *neighbors* are those of them who are closest to Him, such as the Thrones, Cherubim, and Seraphim. Consider the words, *she calleth her friends and her neighbors together.* This seems to indicate two groups, but this may belabor the point.

11-16. And He said, A certain man had two sons: and the younger of them said to his father, Father, give me the portion of the property that falleth to me. And he divided unto them his living. And not many days after the younger son gathered all together, and took his journey into a far country, and there squandered his property with

prodigal living. And when he had spent all, there arose a mighty famine in that land; and he began to be in want. And he went and joined himself to a citizen of that country; and he sent him into his fields to feed swine. And he longed to fill his belly with the pods that the swine did eat: and no man gave unto him. This parable is like those which precede it. For it also presents *a man*, Who is in fact God, the Lover of man. The two sons represent the two kinds of men, righteous and sinners. The younger son said, *Give me the portion of the property that falleth to me.* Of old, from the beginning, righteousness belonged to human nature, which is why the older son [born at the beginning] does not become estranged from the father. But sin is an evil thing which was born later. This is why it is the younger son who alienates himself from the father, for the latter-born son grew up together with sin which had insinuated itself into man at a later time. The sinner is also called the younger son because the sinner is an innovator, a revolutionary, and a rebel, who defies his Father's will. *Father, give me the portion of the property [ousia][1] that falleth to me.* The essential property of man is his rational mind, his logos,[2] always accompanied by his free will [*autexousia*], for all that is rational is inherently self-governing.[3] The Lord gives us logos for us to use, according to our free will, as our own essential property. He gives to all alike, so that all alike are rational, and all alike are self-governing. But some of us use this generous gift rationally, in accordance with logos, while others of us squander the divine gift. Moreover, everything which the Lord has given

---

[1] The more mundane meaning of the Greek word *ousia* is "what belongs to someone," i.e. his property. But *ousia*, a noun derived from the present participle of the verb *eimi, to be*, also means *essence, substance*, and *being* itself. What a man truly is differs not at all from what belongs to him essentially. Because no single word in English captures the related meanings of *ousia*, we have variously translated this word as *property* or *essential property*.

[2] The Greek word *logos*, as understood by the Church, encompasses not only Christ Himself, the *Word* of God, but also the faculties of speech, thought, mind, and reason which God gave of Himself to those created beings, angels and men, whom He fashioned in His own image and likeness. No single English word suffices to translate these many and related meanings. Because *logos* is central to Bl. Theophylact's explanation here, we have identified throughout this parable the word *logos* in the various forms in which it is used (e.g. *to logikon*), so as to alert the reader to the interrelatedness of several concepts which might otherwise seem unconnected in English.

[3] The Greek word *autexousia*, often translated as *free will*, has the literal meaning of *self-authority [auto-exousia]*, or *self-determination*. When God created man with *autexousia*, He ceded to man authority over his own essential property, his logos, that is, He gave man a free will.

us might be called our *property*, that is, the sky, the earth, the whole creation, the law and the prophets. But the later sinful generation, the younger son, saw the sky and made it a god, and saw the earth and worshipped it, and did not want to walk in the way of God's law, and did evil to the prophets. On the other hand, the elder son, the righteous, used all these things for the glory of God. Therefore, having given all an equal share of logos and self-determination, God permits us to make our way according to our own will and compels no one to serve Him who is unwilling. If He had wanted to compel us, He would not have created us with logos and a free will. But the younger son completely spent this inheritance. Why? Because he had gone into *a far country*. When a man rebels against God and places himself far away from the fear of God, then he squanders all the divine gifts. But when we are near to God, we do not do such deeds that merit our destruction. As it is written, *I beheld the Lord ever before me, for He is at my right hand, that I might not be shaken.*[4] But when we are far from God and become rebellious, we both do, and suffer, the worst things, as it is written, *Behold, they that remove themselves from Thee shall perish.*[5] The younger son indeed *squandered* and scattered *his property*. For every virtue is a simple and single entity, while its opposing vice is a many-branched complexity, creating numerous deceptions and errors. For example, the definition of bravery is simple, that is, when, how, and against whom, one ought to make use of one's capacity to be stirred to action. But the vice of not being brave takes two forms, cowardice and recklessness. Do you see how logos can be scattered in every direction and the unity of virtue destroyed? When this essential property has been spent, and a man no longer walks in accordance with logos, by which I mean the natural law, nor proceeds according to the written law, nor listens to the prophets, then there arises *a mighty famine—not a famine of bread, but a famine of hearing the word [logos] of the Lord.*"[7] And he begins *to be in want*, because by not fearing the Lord he has departed far from Him. But *there is no want to*

---

[4] Ps. 15:8

[5] Ps. 72:25

[6] The Greek word which we have translated here as *squander* is *diaskorpizei*, which literally means "scatter".

[7] Amos 8:11

them that fear the Lord.[8] How is there no want to them that fear Him? Because *blessed is the man that feareth the Lord; in His commandments shall he greatly delight.* Therefore *glory and riches shall be in his house,* and far from being himself in want, *he hath dispersed, he hath given to the poor.*[9] Therefore the man who makes a journey far from God, not keeping God's dread face ever before his eyes, indeed is in want, having no divine logos at work in him. *And he went,* that is, he proceeded and advanced in wickedness, *and joined himself to a citizen of that country.* He who is joined to the Lord becomes one Spirit with Him. But he who is joined to a harlot, that is, to the nature of the demons, becomes one body with her,[10] and he makes himself all flesh, having no room in himself for the Spirit, as it was for those men at the time of the flood.[11] The citizens of that country far from God are none other than the demons. The man who joins himself to these citizens, having advanced and become powerful in wickedness, *feeds the swine,* that is, he teaches others evil and filthy deeds. For all those who take pleasure in the muck of shameful deeds and carnal passions are like swine. Pigs are never able to look upward because of the peculiar shape of their eyes. This is why, when a farmer grabs hold of a pig, he is not able to make it stop squealing until he turns it upside down on its back. This quiets the pig, as if, by looking upward, the pig can see things it had never seen before, and it is startled into silence. Such are they whose eyes are ever turned to filthy things, who never look upward. Therefore, a man who exceeds many others in wickedness can be said to *feed swine.* Such are the keepers of brothels, the captains of brigands, and the chief among publicans. All these may be said to *feed swine.* This wretched man desires to satisfy his sin and no one can give him this satisfaction. For he who is habitual in sinful passions receives no satisfaction from them. The pleasure does not endure, but is there one moment and gone the next, and

---

[8] Ps. 33:9

[9] The three preceding quotations are all from Ps. 111.

[10] See I Cor. 6:16.

[11] See Gen. 6:4: *And the Lord God said, My spirit shall certainly not remain among these men for ever, because they are flesh.*

the wretched man is again left empty. Sin is likened to the pods[12] which the swine eat, because, like them, sin is sweet in taste yet rough and harsh in texture, giving momentary pleasure but causing ceaseless torments. Therefore, there is *no man* to provide satisfaction for him who takes pleasure in these wicked passions. Who can both satisfy him and quiet him? Cannot God? But God is not present, for the man who eats these things has travelled a far distance from God. Can the demons? They cannot, for they strive to accomplish just the opposite, namely, that wickedness never end or be satisfied.

17-21. And when he came to himself, he said, How many hired servants of my father's have bread enough and to spare, and I perish with hunger! I will arise and go to my father, and will say unto him, Father, I have sinned against heaven, and before thee, and am no longer worthy to be called thy son: make me as one of thy hired servants. And he arose, and came to his father. But when he was yet a great way off, his father saw him, and had compassion, and ran, and fell on his neck, and kissed him. And the son said unto him, Father, I have sinned against heaven, and in thy sight, and am no longer worthy to be called thy son. The man who until now had been prodigal *came to himself.* This is because he was "outside himself" and had taken leave of his true self so long as he committed foul deeds. Rightly is it said that he wasted and spent his essential property. This is why he was outside himself. For he who is not governed by logos, but lives irrationally without logos, and teaches others to do the same, is outside of himself and has abandoned his reason, which is his very essence. But when a man regains his logos [*analogizetai*] so as to see who he is and into what a state of wretchedness he has fallen, then he becomes himself again, and using his reason, he comes to repent and returns from his wanderings outside reason. He says *hired servants*, signifying the catechumens, who have not yet become sons because they have not yet been illumined by Holy Baptism. Indeed the catechumens have an abundance of the rational bread, the sustenance of the Word

---

[12] In Greek, *keratia*, "little horns," another name for the edible pods of the carob tree. See Vol. 1, *The Explanation* of St. Matthew, p. 33, footnote 4.

[Logos], because they hear each day the readings of Scripture.[13] Listen, so that you may learn the difference between a hired servant and a son. There are three ranks of those who are being saved. The first kind are like slaves who do what is good because they fear the judgment. This is what David means when he says, *Nail down my flesh with the fear of Thee, for of Thy judgments am I afraid.* The second kind, who are like hired servants, are those who are eager to serve God because of their desire for the reward of good things, as David again says, *I have inclined my heart to perform Thy statutes for ever for a recompense.* But if they are of the third kind, that is, if they are sons, they keep His commandments out of love for God. This is what David means when he says, *O how I have loved Thy law, O Lord! The whole day long it is my meditation;*[14] and again, with no mention of fear, *I lifted up my hands to Thy commandments which I have loved,*[15] and again, *Wonderful are Thy testimonies,* and because they are wonderful, *therefore hath my soul searched them out.*[16] One must understand the *hired servants* to refer not only to the catechumens, but also to all those in the Church who obey God out of some lesser motive than love. Therefore when a man is among the ranks of those who are sons, and then is disowned because of his sin, and sees others enjoying the divine gifts, and communing of the Divine Mysteries and of the Divine Bread, such a man ought indeed to apply to himself these piteous words, *How many hired servants of my father's have bread enough and to spare, and I perish with hunger! I will arise,* arise, that is, from my fall into sin, *and go to my Father, and will say unto him, Father, I have sinned against heaven, and before Thee.* When I abandoned heavenly things, I sinned against heaven, preferring shameful pleasure to heavenly things, and choosing the land of hunger instead of my true fatherland, heaven. Just as we have a saying that the man who prefers lead to gold sins against the gold, so too the man who prefers earthly things to heaven, sins against heaven. Indeed he has gone

---

[13] The first part of the Divine Liturgy, called The Liturgy of the Catechumens, consists primarily of the readings from the Psalter, the Epistles, and the Gospel. After this, in the ancient church, the catechumens actually left the temple as they were not able to partake of, or even to witness, the Mystical Bread.

[14] All three of the preceding quotations are from Ps. 118, verses 120, 112, and 97, respectively.

[15] Ps. 118:48

[16] Ps. 118:129

astray from the road that leads to heaven. Understand that when he sinned, he behaved as if he were not acting *in the sight of* God, that is, in the presence of God; but once he confesses his sin, then he realizes that he has sinned *in the sight of* God. *And he arose, and came to his father,* for we must not only desire the things that are dear to God but must get up and do them as well. You see the warm repentance—behold now the compassion of the father. He did not wait for his son to come to him, but he went and met him on the way and embraced him. God is called *Father* on account of His goodness and kindness, even though by nature He is God Who encompasses all things so that He could have restricted a man within His embrace, no matter which way the man might try to turn. As the prophet says, *The glory of God shall compass thee.*[17] Before, when the son distanced himself, it was fitting that God, as Father, release him from His embrace. But when the son drew near through prayer and repentance, it was fitting that God again enclose him within His embrace. Therefore the Father *falls on the neck* of the one who before had rebelled and who now shows that he has become obedient. And the Father kisses him, as a sign of reconciliation, and by this kiss He first makes holy the defiled one's mouth, which is as it were the doorway to the whole man, and through this doorway He sends sanctification into the innermost being.

22-24. But the father said to his servants, Bring forth the first robe, and put it on him; and put a ring on his hand, and shoes on his feet: and bring hither the grain-fed bullock, and kill it; and let us eat, and be merry: for this my son was dead, and is alive again; he was lost, and is found. And they began to be merry. The *servants* you may understand to mean the angels, the ministering spirits who are sent to serve those who are counted worthy of salvation. For the angels clothe the man who has turned from wickedness with *the first robe*, that is, with the original garment which we wore before we sinned, the garment of incorruption; or, it means that garment which is honored above all others, the robe of Baptism. For the baptismal robe is the first to be placed around me, and from it I receive a covering of my former shame and indecency. Therefore you may understand the *servants* to mean the angels

---

[17] Is. 58:8

who carry out all those things that are done on our behalf, and by means of which we are sanctified. You may also understand the *servants* to mean the priests. For they clothe the repentant sinner with Baptism and the word of teaching, placing around him *the first robe*, which is Christ Himself (for all we that have been baptized into Christ have put on Christ[18]). And they put *a ring on his hand,* which ring is the seal of Christ given at Chrismation so that we might execute good deeds in His name. The *hand* is a symbol of action, and the *ring* is a symbol of a seal. Therefore he who has been baptized, and, in general, everyone who has turned from wickedness, ought to have on his hand, that is, on his entire faculty of action, the seal and the mark of Christ, which is placed on him to show that he has been made new in the image of his Creator. You may also understand the ring to signify the *earnest of the Spirit.*[19]   By that I mean that God will give us perfect and complete good things when it is time for them; but for now He gives us gifts as earnest, that is, as tokens of assurance of those good things to come. For example, to some He gives the power to work miracles, to others the gift of teaching, and to others still other gifts; having received these gifts, we have more confident hope in the perfect and complete good things to come. And *shoes* are put on his feet to protect him from scorpions, that is, from the seemingly small and hidden sins described by David,[20] which are in fact deadly. And these *shoes* also protect him from serpents, that is, from those sins which can be seen by all. And, in another sense, shoes are given to him who has been counted worthy of *the first robe*: God makes such a man ready to preach the Gospel and to bring benefit to others. This is Christianity—to benefit one's neighbor. We are not ignorant of what is meant by *the grain-fed bullock*[21] which is slain and eaten. It is none other than the very Son of God, Who as a Man took flesh which is

---

[18] See Gal. 3:27. This verse is also chanted as a hymn at every Baptism and at the great feasts of the Lord.

[19] See II Cor. 1:21-22. *Now He Which establisheth us with you in Christ, and hath anointed us, is God; Who hath also sealed us, and given the earnest of the Spirit in our hearts.*

[20] See Ps. 18:12. *From my secret sins cleanse me.*

[21] To translate *ton moschon ton siteuton* as "the fatted calf", as does the KJV, does not allow the reader to see what is so clear in the Greek: that the animal in question is male, a young bullock, raised on grain, in deliberate anticipation of its slaughter for food or for sacrifice. The Greek adjective *siteutos,* derived from the noun *sitos, grain,* means "of grain" or "made of grain."

irrational and animal by nature, although He filled it with His own glory. Thus Christ is symbolized by the bullock, the Youngling which has never been put under the yoke of the law of sin; and He is *grain-fed* in the sense that Christ was set apart and prepared for this mystery from before the foundation of the world. And though it may seem somewhat difficult to take in, nevertheless it shall be said: the Bread which we break in the Eucharist appears to our eyes to be made of wheat [*sitos*] and thus may be called *of wheat* [*siteutos*]; but in reality it is Flesh, and thus may be called the *Bullock*. For Christ Himself is both Bullock and Wheat. Therefore every one who is baptized and becomes a son of God, or rather, is restored to the status of son, and in general, every one who is cleansed from sin, communes of this Bullock of Wheat. Then he becomes the cause of gladness to the Father and to His servants, namely, the angels and the priests, because he who was dead is alive again, and he who was lost is found. For whoever is dead from the abundance of his wickedness is without hope; but whoever is able, with his changeable human nature, to change from wickedness to virtue, is said to be only *lost*. To be lost is less severe than to be dead.

25-32. Now his elder son was in the field: and as he came and drew nigh to the house, he heard music and dancing. And he called one of the servants, and asked what these things meant. And he said unto him, Thy brother is come; and thy father hath killed the grain-fed bullock, because he hath received him safe and sound. And he was angry, and would not go in: therefore came his father out, and entreated him. And he answering said to his father, Lo, these many years do I serve thee, neither transgressed I at any time thy commandment: and yet thou never gavest me a kid, that I might make merry with my friends: but as soon as this thy son was come, who hath devoured thy living with harlots, thou hast killed for him the grain-fed bullock. And he said unto him, Son, thou art ever with me, and all that I have is thine. It was meet that we should make merry, and be glad: for this thy brother was dead, and is alive again; and was lost, and is found. Here is the celebrated question—how is it that the son who lived a God-pleasing life in all other respects, and who faithfully served his father, could display such envy? The question will be answered if one considers the reason why this parable was told. This parable and the ones preceding it were told because the Pharisees, who considered themselves pure and righteous, were grumbling at the Lord because He received harlots and publicans. The Pharisees murmured indignantly, believing themselves to be more righteous than the publicans, and therefore the Lord taught this parable. Consider that the figure of the son who is seen to grumble is understood to refer to all those who are scandalized at the sudden good fortune and deliverance of sinners. Such men grumble, not because of envy, but because neither they nor we can understand the outpouring of God's compassion for man. Does not David bring forward the figure of a man scandalized at *the peace of sinners*?[22] And Jeremiah likewise, when he says, *Why is it that the way of ungodly men prosper? Thou hast planted them, and they have taken root.*[23] Such thoughts reflect man's weak and poor understanding, which easily ignites with annoyance and questions the good fortune of the wicked, which seems undeserved. In this parable, therefore, the Lord is saying to the Pharisees words like these: ''Let us suppose that you are as righteous as that elder son and well-pleasing to the Father; I entreat you who are righteous and pure not to grumble, as this elder son did, against the gladness which we are showing over the salvation of the sinner, who is also a son.'' Do you see that this parable is not about envy? Instead, by means of this parable, the Lord is instructing the minds of the Pharisees, so that they will not be vexed that the Lord receives sinners, even though they themselves are righteous and have fulfilled every commandment of God. It is no wonder that we do become vexed at those who appear undeserving. For God's compassion is so great, and He gives to us so abundantly of His own good things, that we may even grumble at God's generosity. That criticism follows generosity is a fact to which we refer in everyday speech. If we do good to someone who fails to thank us, do we not say to him, ''Everyone says I am a fool for having been so good to you''? We use this expression, even if no one has actually criticized us, because extreme generosity is so often followed by criticism that to suggest the latter is to prove the former. But let us turn to the particulars of the parable, in brief. The elder son was in the field, that is, in this world, working his own land, meaning his flesh, so that he might have his fill of bread, sowing with tears so that he might reap with rejoicing.

---

[22] Ps. 72:3

[23] Jer. 12:1-2

When he learned what was being done, he did not want to enter into the common joy. But the compassionate father goes out and begs him to come in, and explains to him the reason for the joy, that a man who was dead has come back to life. Because as a man he did not understand, and because he was scandalized, the elder son accused the father of not giving him even a young goat, while for the prodigal son he slaughtered the fatted calf. What does the *kid*, the young goat, signify? You may learn here. Every young goat is considered to be of the portion of sinners who are placed on the left side. The righteous son is saying, then, ''I have passed my life in toil and labor, I have been persecuted, suffered hardships, been oppressed by sinners, and on my behalf you have never slaughtered and killed a kid, that is, a sinner who afflicts me, so that I might have some small measure of rest.'' For example, King Ahab was just such a goat to the Prophet Elijah. Ahab persecuted Elijah, but the Lord did not quickly give this goat over to the slaughter so that Elijah could have some small rest, and take his ease with his friends, the prophets. Therefore Elijah complained to God, *Lord, they have digged down Thine altars, and have slain Thy prophets.*[24] And Saul was a goat to David, as were also all those who slandered David. But the Lord allowed them to tempt him, and did not slay them to give David some rest. Therefore David said, *How long shall sinners, O Lord, how long shall sinners boast?*[25] The elder son in the parable is saying these things: ''You did not count me worthy of any consolation in all my toils; you never handed over to me for slaughter any of these who were afflicting me. But now you save the prodigal son who never had to toil.'' This, then, is the entire purpose of the parable, which the Lord told for the sake of the Pharisees who were grumbling that He had accepted sinners. The parable also instructs us that no matter how righteous we may be, we ought not to rebuff sinners, nor to grumble when God accepts them. The younger son, therefore, represents the harlots and the publicans; the elder son represents those Pharisees and scribes who consider themselves righteous. It is as if God were saying, ''Let us suppose that you are indeed righteous and have not transgressed any commandments; if some others have turned away from wickedness, why do you not accept them

---

[24] III Kings 19:10

[25] Ps. 93:3

as your brothers and fellow laborers?'' The Lord instructs such grumblers as these with this parable. I am not unaware that some have interpreted the elder son to signify the angels, and the younger son, the latter-born nature of men which rebelled against the commandment it was given and went astray. Still others have said that the two sons represent the Israelites and the Gentiles who later believed. But the simple truth is what we have said here, namely, that the person of the elder son should be understood to signify the righteous, and the person of the younger son, to signify sinners who have repented and returned. The entirety of the parable is given for the sake of the Pharisees, to teach them not to be vexed that sinners are received, even if they themselves are righteous. Therefore, let no one be vexed at the judgments of God, but let him be patient with those apparent sinners who prosper, and are saved. For how do you know if a man whom you think is a sinner has not repented, and on this account has been accepted? Or that he has secret virtues on account of which God looks favorably upon him?

CHAPTER SIXTEEN

Concerning the steward of unrighteousness.
That not even one tittle of the law will pass away.
On not divorcing one's wife.
Concerning the rich man and Lazarus.

1-9. And He said also unto His disciples, There was a certain rich man, who had a steward; and the same was accused unto him that he had wasted his goods. And he called him, and said unto him, What is this I hear of thee? Give an accounting of thy stewardship; for thou canst no longer be steward. Then the steward said within himself, What shall I do? For my lord taketh away from me the stewardship: I cannot dig; to beg I am ashamed. I am resolved what to do, that, when I am put out of the stewardship, they may receive me into their houses. So he called every one of his lord's debtors unto him, and said unto the first, How much owest thou unto my lord? And he said, An hundred measures of oil. And he said unto him, Take thy bill, and sit down quickly, and write fifty. Then said he to another, And how much owest thou? And he said, An hundred measures of wheat. And he said unto him, Take thy bill, and write fourscore. And the lord commended the steward of unrighteousness, because he had done wisely; for the sons of this world are in their generation wiser than the sons of light. And I say unto you, Make to yourselves friends from the mammon of unrighteousness; that, when ye fail, they may receive you into everlasting habitations. Each parable indirectly and figuratively reveals the nature of certain things, but it is not similar in every respect to the things which it describes. Therefore it is not necessary to scrutinize in great detail every part of a parable; we should only draw benefit from that part of the parable which is central to its purpose. The other parts, which provide just the structure of the parable and do not contribute to its meaning, we should let alone. Such is the case with this parable. If we attempt to examine every part in detail—who is the steward? who is the one who made him steward? by whom was he accused? who are the debtors? why does one debtor owe wheat and another oil, why in measures of a hundred?—if we examine and belabor every such point, we shall render the entire discourse obscure and unintelligible. We may even make the explanation appear ridiculous because so much of it, by necessity, will be uncertain. Therefore we must attempt to receive from this parable just the benefit that it contains. The Lord here desires to teach us to use well the wealth that has been given to us. First we learn that we are not masters of our own money, for we have nothing that is our own. We are merely stewards of things that belong to another, namely, our divine Master, Who has entrusted those things into our hands so that we might use them well and as He directs. But if we do not handle the stewardship of wealth according to the mind of the Master, but misuse what has been given to us by squandering it on ourselves, we are *accused* stewards. For it is the will of the Master that we use what has been given to us for the needs of our fellow servants,[1] and not for our own pleasures. When we are accused and about to be removed from the office of steward, namely, when we are about to be taken from this life and to give an accounting of our stewardship after our departure from this life, if we are wise, we understand what we must do even at this late hour. We must make friends for ourselves by means of this *mammon of unrighteousness*, which is the money and wealth the Lord has given us to spend for the needs of our brothers and fellow-servants, but which we have hoarded for ourselves. But, even though it is late, we understand where we are headed, and that there will be nothing we can do when that day comes. Then it will not be the time for labor, nor will it be seemly to beg, for the virgins who beg are called foolish.[2] What should we do? We should divide this wealth among our brethren, so that when we *fail* here, that is, when we depart from this life, the poor will *receive* us *into everlasting habitations*. The everlasting habitations have been reserved for the poor in Christ, and these poor are able to welcome into their heavenly habitations those who befriended them in this life by giving them that wealth which should have been given to them in the first place because it is the Master's. These are those debtors of whom it is said, *All day long the righteous showeth mercy, and*

---

[1] The Greek word *oikonomos,* translated here as *steward,* means literally ''the house bursar'', that is, the household servant entrusted with all disbursements relating to the running of the house and the welfare of his fellow servants.

[2] See the parable of the ten virgins in Vol. 1, *The Explanation* of St. Matthew, pp. 214-215.

lendeth,[3] and again, *He that showeth mercy to the poor lends to God.*[4] We ought previously to have given all to these good debtors who pay back a hundredfold. Although we are found to be stewards of unrighteousness who have unrighteously kept back for ourselves that which was appointed for others, let us not persist forever in our inhumanity, but let us distribute to the poor, so that we may be received by them into the everlasting habitations. Therefore, when we understand the parable this way, nothing in the explanation appears excessive, belabored, or fantastic. The words, *The sons of this world are in their generation wiser than the sons of light,* appear to have a strange meaning. But there is nothing here that is strange, or that does not follow. He calls *the sons of this world* those who think only about the things of the earth which bring profit to them; He calls *the sons of light* those who make it their duty to administer spiritual wealth in a God pleasing manner. What He is saying is this: those who become stewards of human affairs do all within their power to insure that when they are removed from their position of stewardship, they might enjoy some comfort. But those who are ranked among the sons of light, that is, those who have been entrusted with the spiritual stewardship of wealth, foolishly ignore how this wealth can benefit them after this life is over.[5] *The sons of this world,* therefore, are those entrusted with the stewardship of human affairs, and *in their generation,* that is, in this life, they administer things shrewdly and with foresight for their own material advantage. *The sons of light* are those who receive monies in order to administer them in a manner pleasing to God. Therefore we find that in positions of worldly responsibility we administer and handle affairs shrewdly for our own advantage, so that if we should lose our position we will have a refuge in the future. But with those monies that ought to be administered according to God's will, we see that we are imprudent and have made no provisions against that day when we are taken from life and must give a reckoning of our stewardship. Then we will find ourselves devoid of any consolation. We are

---

[3] Ps. 36:26

[4] Prov. 19:17

[5] An apostolic example of the spiritual stewardship of wealth, wisely exercised, may be found in the *Life* of the Holy Apostle Thomas. See *The Great Collection of the Lives of the Saints, Volume 2: October,* Chrysostom Press, House Springs, Missouri, 1995, pp. 106-120.

called foolish because we took no thought for the things that might profit us after this life. Therefore, let us make for ourselves friends of the poor, and distribute to them from the wealth of unrighteousness, that is, from the wealth that has been given to us by God to be a weapon of righteousness, but which we have retained for ourselves and thus changed into unrighteousness. And if wealth that has been acquired supposedly by righteous means is considered *unrighteousness* and *mammon* when it is not rightly administered and given to the poor, how much more so will wealth that has been acquired by unrighteous means be deemed iniquitous? Therefore, let us make friends for ourselves from this wealth, so that when we *fail* and depart from this life, and when we are fainthearted as we face judgment, these friends may receive us there into everlasting habitations.

10-13. He that is faithful in that which is least is faithful also in much: and he that is unrighteous in the least is unrighteous also in much. If therefore ye have not been faithful in the unrighteous mammon, who will commit to your trust the true riches? And if ye have not been faithful in that which is another's, who shall give you that which is your own? No servant can serve two masters: for either he will hate the one, and love the other; or else he will hold to the one, and despise the other. Ye cannot serve God and mammon. He is still teaching concerning the need to administer wealth according to God's will. *He that is faithful in that which is least*, that is, he who administers well the wealth that has been entrusted to him in this world, *is faithful also in much*, that is, in the age to come he is worthy to be trusted with true wealth. Earthly wealth He calls *least* because it is small and insignificant; indeed, it is nothing at all, since it is transitory. But the heavenly wealth He calls *much* because it endures forever, and even increases. He who is shown to be unrighteous in his handling of earthly wealth, usurping for himself the things that were given to him for the common need of the brethren, will not be found worthy to be trusted with that heavenly wealth, and he will be cast out as unrighteous. Interpreting what was just said, the Lord adds, *If therefore ye have not been faithful in the unrighteous mammon, who will commit to your trust the true riches?* He names as *unrighteous mammon* that wealth which we have in our possession; if it were righteous wealth, we would no longer have it. But now, since we still have it, it is abundantly clear that we kept it for ourselves and did not distribute it to the poor, and thus it is unrighteous. This is nothing less than embezzlement of money belonging to someone else. This is wealth that belongs to the poor and to withhold it is unrighteousness. Therefore, how can a man who poorly and unfaithfully administers this wealth be entrusted with the true wealth? The wealth we have accumulated in this life is also *another's* in the sense that we were born naked and brought nothing into the world. Therefore, to us who have not been faithful in the money *which is another's*, whether it belongs to the poor or has been derived from another, to us, I say, who have not been faithful in these things, *who shall give* us *that which is* our *own? Our own* is the heavenly and divine wealth, for there in heaven is man's true citizenship and birthright. The money and possessions of man who has been created in the image of God are indeed *another's* and alien to man because neither money nor possessions resemble man. But the enjoyment of divine things and communion with God—these are *our own.* Up to this point, the Lord has been teaching us how we ought to be faithful stewards of wealth, for wealth is *another's* and not our own. We are stewards and not lords and masters. Since the God-pleasing steward-ship of wealth cannot be accomplished without detachment from riches, the Lord adds to His teaching, and says, *Ye cannot serve God and mammon,* that is, it is impossible for a man who is passionately attached to wealth, and who holds back even a part of it, to be a servant of God. Therefore, if you intend to be a faithful steward of wealth, do not *serve* wealth, which means, do not have any tie of affection to wealth, but truly serve God. Everywhere the Gospel condemns the love of money, which is the impassioned bond of affection and devotion to wealth.

14-15. And the Pharisees also, who were loved money, heard all these things: and they derided Him. And He said unto them, Ye are they which account yourselves righteous before men; but God knoweth your hearts: for that which is highly esteemed among men is abomination in the sight of God. The Pharisees were mocking the Lord because they had been stung by His words. Being lovers of money, they were not pleased by what they had heard about non-possession, for as it has been said, *Godliness is an abomination to the sinner,*[6] and

---

[6] Ecclesiasticus 1:24

reproofs are scourges to the impious. The Lord reveals their hidden wickedness and shows that despite their feigned righteousness, they are an abomination in the sight of God on account of their haughty self-conceit. The Lord thus says, *"Ye are they which count yourselves righteous.* You think that only to you has it been given to understand and to teach the things that are important. Therefore you sneer at My words as if they were the words of a foolish man, because you want the multitude to consider you the teachers of truth. But it is not so, for God knows your hearts, and He considers you an abomination on account of your arrogance and your desire to be esteemed by men. *That which is highly esteemed among men is abomination in the sight of God* for every proud heart is unclean in God's eyes. Therefore, O Pharisees, you ought not to live for the praise of men, *for God has scattered the bones of man-pleasers.*[7] You ought rather to make yourselves righteous in the sight of God.''

16-18. The law and the prophets were until John: since that time the good tidings of the kingdom of God are proclaimed, and every man is pressing into it. And it is easier for heaven and earth to pass away, than one tittle of the law to fall. Whosoever putteth away his wife, and marrieth another, committeth adultery: and whosoever marrieth her that is divorced from her husband committeth adultery. These words seem to be disjointed and to have no connection with what was said before. But to him who is attentive, these words are not disjointed; indeed, they follow closely upon what came before. He Himself had introduced the teaching of non-possession in what He said above, and had called wealth *unrighteous mammon,* even though the law spoke of wealth as a blessing,[8] and the prophets promised the good things of the earth.[9] Therefore He wished to forestall anyone who might say to Him in derision, as the Pharisees did, ''Who are You to speak thus? Do You stand in opposition to the law? The law speaks of wealth as a blessing, but You teach non-possession.'' This is why He says, ''Until John it was the season of the law and the prophets, and they

---

[7] Ps. 52:7

[8] See Deut. 28:1-6.

[9] See Is. 1:19.

taught well, as long as their listeners were in their infancy. But then there came John, who was all but immaterial, like an angel, so complete was his non-possession. *Since that time,* I mean, since the time when John proclaimed the kingdom of heaven, it is no longer the time for the good things of the earth; instead, the kingdom of heaven is proclaimed. Therefore, those who long for heaven ought to practice non-possession on earth. Because the prophets and the law made no mention of a kingdom of heaven, it was fitting that they promised the good things of the earth to those who had not yet reached maturity and who were unable to comprehend anything of the ascetic way of life which leads to heaven. Therefore, O Pharisees, I must now teach non-possession, since the time has passed for the imperfect and incomplete commandments of the law.'' Lest they say, "So, then, all the law is rejected because it is useless and empty?'' He answers, "Not at all. Rather, the law now has been fulfilled and completed.'' Whatever the law had sketched in outline, whether speaking in types concerning Christ, or in reference to the commandments, these things have now been filled in. Not a single element of this sketch, not even a tittle, that is, an accent mark, will be shown to be useless. Those things concerning Christ which appeared then in the law in a shadowy fashion have now been perfectly revealed. And the commandments of the law, which at that time were given to fit the understanding of men who were immature, now have a more lofty and perfect sense. It is clear from what the Lord is saying that the law spoke incompletely to those who were imperfect in understanding. The law concerning divorce was spoken in response to the hardness of heart of the Hebrews, so that if a man should hate his wife he might have the authority to divorce her, lest something worse occur. For they were murderous and bloodthirsty, and did not spare those closest to them, but sacrificed even their sons and daughters to the demons. Such was the coarse and imperfect nature of the law, for then it was the time for this kind of lawgiving; but now there is need for another, more perfect teaching. "This is why I say, *Whoso putteth away his wife,* except for reason of fornication,[10] *and marrieth another, committeth adultery.* So it is no wonder that I should speak concerning non-possession, although the law teaches nothing explicitly on this. Behold, the law does not differ

---

[10] See Mt. 19:9.

from Me when it permits divorce on account of the bloodthirstiness of the Jews, whereas I train My listeners to what is more perfect and forbid unjustifiable divorce. I do not speak in opposition to the law; on the contrary, I uphold the intent of the law, which was, to prevent murder between husband and wife. I give the same commandment when I instruct husbands and wives to care for each other and to be forbearing with one another because they are members of each other. This is also what the law intended, but because its listeners were imperfect, the law permitted divorce so that husband and wife might spare, and not kill, each other.'' Therefore, Christ has upheld the law,[11] and so He spoke rightly when He said that not one tittle of the law should fall. How could the law fall? It is being correctly upheld by Christ.

19-22. And there was a certain rich man, who was clothed in purple and fine linen, and fared sumptuously every day. And there was a certain poor man named Lazarus, who was laid at his gate, full of sores, and desiring to be fed with the crumbs which fell from the rich man's table: moreover the dogs came and licked his sores. And it came to pass, that the poor man died, and was carried by the angels into Abraham's bosom: the rich man also died, and was buried. These words follow closely upon what was said before. Because the Lord first taught, above, how we are to be good stewards of wealth, now He appropriately adds this parable which teaches the same thing through the example of the rich man. This is a parable and not, as some have foolishly imagined, something which actually occurred. For good things have not yet been allotted to the righteous, nor punishments to the sinners. The Lord, then, fashioned this story to teach those who show no mercy and give no alms what punishments await them, and to teach those who are suffering what good things they will enjoy on account of the sufferings they patiently endure in this life. The Lord gave no name to the rich man in this parable, because such a man is not worthy to be remembered by God by name. As the Lord says, through the prophet, *nor will I make remembrance of their names through My lips.*[12] But the Lord

---

[11] See Rom: 3:31. *Do we then make void the law through faith? God forbid: instead, we uphold the law.*

[12] Ps. 15:3

mentions the poor man by name, for the names of the righteous are inscribed in the Book of Life. There is a story, according to the tradition of the Hebrews, of a certain Lazarus who lived at that time in Jerusalem, whose lot was one of extreme poverty and sickness. Because he was so well known in the city, the Lord uses his name in the parable. The rich man was awash in wealth, so much so that he clothed himself in purple and costly linen. Not only this, but he also luxuriated in every other kind of luxury. For it says that *he fared sumptuously*, not now and then, but *everyday*, and not in moderation, but *sumptuously*, meaning, extravagantly and at great cost. But Lazarus was destitute and grievously diseased, for it says that he was *full of sores*. It is one thing to be ill; it is another thing to be covered with open sores. But the evil which he suffered goes even further: lying at the gate of the rich man, he had the added torment of seeing others feasting to excess while he himself starved. He desired to be fed, not with their costly foods, but with the crumbs of these foods, the same crumbs which the dogs ate. He was also destitute of any help, for *the dogs licked his sores*, and he had no one to drive them away. Lazarus suffered such terrible things. Did he then blaspheme? Did he revile the luxury of the rich man? Did he condemn his callousness? Did he accuse the Divine Providence? He did none of these things, even in thought; rather, he bravely and wisely endured all. How do we know this? From the fact that the angels took him when he died. For if he had been a grumbler and a blasphemer, he would not have been deemed worthy of such an honor, to be escorted by the angels. *The rich man also died, and was buried.* In truth, while he still lived his soul had been buried alive, entombed within his flesh. Therefore, when he died, his soul was not led away by the angels but instead was borne downwards into hades. He who has never had a single lofty or heavenly thought deserves the lowest place. Thus by saying that he *was buried*, the Lord implies that the rich man's soul received its portion in the lowest and darkest place.

23-26. And in hades he lift up his eyes, being in torments, and seeth Abraham afar off, and Lazarus in his bosom. And he cried and said, Father Abraham, have mercy on me, and send Lazarus, that he may dip the tip of his finger in water, and cool my tongue; for I am tormented in this flame. But Abraham said, Son, remember that thou in thy lifetime receivedst thy good things, and likewise Lazarus evil

**things: but now he is comforted, and thou art tormented. And beside
all this, between us and you there is a great gulf fixed: so that they
which would pass from hence to you cannot; neither can they pass to
us, that would come from thence.** When the Lord cast Adam out of
paradise He settled him in a place just opposite, so that the continuous
sight of paradise before his eyes would keep fresh in his mind the
calamity that had befallen him and would arouse in him a sharper sense
of his fall from good things. In like manner the Lord condemned the rich
man to a place just opposite Lazarus, so that the sight of him in such a
blessed state might awaken in the rich man the realization of the good
things he lost because of his cruelty. Why was it that he saw Lazarus in
the bosom *of Abraham,* and not of any other of the righteous? Because
Abraham showed hospitality to strangers. The rich man sees Lazarus with
Abraham as a reproof of his own inhospitality. For Abraham used to
draw into his own house even those who were just passing by, while the
rich man overlooked a man who was lying within his very courtyard. And
why does the rich man address his words to Abraham, and not to
Lazarus? Perhaps he was ashamed. It may be that he judged Lazarus to
be no different than himself and therefore assumed that Lazarus would
bear a grudge for past wrongs. ''If I, while enjoying such great prosperity, overlooked him while he was suffering such great afflictions, and did
not even give him the crumbs from my table, how much more will he
who was thus despised now remember those past wrongs and refuse to
grant me any favor?'' This is why he addresses his words to Abraham,
thinking that the patriarch would be unaware of what had happened. How
then does Abraham respond? Does he say, ''O cruel and heartless man!
Are you not ashamed? Only now do you remember compassion?'' Not
this, but rather, *Son.* Behold a compassionate and holy soul! For a certain
wise man has said, ''Trouble not a soul that has been brought low.'' This
is why Abraham says, *Son.* By this he also intimates that it is within his
power only to speak to him gently, but more than this he is not permitted
to do. ''That which I have to give, I give you—a voice of compassion.
But to go from here to there I cannot, for all things have been shut. And
you have received your good things, and in like manner Lazarus evil
things.'' Why does he use the [Greek] word *apelabes, thou receivedst,*
and not the [simpler Greek] word *elabes?* We say [in Greek] that a
recipient *receives [apolambanei]* those things which are his due. What
then do we learn? That even if a man is utterly defiled and has reached

the last degree of wickedness, perhaps he has done at least one or two good things. So that even such a man may have some good things, as when he obtains prosperity in this life as his reward, and thus it may be said that he has received these things as his due. Likewise Lazarus received evil things as his due. For perhaps he also did one or two evil things, and he received as his merited reward for these evil things the suffering which he endured in this life. Therefore now he is comforted, while you are in torment. The chasm indicates the separation and the difference that exists between the righteous and the sinners. Just as their choices were far different in this life, so too their dwelling places in the next life are separated by a great distance, each one receiving as his due the reward appropriate to his choices in this life. Mark here a conclusion to be drawn against the Origenists who say that there will be a time when there is an end to hell, that the sinners will be united with the righteous and with God, and that thus God will become all in all. Let us hear what Abraham says, that they who would pass from hence to you, or from thence to us, cannot. Therefore it is impossible for anyone to go from the place apportioned to the righteous to the place of the sinners, and likewise, Abraham teaches us, it is impossible to go from the place of punishment to the place of the righteous. And Abraham, I presume, is more trustworthy than Origen.[13] What is hades? Some say that it is a place of darkness beneath the earth; others have said that hades is the departure of the soul from that which is seen to that which is unseen and invisible. While the soul is in the body, it is manifest through its own energies [which animate the body], but when the soul has departed from the body it becomes invisible.[14] This is hades, they say. *The bosom of Abraham* is the enclosure within which are stored up the good things that await the righteous, who after the storm have found the heavenly haven. We use the same word to name those bodies of water on the sea which are shaped like harbors and havens.[15] Mark this as well, that on that day of judgment, the man who did wrong will see the one he wronged in the glory that is his, and the man who was wronged will likewise see the one

---

[13] Origen's teaching of *apokatastasis*, the ultimate restoration and reconciliation of everyone, even Satan, was condemned as heresy at the Fifth Ecumenical Council held in Constantinople in 553 A.D.

[14] Bl. Theophylact here provides the connection between the Greek word, *adēs*, *hades*, and its etymological root, *aeidēs*, *invisible*.

[15] The Greek word *kolpos* means both *bosom* and *bay*.

who wronged him in that condemnation which befalls him, just as here in this parable the rich man sees Lazarus, and Lazarus the rich man.

27-31. Then he said, I pray thee therefore, father, that thou wouldest send him to my father's house: for I have five brethren; that he may testify unto them, lest they also come into this place of torment. Abraham saith unto him, They have Moses and the prophets; let them hear them. And he said, Nay, father Abraham: but if one went unto them from the dead, they will repent. And he said unto him, If they hear not Moses and the prophets, neither will they be persuaded, though one rose from the dead. The miserable rich man, having failed in his request for himself, now makes supplication on behalf of others. See how punishment has led him to awareness. He who before had overlooked Lazarus as he lay at his feet now thinks of others who are absent, and begs that Lazarus be sent from the dead to his father's house. He asks that not just anyone of the dead, but Lazarus in particular, be sent, so that the rich man's brothers might see him crowned with health and glory. They who once saw him in sickness and in dishonor and were witnesses of his poverty, would be witnesses of his glory. From this it is clear that Lazarus would have appeared to them in glory, had it been necessary to send him as a believable messenger. How then does Abraham reply? *They have Moses.* "You do not take care of your brothers," he is saying, "as well as He Who created them, God Himself. For He has appointed ten thousand teachers for them." But the rich man answers, *Nay, father.* Since he himself had heard the Scriptures and did not believe, considering the readings to be myths, he suspected that it was the same for his brothers. Judging them by what he knew to be true of himself, he said that they gave no more heed to the Scriptures than he did, but that if one should rise from the dead then they would believe. There are those even now who say the same: "Who knows what is in hades? Who has ever come from there to tell us?" But let them hear Abraham who says that if we do not give heed to the Scriptures, we will not believe even those who come from hades. The Jews showed this to be true. Because they gave no heed to the Scriptures, they did not believe when they saw the dead resurrected, but even attempted to slay that other Lazarus who was four days dead. Many of the dead arose at the Lord's Crucifixion, yet this only intensified the Jews' murderous assault against the apostles. If raising the dead would truly help us to believe, the Lord would do this often. But there is no help so great as the close study of the Scriptures. For the devil by trickery has appeared to raise the dead and by this means has deceived the foolish; and concerning those in hades he spreads doctrines worthy of his own wickedness. But no such trickery can prevail against those who make wise study of the Scriptures. For the Scriptures are a lamp and a light,[16] and when light shines, the thief appears and is discovered. Therefore, let us believe the Scriptures and let us not seek out resurrections from the dead. The parable may also be understood in a more figurative sense. The rich man represents the Hebrew people. Of old this people was rich in all knowledge and wisdom, and in the words of God which are more precious than gold and many costly stones. And this people was clothed in purple and fine linen, having both kingship and priesthood, being *a royal priesthood* to God.[17] The purple signifies kingship and the fine linen priesthood, for the Levites used fine linen cloth for the priestly vestments. The Hebrews *fared sumptuously everyday*. Everyday they offered morning and evening sacrifices, which were called the *constant offering*.[18] Lazarus represents the people from among the Gentiles, destitute of divine grace and wisdom, lying before the gates. For the Gentiles were not permitted to enter the house of God; this was considered a defilement, as when, in the Book of Acts, an outcry was made against Paul for bringing Gentiles into the temple and defiling that holy place.[19] The Gentiles were covered with the sores of festering sin, on which impudent dogs, the demons, were feeding. For our sores are pleasure to the demons. And the Gentiles longed for the crumbs which fell from the table of the rich man. They had no share at all of that *bread* which *strengtheneth man's heart*,[20] and they were in need of those most subtle and refined particles of the rational food, like the Canaanite woman desired to be fed from the crumbs, even though she was a Gentile.[21] What then? The Hebrew people died to God, and their bones, which made no movement towards

---

[16] See Proverbs 6:23.

[17] Ex. 19:6

[18] *endelechismos*, Ex. 29:38,42

[19] Acts 21

[20] Ps. 103:17

[21] Mt. 15

the good, became stiff in death. But Lazarus, the Gentile people, died to sin, and the Jews, who died in their sins, burn with the flame of spite. They are envious, as the Apostle says, that the Gentiles have been accepted unto faith,[22] and that the people of the nations, who before were destitute and dishonored, are now in the bosom of Abraham, the father of the nations, and rightly so. For Abraham, himself a Gentile, believed in God, and changed from idolatry to the knowledge of God. Therefore it is right that those who share in his change and in his faith should also find rest in his bosom, and inherit his same portion, dwelling place, and store of good things. The Jew desires just one drop of the old sprinklings and purifications of the law in order to cool his tongue, that he might have the boldness to say to us that the law is still in effect. But he does not obtain his desire. For the law was until John the Forerunner and from then *sacrifice and offering hast Thou not desired*, as the prophet foretold.[23] And Daniel foretold that *the anointing [chrisma] shall be destroyed*,[24] and prophecy shall be sealed,[25] meaning, that prophecy shall cease and be closed. But you, O reader, must also understand the moral meaning of this parable. Do not be rich in wickedness and overlook your mind which is starved and cast down, although it was created to be borne aloft. Do not let it wander outside, nor let it lie idly on the ground, but lead it within and let it act. Then there will be in you the working of the mind and the spirit, and not merely the feasting of the flesh. Likewise, there are other elements of this parable which may easily be understood for your moral benefit.

---

[22] See Rom. 11:11.

[23] Ps. 39:9

[24] Dan. 9:26

[25] See Dan. 12:4, 9.

CHAPTER SEVENTEEN

Concerning offenses.
On forgiving thy brother's sins.
Concerning faith in God.
Concerning the ten lepers.
Concerning the questioning of Jesus
as to when the kingdom of God should come.

1-4. Then said He unto the disciples, It is impossible but that offences will come: but woe unto him, through whom they come! It were better for him that a millstone were hanged about his neck, and he cast into the sea, than that he should offend one of these little ones. Take heed to yourselves: If thy brother trespass against thee, rebuke him; and if he repent, forgive him. And if he trespass against thee seven times in a day, and seven times in a day turn again to thee, saying, I repent; thou shalt forgive him. Because the Pharisees, who were lovers of money, were murmuring against the Lord for speaking about non-possession, He gave them the parable of the rich man and Lazarus to show what kind of punishment awaited them on account of their love of wealth. Now the Lord speaks to the disciples concerning these same Pharisees, revealing the Pharisees to be men who set stumbling blocks and obstacles along the path to God; because of this, the Lord makes clear that woe will be their lot. Let us see what it is He is saying. *It is impossible but that offences will come: but woe unto him through whom they come! Offences* mean hindrances and stumbling blocks to the living of a good and God-pleasing life.[1] Because of the great evil among men, it necessarily follows that there will be many hindrances to the preaching of the Gospel and the Truth. *But woe unto him through whom they come,* woe to the worker of these offences, such as the Pharisees who impeded and obstructed the preaching. But some, who do not understand, might ask, "If it is inevitable that offenses come, and if it is impossible that the preaching not be obstructed, why, O Lord, dost Thou condemn and cry woe to the workers of offences? These things

---

[1] The Greek word *skandalon,* rendered as *offence* in the King James text, is the root of the English word *scandal* and has the literal meaning of *stumbling block* or *obstacle.*

have occurred by necessity, and surely that which is unavoidable may be forgiven.'' But listen: this ''necessity'' follows from a free exercise of will and choice. The Lord saw the wickedness of the people at that time, and how they were inclined towards evil, and how they set their will on nothing good. As a consequence of what He observed, He said that it was inevitable that offences should come. The evil which men practiced was by their own choice, and the stumbling blocks which they made were a necessary consequence of their evil. Therefore, the workers of these offences deserve to be punished. For example, when a doctor sees a man leading a wretched way of life, given over to excessive eating and drinking, he might say, ''It is inevitable that this man will become ill.'' Is the illness indeed inevitable? Yes, inasmuch as it a necessary consequence of his manner of living. Therefore, woe to those who obstruct the preaching of the Gospel! They have attained to such a degree of wickedness that it is inevitable that they will cause others to stumble. It would be better for that man who causes offences and obstructions if a millstone were hanged about his neck and that he be cast into the sea, than he should cause one of those who are little in faith to stumble and fall away. Therefore He protects His disciples, and says, *Take heed to yourselves*. What He is saying is this: ''Behold, I am telling you beforehand that evils will come; and being forewarned, you have no excuse. It is necessary that evils come, but it is not necessary that you should perish, if you protect and arm yourselves. It is inevitable that the wolf should come, but if the shepherd is awake, it is not inevitable that the sheep be destroyed. Instead, the wolf will again depart, its jaws gaping in vain.'' He said these things concerning those who cause offence and harm, that is, who obstruct, because those who do these things are of many different kinds. Some are incurable, as were the Pharisees; others are treatable, as were the brothers of the Lord in their dealings with Him, who did not at first believe in Him. Because there are many different kinds of those who cause offence, it is likely that among them there may even be fellow believers. This is why the Lord says, *If thy brother trespass against thee, go and admonish him between thee and him alone: if he shall hear thee, thou hast gained thy brother. But if he will not hear thee, then take with thee one or two more*, and so on.[2] Luke here is silent

---

[2] Mt. 18:15

concerning those things which Matthew has set forth at greater length, because they have already been spoken by Matthew. If a brother who has trespassed listens to admonishment, he is worthy of forgiveness, but if he does not listen, *let him be unto thee as a Gentile and a publican,*[3] that is, let him be an abomination, and one who is not worthy to be called a brother. The Lord then speaks as if in answer to someone who might say, "Indeed, Lord, Thou hast spoken well; but if this brother has been counted worthy of forgiveness many times, and should cause harm again, what should be done with him?" The Lord replies, "If he repents again, forgive him. Furthermore, if *seven times in a day* he *turn again to thee...forgive him."* *Seven times* here means *many times,* as in the text *the barren woman has born seven.*[4] Therefore, he must be forgiven as many times as he repents. For you must not think that the Lord puts a limit to forgiveness. *Seven* means *countless.* As we say [in Greek] when we speak of *a city of ten thousand*, we do not mean that it has exactly ten thousand inhabitants, for perhaps it has more than that; what we mean is that it is a large city.[5] That this is the meaning here is clear from the Gospel of Matthew. There, to Peter who asked, "Lord, shall I forgive him til seventy times?" the Lord said, "No, but until seventy times seven,"[6] thus indicating an infinite number.

5-10. And the apostles said unto the Lord, Increase our faith. And the Lord said, If ye had faith as a grain of mustard seed, ye might say unto this sycamine tree, Be thou plucked up by the root, and be thou planted in the sea; and it should obey you. But which of you, having a servant plowing or shepherding, will say unto him when he is come from the field, Come at once and sit down at table? And will not rather say unto him, Make ready wherewith I may sup, and gird thyself, and serve me, till I have eaten and drunken; and afterward thou shalt eat and drink? Doth he thank that servant because he did the things that were commanded him? I think not. So likewise ye,

---

[3] Mt. 18:17

[4] I Kings 2:5

[5] The Greek word *myrias* (gen. *myriados*) has the literal meaning of *ten thousand*. But, like its English derivative *myriad,* it also denotes a vast number.

[6] See Mt. 18:21-22.

when ye shall have done all those things which are commanded you, say, We are unprofitable servants: we have done that which was our duty to do. The apostles had faith in the Lord. But they became aware of their weakness, and when they heard the Lord speaking to them about great matters and about the danger they would encounter from the offences and obstacles to come, they asked Him to increase the strength of their faith so that they could accomplish that virtue of which He had spoken, non-possession. For nothing helps a man to achieve non-possession so much as faith and bold confidence in God. On the other hand, nothing is a greater inducement for a man to accumulate wealth than the failure to believe that God is a great dispenser of good things and that His goodness is a treasury which cannot be emptied. Therefore, so that the apostles might have the means with which to withstand offences, they approach the Lord and say, *Increase our faith,* meaning, "Make us more complete and sure in our faith." The Lord shows them that they have asked well, and that they ought to have this sure belief that faith is able to do great things, and He says to them, "*If ye had faith,* ye might transplant this sycamine." Here are two things that are great and marvelous: that a tree rooted in the earth might be moved, and that it might be transplanted into the sea. How could it be planted in water? It is clear that by saying these things the Lord is showing the power of faith. And one might say, in a figurative sense, that the sycamine tree represents the devil, who brings to us the worm that never ceases, and who feeds that worm with thoughts that spring forth from him. For the leaves which spring forth from the sycamine tree feed those worms which produce cocoons of silk.[7] Therefore faith is able to root out this sycamine from the human heart and to cast it into the sea, that is, to destroy it in the abyss. Having said this about faith, the Lord gives another essential teaching: that one must not think highly of oneself because of accomplishments. Faith does accomplish many things: it makes the man who possesses it a fulfiller of the commandments, and it even adorns that man with wonderworking, from which it often happens that he then succumbs to proud thoughts. Therefore the Lord protects His apostles from becoming puffed up with their accomplishments, by means of a

---

[7]The sycamine is a kind of mulberry tree, and it is on the leaves of the mulberry tree that silkworms live and feed.

most apt example. *Which of you*, He says, *having a servant*, and so forth. He shows through this parable that a man must not become proud of any accomplishment, not even if he should fulfill every commandment. For it is the obligation of the servant to fulfill the commandments of his lord, and by no means should he consider this to be an accomplishment. If he had not done his duty, he would have deserved a beating; if he has performed it, let it suffice that he has escaped a beating, and by no means should he seek to be honored for this. It is his master's choice whether to give him honor, or indeed, whether to bestow anything at all upon him. For the same reasons, a servant of God should never become proud when he has accomplished the commandments, for he has done nothing magnificent. But woe to him if he should not keep the commandments! As the Apostle says, *Woe is unto me, if I preach not the Gospel!*[8] Nor should he think highly of himself if he has received spiritual gifts. For the gifts are bestowed upon him by the mercy of God, and not because the Master owes them to him. Rather, the servant owes it to the Master to keep all His commandments. And if we ought not to think any great thoughts even if we have kept all the commandments, what will become of us if we are proud and yet have not accomplished the least part of the commandments of God? Understand, O reader, the wording of the parable. He mentions first the servant who was plowing, and then the servant who was shepherding. One must first be a plowman before he may be entrusted with shepherding. It is the man who has thoroughly plowed his own flesh like a piece of ground who is worthy to become a shepherd of others. How can someone take care of the Church who does not govern his own house as he should? First plow yourself, and then you may shepherd others. As Jeremiah says, *Break up fresh ground for yourselves,*[9] and then *light ye for yourselves the light of knowledge,*[10] indicating the most important part of being a pastor.

11-19. And it came to pass, as He went to Jerusalem, that He passed through the midst of Samaria and Galilee. And as He entered into a certain village, there met Him ten men that were lepers, who

---

[8] I Cor. 9:16

[9] Jer. 4:3

[10] Hos. 10:12

stood afar off: and they lifted up their voices, and said, Jesus, Master, have mercy on us. And when He saw them, He said unto them, Go show yourselves unto the priests. And it came to pass, that, as they went, they were cleansed. And one of them, when he saw that he was healed, turned back, and with a loud voice glorified God, and fell down on his face at His feet, giving Him thanks: and he was a Samaritan. And Jesus answering said, Were there not ten cleansed? But where are the nine? There are not found any that returned to give glory to God, save this stranger. And He said unto him, Arise, go thy way: thy faith hath made thee whole. From this one may learn that nothing prevents a man from living in a manner pleasing to God, not even if he belongs to a despised race, if only he has a good will and disposition. For behold, ten lepers met Jesus as He was about to enter a certain city. They met Him outside the city, for those who were considered unclean were not permitted to go into the city. They *stood afar off*, as if ashamed of their supposed uncleanness, and did not dare to draw near, thinking that Jesus abhorred them, as did the others. *They lifted up their voices* and made supplication. By physical location they were standing afar off, but in their supplication they were near. For *the Lord is nigh unto all that call upon Him in truth.*[11] And they did not make supplication to Him as to a mere man, but as to One greater than a man. For they called Him *Master*, meaning Lord, Protector, and Guardian, which is not far from thinking of Him as God. The Lord instructs them to show themselves to the priests. [Initially] the priests would examine men such as these to determine whether they were lepers or not. For there were certain signs by which the priests could recognize incurable leprosy. But in addition to this, if it were the case that someone who had been suffering from leprosy were healed, the priests would [again] examine him to verify the cure, in which event the gift commanded by the law would be offered.[12] In this case, since these men were already confirmed lepers, why should they show themselves to the priests, unless indeed they were about to be cleansed? To command them to go the priests indicated nothing other than that they would be healed. This is why the Evangelist says that *as they went, they were cleansed.* Of the

---

[11] Ps. 144:19

[12] Leviticus, ch. 14

ten lepers, the nine who were Israelites showed themselves to be ungrateful, while it was the Samaritan, an accursed foreigner, as we said earlier, who returned to voice his gratitude. The Samaritans were Assyrians; therefore, let no Gentile despair, and let no one descended from holy forebears boast. This miracle also signifies the common salvation that came to the whole human race. For the ten lepers represent all of human nature, and that nature was leprous with wickedness, carrying about with it the ugliness of sin, passing its life outside the heavenly city on account of its uncleanness, and standing afar off from God. But this very distance from God is itself a supplication. For when the Lover of mankind, Who wills that all should be saved and receive good things, sees someone who is not sharing in His goodness, then He is most quick to show mercy and to heal those who are so miserably afflicted. But He also healed the whole leprous nature of man, when, for every man's sake, He took flesh and tasted of death. Although the Jews had been cleansed of the uncleanness of their leprous sin, as far as it was the Lord's part to do, they showed themselves ungrateful and did not return from the path of their vain foolishness to give glory to God Who saved them, that is, to believe in Him Who is God and Who endured the extremes of suffering. For this is the glory of God: His Flesh and His Cross. These Jews, then, did not confess the incarnate and crucified Lord of glory. But the foreign and accursed people of the Gentiles recognized the One Who makes clean, and they glorified Him by believing in Him. They believed that God loves man so much and is so powerful that He accepted the very depth of dishonor for our sake—this is His love of man—and having accepted it, He suffered no harm to His own nature—this is His power.

20-25. And when He was asked by the Pharisees, when the kingdom of God should come, He answered them and said, The kingdom of God cometh not with observation; neither shall they say, Lo here! or, lo there! For, behold, the kingdom of God is within you. And He said unto the disciples, The days will come, when ye shall desire to see one of the days of the Son of Man, and ye shall not see it. And they shall say to you, See here; or, see there: go not after them, nor follow them. For as the lightning, that flasheth out of the one part under heaven, shineth unto the other part under heaven, so shall also the Son of Man be in His day. But first must He suffer

many things, and be rejected by this generation. Many times the Lord mentioned the kingdom of God in His teachings. But when the Pharisees heard these things, they would ridicule Him. This is why they approached Him with the question as to when the kingdom would come, mocking Him as an eccentric who was preaching something strange and foreign. For none of the previous teachers and prophets had made mention of the kingdom of God. Or perhaps, since they had it in mind to kill Him, they approached Him and questioned Him with derision and sarcasm, as much as saying, "You make sermons about the kingdom—when will your kingdom be? As for you, soon you will be killed by us and meet your end on the cross, with all the dishonor that goes with it." How does Christ reply? He does not answer these senseless men according to their foolish and senseless way of thinking, but He lets them be deceived by the several meanings of *kingdom* and does not reveal to them what He means. For they would not have accepted what He said concerning this kingdom, that it is not a worldly, but an other-worldly, kingdom. They were not worthy of hearing this, on account of their willful deafness, and so the Lord lets it be, and speaks instead of the time of the kingdom, saying that its time is not knowable to us by means of observation. It has no fixed date: instead, the kingdom of God is always present for him who desires and wills it. When a man's disposition and way of life are like that of an angel, most assuredly this is the kingdom of God. For God indeed is said to rule as King when nothing worldly meddles in the governing of our souls and when in every respect we live not of this world. This manner of life we have within us, that is to say, we have it within us when we desire and will it. We do not need to wait a long time, or until our departure from this life; instead, faith and a God-pleasing life which accompanies faith are very near us. The Apostle said the same thing: *The word is nigh thee, even in thy mouth, and in thy heart; that is, the word of faith.*[13] To have faith, and, together with faith, to walk in a manner worthy of our calling, is indeed something within us. The Pharisees, then, were mocking the Lord for preaching about the kingdom, which no one had preached before. But the Lord shows that they are ignorant of that which is within them, although those who so desire may easily understand it. "Now, while I am among you, it is entirely within

---

[13] Rom. 10:8

your ability to have the kingdom of God, by believing in Me and by choosing to live according to My commandments.'' To His disciples He said, *The days will come, when ye shall desire to see one of the days of the Son of Man, and ye shall not see it.* This means, ''For you also the kingdom of God is present, while I am with you. It is present with you not only in that you have believed in Me and followed Me, but also in that you now live free of any cares while I am here to watch over you and to provide for you. But *the days will come* when I will be absent and you will be delivered over to dangers. When you are led before rulers and kings, you will long for the time you have now, free of dangers and cares while I am with you, as the kingdom of God. And often you will desire to have just one of the days of the Son of Man, that is, to have one day of this present life with Me, because it is free of danger.'' On the one hand, the disciples, while they were with the Lord, did not in fact have a life that was altogether free of pain and danger, for they suffered hardships when they had to flee with Him when He fled, and were reviled with Him when He was reviled. But, by comparison with the dangers that were to come, the things that happened to the apostles while Christ was among them would appear to have been without danger. Thus, the kingdom of God was within the apostles in this sense also, that they lived without danger and pain while they were with the Lord. For after the Resurrection they went about from place to place like hunted men and prisoners. With these words the Lord is preparing the hearts of the apostles to be strong and to endure pains, and He forewarns them lest they be deceived. He says to them, ''And if they should say, *See here; or, see there: go not after them.* Let no one persuade you,'' He is saying, ''that I have come here, or that I have come there. For My second coming, which will be more brilliant and more glorious than the first, will not be limited to any one place. Just as lightning does not escape anyone's notice, but is visible from one end of the earth to the other, so too My coming will be dazzling and in full view, not hidden from anyone. Therefore, do not be deceived by false christs and messiahs. When I come again I will not appear as I did before, in a manger and in poverty for thirty years, but all in glory, escorted by the angels, and in the twinkling of an eye.'' Because He had foretold to them the fearful things which they would face, He then consoles them and encourages them to be brave, strengthening them by His own example. ''Do not marvel,'' He says, ''if you should experience such pains and tribulations

that you desire to return to this life which you now live with Me. For I
Myself, Who will appear like the lightning, must first suffer many things,
and be rejected, and only then come in glory. Let this be an encouragement to you to show valor, let this make you eager to endure. Look to
Me, and hope in that glory which will result for you from enduring
dangers and being rejected, just as it will for Me.''

**26-30. And as it was in the days of Noah, so shall it be also in the
days of the Son of Man. They did eat, they drank, they married, they
were given in marriage, until the day that Noah entered into the ark,
and the flood came, and destroyed them all. Likewise also as it was
in the days of Lot; they did eat, they drank, they bought, they sold,
they planted, they builded; but the same day that Lot went out of
Sodom it rained fire and brimstone from heaven, and destroyed them
all. Even thus shall it be in the day when the Son of Man is revealed.**
By further examples the Lord indicates the suddenness and the unexpectedness of His second coming. Just as the flood came suddenly at the time
of Noah and carried everyone away, just as suddenly will He come again.
By referring to the men at the time of flood, and to the Sodomites, He
also indicates that when the Antichrist comes shameful pleasures will be
commonplace among people, and they will become lewd sensualists,
abandoning themselves to unlawful pleasures. This is just as the Apostle
said, that in the last days men would become *lovers of pleasures more
than lovers of God.*[14] It is fitting that wickedness should flourish during
the reign of the deceiver, for he is the vile haunt of every evil and every
sin. For what other way of life than his own would he make to prevail
among the wretched generation of men at that time? Can anything pure
arise out of uncleanliness? Therefore the people of that time will be given
over to every voluptuous pleasure just as in the time of Noah, not
expecting anything unpleasant in the future, and disbelieving anyone who
speaks to them of unpleasant things that will happen to them. Even so did
the people disbelieve the warnings of Noah and Lot.

**31-33. In that day, he which shall be upon the housetop, and his
goods in the house, let him not come down to take them away; and**

---

[14] II Tim. 3:4

he that is in the field, let him likewise not return back. Remember Lot's wife. Whosoever shall seek to save his life shall lose it; and whosoever shall lose his life shall preserve it. In that day of the coming of the Antichrist, he who is on the housetop, that is, he who has attained the heights of virtue, let him not come down from that place, nor let him become lax in the practice of virtue for any worldly reason. For all the things of this life, no matter whether they be used by one man unto virtue, or by another unto vice, are nothing more than pots and pans. Therefore let him who is standing on the heights of virtue not come down for the sake of anything worldly, nor let him fall from that height. Instead let him stand firmly against wickedness and not become weak and cowardly. *And he that is in the field, let him likewise not return back.* He that is in the field, meaning, in this world laboring for virtue, should not turn back but should reach forward to the things that are before him. As the Lord says in another place, *No man, having put his hand to the plough, and looking back, is fit for the kingdom of God.*[15] He adds the example of Lot's wife, who looked back and was turned into a pillar of salt.[16] This signifies that she had not fled from wickedness, but had stayed behind in that foul and brackish state, and became completely wicked. And thus immobile and fixed in her wickedness, it was as if the defeat she had suffered had been inscribed on a pillar for all to read as a memorial. Then the Lord speaks words which follow from what He has just said. *Whosoever shall seek to save his life shall lose it.* During the persecutions of the Antichrist, He is saying, let no one indulge himself in cares for his own life. If he does so, he shall lose it. But whoever gives himself over to danger and slaughter shall be saved, because he did not submit to the Antichrist's tyranny on account of his love of life. The Lord had just said, "Let him who is on a high place of virtue not come down because he regards the affairs of this life and his resolve is weakened by wealth and possessions, and thus he abandons his resistance." Now He says, "Let him go forward on the path, [as did Lot]. I do not only say, Let him not come down from virtue because of worldly goods, but I go further: let him not abandon virtue for the sake of anything external whatsoever. Let not even the desire to preserve his life incline him to-

---

[15] Lk. 9:62

[16] See Gen. 19:26.

wards that deceiver and persecutor, the Antichrist.'' Matthew says that the Lord spoke all these things in regard to the capture of Jerusalem, indicating the assault of enemies and that when the Romans attacked, they should flee without turning back; and those on the rooftops should not come down to get anything that they might need, but should flee at once, for there would be no time to spare in which to make preparations; nor should those in the fields return to the house. And those in the house should flee.[17] Do not wonder [that in Luke's Gospel the Lord speaks of these things in reference to His second coming]. Because these things happened when Jerusalem was captured, it does not follow that they will not happen again when the Antichrist comes. Indeed, at the time of the end of the world, there will be unendurable affliction.

34-37. I tell you, in that night there shall be two on one couch; the one shall be taken, and the other shall be left. Two women shall be grinding together; the one shall be taken, and the other left. Two men shall be in the field; the one shall be taken, and the other left. And they answered and said unto Him, Where, Lord? And He said unto them, Where the corpse is, there also will the eagles be gathered together.[18] Here again we learn how sudden and unexpected His second coming will be. By saying that there will be two on one couch, He shows the leisure and unconcern in which His coming will find them. The two women grinding together are another indication that His coming will be unexpected. We also learn that His coming will be in the night. He is saying, therefore, that of the wealthy, whose riches allow them to take their ease upon their couches, some will be saved, and some will not. Because He had said before that it is hard for a rich man to be saved,[19] now He shows that not all the rich perish and that not all the poor are saved. Of the rich, one is taken and caught up into the resurrection of the Lord,[20] because he is light in spirit and heavenly, while

---

[17] See Vol. 1, *The Explanation* of St. Matthew, pp. 206-207.

[18] Verse 36, *Two men shall be in the field...*, does not appear in Bl. Theophylact's text of St. Luke, nor does it appear in the majority of Byzantine Gospel manuscripts. However, because it does appear in certain Orthodox lectionary manuscripts, in the Slavonic Gospel, and in the KJV, it has been included here.

[19] See Mt. 19:23 and Mk. 10:23.

[20] I Thess. 4:17

another is left below, condemned. Likewise, of the poor, whom He signifies by mentioning those who grind flour, one will be saved and another will not. Not all the poor are righteous; some of them are thieves and pickpockets. By those grinding, therefore, He indicates the toilsome life of the poor. The disciples ask, *"Where, Lord,* will they go who shall be taken?"* and He answers, *Where the corpse is, there also will the eagles be.* This means, Where the Son of Man is, there also will all the saints be, for they are light and soaring, unlike those heavy with sin who are left below. When the Son of Man, Who died for our sake and was laid out as a corpse, appears from the heavens, all the saints and angels will gather around Him, just as all the birds which feed on flesh gather around a dead body. With them He will come in the glory of the Father and with ineffable splendor. He called the time of His coming *night* because of its unexpectedness and because it would bring darkness to sinners. But for the righteous, Light will arise, and indeed they themselves will shine like the Sun.

CHAPTER EIGHTEEN

On unceasing prayer.
Concerning the judge of unrighteousness.
Concerning the Pharisee and the Publican.
Concerning the children, of whom is the kingdom of God.
Concerning the man who asked Jesus what he should do
to inherit eternal life.
Concerning the blind man at Jericho.

1-8. And He spake a parable unto them to this end, that men ought always to pray and not to grow faint, saying, There was in a city a judge, who feared not God, neither had he any shame before man. And there was a widow in that city; and she came unto him, saying, Vindicate me against mine adversary. And he would not for a while: but afterward he said within himself, Though I fear not God, nor have any shame before man, yet because this widow troubleth me, I will vindicate her, lest by her continual coming she weary me. And the Lord said, Hear what the judge of unrighteousness saith. And shall not God vindicate His own elect, who cry day and night unto Him, though He bear long with them? I tell you that He will vindicate them speedily. Nevertheless when the Son of Man cometh, shall He find faith on the earth? Because He had spoken to them of dangers and tribulations, here He provides the remedy for these things, namely, prayer. But not simply any kind of prayer; rather, persistent and attentive prayer. All these tribulations will befall the men of those times, He is saying, but prayer is a great ally, and we must offer prayer persistently and continuously, remembering how the persistence of the widow shamed the judge of unrighteousness. If perseverance softened this man who was full of every wickedness and had no shame before God or man, how much more so shall we move God, the Father of mercy, to take pity, even though He should delay for the present? See that not being ashamed before men is a sign of even greater wickedness. There are many who do not fear God, but who nevertheless are ashamed before men and thus commit less sin. But when a man has no shame even before men, this is the height of wickedness. This is why the Lord spoke the words *neither had he any shame before man* after saying that the judge *feared not God*. It is as if He were saying, ''There was a judge who did not fear God; but why do I merely say that he did not fear God? There is an even greater sign of his wickedness: that he had no shame before men.'' Therefore the parable teaches us, as we have said, not to grow faint in our prayers, just as the Lord said on another occasion, ''Which of you shall have a friend, and then when he comes and knocks at night will send him away? Out of shame, if for no other reason, you will open to him.''[1] And again, *What man is there of you, whom if his son ask bread, will he give him a stone?*[2] In all these passages, the Lord is directing us to pray without ceasing. Some have attempted to understand this parable in a more elaborate manner, and have made bold to declare their interpretation to be true. The widow, they have said, represents every soul which has cast off the husband which she had before, namely, the devil, who, because of this, is now her adversary, constantly assailing her. The widow approaches God, the judge of unrighteousness, that is, He Who condemns unrighteousness, and Who fears not any god. For He alone is God, and there is no other god whom He should fear. Neither is He ashamed before any man, for *God regardeth no man's person.*[3] Moved by her perseverance, God takes pity on this widow, the soul, who prays to God continuously because of her adversary, the devil. Let him who so desires accept this interpretation: it has been set forth so that you may not be ignorant of it. But in any event the Lord taught us these things concerning the need to pray, and showed us that if this lawless man, full of every unrighteousness, was moved to pity by the constancy of the request made to him, how much more will God, the Source of all righteousness, make speedy vindication, *though He bear long with them*, and appears not to hear those who pray to Him day and night? Therefore, having taught us these things and shown us that at the time of the end of the world we will need this kind of prayer in order to meet the dangers that will confront us, He adds, *Nevertheless when the Son of Man cometh, will He find faith on the earth?* By using the form of a question, He indicates how few faithful He will find then. For the son of lawlessness will prevail to such a degree at that time that he would deceive even the

---

[1] See Lk. 11:5-8.

[2] Mt. 7:9

[3] Gal. 2:6

elect, if it were possible.[4] The Lord often used the question form to speak of that which is rarely found, as when He said, *Who then is a faithful and wise servant?*[5] Here too He indicates the same thing by using the form of a question, saying that there are very few who will keep their faith in God and in each other. It is fitting that the Lord should add a word on faith to His exhortation concerning prayer. Faith is the foundation and support of prayer. When a man asks God for something, unless he believes he will receive that which is to his own benefit, his prayer is in vain. This is why the Lord mentions faith while He is teaching about prayer, showing in a hidden manner that few will pray then, because few will be found then who have faith. Therefore, when the Lord comes in the clouds He will not find faith on the earth, except in a few. But with His coming He will put an end to faithlessness, for all will confess, willingly or no, that Jesus is Lord to the glory of God the Father.[6] Not indeed by true faith, but by necessity, [on account of Christ Himself before their eyes,] every unbeliever will then believe that the One they had blasphemed before is none other than the Saviour.

9-14. And He spake this parable unto certain who trusted in themselves that they were righteous, and despised others: two men went up into the temple to pray; the one a Pharisee, and the other a publican. The Pharisee stood and prayed thus within himself, God, I thank Thee, that I am not as other men are, extortioners, unjust, adulterers, or even as this publican. I fast twice in the week, I give tithes of all that I possess. And the publican, standing afar off, would not lift up so much as his eyes unto heaven, but smote upon his breast, saying, God be merciful to me a sinner. I tell you, this man went down to his house counted righteous rather than the other: for every one that exalteth himself shall be humbled; and he that humbleth himself shall be exalted. The Lord ceaselessly purges the passion of pride in many ways. This passion, more than any other, disturbs our thoughts, and for this reason the Lord always and everywhere teaches on this subject. Here He is purging the worst form of pride. For

---

[4] See Mt. 24:24.

[5] Mt. 24:45

[6] Phil. 2:11

there are many offshoots of self-love. Presumption, arrogance, and vainglory all stem from this root. But the most destructive of all these kinds of self-love is pride, for pride is contempt of God. When a man ascribes his accomplishments to himself, and not to God, this is nothing less than denial of God and opposition to Him. Therefore, like enemy to enemy, the Lord opposes this passion which is opposed to Him, and through this parable He promises to heal it. He directs this parable towards those who trust in themselves and who do not attribute everything to God, and who, as a result, despise others. He shows that when righteousness, which is marvelous in every other respect and sets a man close to God, takes pride as its companion, it casts that man into the lowest depths and makes demonic what was God-like just a short time before. The words of the Pharisee at first resemble the words of a grateful man. For he says, *God, I thank Thee.* But the words that follow are full of foolishness. For he does not say, "that Thou hast made me to depart from extortion and iniquities." Instead he says, "*I thank Thee that I am not* an extortioner or worker of iniquity." He attributes this accomplishment to himself, as something done by his own strength. How can a man who knows that what he has, he has received from God, [compare other men to himself unfavorably] and judge them? For certainly if a man believed that he had received as a gift good things that in truth belong to God, he would not despise other men. He would instead consider himself just as naked as his fellow men in regards to virtue, except that by the mercy of God his nakedness has been covered with a donated garment. The Pharisee is proud, ascribing his deeds to his own strength, and that is why he proceeds to condemn others. By saying that the Pharisee *stood,* the Lord indicates his haughtiness and lack of humility. In the same way that a humble-minded man is likewise humble in his demeanor, this Pharisee by his bearing displays his pride. Although it is also said of the publican that he stood, see what follows, that he *would not lift up so much as his eyes unto heaven,* so that he was stooped in posture. But the eyes of the Pharisee, together with his heart, were lifted up to heaven in boastful exaltation. Nonetheless, how the Pharisee arranged the words of his prayer can still instruct us. First he says what he is not, and then he declares what he is. For after he says, *God, I thank Thee, that I am not as other men are,* naming this, this, and this, then he declares his good deeds, fasting twice a week and giving tithes of all that he possesses. [The order of his prayer shows us that] we must first refrain from wickedness, and then set our hand to virtue. For one must not only turn away from evil, but also do good.[7] In the same way, a man who wants to draw pure water from a muddy spring first cleans out the mud and only then can he draw pure water. Consider this as well, that the Pharisee did not say, "I thank Thee that I am not an extortioner or an adulterer, as other men are." He could not endure even the association of his name with such vile terms, and so he uses them in the plural, casting these terms at other men, and avoiding the singular, which might associate him with sin. Having said, *I thank Thee, that I am not as other men are,* by contrast he points to himself, saying, *I fast twice in the Sabbath,*[8] meaning, twice in the week, for the week was called "the Sabbath," taking its name from the last day of the week, the day of rest. The day of rest was called *Sabbat,* and the week was called *Sabbata,* being the plural form of *Sabbat.* Whence it is that *mian Sabattōn*[9] is the first day of the week, which we call "the Lord's Day" [Sunday]. Among the Hebrews *mian* means the same thing as *first.*[10] There is also another, more profound, explanation of this parable. Against the passion of adultery, the Pharisee boasted of his fasting, for lustful desires arise from eating and drinking to excess. By restraining his body through fasting on Mondays and Thursdays, as was the practice of the Pharisees,[11] he kept himself far from such passions. He also resisted extortion and injustice by giving tithes of all his possessions. I am so opposed to extortion and to wronging others, he says, that I give alms of everything I have. Some believe that a simple and single tithe is prescribed by the law; but those who carefully examine the law will find three forms of tithing prescribed.

---

[7] Ps. 33:14

[8] In Greek, *nēsteuō dis tou Sabbatou.* The King James text does not preserve the Hebrew expression, as does the Greek text, but translates it simply as *week.*

[9] See Mk. 16:2.

[10] *Mian* is the Greek cardinal number, meaning *one,* used in this idiom instead of what would be expected, the ordinal number, *prōtēn.* This echoes the Hebrew expression.

[11] Guided by the Holy Spirit, the Church has always taught the faithful to fast instead on Wednesdays and Fridays, in remembrance of the Lord's betrayal by Judas and His crucifixion. The earliest documentary proof of this practice is to be found in *The Teaching of the Twelve Apostles,* dating from the year 120 A.D. See *The Ante-Nicene Fathers, Volume 7,* Hendrickson Publishers, Peabody, Massachusetts, 1994, p. 379.

You may learn this from Deuteronomy if you apply yourself diligently.[12] So much for the Pharisee. Now we turn to the publican and see that he is the Pharisee's exact opposite in every regard. He *stood afar off*, and kept himself at a great distance, not only in physical location, but in his demeanor, in his words, and in his compunction of heart. He was ashamed to lift up his eyes to heaven, for he considered his eyes unworthy of heavenly vision because they had desired to see and to enjoy the good things of earth. And he smote himself upon the breast, striking his heart, as it were, because of its evil designs, and awakening it because it had been sleeping. And the publican said no other words than, *God be merciful to me a sinner*. Because of all these things he *went down to his house counted righteous, rather than the other*. For every proud heart is unclean in the Lord's eyes, and *the Lord resisteth the proud but He giveth grace to the humble*.[13] But one might wonder why it is that the Pharisee is condemned for speaking a few boastful words, while Job receives a crown for speaking many such words.[14] The answer is that the Pharisee stood and spoke these vain words under no compulsion, and he condemned others for no reason. But with Job, his friends pressed him and bore down upon him more fiercely than did his own calamities, telling him that he was suffering these things because of his sins. Job was compelled to enumerate his good deeds, but he did so for the glory of God, and so that men would not be misled from the path of virtue. For if men came to hear that Job was suffering because what he had done was sinful, they would not act as Job had. As a result they would become haters of strangers instead of hospitable to strangers, merciless instead of merciful, and unrighteous instead of righteous; for such were the good deeds of Job. Therefore Job enumerated his virtues so that others would not be misled and harmed, and this was why he spoke as he did. Shall we not say that his words, which may seem boastful, in fact are radiant with humility? *Oh that I were as in months past*, he said, *wherein God*

---

[12] Deut. 12:11,17; 14:22,28; 26:12.

[13] Prov. 3:34, I Pet. 5:5.

[14] See Job 29, wherein Job states that he had saved the poor out of the hand of the oppressor, helped the fatherless, put on righteousness, been the eye of the blind and the foot of the lame, and much more.

preserved me![15] Do you see that he attributes everything to God and does not judge others? Instead he is judged by his friends. But condemnation rightly falls upon the Pharisee, who attributed everything to himself and not to God and judged others for no reason whatsoever. *For every one that exalteth himself shall be humbled* and condemned by God; *and he that humbleth himself* when he is condemned by others *shall be exalted* and counted righteous by God. The Lord is saying, "You, O Christian, be the first to tell your sins, so that you may be counted righteous."

15-17. And they brought unto Him also infants, that He would touch them: but when His disciples saw it, they rebuked them. But Jesus called them unto Him, and said, Let the little children come unto Me, and forbid them not: for of such is the kingdom of God. Verily I say unto you, Whosoever shall not receive the kingdom of God as a little child shall in no wise enter therein. This account of the Lord receiving the little children also instructs us in humility. By means of it the Lord is teaching us to be humble-minded, to welcome all, and to despise no one. His disciples thought it undignified to bring little children to such a great teacher. But He showed them that it is necessary to be so humble-minded that we do not turn away even the most insignificant. Thus He teaches humility, first through His actions by not sending the children away, but gladly receiving them, and then through His words, saying that the kingdom of heaven belongs to those who are like little children. A little child is not haughty, he does not despise anyone, he is innocent and guileless. He does not inflate himself in the presence of important people, nor withdraw from those in sorrows. Instead he lives in complete simplicity. So it is that he who lives humbly and innocently will be accepted by God, as well as he who receives the kingdom of God the way a little child does, without guile or skepticism, but with trust and faith. For a man who is skeptical and always asking "How can this be?" will be destroyed by his unbelief and *shall in no wise enter* the kingdom which he would not accept simply, humbly, and trustingly. Therefore, all the apostles and, indeed, all those who believe in Christ, may be called *children*. The Lord Himself called the apostles

---

[15] Job 29:2

such, when He said, *Children, have ye any thing to eat?*[16] But the so-called wise among the pagan Greeks sought their kind of wisdom in the Mystery which is the kingdom of God, and they would not accept this Mystery without logical proofs; therefore it is fitting that they were shut out from this kingdom. The Lord did not say, "Of these is the kingdom of God," but, *of such* as these *is the kingdom of God*, namely, those who have chosen by their own will to acquire guilelessness and humility, qualities which little children possess by nature. Therefore, not with skepticism but with faith and humility, let us accept everything that pertains to the Church, which is the kingdom of God. For skepticism comes from presumption and self-conceit, and from glorifying mere intelligence.

18-23. And a certain ruler asked Him saying, Good Teacher, what shall I do to inherit eternal life? And Jesus said unto him, Why callest thou Me good? None is good, save One, that is, God. Thou knowest the commandments: Do not commit adultery, Do not murder, Do not steal, Do not bear false witness, Honour thy father and thy mother. And he said, All these have I kept from my youth up. Now when Jesus heard these things, He said unto him, Yet lackest thou one thing: sell all that thou hast, and distribute unto the poor, and thou shalt have treasure in heaven: and come, follow Me. And when he heard this, he was very sorrowful: for he was very rich. Some think that this man was cunning and sought to trap the Lord with words. But this is not how he appears; rather, he was a lover of money, and Christ Himself rebuked him as such. Mark says that the man came running, and knelt before Jesus, and asked Him his question, and that Jesus, beholding him, loved him.[17] The man is a lover of money, and he approaches Jesus eager to learn how he, along with his wealth, might inherit eternal life. For there is no one who loves prolonged life as much as a man who loves money. Therefore this man thought that Jesus could show him some way in which he could live forever enjoying his possession of wealth. But when the Lord told him that non-possession is what bestows eternal life, he went away as if he regretted both his

---

[16] Jn. 21:5

[17] See Mk. 10:17-22.

question and Jesus' answer. For in his mind he needed eternal life for the very reason that he had great wealth. If he were to give up his possessions, why would he want eternal life, he thought, since that life was to be the life of a pauper? He approached the Lord as if the Lord were merely a man and a teacher. Therefore the Lord shows him that he ought not to approach Him in this manner, saying, *None is good, save One, that is, God.* By this He means, "You call Me good; why then do you also call Me a teacher? It appears that you think that I am one among many men. But if this were so, I would not be good, for no man is good in and of himself. Only God is. If you want to call Me good, you must call Me good because I am God; do not approach Me then as if I were merely a man. But if you think I am only a man, do not call Me good. For in truth God is good, and the source of goodness, and the first cause of goodness itself. If any man is good, he is not good in and of himself, but only because he receives a share of God's goodness. Moreover, what goodness a man has is changeable." *Thou knowest the commandments: Do not commit adultery, Do not murder, Do not steal, Do not bear false witness,* and so forth. The law remedies first those sins into which we fall easily, and then those less frequent sins to which fewer men fall. And so adultery and murder are mentioned, first, because lust and anger are difficult to control: lust is a raging fire, inflaming both the outer and inner man, and anger is a great wild beast.[18] But stealing comes from a less fierce passion and bearing false witness occurs rarely. Therefore, the law remedies first those sins into which we fall most easily, and which are the most grave. But the other sins, such as stealing and bearing false witness, He places second because they lead astray less often and are less grave than murder and adultery. To sin against one's parents He mentions last of all; for although it is a grave sin, it does not occur often. Rarely is there found a man so cruel that he abuses his parents. Because the young man said that he had kept all these commandments from his youth, the Lord enjoins him to keep that commandment which stands at the head of all: non-possession. Behold the laws of the true Christian life. *Sell all that thou hast,* the Lord says. If anything remains, you are its slave. *And distribute,* not to your rich relatives, but *unto the poor.* I think

---

[18] Bl. Theophylact here includes lust with adultery, and anger with murder, in accordance with Christ's commandments and teaching. See Mt. 5:21-22, 27-28.

that the word *distribute* implies that the meting out of wealth is to be done with discernment and not haphazardly. And because a man must have all the other virtues as well as non-possession, the Lord then said, *And come, follow Me,* meaning, "Be My disciple in all things, and always keep following Me.[19] Do not follow Me today only, and leave Me tomorrow." Because the ruler was a lover of money, the Lord promised him treasure in heaven, but the ruler did not give heed, because he was a slave of his money. Therefore when he heard what the Lord had asked of him, he was sorrowful. For the Lord had counselled him to deprive himself of his wealth; yet that was the very reason he wanted eternal life in the first place, so that he could live forever enjoying his many possessions. That he was sorrowful shows that he was sincere and not devious. Not one of the Pharisees was ever sorrowful; instead, they raged even more against the Lord [when they heard His answers to their questions]. I am not unaware that the great light of the world, John Chrysostom, believed that this young man truly desired eternal life, but that he was held fast by the love of money, a passion that was stronger than his love for eternal life. What we have said here is not inconsistent, namely, that the young man desired to have eternal life along with his wealth.

24-30. And when Jesus saw that he was very sorrowful, He said, How hard it shall be for them that have riches to enter into the kingdom of God! For it is easier for a camel to go through a needle's eye, than for a rich man to enter into the kingdom of God. And they that heard it said, Who then can be saved? And He said, The things which are impossible with men are possible with God. Then Peter said, Lo, we have left all, and followed Thee. And He said unto them, Verily I say unto you, There is no man that hath left house, or parents, or brethren, or wife, or children, for the kingdom of God's sake, who shall not receive many times more in this present time, and in the age to come life everlasting. Because the rich man was sorrowful when he heard that he should give up his riches, the Lord said, as though He were marvelling, *How hard it shall be for them that have riches to*

---

[19] In the Greek text, the word for *follow, akolouthei,* is in the present imperative, implying a continuous action. By contrast, the two previous imperatives, *pōlēson, sell,* and *diados, distribute,* are in the aorist imperative, implying a single, finite action.

enter into the kingdom of God! He did not say that it would be impossible for those with wealth to enter, but that it would be difficult. It is not impossible for such as these to be saved. Those who give away their riches are able to obtain the heavenly things above. However, this is difficult, for money is stickier than glue and it is hard for a man to free himself when he is held fast by money. In His very next words the Lord indicates that this is so difficult that it is all but impossible, when He says, *It is easier for a camel to go through a needle's eye*, than for a rich man to be saved. It is indeed impossible for a camel to pass through the eye of a needle, whether you understand *camel* to mean the animal or the thick rope used on a ship. Therefore, if it is easier for a camel to go through the eye of a needle—which is impossible—than it is for a rich man to be saved, then it is even more impossible for a rich man to be saved. What does the Lord mean? First, that this statement is true: it is impossible for a rich man, while he is a rich man, to be saved. Do not say to me that such and such a rich man gave away his riches and was saved. He was not saved as a rich man; he was saved either as a man who had attained non-possession, or who had become a steward, but not as a rich man. A steward and a rich man are not the same. The rich man keeps riches for himself, while the steward, as a trustee, holds wealth for the benefit of others. Therefore, if such a man is saved, he is not saved as a rich man, but, as we have said, because he has given away all that he has, or because he has spent his wealth as a good steward. Consider this as well: while it is impossible for *a rich man* to be saved, it is not impossible, but only difficult, for *them that have riches* to be saved. It is as if the Lord had said, "The rich man who is possessed by riches and is a slave to them and is held fast by them, shall not be saved. But he who only *has riches*, that is, who is master of riches, owning them without being owned by them, shall be saved with difficulty." That difficulty is because of human weakness. For it is impossible for us not to misuse what we have. As long as we have riches, the devil strives in every way to deceive us into using that wealth in ways that violate the canons and laws of stewardship, and only with great difficulty do we escape the devil's traps. This is why non-possession is better, and almost unassailable by the evil one. *And they that heard it said, Who then can be saved? And He said, The things which are impossible with men are possible with God.* With men who have merely a human outlook, that is, those who desire earthly things and are pulled downwards, it is impossible for them to be saved, as we have said. But *with God* it is possible. That is to say, with God's help, when a man has God as his Counsellor, and takes as his teachers the judgments of God and His commandments concerning non-possession, and calls upon God for help, then it is possible to be saved. We, for our part, must desire what is good; God will then accomplish and perfect it in us. If we can only rise above our timid littleness of soul as concerns our wealth, and make for ourselves friends from the mammon of unrighteousness, we will be saved by those friends when they escort us to the eternal mansions.[20] It is better if we give away all our wealth; and if not all, then at least let us share it with the poor. Thus the impossible becomes possible. For though it is impossible for the man who does not distribute all to be saved, yet through God's love for man, even a partial distribution brings a partial benefit. In response to this, Peter asks, *"Lo, we have left all.* [What do we have to give to the poor?]" He does not ask this for his own sake alone, but in order to find some consolation for all the poor. Peter asks his question for fear that only the rich have the good hope to obtain much because they despised much, and that the poor have little hope because they had little to give away and thus can expect only a little reward. Peter asks, and hears the answer, that everyone who despises, for God's sake, whatever goods he may have, even if they are few, shall receive his reward both in this age and in the age to come. Do not consider those goods to be few; rather, for that poor man, his few things are his whole life. Just as you, the rich man, expect to pass your life with your many and great possessions, the pauper, likewise, expects to pass his life with his belongings, no matter how few and small they may be. Though his belongings are few, I will say that a man's attachment to his possessions is even greater when he owns little. This is clearly shown to be true with parents. The attachment of a parent to his only child is much greater than that of a parent to his many children. Likewise, the poor man has a keener love for his single house and single field than you have for your many houses and fields. And even if it is the case that a poor man is attached to his possessions to the same degree as a rich man, then, at a minimum, the loss is the same for each. Even in this present age, those

---

[20] See Bl. Theophylact's explanation of Luke 16:9, the parable of the steward of unrighteousness, on pp. 207-208 of the present volume.

who give of the little they have receive their reward many times over, as did these very apostles. For each apostle left his own hut, and now each one has magnificent temples in his name, with lands and triumphant processions, and, instead of a single wife, many women bound to him in fervent faith; in short, for everything they gave up, they have received many times over. And in the age to come they receive, not a multiplication of fields such as these and other tangible rewards, but eternal life.

31-34. Then He took unto Him the twelve, and said unto them, Behold, we go up to Jerusalem, and all things that are written by the prophets concerning the Son of Man shall be accomplished. For He shall be delivered unto the Gentiles, and shall be mocked, and spitefully treated, and spitted on: and they shall scourge Him, and put Him to death: and the third day He shall rise again. And they understood none of these things: and this saying was hid from them, neither knew they the things which were spoken. He foretells to them the events of His Passion for two reasons: first, to show that He is not crucified against His will or as a mere man who cannot foresee the circumstances of his death. Instead, He knows these things beforehand and suffers willingly. If He had not wanted to suffer, through His foreknowledge He could have avoided death; it is only those who do not know what will happen who are caught by the enemy. The second reason He forewarns them of His Passion is to enable them to bear more easily the events that will take place, by hearing of them beforehand and not being suddenly overtaken by them. But, O Lord, if the things are about to be accomplished concerning Thee which the prophets foretold of old, why dost Thou go up to Jerusalem? "I go up, that I may accomplish the salvation of man." Thus, He goes willingly. But the disciples at that time *understood none of these things, and this saying was hid from them,* most of all, the saying concerning His Resurrection. The disciples did not understand the other things the Lord had said, for example, that He would be handed over to the Gentiles; but His words concerning the Resurrection were completely beyond their comprehension. The idea that a man might rise from the dead was not prevalent at that time in the ancient world. Few Jews believed it possible, and there was even disbelief in general resurrection from the dead, as is clear from the Sadducees. You might ask, "If the disciples did not understand, why did the Lord foretell these things to them? How could it comfort them at the time of the

Crucifixion if they did not understand what had been said?'' But it was of great benefit to them later when they remembered that these were the events which the Lord had foretold and which they had not then understood. There are many indications that this was so, and especially from what John says: *These things understood not His disciples at the first: but when Jesus was glorified, then remembered they that these things were written of Him.*[21] And the Holy Spirit, the Comforter, caused them to remember all these things, giving them a surer testimony concerning Christ. Concerning how the three days of His burial are counted, enough has been said in the previous Gospels.[22]

35-43. And it came to pass, that as He was come nigh unto Jericho, a certain blind man sat by the way side begging. And hearing the multitude pass by, he asked what it meant. And they told him, that Jesus of Nazareth passeth by. And he cried, saying, Jesus, Son of David, have mercy on me. And they which went before rebuked him, that he should keep silent; but he cried so much the more, Son of David, have mercy on me. And Jesus stood, and commanded him to be brought unto Him: and when He was come near, He asked him, saying, What wilt thou that I shall do unto thee? And he said, Lord, that I may receive my sight. And Jesus said unto him, Receive thy sight: thy faith hath made thee whole. And immediately he received his sight, and followed Him, glorifying God: and all the people, when they saw it, gave praise unto God. The Lord performed this wayside miracle of the blind man so that even His passage along a road would yield a profitable teaching for His disciples and for us: that we should in all things, at all times, and in every place do what is beneficial and never be idle. The blind man believed that Jesus was the awaited Messiah; having been raised among the Jews, it is certain that he knew that the Christ would be of the seed of David. Therefore he cries out with a great voice, *Son of David, have mercy on me.* His words *have mercy on me* show that he understood Jesus to be divine and not merely a man. Marvel at his staunch confession: although rebuked by many, he did not keep silent, but cried out all the more, urged on by the fervent zeal within him.

---

[21] Jn. 12:16

[22] See Vol. 1, *The Explanation* of St. Matthew, p. 254.

Therefore Jesus summons him as one who is truly worthy to approach Him, and asks him, *What wilt thou that I shall do unto thee?* He asks the question, not in ignorance of what the blind man wanted, but so that it would not appear to the others who were present that the Lord gave something different from what the man wanted. Otherwise, some might have said that the Lord, in a vainglorious show of power, healed the man's blindness when the man had only been begging for alms.[23] Envy might well have inspired some to slander the Lord with such foolishness as this. Therefore the Lord asked the blind man what he wanted, and when He heard that he wanted his sight, He gave him his sight. See the absence of vainglory: the Lord says, *"Thy faith hath made thee whole. For you have believed with faith that I am the Son of David, the Christ, Who is now revealed, and you have shown such zeal that you did not keep silent even when rebuked."* We may learn from this that when we ask with faith, God does not give something other than what we ask for, but the very same thing. However, when we ask for one thing and receive something else, it is clear that either we did not make a good request or we did not ask with faith.[24] See also the power of the Lord: *Receive thy sight.*[25] Which of the prophets ever healed in this manner, with such power? His voice, proceeding from Him Who is the true Light, became light to the blind man. See also the gratitude of the healed man: he followed Jesus, glorifying God, and causing others to do the same.

---

[23] The Greek word *eleos, mercy,* is also commonly used to mean *alms,* i.e. compassion shown to the poor.

[24] James 4:3. *Ye ask, and receive not, because ye ask amiss.*

[25] In Greek, the Lord responds with a single word, *anablepson, receive [thy] sight.*

CHAPTER NINETEEN

Concerning Zacchaeus.
Concerning the man who went to receive for himself kingship.
Concerning the ten servants who received the ten pounds.
Concerning the colt.
Concerning Jesus weeping over Jerusalem.
On the casting out from the temple of those who bought and sold.
Concerning the chief priests and scribes who asked the Lord
by what authority He did these things.

1-10. And Jesus entered and passed through Jericho. And, behold, there was a man named Zacchaeus, who was a chief publican, and he was rich. And he sought to see Jesus Who He was, and could not for the crowd, because he was of little stature. And he ran before, and climbed up into a sycamore tree to see Him: for He was to pass that way. And when Jesus came to the place, He looked up, and saw him, and said unto him, Zacchaeus, make haste, and come down: for today I must abide at thy house. And he made haste, and came down, and received Him joyfully. And when they saw it, they all murmured, saying, He has gone to be guest with a man that is a sinner. And Zacchaeus stood, and said unto the Lord; Behold, Lord, the half of my goods I give to the poor; and if I have taken any thing from any man by false accusation, I restore him fourfold. And Jesus said unto him, This day is salvation come to this house, forsomuch as he also is a son of Abraham. For the Son of Man is come to seek and to save that which was lost. The Lord seizes the mightiest of the devil's vessels and destroys his cities. See how the Lord not only makes publicans His disciples, but He even takes prisoner, in order to save him, the chief of publicans, Zacchaeus. No one doubts that a publican is an abomination: how much more so is the chief publican, who is foremost in wickedness? For the publicans derived their living from no other source than the tears of the poor. But even this chief publican is not despised by the Lord. In return only for showing eagerness to see Jesus he receives salvation. He desired to see Jesus, which is why he climbed up into the sycamore tree, but before he had caught sight of Jesus, the Lord had already seen him. In the same manner, the Lord always anticipates us if only He sees that we are willing and eager. When the Lord sees Zacchaeus, He urges him to come down quickly, for He intends to stay at his house. And Zacchaeus was not slow to obey—for when Christ commands anything, we must not hesitate—but *he came down and received Him joyfully,* even though many people murmured. Let us see how Zacchaeus reaped the benefit of Christ's entrance into his house. He says, *The half of my goods I give to the poor.* Do you see his fervor? He began to disburse without stint, not giving just a little, but all that he had. Even what he held back, he held back so that he could give to those whom he had wronged. From this we learn that there is no benefit at all to a man who gives alms to others of money he has obtained unrighteously and ignores those whom he defrauded in obtaining that money. See what Zacchaeus does with this money: if he defrauded anyone, he restores to him fourfold, thus remedying the harm he had done to each man he defrauded. This is true almsgiving. He not only remedies the harm, but he does so with increase. This is in accordance with the law, which commanded that the thief make fourfold restitution.[1] If we consider this well, we see that nothing at all remained of Zacchaeus' money. Half he gave to the poor, and of the half that remained to him, he gave fourfold to those whom he had wronged. But since the living of the chief publican was derived from fraud and extortion, and since he paid back fourfold all that he wrongly taken, it follows that he stripped himself of everything that he had. From this we see that his thinking goes beyond the prescription of the law, for he had become a disciple of the Gospel, and he loved his neighbor more than himself. And what he promised to do, he did: he did not say, "I shall give half, and I shall restore fourfold," but instead, *Behold, I give* and *I restore.* For he had heard the counsel of Solomon, *Say not, Come back another time, tomorrow I will give.*[2] Christ proclaims to him the good tidings of his salvation, saying, "Today you give, today salvation is come to you." By saying, *to this house,* the Lord indicates that Zacchaeus himself has received salvation. By *this house* He means Zacchaeus, for the Lord would not call a building without a soul *a son of Abraham.* It is clear that the Lord named this living master of the house a son of Abraham, because Zacchaeus was like the Patriarch in two respects: he believed and was counted righteous by faith, and with money he was

---

[1] See Ex. 22:1.

[2] Proverbs 3:28

magnanimous and generous to the poor. See that the Lord says that Zacchaeus is now a son of Abraham, and that in his present behavior the Lord sees the likeness to Abraham. The Lord did not say that Zacchaeus had always been a son of Abraham, but that he is now a son of Abraham. Before, when he was a chief publican and tax collector, he bore no resemblance to that righteous man, and was not his son. To silence those who were complaining that the Lord went to be the guest of a sinful man, He says, *The Son of Man is come to seek and to save that which was lost.* This is the explanation of the literal words; but it is easy to understand these things in another sense as well, for moral benefit. Anyone who is *chief* among many in wickedness is little in spiritual stature, for the flesh and the spirit are opposites to one another, and for this reason he cannot see Jesus *for the crowd.* Crowded in by a multitude of passions and worldly affairs, he is not able to see Jesus acting, moving, and walking about. Such a man as this cannot recognize Christian acts for what they are, namely, Christ acting and moving in us. But such a man, who never sees Jesus passing by and cannot perceive Christ in Christian acts, will sometimes change from negligence and come to his senses. Then he will climb up to the top of the sycamore-fig, passing by every pleasure and sweetness, as signified by the figs, and counting them as foolish and dead. Becoming higher than he was and making *ascents in his heart,*[3] he is seen by Jesus and can see Jesus, and the Lord says to him, *Make haste, and come down,* which means, ''Through repentance you have ascended to a higher life; come down now through humility lest pride and high mindedness make you fall. Make haste, and humble yourself. If you humble yourself, I must abide at your house, for it is necessary that I abide in the house of a humble man. *Upon whom shall I look, if not upon him who is humble and meek, who trembles at My words?''*[4] Such a man gives half of his goods to the destitute demons. For our substance is twofold: flesh and spirit. The righteous man imparts all his fleshly substance to the truly poor, the demons who are destitute of everything good. But he does not let go of his spiritual substance, for as the Lord likewise said to the devil concerning Job, *Behold, I give into thine hand*

---

[3] Ps. 83:6

[4] Is. 66:2

all that he has, but touch not his soul.[5] And if he has taken any thing from any man by false accusation, he restores it to him fourfold. This suggests that if a man repents and follows a path that is opposite to his former way of wickedness, he heals his former sins through the four virtues,[6] and thus he receives salvation and is called *a son of Abraham.* For, like Abraham, he also goes out of his land and out of his kinship with his former wickedness and out of the house of his father,[7] meaning, he comes out from his old self and rejects his former condition. He himself was *the house of his father*, the devil. Therefore, when he went out of the house of his father, that is, when he went out of himself and changed, he found salvation, as did Abraham.

11-14. And as they heard these things, He added and spake a parable, because He was nigh to Jerusalem, and because they thought that the kingdom of God should immediately appear. He said therefore, A certain nobleman went into a far country to receive for himself kingship, and to return. And he called his ten servants, and gave them ten pounds, and said unto them, Trade with them till I come. But his citizens hated him, and sent a message after him, saying, We will not have this man to reign over us. It seems to me that when these men heard the Lord speak of *the kingdom of God*, they understood it to mean a kingdom of this world which God wanted to establish for the liberation of the Hebrew race. Therefore they thought that Jesus was going up to Jerusalem to receive this kingdom. But the Lord shows them that their thoughts are foolish, for His kingdom is not one perceived by the senses. At the same time He reveals to them that He is God, because He knows their thoughts. He tells them this parable and presents Himself in it as a highborn *nobleman.* For though He became a man, He remained in the heights and never relinquished the nobility of His divinity. And when He had accomplished the mystery of His dispensation in the flesh, *He went into a far country*, which means,

---

[5] Job 1:12. *tēs psychēs autou mē apsē.* The Septuagint text of this passage from Job as given by Bl. Theophylact differs from the text given by Brenton, which reads *Touch not himself, autou mē apsē.*

[6] The four universal virtues are: courage, prudence, righteousness, and self-control. See Vol. 1, *The Explanation* of St. Matthew, p. 7.

[7] See Gen. 12:1.

heaven, *to receive for himself kingship*, that is, so that as a Man in the flesh He might sit at the right hand of the throne of majesty in the highest. As God, He was always co-enthroned with the Father, but as Man He sat upon the throne after His Ascension, *waiting till His enemies be made His footstool.*[8] This will take place at the end of the world when everyone, willingly or not, shall be made subject to Him and shall believe that Jesus Christ is Lord to the glory of God the Father. *His citizens* are those Jews who hate Him. For *they have seen*, He says, *and have hated both Me and My Father,*[9] and they did not want Him to reign over them. Rejecting His kingship they said to Pilate, *We have no king but Caesar*, and, *Write not, The King of the Jews.*[10] Yet Zechariah cries out, *Rejoice greatly, O daughter of Sion; thy King is coming to thee, righteous and saving;*[11] and Isaiah, *Behold, a righteous King shall reign;*[12] and David says, *But as for Me, I was established as King by Him.*[13] The Jews hated the Lord, but to His servants He gave ten pounds. His servants are those who have been entrusted with serving in the Church, and they are said to be ten in number, indicating the completeness and perfection of authority resting upon those who preside in the Church.[14] For there is a full and perfect order in the Church in the ranks of those who preside, and there is nothing lacking or to excess. For example, we see in the Church these three things: cleansing, enlightenment, and perfecting. And these three activities have been allotted to the three ranks of clergy. The deacons cleanse by instruction and teaching, the presbyters illumine through baptism, and the hierarchs establish the priestly ranks and bring them to completion and perfection, that is to say, the hierarchs ordain by the laying on of hands.[15] Do you see that each rank fulfills its function, and

---

[8] See Heb. 10:12-13.

[9] Jn. 15:24

[10] Jn. 19:15,21

[11] Zech. 9:9

[12] Is. 32:1

[13] Ps. 2:6

[14] *to teleion tēs ekklēsiastikēs prostasias*

[15] The connection between "perfecting and completing," on the one hand, and "ordaining," on the other, may be found in the prayer that is said aloud by the presiding bishop at the ordination of a bishop, priest, or deacon: "The divine grace, which always healeth that which is infirm, and

that there is no need for either more or less? Therefore, to His servants the Lord distributes ten pounds, representing the gifts He bestows on each servant according to what is profitable for each. Thus each man who has been entrusted to preside in the Church, though he be unworthy, receives his gift from this consecration. This is truly a great Mystery and Sacrament of God's love and providence for mankind.

15-28. And it came to pass, that when he was returned, having received the kingship, then he commanded these servants to be called unto him, to whom he had given the money, that he might know how much every man had gained by trading. Then came the first, saying, Lord, thy pound hath gained ten pounds. And he said unto him, Well done, thou good servant: because thou hast been faithful in a very little, have thou authority over ten cities. And the second came, saying, Lord, thy pound hath gained five pounds. And he said likewise to him, Be thou also over five cities. And another came, saying, Lord, behold, here is thy pound, which I have kept laid up in a napkin. For I feared thee, because thou art a severe man: thou takest up what thou layedst not down, and reapest what thou didst not sow. And he saith unto him, Out of thine own mouth will I judge thee, thou wicked servant. Thou knewest that I was a severe man, taking up what I laid not down, and reaping what I did not sow. Why then gavest not thou my money into the bank, that at my coming I might have demanded it with interest? And he said unto them that stood by, Take from him the pound and give it to him that hath ten pounds. (And they said unto him, Lord, he hath ten pounds.) I say unto you, Unto every one which hath shall be given; and from him that hath not, even what he hath shall be taken away from him. But those mine enemies, which would not that I should reign over them, bring hither, and slay them before me. And when He had thus spoken, He went ahead, going up to Jerusalem. Christ is this highborn nobleman, not only in His divine nature, but also in His human nature descended as He is from the royal line of David. When He

---

perfecteth [and completeth] that which is lacking, elevateth through the laying-on of hands, N., ... to be a Deacon [or Priest, or Bishop]. Wherefore let us pray for him, that the grace of the all-holy Spirit may come upon him.'' It is the Holy Spirit which perfects and completes, through the sacramental actions and prayers of the presiding bishop(s).

returns, that is, when at His second coming He will appear as King with
the angels, coming in the glory of the Father, and every knee shall bow
to Him,[16] then indeed He shall make a reckoning of His servants who
received the gift. Then it shall be seen who has brought benefit to many,
increasing his gift tenfold; who has brought benefit to others, but to fewer
than the first; and who has brought benefit to no one but has spent in
slothfulness the time for trading. He who has increased tenfold what he
received is set over ten cities, that is, he receives the rule of ten cities,
meaning that he receives a reward many times over. And the next servant
is likewise rewarded. But he who gained nothing is condemned. Let us
see what it is this man is saying, *"Lord, behold, here is Thy pound;* take
it, for *I have kept it laid up in a napkin."* A *napkin* was wrapped about
the Lord when He was dead, and the face of Lazarus in the tomb was
covered about with a *napkin.*[17] It is fitting, therefore, that this lazy man
deposited his gift in a napkin, for he made it dead and inactive, not
trading with it, nor producing any gain. *For I feared Thee,* he says. *Thou
takest up what Thou layedst not down.* There are many who make this
kind of excuse. Not wanting to bring benefit to others they say, "Where
God has not sown a natural aptitude, do not seek to find any harvest.
This particular man God has not made suited and well disposed for
learning—why then does God demand of me that I produce in him some
gain?" But the Lord says, "Thou, servant, teach him! Deposit My wealth
with the bankers, that is, with him and with everyone whom you find
before you in need of the benefit [you can bestow]. For every man is a
banker preordained by God to trade in this great market place of the
world, and each man is capable of producing a return on what wealth of
Mine you deposit with him. And when I come I shall demand that wealth
from you, with interest." Therefore we must do now what is ours to do;
as for the consequences, let God judge those who do not wish to receive
benefit. Thus the gift is taken away from that indolent man and given to
the good trader. And if the good trader already has, it is all the more
reason for him to receive more. *Unto everyone which hath shall be given,*
that is, to him who has gained much by trading well, even more shall be
given. If he increased his small gift tenfold, it is clear that greater gifts

---

[16] See Philippians 2:10.

[17] Jn. 11:44

he will also increase tenfold, and thus bring even more profit to his master. From the negligent and slothful man who did not try to increase what he had been given, even that which he has will be taken away, so as not to leave idle the master's gift which can be given to another and increased many times over. But we do not understand this parable only in terms of its literal meaning and teaching, but also in regards to the moral virtues. If God has given gifts to us—to one fasting, to another almsgiving, to another meekness, to another humility—if we are sober and vigilant we multiply these gifts. But if we are lazy and deaden ourselves by our own choice, later we will put the blame on God. We will say, as we so often do, "What can I do? If such and such a man is holy, it is because God wants him to be holy and so he is. But He does not want me to be holy, and so I am not. Some are born Peter, and some are born Paul. I was not." O foolish man! The single pound which you received can make you a Peter or a Paul. Labor hard, and bring in some yield for the Giver, even if it is less than Peter and Paul brought. You have received the very same gift as Peter and Paul. If they received a pound, and you also received a pound, but then did not bestir yourself at all to labor for the good, why do you blame God? Therefore, if we are found unworthy of these gifts, we are stripped of them. "But My enemies," the Lord says, "who do not want Me to reign over them, bring them here and slay them." He speaks here of the unbelieving Jews whom He delivers to destruction, consigning them to the outer fire. Although these wretched ones were slaughtered even here in this world by the Roman armies, they are held and kept for destruction in the next world as well.

29-40. And it came to pass, when He was come nigh to Bethphage and Bethany, at the mount called the Mount of Olives, He sent two of His disciples, saying, Go ye into the village over against you; in the which at your entering ye shall find a colt tied, whereon yet never man sat: loose him, and bring him hither. And if any man ask you, Why do ye loose him? thus shall ye say unto him, Because the Lord hath need of him. And they that were sent went their way, and found even as He had said unto them. And as they were loosing the colt, the masters thereof said unto them, Why loose ye the colt? And they said, The Lord hath need of him. And they brought him to Jesus: and they cast their garments upon the colt, and they set Jesus thereon. And as

He went, they spread their clothes in the way. And when He was come nigh, even now at the descent of the Mount of Olives, the whole multitude of the disciples began to rejoice and praise God with a loud voice for all the mighty works that they had seen, saying, Blessed be the King that cometh in the name of the Lord: peace in heaven, and glory in the highest! And some of the Pharisees from among the multitude said unto Him, Teacher, rebuke Thy disciples. And He answered and said unto them, I tell you that, if these should be silent, the stones would immediately cry out. The Lord shows two things by sitting upon the colt. First, He fulfills the prophecy which says, Behold, thy King cometh, sitting upon an ass.[18] But in addition, He suggests to us figuratively that He shall be conveyed by a young, unclean, and untamed Gentile people. It was not that He needed this donkey because of the length of the journey. How could He, Who had traversed all of Galilee and Judea on foot, have needed a colt to go from Bethany to Jerusalem, as short a distance as that is, as everyone knows? As I have said, He does this for a mystic purpose. The colt was tied up and it had many masters, but it is loosed by the apostles, that is, by *them that were sent.*[19] *Bethany* means *house of obedience* and *Bethphage* means *house of jawbones*, so named because it was a priestly place. For jawbones were given to the priest, as is written in the law.[20] The jawbones symbolize the word of teaching which spiritual jaws chew well and make refined. Therefore the Lord's disciples are sent to the house of the word of teaching and to the house which is obedient to that word. They loose the people that are bound by their sins and by their many cares of life. And instead of the Gentiles having many lords and gods, the apostles make them to have one Lord, Jesus, and one God, the Father. But where there is no house of obedience and no acceptance of the word of teaching, nothing like this can take place and the colt is not set loose. Two are sent, signifying that there are two ranks of servants who bring in the Gentile people and make them subject to Christ: prophets and apostles. They lead the untrained colt in from a country village, teaching us that

---

[18] See Zech. 9:9.

[19] In verse 32 the participial phrase, *oi apestalmenoi*, *them that were sent*, is a form of the verb *apostellō, I send.* The noun *apostolos, apostle,* is of course derived from the very same verb.

[20] Deut. 18:3

this Gentile people was coarse and ignorant, for it had carried neither the Mosaic nor the prophetic word. Another Evangelist says that there were children crying out, *Hosanna to the Son of David,*[21] and these children also signify this same young people, who sent up glory to God because they believed in Jesus Who had appeared in the flesh of the seed of David. As it is written, *the people that is being created shall praise the Lord.*[22] The spreading of garments in the way signifies that those who are worthy to praise Jesus shed the old man and spread it beneath Jesus and subject it to Him, so that He may walk upon it and sanctify it. Then no longer will the flesh rise up against the spirit, for as it is said, *Submit thyself unto the Lord and supplicate Him.*[23] Luke says that *the whole multitude of the disciples began to praise God.* It is not only the twelve, or the seventy, whom he calls *disciples,* but in general all those who were following Jesus, some because of the miracles and some who were attracted for a while by His teaching. Among this multitude it is likely that there were also children, as the other Evangelists say. All these were inspired by God, confessing Christ to be the King Who comes in the name of the Lord, that is, confessing Him to be God. And they say, *Peace in heaven,* meaning, "The ancient war which we waged against God has been ended." God had not been their King on earth. But now that God has come to earth, there is peace in heaven. Therefore there is *glory in the highest,* for the angels are giving glory that the King and God Who comes upon a colt has granted us such terms of union and reconciliation. The very fact that God has appeared on earth and walks about in enemy territory, for we had been His enemies, shows that treaties have been forged between us and Him. But the Pharisees grumbled that the multitude both called Him King and praised Him as God. For they thought that to name Him King amounted to insurrection against Caesar, and that to praise Him as God was blasphemy. But He says, "*If these should be silent, the stones would immediately cry out.* They are not saying these things to curry favor with Me; rather, they are compelled to offer this doxology of praise because of the mighty works they have seen."

---

[21] Mt. 21:15

[22] Ps. 101:18

[23] Ps. 36:7

**41-44. And when He was come near, He beheld the city, and wept
over it, saying, Would that thou knewest, even thou, at least in this
thy day, the things which are for thy peace! But now they are hid
from thine eyes. For the days shall come upon thee, that thine
enemies shall raise up a rampart about thee, and compass thee
round, and keep thee in on every side, and shall make thee even with
the ground, and thy children within thee; and they shall not leave in
thee one stone upon another; because thou knewest not the time of
thy visitation.** He weeps over the city because He is the Lover of
mankind and did not want to destroy those in the city on account of their
outrage against Him. By weeping He shows His compassionate mercy.
That He took pity on them, not only before the Cross but after the Cross
as well, and thirsted for their repentance, is clear from the fact that so
many years went by, some thirty-five years, until they were delivered into
the hands of the Romans. For it is certain that He delayed their punishment for no other reason than that He desired their repentance. He weeps,
therefore, over the senselessness of Jerusalem and says, *Would that thou
knewest, even thou, at least in this thy day, the things which are for thy
peace,* that is, "If only you would realize even now the things that are to
your advantage and which would bring you peace and rest, namely, faith
in Me and the abandonment of your plot against Me. *But now they are
hid from thine eyes* because you rejected, unbearable evils shall be
brought upon you, and you shall suffer this and this and this, *because
thou knewest not the time of thy visitation,* that is, the time of My coming
when I came to care for you and to save you. You ought to have
recognized the things which were for your peace, and you ought to have
believed in Me. Then you would have had peace from the Romans, and
deliverance from every affliction." For all those in Jerusalem who
believed in Christ were saved from the taking of the city; if all had
believed, no one would have been destroyed.

**45-20:8.[24] And He went into the temple, and began to cast out
them that sold therein, and them that bought, saying unto them, It
is written, My house is the house of prayer: but ye have made it a**

---

[24] The ancient manuscripts of Scripture were not divided into chapters and verses. These were
added much later. Bl. Theophylact's twelfth century text includes at the end of its "Chapter 19"
what later was arranged as the first eight verses of "Chapter 20."

den of thieves. And He taught daily in the temple. But the chief priests and the scribes and the chief of the people sought to destroy Him, and could not find what they might do: for all the people hung on Him to hear. And it came to pass, that on one of those days, as He taught the people in the temple, and preached the Gospel, the chief priests and the scribes with the elders came upon Him, and spake unto Him, saying, Tell us, by what authority doest Thou these things? Or who is he that gave Thee this authority? And He answered and said unto them, I will also ask you one thing, and answer Me: The baptism of John, was it from heaven, or of men? And they reasoned among themselves, saying, If we shall say, From heaven, He will say, Why then believed ye him not? But if we say, Of men, all the people will stone us: for they be persuaded that John was a prophet. And they answered, that they knew not whence it was. And Jesus said unto them, Neither tell I you by what authority I do these things.
Having entered into Jerusalem with glory, the Lord now shows the mark of His own authority by cleansing the peddlers from His Father's house. Although He had done this before at the beginning of His preaching, as John relates,[25] He does it now for the second time as an even greater condemnation of the Jews; for they did not amend their ways after His first correction but continued their profiteering. They even called Him an enemy of God at the very moment that He was honoring God the Father by cleansing the peddlers from the Father's house. Therefore He brings against them as their accuser Isaiah, who said, *My house shall be called a house of prayer.*[26] It was foolish for them to ask Him, *By what authority doest Thou these things?* for they were well able to answer their own question. Had He not provided them with the testimony of the prophet's words, that the house of God is a house of prayer and not a place of business or a den of thieves (for greed and profiteering are thievery)? Therefore, what need was there to ask Him by what authority He did these things? It should have been obvious to them that it was God Who had commanded these things, through His prophet. But they ask, *"By what authority doest Thou these things?* The law directs those descended from Levi to keep in good order the affairs of the temple. But

---

[25] Jn. 2:14-16

[26] Is. 56:7

You, Who are not descended from the tribe of Levi, how dare You usurp the duties of a priest?'' But remember, O Jews, what David said of Christ, *Thou art a priest forever, after the order of Melchizedek.*[27] Melchizedek was called a priest; yet he was not a priest according to the law, nor was he of the tribe of Levi. How could he have been, having been born before Levi? In the same vein, why do you seek to place Christ within the classifications of the law? Laws do not apply to God. When it was the time to do so, God commanded that the priests come from the tribe of Levi. But now He transfers duties, giving preference to the priesthood of Melchizedek.[28] This is why the Lord casts out from the temple those buying and selling the animals of sacrifice, such as sheep and doves, not only out of concern for reverence and orderliness in the temple, but also to show that it is no longer necessary to believe that God is moved to mercy by the sacrifice of animals. It would have been easy for the Lord to answer them, as we have said, and to say that it is the prophet, or, more correctly, God Himself, Who commands Him to do these things. Instead He asks them a question in return in order to show them that they always disbelieve the Holy Spirit, refusing to believe not only Isaiah, the prophet of old, whom perhaps they cannot remember, but even John, who appeared only yesterday and who lived a miraculous life that was little short of being immaterial and fleshless. The Lord asks this marvelous question and shuts their mouths. He shows that if they would not believe even such a great prophet as John, who seemed to them greater than Christ and who bore witness to Christ, why would they believe Christ if He told them by what authority He did these things? If He had told them, it is certain that they would have slandered and rejected Him, just as they had rejected the words of John who was, in their eyes, more glorious than Jesus.

---

[27] Ps. 109:4

[28] See Hebrews, chapters 7-8.

CHAPTER TWENTY

Concerning the parable of the vineyard.
Concerning those who craftily asked Him about the tribute.
Concerning the Sadducees who denied the resurrection.
Concerning the Lord's questioning of the Pharisees.

9-16.[1] Then began He to speak to the people this parable. A certain man planted a vineyard, and let it out to husbandmen, and went into a far country for a long time. And at the season he sent a servant to the husbandmen, that they should give him of the fruit of the vineyard; but the husbandmen beat him, and sent him away empty. And again he sent another servant; and they beat him also, and treated him shamefully, and sent him away empty. And again he sent a third; and they wounded him also, and cast him out. Then said the lord of the vineyard, What shall I do? I will send my beloved son: it may be they will reverence him when they see him. But when the husbandmen saw him, they reasoned among themselves, saying, This is the heir: come let us kill him, that the inheritance may be ours. So they cast him out of the vineyard, and killed him. What therefore shall the lord of the vineyard do unto them? He shall come and destroy these husbandmen, and shall give the vineyard to others. This parable is short, yet it holds for us many weighty teachings: it shows the providence of God bestowed so abundantly upon the Hebrews, who from the very beginning displayed in return a propensity for murder; it teaches that the God of the Old Testament and the God of the New are one and the same God, and that the Gentiles will be brought in, and the Jews cast out. This *vineyard*, then, is the assembly of the Jews, and the *husbandmen* are the scribes and Pharisees who are the leaders and guardians of the people. Moreover, we ourselves, individually, are both the vineyard and the husbandmen, for we must cultivate ourselves. Therefore, God, the Lover of Man, gave this vineyard to the husbandmen, and then *went into a far country*, that is, He allowed the husbandmen to act according to their free will. God sent various servants, meaning, the prophets, so that He might have some small gain, for the parable says that He wished to

---

[1] See footnote 24 on p. 257 (end of Chapter 19).

receive something *of the fruit of the vineyard*, not all the fruit. What is it that God profits from us, if not our knowledge of Him? To acknowledge God as our Master is in fact our gain, yet God counts our salvation and our gain as His own gain. The wicked husbandmen abused those who were sent, first beating them and then sending them away empty-handed. This signifies that they had reached such a state of ingratitude towards God that they not only turned away from the good, rendering no good fruit, but also did what was evil, and for this great wrong they deserved even greater punishment. After the prophets had suffered these terrible things, God's Son was sent. "For *it may be they will reverence* My Son." He did not say this in ignorance of what would happen, namely, that they were about to treat His Son even worse than they had the prophets; instead, He said what ought to have happened, for they ought to have reverenced the Son. And if they showed such irreverence for Him that they killed Him, this is to their greater condemnation, that even after God had declared that it was good that they reverence His Son,[2] they themselves determined to do just the opposite. To speak as if God did not know what would happen is a manner of expression often found in Scripture, as, for example, when it is written, *If they shall hear.*[3] He does not say this in ignorance of the future; instead, He shapes His speech as He does to prevent anyone from later saying that God's foreknowledge was the necessary cause of the disobedience of the people. There is an explanation right at hand for the words, *they cast him out of the vineyard and killed him*: that they will cast Jesus outside of Jerusalem, for Christ indeed underwent the Passion outside the gate of the city.[4] But since we explained above that the vineyard means the people, not Jerusalem, perhaps it would be more fitting to say that the people killed Him outside of the vineyard. That is to say, the people did not kill Him with their own hands, but handed Him over to Pilate and to Gentiles. *Outside the vineyard* means, therefore, that the Lord suffered and died *outside* the hands of the people. It was not lawful for them [being under occupation] to kill anyone, and so He died at the hands of Roman soldiers. Some have also understood the vineyard to mean Scripture; understood this

---

[2] See, for example, Mt. 3:17: *This is My beloved Son, in Whom I am well pleased.*

[3] Ezekiel 2:5; 3:11.

[4] See Heb. 13:12.

way, the Lord suffered outside the Scriptures, that is, He was slain by
those who did not believe Moses. If they had believed Moses and if they
had been searching the Scriptures, they would not have slain the Master
of the Scriptures. Having said these things, the Lord then gives the
sentence which will fall upon them, that He *shall give the vineyard to
others*, that is, the grace of being called "My people" will be given to
others. See that those who say that the vineyard signifies Scripture appear
to hit the mark, as is shown here. For Scripture has indeed been taken
from the Hebrews and given to us. One could also say boldly that the
vineyard represents everything spiritual, whether it is found in Scripture
and the law, or in the actions and events of life, past and present. The
Jews have been deprived of everything spiritual; what they have lost, we
now enjoy.

**16-19. And when they heard it, they said, God forbid! And He
beheld them and said, What is this then that is written, The stone
which the builders rejected, the same is become the head of the
corner? Whosoever shall fall upon that stone shall be broken; but on
whomsoever it shall fall, it will crush him to powder to be scattered.
And the chief priests and the scribes the same hour sought to lay
hands on Him; but they feared the people. For they perceived that
He had spoken this parable against them.** Luke says, as you have just
heard, that it is the Lord Who states that the master of the vineyard
would destroy those ungrateful husbandmen and give the vineyard to
others, and hearing this the Pharisees said, *God forbid!* But Matthew says
that the Lord asked a question, "*What will* the master of the vineyard *do
unto those husbandmen?*" and the Jews gave the answer, *He will
miserably destroy those wicked men, and will let out his vineyard unto
other husbandmen.*[5] Do these two accounts, then, contradict each other?
Far from it! It is altogether reasonable that both things occurred; that first,
as Matthew says, the Jews themselves answered the Lord's question, and
then, when they sensed where the parable was leading and that it was
spoken against them, that they altered their course and exclaimed *God
forbid!* as Luke records. How does Christ respond? He introduces further
testimony from David, calling Himself *the stone* and these false teachers

---

[5] Mt. 21:40-41

the builders, just as Ezekiel says of the false prophets and teachers of Israel, that *one builds a wall, and they plaster it—it shall fall.*[6] This means that these teachers speak to curry favor, covering up the faults of the people as plasterers do to the surface of faulty segments of a wall. How did they reject this stone? By saying, "He is not of God." The Lord then makes reference to two destructions: first, the destruction of their souls which they suffered when they took offence at Christ, *for whosoever shall fall upon that stone shall be broken*; and secondly, the destruction at the time of the captivity of Jerusalem, which was brought upon them by the Stone which they had despised: *but on whomsoever it shall fall, it will crush him to powder.* The Jews indeed were crushed to powder and scattered like chaff from the threshing floor, that is, from Judea into all the world. Note that first they fell on the stone, that is, they took offence, [tripping upon the Rock that lay in their path,] and then as a result the Stone fell on them in punishment. First comes my own sin, and then the righteous punishment of God upon me. The Jews rejected this Stone, which was so beautiful and elect that it was set as the head of the corner, joining together two walls, the Old and the New, and making them one. They ought to have given heed to Isaiah who said, *Sanctify ye the Lord Himself; and He shall be thy fear. Ye shall not come against Him as against a stone in stumbling, nor as against a rock in falling.*[7] Because they knew that He had spoken this parable against them, they plotted against Him, and had they not been afraid of the people they would have laid hands on Him then. Heedless of the law which says, *Thou shalt not slay the innocent and righteous man,*[8] they feared only the anger of men, and therefore abandoned their open attack, choosing instead to plot against Christ secretly.

20-26. And they watched Him, and sent forth spies, who should feign themselves righteous men, that they might take hold of His words, that so they might deliver Him unto the power and authority of the governor. And they asked Him, saying, Teacher, we know that Thou sayest and teachest rightly, neither considerest Thou the person

---

[6] Ezekiel 13:10

[7] Is. 8:14. Brenton's translation has been corrected here.

[8] Ex. 23:7

of any, but teachest the way of God truly: Is it lawful for us to give tribute unto Caesar, or no? But He perceived their craftiness, and said unto them, Why tempt ye Me? Show Me a penny. Whose image and superscription hath it? They answered and said, Caesar's. And He said unto them, Render therefore unto Caesar the things which be Caesar's, and unto God the things which be God's. And they could not catch Him in His words before the people; and they marvelled at His answer, and kept silent. The Pharisees set what they thought was an inescapable trap: but their own feet were caught in it. See their vicious cunning: if He said that they ought to give tribute to Caesar, He would be condemned by the people for leading their race into slavery, this race which is the seed of Abraham and no man's slave. But if He forbade them to give tribute, the Pharisees could bring Him before the governor on the charge of sedition. But He leaps from their snare like a gazelle (for so the bride names Him in the Song of Solomon[9]); and He teaches us that to subject ourselves bodily to a king or ruler who has authority over our bodies in no way interferes with our ability to lead a spiritual life pleasing to the God of spirits. For He says, *Render unto Caesar the things which be Caesar's, and unto God the things which be God's.* See that He did not say simply *give* [*dote*], but *render* [*apodote*], that is, give back what it is due. It is obligatory, Christ says, to render that which is due. Your ruler guards you from enemies and makes your life peaceful: in return for these things, you owe him the tax. It is obligatory for another reason as well: the coin which you give comes from your ruler in the first place. Therefore give back to the king his own coin, for all this time you have made a profit doing business with it, and you have used it to acquire the necessary things of life. You must likewise render to God the things of God. He has given you intellect [*nous*]; render it to God by governing your actions by this intellect. He has given you logos; render it to Him by doing everything as a reason-endowed creature, not becoming like the mindless beasts. In short, He has given you both soul and body; give back all that you owe Him, which is nothing less than the image of Himself in you, which you must restore by walking in faith, hope, and love. In yet another way we must render unto Caesar the things of Caesar: each one of us bears the image either

---

[9] Song 2:9

of God or of the ruler of this world. When we make ourselves like "Caesar", we become sons of the devil. If we bear the devil's image, we ought to return it to the devil and cast it away from us so that he can have what is his and find nothing in us that belongs to him. This is how we preserve in ourselves the unadulterated image of God. Therefore Paul exhorts, *As we have borne the image of the earthen, we shall also bear the image of the heavenly;*[10] and in another place, *that ye put off the old man.*[11] What the Lord here says to *render* and give back, Paul says to *put off*; and what is here spoken of as the image of Caesar is there described by Paul as the image of the earthen sinner, of Adam and the old man. For *the image of the earthen* is none other than the corruption and sin which we acquired when we made ourselves like that traitorous renegade, the devil, and defaced our likeness to God, the true King. And so the Pharisees were not able to catch Jesus in His words in front of the people. What they were striving to do was just that, to slander Christ before the people as a man who would enslave the Hebrews to the Romans. But they were unable to accomplish their desire because of His exceedingly wise answer.

27-40. Then came to Him certain of the Sadducees, who deny that there is any resurrection; and they asked Him, saying, Master, Moses wrote unto us, If any man's brother die, having a wife, and he die without children, that his brother should take his wife, and raise up seed unto his brother. There were therefore seven brethren: and the first took a wife, and died without children. And the second took her to wife, and he died childless. And the third took her; and in like manner the seven also: and they left no children, and died. Last of all the woman died also. Therefore in the resurrection whose wife of them is she? For seven had her to wife. And Jesus answering said unto them, The children of this age marry, and are given in marriage: but they who shall be accounted worthy to obtain that age, and the resurrection from the dead, neither marry, nor are given in marriage; for neither can they die any more, for they are equal unto the angels, and are the children of God, being the children of the

---

[10] I Cor. 15:49

[11] Eph. 4:22; see also Col. 3:8-9.

resurrection. Now, that the dead are raised, even Moses showed at the bush, when he calleth the Lord the God of Abraham, and the God of Isaac, and the God of Jacob. For He is not God of the dead, but of the living: for all are alive in Him. Then certain of the scribes answering said, Master, Thou hast well said. And after that they dared not ask Him any question at all. The Sadducees did not believe in the resurrection of the dead because their reasonings stood on a faulty and deceptive foundation which led them inevitably into error: they supposed that life in the resurrection would be fleshly. Therefore they slandered the doctrine of the resurrection as absurd by concocting this ridiculous scenario. The Lord first shakes their foundation by showing that there is no fleshly existence in the resurrection, and then immediately hurls down their teaching together with its faulty premise and supposition, saying, *"Ye are deluded, not knowing the Scriptures,*[12] and distorting their meaning. For *the children of this age*, begotten and begetting in this world, *marry and are given in marriage*. But the children of the resurrection do nothing of the kind, *for neither can they die any more*; therefore, in that age there is no married life, but instead an angelic and divine life. Here, there is marriage because there is death, and there is death because there is marriage. There, where death has been abolished, what need is there of marriage? Marriage is for the help of mortals and for the replenishing of what is lacking [because of death]. But where nothing is lacking, what need is there for replenishing? Therefore *they are equal unto the angels and are the children of God.* Why? Because they are *children of the resurrection."* What He means is this: "I have said that they are the children of God because nothing in their begetting is carnal—all is divine. Their birth into resurrection is preceded by neither intercourse, nor seed, nor womb, nor conception; it is God Who begets their resurrected bodies by ways known only to Him. Therefore, since it is God Who is at work in the resurrection, it is fitting that those who have been reborn of the resurrection should be called the children of God." To this reasoning the Lord adds the witness of Scripture. Moses says that God spoke to him out of the burning bush, saying, *I am the God of Abraham, and the God of Isaac, and the God of Jacob.*[13] If the

---

[12] Mt. 22:29

[13] Ex. 3:6

Patriarchs had altogether perished and no longer lived with God in the hope of the resurrection, God would not have said, *I am the God of Abraham,* but "I was the God of Abraham." For this is how we speak of things that have corrupted and perished: "I was the owner of such and such a thing." But here, by saying *I am,* He shows that He is Master and God of the living, and not of things that have completely corrupted. Though the Patriarchs are dead, they are alive in the hope of the resurrection, even as Adam had death even while he lived. For it is said that Adam died [spiritually and began to die physically] at the very hour at which he ate of the fruit.[14] When the Sadducees had thus been put to shame, the scribes applauded Jesus as an adversary of the Sadducees and took pleasure in their defeat.

41-47. And He said unto them, How say they that Christ is David's son? For David himself saith in the book of Psalms, The Lord said unto My Lord, Sit Thou at My right hand, till I make Thine enemies the footstool of Thy feet. David therefore calleth Him Lord; how is He then his son? Then in the audience of all the people He said unto His disciples, Beware of the scribes, who desire to walk in long robes, and love greetings in the markets, and the chief seats in the synagogues, and the places of honour at feasts; who devour widows' houses, and for a pretence make long prayers: the same shall receive greater condemnation. Because He is shortly to go to His Passion, He now proclaims His divinity; but He does not do so openly and brazenly, but in a most humble fashion. He asks them a question, first causing them to be perplexed and then allowing them to figure out for themselves the consequences of the answer. For *David,* He says, *calleth Him Lord; how then is He* merely *his son?* Christ was the son of David according to the flesh, but He is also David's God. But the scribes thought that Christ was only David's son. Therefore He first refutes their opinion that Christ is merely the son of David, and then He reveals that He is in no way opposed to the Father; on the contrary, He has such oneness of mind with Him, that the Father makes war against Christ's enemies. This much He addresses to the scribes, and then He turns to His disciples. Because He sent them out to be the teachers of the whole world, it is fitting that

---

[14] See Bl. Theophylact's explanation of Lk. 21:28-33 on p. 275 of this volume.

He exhort them not to imitate the Pharisees with their vainglory and love of being first, and in general, their worldliness and desire to please men. For those who give grand salutations in the market places do so to flatter those whom they meet and to honor them as virtuous and upstanding men, or else they make a show of their salutations in order to receive donations. Not only this, the Lord says, but with their greedy appetites they also *devour widows' houses*, eating them out of house and home. They use piety as a pretext to gain entry, and then, masking their purpose with prayers and blessings, they teach drunkenness and gluttony instead of fasting. For this reason, the Lord says, they *shall receive greater condemnation,* in that they not only do evil, but make a pretence of prayer. They make a show of piety and under the pretext of virtue do evil. They shall receive a greater condemnation because their actions defame piety. They ought to take pity on the widows; instead they enter the widows' houses supposedly to bless them with long prayer, and the widows feel obliged to lavish hospitality on them, and thus impoverish themselves.

CHAPTER TWENTY-ONE

Concerning the widow who cast in two mites.
Concerning the question about the end.
Concerning the captivity of Jerusalem,
and the Lord foretelling to His disciples her desolation.
Concerning the signs.

1-4. And He looked up, and saw the rich men casting their gifts into the treasury. And He saw also a certain poor widow casting in thither two mites. And He said, Of a truth I say unto you, that this poor widow hath cast in more than they all. For all these have from their abundance cast in unto the offerings of God: but she of her destitution hath cast in all the living that she had. The temple treasury, to which those who loved God made contributions, was used for the upkeep and repair of the temple precincts, for the adornment of the temple itself, and for the feeding of the poor. In later times the priests appropriated this money, dividing it among themselves and using it for purposes other than those for which the treasury had been instituted. The Lord praises the widow more than all the others because she cast into the treasury everything she had to live on, despite her destitution. These two coins, although they may seem trifling, were in fact the entire living of this widow who was so destitute that she fed herself by begging. When the Lord renders to each his due reward, He does not consider the amount given but the amount left. Therefore what those rich men gave was small and trifling because there was so much more left to them in their houses. But the house of the widow was empty and nothing remained. It is altogether fitting, then, that she was more worthy of praise than they. Some have also understood the *widow* to represent every soul that has buried her first husband, the old law, but is not yet worthy to be wedded to God the Word. But she offers as the pledge of her betrothal what little she has: her still small faith and a good conscience. For we must offer not only faith but a good conscience as well, which means, an upright life. If any one approaches God in this manner, he is seen to cast in more than those who are rich in learning and have pagan virtues in abundance.

5-11. And as some were speaking of the temple, how it was adorned with goodly stones and gifts, He said, As for these things

which ye behold, the days will come, in the which there shall not be
left one stone upon another, that shall not be thrown down. And they
asked Him, saying, Master, but when shall these things be? And what
sign will there be when these things shall come to pass? And He said,
Take heed that ye be not deceived: for many shall come in My name,
saying, It is I; and, The time hath drawn near. Go ye not therefore
after them. But when ye shall hear of wars and tumults, be not
terrified; for these things must first come to pass; but the end will
not come at once. Then He said unto them, Nation shall rise against
nation, and kingdom against kingdom: and great earthquakes shall
be in divers places, and famines, and pestilences; and fearful sights
and great signs shall there be from heaven. Inasmuch as He is shortly
to go to His Crucifixion, it is fitting that the Lord now prophesies
concerning Jerusalem, so that we might have these words as further, and
overwhelming, proof that He is truly God. Therefore, when certain people
praised the buildings of the temple precincts and its votive offerings—I
think that these were perhaps the carvings and sculptures, such as the
carved palm trees and cherubim[1]—the Lord did not turn to admire these
things, but instead foretold their destruction. They thought He was
speaking of the end of the world, when in fact He was speaking of the
taking of Jerusalem by the Romans. For this reason He condescends [to
their misunderstanding]. He ceases to speak only of the capture of
Jerusalem, and now begins to weave together into a single account the
destruction of Jerusalem and the end of the world, forewarning them not
to be led astray by the false prophets that will appear before His second
coming. There will be wars and tumults, for when all love has vanished,
it is only fitting that wars and tumults should take its place. After the
wars, famines and pestilences will come: disease, because the air will be
corrupted by the corpses of the slain, and famine, because there will be
no one left to till the soil. Some have understood the famines, pestilences,
and other tribulations to be not only those which will occur at the end of
the world, but also those which took place at the time of the capture of
Jerusalem. For Josephus says that unspeakable horrors took place at that
time because of starvation; and Luke says in Acts that there was a famine
during the reign of Claudius Caesar; and many *fearful sights* occurred

---

[1] III Kings (I Kings) 6:23-30

indicating the capture of Jerusalem, as Josephus relates.[2] All these things together, the tumults, the wars, and all the rest, can be understood to refer both to the time of the end of the world and of the capture of Jerusalem.

12-19. But before all these, they shall lay their hands on you, and persecute you, delivering you up to the synagogues, and into prisons, being brought before kings and rulers for My name's sake. And this shall prove unto you a witnessing. Settle it therefore in your hearts, not to meditate beforehand what ye shall answer: for it is I Who will give you a mouth and wisdom, which all your adversaries shall not be able to contradict nor resist. And ye shall be betrayed both by parents, and kinsfolk, and friends, and brethren; and some of you shall they put to death. And ye shall be hated by all for My name's sake. But there shall not a hair of your head perish. In your patient endurance, ye shall gain your souls. The Lord says, *Before all these*, that is, before all these things that will mark the end of the world, and the capture of Jerusalem as well. For, as I have said above, the Lord weaves His words concerning the capture of Jerusalem into His words concerning the end. *"They shall lay their hands on you, My disciples,"* He says. Indeed, before the capture of the city, the apostles were persecuted and driven out of Jerusalem; this was done by God's providence so that the terrible calamities would fall only upon the crucifiers of the Lord, while they, the apostles, filled the whole world with the preaching of the Gospel. For this the apostles were brought before kings and rulers, as Paul was brought before Festus and Agrippa and Caesar himself.[3] This happened to them so that they might have the glory of giving testimony. The apostles were simple and unlearned men; therefore, so that they would not be distressed when they would be examined and have to give an accounting before learned men, the Lord says, "Take no thought beforehand concerning this, for you will receive from Me wisdom and eloquence for this situation, so that not even all your adversaries gathered together into one assembly will be able to withstand you, either in wisdom, that is, in the power of your thoughts, or in unhesitating eloquence." It often happens that one who is wise in reasoning and

---

[2] See Acts 11:28 and Josephus, *Jewish Wars*, Bk. V, Ch. X.

[3] Acts 25 and 26

thought is easily upset when there is a turmoil and commotion, and he is thrown into confusion when it is time for him to speak publicly. But the apostles were given the gift of both wisdom and eloquence, and thus the high priest and his kindred were astonished at the sudden wisdom of Peter and John when they learned that before this they were ordinary, unlearned men.[4] Likewise Festus said to Paul, *Paul, thou art beside thyself; much learning doth make thee mad.*[5] When the Lord had said these things, and removed their fear of being unlearned, He added something that was distressing and sufficient to shake their souls: "*Ye shall be betrayed* by friends and kinsfolk." He foretells this to them so that they will not be overwhelmed when it suddenly occurs. Such a thing bears grievously upon the soul, for, as David says, *If mine enemy had reviled me, I might have endured it,* and further, *The man...who ate of my bread hath magnified the lifting of heels against me.*[6] Having said these things, and also that they shall be hated and some of them put to death, the Lord adds these words of supreme comfort: *But there shall not an hair of your head perish.* "You will be saved," He says, "and not destroyed at all, even though it will seem to many that you have been destroyed. You must only endure patiently, and in your patient endurance you shall be able to gain your souls. For the enemy will fall upon you like a spearman to take you prisoner, trying to snatch away your soul by the onslaught of terrible things. But as a ransom give him patience instead of silver, and by this exchange you will gain your soul and not suffer any loss." Give heed to the words, *some of you shall they put to death,* and you will understand in them something more profound. They will not put all of you to death: we consist of two parts, soul and body, and of these two parts *of you* they will put to death only one, namely, the body, but your soul you will gain by your patient endurance. The Lord says the same elsewhere, *Fear not them which kill the body, but are not able to kill the soul.*[7]

20-27. And when ye shall see Jerusalem compassed with armies,

---

[4] See Acts 4:13-14.

[5] Acts 26:24

[6] Ps. 54:12, Ps. 40:9

[7] Mt. 10:28

then know that the desolation thereof is nigh. Then let them which are in Judea flee to the mountains; and let them which are in the midst of it depart out; and let not them that are in the country enter thereinto. For these be the days of vengeance, that all things which are written may be fulfilled. But woe unto them that are with child, and to them that give suck, in those days! For there shall be great distress in the land, and wrath upon this people. And they shall fall by the edge of the sword, and shall be led away captive into all nations: and Jerusalem shall be trodden down by the Gentiles, until the times of the Gentiles be fulfilled. And there shall be signs in the sun, and in the moon, and in the stars; and upon the earth distress of nations, with perplexity; the sea and the waves roaring; men fainting from fear and foreboding of those things which are coming upon the earth: for the powers of heaven shall be shaken. And then shall they see the Son of Man coming in a cloud with power and great glory. Now He is speaking quite clearly of the capture of Jerusalem. Therefore I think that what He says above, *But before all these,* ought to be understood in this manner: "Before the famines, and pestilences, and the terrible things which will occur at the time of the end of the world, you, the apostles, will be persecuted," and so forth. Then the disaster will befall Jerusalem. Because they had thought that the buildings of the temple would be destroyed at the end of the world, the Lord says, "No, it is not so; at the time of the end of the world there will be false prophets, and famines and pestilences arising from the many wars that will occur because love has grown cold. But it is before the end of the world that, you, the apostles, will be persecuted, and Jerusalem will be captured, and these stones will be destroyed. For *when ye shall see Jerusalem compassed with armies, then know that the desolation thereof is nigh.*" In words full of tragedy He foretells the terrible siege of the city. *Let them which are in Judea flee to the mountains,* He says, *and let not them that are in the country* expect to find protection in the city, even though it has strong walls; but let them flee, together with those in the city. For these are *days of vengeance,* so that the things which were written, especially in the book of Daniel,[8] may be fulfilled. *Woe unto them that are with child,* for they will not be to able to flee because of

---

[8] See Dan. 10.

the burden of the womb; and woe *to them that give suck,* because, on account of their love for their infants, they will neither be able to abandon them nor take them along. Some say that the Lord here is referring to the eating of children of which Josephus gives an account[9] and Jeremiah prophesied.[10] Then, the Lord says, *Jerusalem shall be trodden down by the Gentiles.* To this point He has been speaking of the captivity. Now He turns again to the events of the end of the world. *There shall be signs in the sun, and in the moon, and in the stars.* For when creation is changed, it is fitting that its elements be altered. There will be *distress of nations,* which means, tribulation, together with bewilderment, and the sea will roar with a fearful noise. There will be such storms and upheavals that men will faint merely out of fear and foreboding of the things that are coming upon the earth. Here you see the Lord clearly speaking about the end. Above He spoke only of Jerusalem being surrounded and trodden upon by the armies of the Gentiles; here He speaks of the evils coming upon the whole world, so that now His words refer to the end of all things. *For the powers of heaven shall be shaken.* "Do I say that only mankind will be distressed when all creation is changed? No, even the angels and the commanding powers of the heavenly host will be shaken and astounded at the fearful changes of the universe." *And then shall they see the Son of Man.* Who shall see Him? All shall see Him, both those who believe and those who do not believe. They shall see Him *coming in a cloud,* that is, as God, *with power and great glory,* and both He and His Cross will shine more brightly than the sun and will be recognized by all.

28-33. And when these things begin to come to pass, then look up, and lift up your heads; for your redemption draweth nigh. And He spake to them a parable: Behold the fig tree, and all the trees; when they now shoot forth, ye see and know of your own selves that summer is now nigh at hand. So likewise ye, when ye see these things come to pass, know ye that the kingdom of God is nigh at hand. Verily I say unto you, This generation shall not pass away, till all be fulfilled. Heaven and earth shall pass away: but My words shall not

---

[9] See Josephus, *Jewish Wars,* Bk. VI, Ch. III, 4.

[10] See Jer. 19.

pass away. Just as the first coming of the Lord was for the re-fashioning and rebirth of our souls, so the second coming will be for the rebirth of our bodies. Death came first to the souls of Adam and Eve when they disobeyed, and nine hundred years after their disobedience their bodies underwent death in physical actuality. Consequently, our souls are reborn and made better by the first coming of Christ, and our bodies, by the second coming. Therefore the Lord says, "When these things come to pass, look up, you who are weighted down by corruption, and you will be set free. For your redemption is at hand, that is, the perfect liberation of both your soul and body together." The prefix *apo*, [of the Greek word *apolytrōsis, redemption*] intensifies the sense that the body at the second coming will be completely and totally delivered from corruption by the grace of the Lord Who abolishes the final enemy, death. First He overthrew the dark principalities and powers and redeemed our souls. But death remained, feeding upon our bodies. When the Lord abolishes death, it will result in our complete freedom and redemption. And when all this comes to pass, the kingdom of God will at once be present. When the fig tree puts forth leaves, it indicates that summer is near; so too when these fearful signs and changes in the universe occur, they indicate that summer is coming, that is, the kingdom of God, which comes upon the righteous like summer after the storms of winter; but for sinners their stormy winter will then begin, for they consider this age to be summer and the age to come a winter of violent storms. *Verily I say unto you, This generation shall not pass away, till all be fulfilled.* He says *generation*, meaning, not only those who lived at that time, but the generation of all believers who alike have been baptized and reborn in Christ. Scripture uses *generation* to refer to those who are alike in some way; for example, *This is the generation of them that seek the Lord.*[11] Christ had said that tumults and wars and changes would occur in the elements and in human affairs; therefore, lest anyone imagine that Christianity would also be destroyed, He says, "No, *this generation* of Christians *shall not pass away.* Heaven and earth shall be changed, but My words and My Gospel shall not be

---

[11] Ps. 23:6

destroyed, but shall remain.[12] Though all is shaken, faith in Me shall not fail.'' Here He shows that He holds the Church in greater honor than all creation; for if all creation is changed, then no part of it outlives or is superior to His words and the Church of the faithful, which shall not pass away.

34-36. And take heed to yourselves, lest at any time your hearts be weighed down with overindulgence and drunkenness, and cares of this life, and so that day come upon you unawares. For as a snare shall it come on all them that sit upon the face of the earth. Watch ye therefore, and pray always, that ye may be accounted worthy to escape all these things that shall come to pass, and to stand before the Son of Man. You have heard Me speak, He says, of terrors and tumults; all these things are visible symbols of the evils that will overtake the sinners. Against these terrible things there is a powerful medicine and antidote: prayer and attentiveness. To be always in readiness and expectation of the end will help you more than anything else. You may achieve this, the Lord says, if you are sober and your hearts are not *weighed down with overindulgence, and drunkenness, and cares of this life.* For that day *cometh not with observation,*[13] but unexpectedly and secretly, like a trap which snaps shut on those who are not paying attention. Let us examine more closely the expression *them that sit upon the face of the earth.* That day will ensnare those *that sit,* who are passing their lives carelessly and slothfully. It is they who are caught in the trap. But an active and vigorous man, alert in doing good, and always moving towards virtue, does not sit or rest among earthly things, but gets up from this place and says to himself, *Arise thou, and depart; for this is not thy rest.*[14] He always longs for the better fatherland. For such a man, that last day is neither snare nor peril; it is instead a feast day. This is why we must keep watch and pray to God: so that we may be able *to escape all*

---

[12] Having explained it elsewhere (see Vol. 1, *The Explanation* of St. Matthew, pp. 21-22), Bl. Theophylact does not need to mention here that the word *until* [eōs] of *until all be fulfilled*, does not mean that after all has been fulfilled, *this generation* shall then pass away. Instead it means, in keeping with this common usage of *until* in Scripture, that *this generation* shall never pass away, even after all has been fulfilled.

[13] Lk. 17:20

[14] Micah 2:10

these things that shall come to pass. What things? First of all, the famines, and pestilences, and all the rest, which will not press so heavily upon God's elect as they will upon the others. Indeed, [so great is God's solicitude for His elect that] for their sake He will shorten these calamities even for those not among the elect, although such tribulations will occur eternally for sinners. Only through watchfulness and prayer can we escape all these things. It is not enough for those who may be courageous merely to flee these evils; they must also attain what is good. Therefore, after saying, *That ye may be* able *to escape all these things that shall come to pass,* the Lord adds the words, *and to stand before the Son of Man.* This is the enjoyment of good things. We must not only flee from evil things but also strive to receive the Christian glory. It is an angelic rank to stand before the Son of Man and our God. *For their angels,* He says, *do always behold the face of My Father.*[15]

37-38. And in the day time He was teaching in the temple; and at night He went out, and abode on the mount called the Mount of Olives. And all the people came early at dawn to Him in the temple, for to hear Him. The Evangelists, especially the three, did not reveal most of what Jesus taught. Even John himself was silent concerning the greater part, although he did set forth certain teachings more sublime than those recorded by the three. We can infer that the Lord conversed on many and exalted themes with those assembled in the temple. That the Evangelists, who did not want to make a pretentious show, told only a few things of what the Lord taught, is clear from many indications, not the least of which is the fact that, although the Lord preached for almost three years, few of His teachings are written down. And if a man said that these teachings which were written down could be spoken in a single day, I think he would not be mistaken. The holy Evangelists, therefore, wrote down for us a few things from very many, just enough for us to get a taste of sweetness. And the Lord did not speak in one manner only, but set forth for each listener something that was to his benefit. This is why the multitude *came early at dawn to Him,* for grace flowed from His lips. But at night He departed to the mountain, showing us that we must converse with God at night, because then it is quiet, and in the day come

---

[15] Mt. 18:10

down to men to bring them benefit. We must gather by night, and then distribute by day what we have gathered. The Lord Himself had no need of prayer, or to be with God: He Himself is God and lacks nothing. But He did this as an example for us, so that at night, like wells collecting the water that trickles into them through the veins of the earth, we might receive the grace which seeps into us through the spiritual channels of prayer. Then by day we can draw from this living water for those who thirst and ask us for spiritual help. If a man saw those people rising early at dawn to hear Christ, he might say that the words of David fitted them: *O God, My God, unto Thee I rise early at dawn. My soul hath thirsted for Thee.*[16]

---

[16] Ps. 62:1

CHAPTER TWENTY-TWO

Concerning the Pascha.
Concerning those who disputed who was the greatest.
Concerning Satan's demand to have Peter
that he might sift him as wheat.
Concerning Christ's arrest.
Concerning Jesus when He was led away to the high priest.

1-6. Now the feast of the unleavened bread drew nigh, which is called Pascha. And the chief priests and scribes sought how they might kill Him; for they feared the people. Then entered Satan into Judas surnamed Iscariot, being of the number of the twelve. And he went his way, and spoke with the chief priests and captains, how he might betray Him unto them. And they were glad, and covenanted to give him money. And he agreed, and sought opportunity to betray Him unto them in the absence of the multitude. The scribes were seeking to kill Christ. But with the time of Pascha fast approaching, they saw how dangerous it would be for them to attempt this while the people were gathered together in Jerusalem for the feast. So they sought another way to kill Him, one that would not put them in such danger. *Then entered Satan into Judas...being of the number of the twelve,* which means, "despite the fact that Judas was from the inner circle of the Lord's own disciples." By saying this, the Evangelist shows that no one should have bold confidence in himself. Instead, we should always keep close watch over our own lives because we have such a terrible opponent. Some have understood the words, *being of the number of the twelve,* to mean that Judas filled only the number of the apostolic rank, but was not a true apostle and disciple. How could he be a true disciple when he stole from the contents of their purse?[1] Therefore, when Satan entered into him, Judas welcomed him, and made an agreement with those who wanted Jesus handed over to them. The word *exomologēsen, he agreed,* means "he made a perfect agreement [*omologia*] and pact with them." And *he sought opportunity* when he might find Jesus *in the absence of the multitude,* that is, alone, to *betray Him unto them. Captains* here

---

[1] See Jn. 12:6.

mean the overseers of the temple buildings, or those in charge of keeping order in the temple precincts. The Romans had appointed such overseers over the people to prevent tumults, because the people were rebellious. These the Evangelist calls *captains*. Perhaps they were named *captains* because they also had military duties, although they were still members of the priestly rank. They were diseased with the love of being first, and it greatly pleased them to apply such titles to themselves. Therefore the Evangelist rebukes them all the more openly by calling them *captains* of the temple.

7-13. Then came the day of unleavened bread, when the Pascha must be sacrificed. And He sent Peter and John, saying, Go and prepare us the Pascha, that we may eat. And they said unto Him, Where wilt Thou that we prepare? And He said unto them, Behold, when ye are entered into the city, there shall a man meet you, bearing a pitcher of water; follow him into the house where he entereth in. And ye shall say unto the master of the house, The Master saith unto thee, Where is the guestchamber, where I shall eat the Pascha with My disciples? And he shall show you a large upper room furnished: there make ready. And they went, and found as He had said unto them: and they made ready the Pascha. Many have said that *Pascha*, in Hebrew *Phasek*, means the passage out of Egypt; the saints have interpreted it to mean in general everything that is performed during the feast of Pascha.[2] Now we must explain *the day of unleavened bread.* It means Thursday, on the evening of which they intended to slay the paschal lamb.[3] The Lord, therefore, perhaps on the morning of Thursday, sends out His disciples Peter and John, the one who loved and the other who was beloved. He sends them to a stranger's house, for He Himself had no house, nor did His disciples. If they had, He would have

---

[2] In Scripture *Pascha* may mean the feast itself, the paschal supper that is eaten, or the paschal lamb that is slain.

[3] St. Matthew (26:17) and St. Mark (14:12) call this Thursday *the first day of unleavened bread,* that is, the day before the Feast of Unleavened Bread, the Passover, which began on Friday, the fourteenth day of the Jewish month of Nisan (Abib). The Lord and His disciples made preparations for the Passover meal one day before the time appointed by the law, because on Friday Christ Himself would be slain as the true Paschal Lamb, fulfilling in His own Person the types and foreshadowings of the Old Testament.

kept the Pascha in the house of one of them. Behold the non-possession
of the Lord and His disciples. He sends them to a man they do not know
to show that He willingly accepted His Passion. He Who from afar
convinced the mind of a stranger to accept the disciples could likewise
have made the Jews do whatever He wanted them to do, had He not
willed to accept His death on the Cross. Some give another reason why
the Lord did not say the name of the man nor reveal his identity, but
instead led them by a sign to the house of the man: so that the betrayer
would not learn the name and report the house to the Pharisees, who
could then come and arrest Him before He had finished the supper and
delivered to them His spiritual Mysteries. This is why, further down,
Christ says, *With desire I have desired to eat this Pascha with you before
I suffer.*[4] This means, "I have taken great care to conceal My intentions
from the betrayer so that I do not undergo the Passion before it is time,
before I have delivered to you the Mysteries." He who wishes may
accept this explanation. Why does He keep the Pascha? To show in
everything He does, until His last breath, that He is not an opponent of
the law. Let us who are Christians also eat the Passover supper. But we
must do so noetically, by spiritually understanding the *day of unleavened
bread*. What is that day? It is when all our life is lived [in Christ] in the
light of the Spirit, not mixed with any of the old and corrupting leaven
of our former disobedience that was in Adam. Only when we live in this
manner may we feast on the Mysteries of Jesus. These Mysteries shall be
prepared for us by Peter, who represents action and fervent zeal, and by
John, who represents divine vision and peaceful meekness. For the
believer must be fervent in doing good and be zealous against evil, and
yet be meek and gentle to those who do evil. It is evil we must hate, not
the doer of evil; he, instead, must be healed, for he is suffering. For when
a man does evil, he is being harassed by the evil one and is suffering
from this evil. Therefore, if we have the supper prepared for us by Peter
and John, by which I mean the supper made ready by a good life—this
is Peter—and by true dogmas—this is John the Theologian—a *man* shall
meet such preparers as these. This means, then we shall find *a man*, our
true human condition as it was created in the image of our Maker, God
the Creator, *bearing a pitcher of water*. For water signifies the grace of

---

[4] Lk. 22:15

the Holy Spirit, as the Evangelist John teaches,[5] and the pitcher represents a heart that is easily broken and humbled. He that receives spiritual
grace is humble and contrite in heart. *The Lord gives grace to the
humble.*[6] He who knows that he is earth and dust (saying with Job, *From
the earth hast Thou fashioned me*[7]) bears the grace of the Holy Spirit in
his heart, a vessel quickly moved to compunction and contrition. If we
follow such a man, the true human condition, we shall reach the house
of the mind [*nous*]. The master of this house, the mind, will show us *a
large upper room furnished.* The *upper room* is the lofty and sublime
capacity of the mind; it signifies those divine and noetic things among
which such a mind gladly dwells and mingles.   These things are
furnished[8] and well in order. There is nothing jagged or rough or out-of-
place, and whatever was crooked or twisted has been made straight and
right by this mind. For, as Solomon said, *All things are straight to those
that understand, and right to those that find knowledge.*[9] You would not
miss the mark if you were also to say that, although the mind does
produce something lofty when it acts according to its own energy, its
knowledge does not rise above itself, and remains a lowly thing. But truly
lofty is the knowledge, and above every height is the unknowing beyond
the mind, when the mind no longer acts but is acted upon. First we must
act with our mind, and then we are acted upon by the grace of the Lord
which takes hold of us [*lambanontes*] just as it did the prophets, taking
us outside the realm of mere natural and physical activity. It is written

---

[5] Jn. 7:38-39

[6] Proverbs 3:34

[7] Not an exact quotation; see Job 10:8-9.

[8] *estrōmenon, furnished.* The Greek word is a past participle of a commonly used verb *strōnnymi,
to spread* (i.e. the bed clothes over a bed), to make smooth, level, or calm. The sense of *furnished*,
as of a room, is unique to the Gospels, implying that couches had been "spread" or prepared for
reclining at dinner. The Greek reader would have no difficulty in sensing the common meaning of
the word, something spread level and smooth, and to him the elaborate metaphor used by Bl.
Theophylact is quite clear.

[9] Prov. 8:9. Note that the Greek text of this verse of Proverbs used by Bl. Theophylact is not
exactly the same as that used in Lancelot Brenton's translation of the Septuagint.

that there was a *burden* [*lēmma*] *of the Lord* in such and such a prophet.[10] Therefore, as it is here, when this *upper room* has been *furnished,*
Jesus comes with His disciples, and performs the Mysteries. He Himself
comes to us and reveals in us His own divine energy, no longer waiting
for us to come to Him. The *disciples* of God the Logos are all the minds
that have come into being, each with its own logos. Therefore when the
divine Logos acts within us, then we shall understand the communing and
the sharing of the Pascha; moreover, we shall then be enlightened to
understand the logos of all those who have been begotten [of the Spirit],
for as it is written, *I will behold the heavens, the works of Thy fingers.*[11]

**14-20. And when the hour was come, He sat down, and the twelve
apostles with Him. And He said unto them, With desire I have
desired to eat this Pascha with you before I suffer. For I say unto
you, I will not any more eat thereof, until it be fulfilled in the
kingdom of God. And He took the cup, and gave thanks, and said,
Take this, and divide it among yourselves. For I say unto you, I will
not drink of the fruit of the vine, until the kingdom of God shall
come. And He took bread, and gave thanks, and broke it, and gave
unto them, saying, This is My Body which is given for you: this do
in remembrance of Me. Likewise also the cup after supper, saying,
This Cup is the New Testament in My Blood, which is shed for you.**
The Pascha was eaten standing; why then does it say that the Lord sat
down? Some say that they first ate the Pascha of the law, and then they
sat down in the usual manner to eat some other foods. He says to His
disciples, *With desire I have desired to eat this Pascha with you before
I suffer.* It is as if He were saying, "This is My last supper with you;
therefore I come to it with love and yearning. I will not eat with you
again." It is the same with those about to leave on a far journey: the last
words with their family and close friends are spoken with greater
sweetness and yearning. And in another sense as well the Lord says, "*I
have desired to eat this Pascha with you,* because at this time I intend to

---

[10] See Habakkuk 1:1, Zechariah 9:1, and Malachi 1:1. *lēmma, burden,* is a noun derived from the
perfect passive of the verb *lambanō, to take or receive,* used by Bl. Theophylact in the preceding
sentence where it was translated as *take hold of.* Bl. Theophylact interprets *lēmma* to mean the state
of mind when a prophet "has been taken hold of" by the Lord to utter God's oracles.

[11] Ps. 8:3

deliver unto you the great Mysteries of the New Testament." He shows by this that He goes willingly to His Passion. Knowing that He was about to suffer, it was indeed within His power to withdraw and elude His enemies as He had done on previous occasions. Some of the saints have understood His words, *I will not drink of the fruit of the vine until the kingdom of God shall come,* to mean, "until I am risen from the dead." When He met with His disciples after His Resurrection, He ate and drank with them, as Peter says to Cornelius, "We *did eat and drink with Him after He rose from the dead.*[12] That the Resurrection is the kingdom of God is plainly evident. The Resurrection is the overthrow of death. Death had reigned as king from Adam until Christ. Then death was overthrown, conceding victory and kinship to the Lord. Hence it is said, *O death, where is thy victory?*[13] And David says, *The Lord is King,* and then, to explain what kind of kingship He has, adds, *He is clothed with majesty,*[14] meaning that man's body has shed its corruption and has been adorned with divinity. Likewise, Isaiah says, *He is fair in His apparel, with mighty strength.*[15] And the Lord Himself said, after His Resurrection, *All authority has been given unto Me.*[16] But when the Resurrection came, which the Lord here calls *the kingdom of God* because it overthrew the reign of death, He again drank with His disciples to assure them that His Resurrection was not a phantasy. Some also say that the *kingdom of God* is life in the age to come, and the Lord drinking with us there means His revelation to us of the Mysteries. When the Lover of Man makes us glad, He is glad, and when He feeds us, He is fed, in that He counts our food and drink, namely, our instruction, as His own sustenance. Therefore, the Lord then will drink a new drink with those who are worthy,[17] ever revealing to them new and extraordinary things. Luke appears to mention two cups. The first cup, when the Lord says, *Take this, and divide it among yourselves,* might be explained as a type of the Old Testament; the second Cup, after He has broken and distributed the Bread,

---

[12] Acts 10:40-41

[13] See I Cor. 15:55.

[14] Ps. 92:1

[15] Is. 63:1

[16] Mt. 28:18

[17] See Mk. 14:24.

He Himself distributes to His disciples, calling it the Cup of *the New Testament,* and He says that it is initiated with His Blood. At the time of the Old Testament, when the law was given [and put into effect], there was the blood of irrational animals, beasts without logos.[18] Now, when God the Logos has became Man, blood is the seal of the New Testament, putting it into effect for us. When the Lord says, *which is given for you* and *which is shed for you,* He does not mean that His Body was given and His Blood was shed only for the apostles, but for human nature itself. Therefore, whenever He says, *Given for you,* understand it to mean, ''Given for the human nature which belongs to you all.'' The old Pascha was performed for the deliverance from slavery in Egypt, and the blood of the lamb was shed for the preservation of the first born. But the new Pascha is celebrated for the remission of sins and for the preservation in us of pure and holy thoughts, consecrated to God like first-born sons. First the Bread is given, and after that, the Cup. First comes activity, which is toilsome and difficult to complete, for sweat precedes virtue. Not only is bread produced by the sweat of the brow, but it is more laborious to consume than wine. Likewise, only after toil comes the gladness of the grace of God, which is the Cup. Only when a man has labored for virtue, which is hard to achieve, does he become worthy of the gifts. Then he delights in that good inebriation by which in ecstasy he stands outside this world, as did Paul and David, and, may I dare to say it, as does God, according to Habakkuk.[19]

21-27. But, behold, the hand of him that betrayeth Me is with Me on the table. And the Son of Man goeth as it has been determined: but woe unto that man by whom He is betrayed! And they began to inquire among themselves, which of them it was that should do this thing. And there was also a strife among them, which of them should be accounted the greatest. And He said unto them, The kings of the Gentiles exercise lordship over them; and they that exercise authority upon them are called benefactors. But ye shall not be so: but he that is greatest among you, let him be as the younger; and he that is chief, as he that doth serve. For who is greater? He that sitteth at table, or

---

[18] See Heb. 9:18-21.

[19] See II Cor. 5:13; Ps. 115:2; and Habakkuk 3:14.

**he that serveth? Is not he that sitteth at table? But I am among you
as He that serveth.** There is nothing more wretched than a soul turned
to stone. Behold, then, that when the Lord says, *The hand of him that
betrayeth Me is with Me on the table,* he who had become senseless
senses nothing. The Lord says this, not only to show that He is not
unaware of what will take place, but also to show us His own goodness
and the evil of the betrayer, whose face did not redden with shame that
he shared supper with the man he was to betray. The Lord did not, even
then, cease to do His work, setting before us the example of how we
must strive until the very end to win the souls of those who have sinned.
And the Son of Man goeth, He says, not because He is unable to defend
Himself, but because He has determined upon and chosen death for
Himself for the salvation of mankind. *But woe unto that man by whom
He is betrayed.* "It has been appointed for Me to suffer, but why are you
found to be so wicked that you are ready to betray Me? Therefore *woe*
and condemnation are your lot, because you were found to be capable of
betrayal. Likewise the serpent was cursed because it submitted to the
counsel of the devil." The disciples were troubled when they heard these
things; you may learn of this at greater length in the Gospel according to
St. John.[20] Here they are not troubled only by the suspicion of betrayal;
out of the distress of this suspicion they come to strife, and begin to
quarrel with one another as to which of them is the greatest. Their
quarreling is a consequence of the suspicion. For it is altogether likely
that one said to another, "You are going to betray Him," and the other
replied, "No, you are." From this they were led on to say, "I am
better," and "I am greater," and so forth. What does the Lord do? He
puts an end to their turmoil by giving two examples. In the first He refers
to the Gentiles, whom the disciples considered an abomination, and
shows that if the disciples strive with one another in this fashion they will
be just like the Gentiles. In the second example He refers to Himself,
guiding them towards humility by His own actions and showing that He
Himself is a servant to them. For at that very time, as it has been said,
He Himself had distributed the Bread and the Cup to them. Therefore, He
says, "If I, Who am worshipped by every angelic and rational creature,
am among you as He that serveth, how can you dare to esteem your-

---

[20] Jn. 13:21-30

selves highly and to strive with one another for the privilege of being first?'' It seems to me that the Lord purposefully mentions their sitting at table and His serving them, to remind them of a truth: "If you have all eaten from one Bread and have drunk from one Cup, the one Table unites you all as friends. Why then do you have such unworthy thoughts? For I did not serve only one of you and not the others; I was the servant of you all. Therefore all of you must think and be as one." You, O reader, will understand from this that the disciples were not yet mature and perfected. But see how they later shone forth. Let the Manichees be put to shame who say that some are ignorant and unlearned by nature and that it is impossible for such to change.

28-34. Ye are they which have continued with Me in My temptations. And I appoint unto you a kingdom, as My Father hath appointed unto Me; that ye may eat and drink at My table in My kingdom, and sit on thrones judging the twelve tribes of Israel. And the Lord said, Simon, Simon, behold, Satan hath demanded to have you, that he may sift you as wheat; but I have prayed for thee, that thy faith fail not: and when thou hast turned back, strengthen thy brethren. And he said unto Him, Lord, I am ready to go with Thee, both into prison, and to death. And He said, I tell thee, Peter, the cock shall not crow this day, before that thou shalt thrice deny Me that thou knowest Me. The Lord had said to His disciples, "*Woe unto that man* who betrayeth Me," and in their midst He had taught them to be humble-minded. Just as He had apportioned *Woe!* to the betrayer, now He promises the opposite to the others: "*Ye are they which have continued with Me in My temptations.* Therefore *I appoint unto you* your reward, namely, I make this promise to you: because *My Father hath appointed unto Me* the kingdom, you shall *eat and drink at My table.*" He did not speak of eating and drinking because there would be food there, or because His kingdom is perceptible to the material senses. On the contrary, He Himself had taught them, when He spoke to the Sadducees, that the manner of life in His kingdom is angelic, and Paul teaches that *the kingdom of God is not food and drink.*[21] Therefore, let no one be deceived here when they hear the words, *that ye may eat and*

---

[21] Rom. 14:17

drink at My table. Understand that the Lord is speaking metaphorically when He refers to the way in which men are honored by kings in this world. For those who are the supper companions of the king are considered to hold first place in the king's esteem. Therefore the Lord says this concerning the apostles, showing that they will be honored by Him above all others. And when you hear Him speaking of sitting on thrones, do not understand Him to mean actual seats, but instead honor and glory. No created being will sit in that kingdom, for the Holy Trinity, the uncreated God and King of all, alone will sit. Created beings, subservient by nature, must stand. But even these words, *sit* and *stand,* we use metaphorically. *Judging the twelve tribes of Israel* means condemning those of the twelve tribes who finally did not believe. The apostles themselves will be a great condemnation to those men of Israel who did not believe, for the apostles too were Israelites and yet they believed. Because the Lord gave the betrayer *woe* as his reward and foretold such a great reward to those who remained with love towards Him, He speaks further, lest they become proud of having accomplished something great by remaining in His love and not betraying Him. He says, *Satan hath demanded to have you, that he may sift you,* that is, "that he may shake, and harm, and tempt all of you." *But I have prayed for thee.* The Lord is saying, "Do not think that your faithfulness to Me is entirely your own accomplishment. For the devil has pressed hard against you, seeking to cast you outside My love, and to reveal you as traitors." He addresses these words to Peter because he was bolder than the others and more likely to have proud thoughts concerning the rewards which Christ promised. Therefore He humbles Peter by saying to him, "Satan has striven mightily against you all, *but I have prayed for thee,* Peter."[22] The Lord said this according to His human nature, for what need had He as God to ask for anything in prayer? *"I have prayed for thee,"* He says, *"that thy faith fail not.* Though you will be shaken for a short time, you have stored up within you the seeds of faith. Though the wind of the tempter may tear off the leaves, the root still lives and your faith shall not fail." *And when thou hast turned back, strengthen thy brethren.* Understand this to mean, "Because I have made you chief of

---

[22] In the words of the Greek New Testament text, *Satan hath demanded to have you,* the word *you* is plural, referring to all the disciples. But when the Lord says, *But I have prayed for thee,* the word *thee* is singular, referring to Peter.

the disciples, strengthen the others, after you have denied Me and wept and returned in repentance. This befits who you are: after Me, the rock and firm support of the Church.'' *Strengthen thy brethren* may also be understood to refer not only to the apostles of that time, who were indeed strengthened by Peter, but also to all the faithful until the end of the world. ''When you turn back, O Peter, you will become to all a beautiful example of repentance. No one who believes in Me will despair for himself when he looks at you and sees the apostle who denied the Lord, and then, by repentance, received back the first place of honor among all and was once again entrusted as an apostle with the care of the whole world. Therefore Satan demanded to have you, that he might sift you and harm you, the pure wheat, by mixing in his defilement, because he envies your love for Me, as he always does. For he likewise envied Job's love. But I have not abandoned you altogether lest your faith completely fail. Though I Myself have prayed for you, nevertheless you will fall. But when you have *turned back*, that is, repented, and shed tears, and fled from your denial, you will become for all the faithful a type and figure of repentance and the avoidance of despair.'' What does Peter then do? Emboldened by his great love, he promises what he is not yet able to do. But when the Lord sees that Peter spoke impetuously (for once Peter had heard Truth Itself say to him that he would be tempted, he ought not to have contradicted), the Lord reveals to Peter the kind of trial it would be, a denial. Here we learn the lesson that the willingness of man is not enough without the help of God. For Peter was abandoned for a short time; and though he appeared to retain his love and zeal, when God left him, he was tripped up by the enemy. By the same token, the help of God is not enough without the willingness of man. For Judas received no benefit, although the Lord did everything to gain him, because Judas lacked a good will and disposition. Therefore let us tremble when we understand that the plots of the devil prevail over those who are slack. Here let us behold how Peter, though held by God, was abandoned for a short time in accordance with God's economy, and fell away into denial. If he had not been preserved by God, and if the good seeds of faith had not been stored up within him, what calamity would he not have suffered? It was the purpose of the devil to cast even zealous Peter into betrayal; for, as the prophet says, the foods of the devil are chosen from the finest.[23] Thanks be to God, Who does not abandon those who are holy, righteous, and have good in their hearts. Such a man was Peter: full of love, and a stranger to any wicked thought concerning his Teacher.

35-38. And He said unto them, When I sent you without purse, and satchel, and shoes, lacked ye any thing? And they said, Nothing. Then said He unto them, But now, he that hath a purse, let him take it, and likewise his satchel: and he that hath no sword, let him sell his garment, and buy one. For I say unto you, that this that is written must yet be accomplished in Me: And He was reckoned among the transgressors. For the things concerning Me have a fulfillment. And they said, Lord, behold, here are two swords. And He said unto them, It is enough. When the Lord sent His disciples into the villages and cities at the beginning of the proclamation of the Gospel, He sent them out with no possessions, not even the necessities, without, in fact, any cares for anything other than the preaching. He did this so that they would learn His power in such conditions. He Himself took care of them because they were weak, and He showered upon them what they needed without their having to give it any thought. But now He commands the opposite, not contradicting himself, but showing them that up to now He had taken care of them like children, not letting them worry about anything. But from now on it was necessary for them to think like men and to have forethought for themselves. "I have cared for you like a father," the Lord says, "but now I am going away. From now on you must begin to take care of yourselves, instead of depending on Me for everything. The physical necessities of life will no longer come to you easily and without effort; instead you will find yourselves beset by hunger, thirst, and many adversaries." The Lord implies all this when He speaks of *purse*, *satchel*, and *sword*. Therefore, rise up like men who will soon experience hunger and be in want of food—this is implied by *satchel*—and be stalwart like brave men beset by many enemies—this He indicates by *sword*. The Lord says this, not in fact proposing that they use weapons, but, as I have said, to hint to them of wars and dangers to come, and to teach them to prepare themselves for every eventuality. The Lord did not want those who came later to think that the apostles contributed nothing of them-

---

[23] See Hab. 1:16.

selves towards their own virtue, and that everything was bestowed by God, and so He says, "It shall not be so. I do not wish to use My disciples like lifeless tools; instead I desire that they themselves offer for My use that which is their own." Most assuredly you will find that the apostles, and especially Paul, accomplished many things by means of human plans (read the Book of Acts), yet in these human plans God's help was not absent. In this manner, the Lord helped the apostles to preserve their humility. Had they taken no thought for themselves, but had waited upon God for everything and then received it, they would have become proud of obtaining things that are beyond the reach of human nature. Furthermore, a man's nature becomes lazy and corrupt when he takes no thought for himself but expects everything to be handed to him on a platter, as the saying goes. This is why the Lord says to them, "From now on, carry a satchel," that is, be prepared in thought and disposition to face hunger; "and buy swords," that is, plan beforehand how to resist dangers and enemies. Others have interpreted differently the command to buy a sword. It indicates, they say, the assault that is shortly to be made against Christ, and that murderous men will soon lay hold of Him. Because the disciples had been quarrelling with each other over their respective rank and honors, the Lord says to them, "This is no time for love of honors. Danger and bloodshed are upon us. I, your Teacher, will soon be led away to death, and to a shameful death at that. Even the Scripture, *He was reckoned among the transgressors,*[24] will be fulfilled in Me." The Lord speaks of swords, these others say, to suggest the violent and lawless assault that will soon be made against Him. He did not completely reveal this assault to them, lest they be shaken by cowardice; nor did He remain totally silent about it, lest they be thrown into confusion by the sudden attack. Instead, when they later remembered what He had said about the swords, they would marvel at His foreknowledge and be astonished how He had voluntarily given Himself over to His Passion for the salvation of mankind. Mindful of this, neither would they flee the pains and sorrows that would accompany their efforts to save others. I think the Lord was speaking enigmatically so that later, when His apostles remembered His words, they would

---

[24] Is. 53:12

understand and receive benefit. Indeed, at the time these words were spoken, the apostles were so lacking in understanding that they replied, *Lord, behold, here are two swords.* Because the Lord knew they had not understood, He said, *It is enough,* although in fact it was not enough. If He had needed human assistance against those swooping down on Him like bandits, a hundred swords would not have been enough; but if He had needed divine aid, two swords were excessive. Because they did not understand, the Lord did not want to rebuke them, and so by saying, *It is enough,* He passes over the matter without comment. We do the same ourselves when we see that someone with whom we are talking does not understand what we are saying, and we say, "Fine, let it be," although it is not fine. We let it go so as not to cause a disturbance. This is what the Lord is doing here when He sees that the disciples have not understood what was said. He lets it pass by, permitting the understanding of his words to emerge later from the outcome of the events. He did the same when He said, *Destroy this temple, and in three days I will raise it up,*[25] and the disciples did not understand the meaning until after His Resurrection. Some others have interpreted the Lord's words, *It is enough,* to have been spoken ironically. When the disciples said, *Behold, here are two swords,* the Lord answered with irony, as if to say, "Yes, you have two swords, more than enough to deter the great multitude that comes against us."

39-46. And He came out, and went, as He was wont, to the Mount of Olives; and His disciples also followed Him. And when He was at the place, He said unto them, Pray that ye enter not into temptation. And He withdrew from them about a stone's throw, and kneeled down, and prayed, saying, Father, if Thou be willing, remove this cup from Me: nevertheless not My will, but Thine, be done. And there appeared an angel unto Him from heaven, strengthening Him, and being in an agony He prayed more earnestly: and His sweat was as it were great drops of blood falling down to the ground. And when He rose up from prayer, and was come to His disciples, He found them sleeping for sorrow, and said unto them, Why sleep ye? Rise and pray, lest ye enter into temptation. After supper the Lord did not

---

[25] Jn. 2:19

relax with idleness, games, diversions, and sleep, but instead He taught and prayed, setting an example for us. Therefore, woe to them who put their hands to deeds of shameful fornication after supper! After teaching the disciples, the Lord goes up to the Mount of Olives to pray. It was His custom to do this alone, which is why He withdraws from the disciples. He does not take all of the disciples with Him, but only those three who had seen Him in glory on Mount Tabor.[26] Because He was agonizing as He prayed, He did not want these things to appear as cowardice. He takes with Him those who were eye-witnesses of His divine glory and hearers of the Voice from above which bore witness to Him,[27] so that when they see Him struggling and agonizing, they would understand this to be His human nature. To confirm that He was truly man, He permitted His human nature to do what is natural to it. Christ, as man, desires life and prays for the cup to pass, for man has a keen desire for life. By doing these things, the Lord confutes those heretics who say that He became man in appearance only.[28] If they found a way to utter such nonsense even though the Lord showed here such clear signs of His human nature, what would they not have dared to invent if He had not done these things? To want the cup removed is human. By saying without hesitation, *Nevertheless not My will, but Thine, be done,* the Lord shows that we too must have the same disposition and the same degree of equanimity, yielding in all things to the will of God. The Lord also teaches here that when our human nature pulls us in a different direction, we ought not to yield to that temptation. "Not My human will be done, but Thine, yet Thy will is not separate from My divine will." Because the one Christ has two natures, He also had two natural wills, or volitions, one divine and the other human. His human nature wanted to live, for that is its

---

[26] St. Luke does not mention the three disciples, Peter, James, and John, whom the Lord took with Him at Gethsemane, apart from the others. This is told by St. Matthew [26:37] and St. Mark [14:33].

[27] See the account of the Lord's Transfiguration in Lk. 9:28-36, and in the first two Evangelists.

[28] The Docetists, 'Appear-ists,' were a heretical sect dating back to apostolic times. They held that God the Word did not become flesh in any literal manner, but only appeared to do so. Thus they denied that Christ's body, Passion, or His human nature were real. This false and blasphemous heresy, which is contrary to the very doctrine of the Incarnation and the salvation of man, has been condemned by the Church whenever it has arisen: in the Gnostics of the apostolic era, in the Manichees a few centuries later, in the Bogomils of the later Byzantine era, and in the Theosophists and spiritualists of the nineteenth century.

nature. But then, yielding to the divine will common to the Father, Son, and Holy Spirit—namely, that all men be saved—His human nature accepted death. Thus His two wills willed one and the same thing: Christ's salvific death. The praying in Gethsemane was from His human nature which was permitted to suffer the human passion of love of life. It was not from His divine nature, as the accursed Arians say, and this is made clear by His sweat and by His agony which was so great that, as the saying goes, drops of blood fell from Him. For it is a saying that those who labor extremely hard "sweat blood," and that those in bitter sorrow "weep blood." This is why the Evangelist uses the image of sweating drops of blood, to show that the Lord was not merely damp with perspiration as a token of His humanity, but was completely drenched with sweat. This makes it clear that the nature which sweated and agonized was the Lord's human nature, not His divine. His human nature was permitted to suffer these things, and consequently did suffer them, to prove that the Lord was truly human, and not a man in appearance only. And, in a more mystical sense, the Lord voluntarily suffered these things in order to heal human nature of its cowardice. He did this by using it all up Himself, and then making cowardice obedient to the divine will. It could be said that the sweat which came out from the Lord's Body and fell from Him indicates that our cowardice flows out of us and is gone as our nature is made strong and brave in Christ. Had He not desired to heal the fear and cowardice of mankind, the Lord would not have sweated as He did, so profusely and beyond even what the most craven coward might do. *There appeared an angel unto Him,* strengthening Him, and this too was for our encouragement, that we might learn the power of prayer to strengthen us, and having learned this, use it as our defense in dangers and sufferings. Thus is fulfilled the prophecy of Moses, *And let all the sons of God be strengthened in Him,* as it is written in the great ode.[29] Some have interpreted what was said concerning the angel to mean that the Lord saw an angel glorifying Him, and saying, "Thine is the strength, O Lord, for Thou hast power over death and hades, to free the race of man." When the Lord finds the

---

[29] Deut. 32:43. This is part of the Second Ode of the Nine Prophetic Odes. These nine Odes, or Canticles, taken from the Old and New Testaments, are printed together with the Psalms in the Psalter Book. They provide the underlying Scriptural structure for one of the most important parts of the Matins service, the Matins Canon.

disciples sleeping, He both rebukes them, and exhorts them to pray when they are in temptation, so that they not be overcome by temptation. For this is what it means, not to *enter into temptation*, namely, not to be swallowed up by temptation or held in its grip. He is also giving us the simple command to pray that our lives be peaceful and that we not fall into any distress. It is demonic, and arrogant, for us to throw ourselves into temptations. How then does James say, *Count it all joy when ye fall among divers temptations?*[30] How can this be? Have we not just said the opposite? But look: James did not say, "Throw yourselves," but rather, *when ye fall*; that is, when it happens that you fall among temptations, do not fall down, but *count it all joy*, and willingly accept the trial, though you had not desired it before. It would be better had it not come upon you. But since it has come, why should you foolishly lament? Show me the words where we are commanded, "Pray that you fall into temptations." You will find no such text. I know that there are two kinds of temptations, and that some understand the Lord's command to pray that we enter not into temptation to mean that we enter not into that temptation which may conquer the soul, such as the temptation of fornication or the temptation of anger, but that we should count it all joy when we fall into such temptations as bodily afflictions and trials. The more the outer man is consumed, the more the inner man is renewed. We know these things, but I prefer the explanation which is closer to and more consistent with the intent of the text itself.

47-53. And while He yet spake, behold a multitude, and he that was called Judas, one of the twelve, went before them, and drew near unto Jesus to kiss Him. But Jesus said unto him, Judas, betrayest thou the Son of Man with a kiss? When they which were about Him saw what would follow, they said unto Him, Lord, shall we smite with the sword? And one of them smote the servant of the high priest, and cut off his right ear. And Jesus answered and said, Permit ye them even this. And He touched his ear, and healed him. Then Jesus said unto the chief priests, and captains of the temple, and the elders, which were come to Him, Be ye come out, as against a thief, with

---

[30] James 1:2. Note the Greek text of this verse uses the word *peripesēte*, which means literally *fall among*. This accounts for the distinction here drawn by Bl. Theophylact between falling among and falling into temptations.

swords and staves? When I was daily with you in the temple, ye stretched forth no hands against Me: but this is your hour and power of darkness. Judas gave a kiss as a signal to the Lord's assailants. He did not point out the Lord from a distance lest those who followed behind him with torches and lamps be deceived by the darkness of the night, thereby allowing Jesus to evade them and escape. What, then, does the Lord do? He accepts this hostile kiss. Thunderbolts did not strike this treacherous ingrate, teaching us the forbearance of the Saviour. He only reproaches him, saying, ''Judas, with a kiss dost thou betray? Are you not ashamed of the manner of your betrayal? Do you mix the work of an enemy—betrayal—with the embrace of a friend? And Whom do you betray? It is the *Son of Man*, the meek, the gentle, the compassionate One, Who became man for your sake, and in all these things never ceases to be God.'' The Lord said these things to Judas, showing until the very last hour His fervent care for him. This is why He did not hurl insults at him, or say, ''You inhuman and ungrateful man,'' but instead simply called him by his first name, *Judas.* Nor would the Lord have reproached him at all, had it not been to help Judas, if only Judas had wanted to be helped. Judas was rebuked so that he would not think that his treachery had escaped the Lord's notice, and so that even then he might clearly recognize Christ as the Master Who knows all things, and fall down before Him and repent. For no other reason did the Lord speak to Judas and appear to reproach Him. Although the Lord already knew that Judas would not accept correction, He nonetheless continued to do His saving work, just as His Father did in the Old Testament when He sent the prophets to the Hebrews, though He knew they would not obey. At the same time, the Lord is teaching us to do as He does: when we correct those who have sinned we should not treat them abusively. But the disciples are zealous and draw their swords. From where did they obtain swords? It is likely that they had kept them when they left the table in the upper room after sacrificing the lamb. Fervent Peter is rebuked for using zeal in a manner contrary to the Lord's purpose. The other disciples asked, *Shall we smite?* but Peter did not wait for the answer, so ardent was he for his Teacher on every occasion. He strikes the servant of the high priest and cuts off his right ear. This did not happen by chance, but signifies that those high priests were all servants who had lost their right hearing. For if they had heeded Moses, they would not have crucified the Lord of glory. But Jesus restores the servant's ear; it befits the great power of the Word to heal the deaf and the heedless and to give them ears with which to hear. Jesus works this unmistakable miracle to show His forbearance and to induce them to abandon their madness. He speaks to the chief priests and captains of the temple, calling *captains* those officers who were appointed to direct the affairs of the priests, or those who were entrusted with the work of repairing and supplying the temple building. He says to them, "Every day I was teaching in the temple, and you showed no desire to arrest Me. But now you come upon Me like thieves. Truly you stretch forth your hands to deeds of the night, and your power is the power of darkness. This is why you have come out at such an hour which befits you and the work you have undertaken."

54-62. Then took they Him, and led Him, and brought Him into the high priest's house. And Peter followed afar off. And when they had kindled a fire in the midst of the courtyard, and had sat down together, Peter sat down among them. But a certain maid beheld him as he sat by the fire, and earnestly looked upon him, and said, This man was also with Him. And he denied Him, saying, Woman, I know Him not. And after a little while another saw him, and said, Thou art also of them. And Peter said, Man, I am not. And after about the space of one hour, another confidently affirmed, saying, Of a truth this fellow also was with Him: for he is a Galilean. And Peter said, Man, I know not what thou sayest. And immediately, while he yet spake, the cock crew. And the Lord turned, and looked upon Peter. And Peter remembered the word of the Lord, how He had said unto him, Before the cock crow, thou shalt deny Me thrice. And Peter went out, and wept bitterly. As Christ had foretold, Peter weakened, denying the Master Christ not once, but three times, and making his denial with an oath. For Matthew says that he *began to curse and to swear, saying, I know not the man.*[31] He was gripped by cowardice to such a degree as this, and was abandoned for a short time by God, because he was over-bold, so that when he had been corrected he might be more forgiving towards others. He was so impetuous that if he had not been chastened here, he would have become self-willed, arrogant, and unforgiving towards others. But at this time Peter was in the grip of such

---

[31] Mt. 26:74

fear that he would not have been aware of his fall if the Lord had not turned and looked at him. What goodness! Though undergoing His own condemnation, He did not neglect the salvation of His disciple. And rightly so, for it was for the sake of the salvation of men that He was enduring this condemnation. The disciple denied once and then the cock crew; he denied a second and third time and then the cock crew the second time. Thus Mark records the events more precisely and in greater detail,[32] recording them as one who had learned them from Peter himself, for Mark was Peter's disciple. Therefore Luke simply summarizes here the things spoken by Mark, not going into detail. And what Luke says does not contradict Mark's account. When a cock crows, it usually does so two or three times. Peter had been so numbed and dulled by his human weakness that he was not brought to his senses by the first crowing of the cock, but even after it had crowed he denied again, and again, until he was brought to remembrance by the compassionate glance of Jesus. *And Peter went out, and wept bitterly.* Peter had gone out after he denied the first time, as Mark says. Then it is likely that he went back in so as not to cause a greater suspicion that he was one of Jesus' followers. Returning to his senses, now he goes out and weeps bitterly. He goes out and hides himself from them so as not to be seen by those in the hall. Some have put forward, I do not know how, a foolish defense of Peter, boldly saying that Peter did not deny the Lord, and that his words, *I do not know the man,*[33] mean "I do not know Him as mere man, but as God Who became man." Let us leave this foolish argument to others. For they make the Lord a liar and contradict the content of the Gospel. They utterly fail to make their idea agree with the context of the account. Why did Peter weep if he had not denied?

63-71. And the men that held Jesus mocked Him, and smote Him. And when they had blindfolded Him, they struck Him on the face, and asked Him, saying, Prophesy, who is it that smote Thee? And many other things blasphemously spake they against Him. And when it was day, the elders of the people and chief priests and the scribes came together, and led Him into their council, saying, Art Thou the

---

[32] Mk. 14:66-72

[33] Mt. 26:72

Christ? Tell us. And He said unto them, If I tell you, ye will not believe; and if I also ask you, ye will not answer Me, nor let Me go. Henceforth the Son of Man shall sit at the right hand of the power of God. Then said they all, Art Thou then the Son of God? And He said unto them, Ye say that I am. And they said, What need we any further witness? For we ourselves have heard from His own mouth. The men who did this to Jesus were depraved tormentors. Yet it was for our benefit that the devil did not omit any form of wickedness, but emptied it all out upon Christ, so that our nature, found in Christ to be holy in all things, might conquer the devil and dash him to pieces. This is why the Lord assumed our nature, to show its ability to be strong against all the devices of the devil, and to show, even from the beginning, that if Adam had been watchful and sober, he would not have been overcome. This is why He endures every kind of wickedness of the devil poured out upon Him, so that we who come after might not be afraid of anything which seems abusive and grievous, but be bold because our nature in Christ has vanquished the enemy. Therefore He is mocked and struck, and the Lord of the prophets is ridiculed as a false prophet. Their words, *"Prophesy to us, who is it that smote Thee?"* show that they were mocking Him as an imposter who claimed to be a prophet. *And when it was day,* for the mockeries and blasphemies were done at night by the drunken servants, the elders and those of higher rank ask Him if He is the Christ. But knowing their minds, and that if they had not believed His deeds which had even more power to persuade, they would not believe His words, He says to them, *"If I tell you, ye will not believe. If you believed My words, what need would there be for this council now? And if I also ask you, ye will not answer Me."* For many times when He asked them a question, they had remained silent, for example, when He asked them about the baptism of John, or how David could say, *The Lord said unto my Lord,* and when He questioned them concerning His healing of the woman bent over in infirmity.[34] "How then will you believe when you hear My words now? And when you are questioned, will you not again keep silent? Therefore I say only this: from now on it is no longer the time for you for words and teachings concerning Who I am. If you had so desired, you would have known Me from the signs that

---

[34] Mt. 21:25; Mt. 22:44; Lk. 13:17.

have taken place. From this moment on is the time of judgement. Therefore you will see Me, the Son of Man, sitting at the right hand of the power of God.'' They ought to have trembled; instead, after his words, they raged all the more, and demanded in a fury, *Art Thou the Son of God?* And He answers in an ambiguous and ironic manner, *Ye say that I am.* For He disdained their rage, and spoke to them fearlessly. From this it is clear that the disobedient and heedless receive no benefit when mysteries are revealed to them, but receive instead greater condemnation. Therefore we should hide these mysteries from them, as an act of compassion.

CHAPTER TWENTY-THREE

How the Saviour was led away to Pilate.
How He was mocked by Herod.
Concerning the women who bewailed Him.
Concerning the Crucifixion of Christ.
Concerning the repentant thief.
Concerning the burial of Christ.

1-5. And the whole multitude of them arose, and led Him unto Pilate. And they began to accuse Him, saying, We found this fellow perverting the nation, and forbidding to give tribute to Caesar, saying that He Himself is Christ a king. And Pilate asked Him, saying, Thou art the King of the Jews? And He answered him and said, Thou sayest it. Then said Pilate to the chief priests and to the people, I find no fault in this man. And they were the more vehement, saying, He stirreth up the people, teaching throughout all Judea, beginning from Galilee to this place. Clearly these men are enemies of the truth. How could Jesus have forbidden the people to give tribute when, on the contrary, He put them under strict obligation to pay the tribute, saying, *Render unto Caesar the things which are Caesar's?*[1] How was He stirring up the people? By making an attempt on the throne? But this is altogether implausible. When the multitude wanted to make Him a king, Jesus perceived it and departed.[2] Hence even Pilate understood this to be a false accusation and declared, *I find no fault in this man.* It seems to me that even when he asks the question of Christ, *Thou art the King of the Jews?* he is mocking and ridiculing this accusation. It is as if he were saying, "You—penniless, low-born, naked, and all alone—you are accused of making an attempt against the throne?" He is ridiculing, as we have said, those who had fabricated this charge against Jesus, because the commission of such an act requires considerable money and assistance. These accusers had no support for their slander except their own shrill voices, and so they cried out against God the Word. *He stirreth up the people,* they say, meaning "He is

---

[1] Mt. 22:21

[2] See John 6:15.

fomenting an insurrection, and not just in one place only; He started in Galilee, and after passing through Judea, has reached even here.'' It is not by accident, it seems to me, that they mentioned Galilee. They wished to frighten Pilate; and the Galileans, such as Judas of Galilee,[3] were well-known instigators of rebellion and revolt. It is likely that they wanted to remind Pilate of this. It is as if they were saying, ''Governor, consider well Judas the Galilean, who caused such trouble for the Romans when he led a large faction of the people in revolt. This man is like him, and you ought to do away with Him.''

6-27. When Pilate heard of Galilee, he asked whether the man were a Galilean. And as soon as he knew that He belonged unto Herod's jurisdiction, he sent Him to Herod, who himself also was at Jerusalem at that time. And when Herod saw Jesus, he was exceeding glad: for he had long desired to see Him, because he had heard many things of Him; and he hoped to see some miracle done by Him. Then he questioned Him with many words; but He answered him nothing. And the chief priests and scribes stood and vehemently accused Him. And Herod with his men of war set Him at nought, and mocked Him, and arrayed Him in a gorgeous robe, and sent Him again to Pilate. And the same day Pilate and Herod were made friends with one another; for before they were at enmity between themselves. And Pilate, when he had called together the chief priests and the rulers and the people, said unto them, Ye have brought this man unto me, as one that perverteth the people: and, behold, I, having examined Him before you, have found no fault in this man touching those things whereof ye accuse Him. No, nor yet Herod: for I sent you unto him, and, lo, nothing worthy of death has been done by Him. I will therefore chastise Him, and release Him. (For of necessity he must release one unto them at the feast.) And they cried out all together, saying, Away with this man, and release unto us Barabbas: (who for a certain sedition made in the city, and for murder, was cast into prison.) Pilate therefore, desiring to release Jesus, spake again to them. But they cried, saying, Crucify Him, crucify Him. And he said unto them the third time, Why, what evil hath He done? I have

---

[3] See Acts 5:37 and Josephus, *Jewish Wars,* Bk. II, Ch. VIII, 1.

**found no cause of death in Him: I will therefore chastise Him, and
let Him go. And they pressed urgently with loud voices, demanding
that He be crucified. And the voices of them and of the chief priests
prevailed. And Pilate gave sentence that it should be as they
demanded. And he released unto them him that for sedition and
murder was cast into prison, whom they had demanded, but he
delivered Jesus to their will. And as they led Him away, they laid
hold upon one Simon, a Cyrenian, coming out of the country, and on
him they laid the Cross, that he might bear it after Jesus. And there
followed Him a great company of people, and of women, who also
bewailed and lamented Him.** Pilate sent the Lord to Herod, following
the Roman law which required that every man be judged by the ruler of
the province in which he lived. This is why Pilate sent Jesus, a Galilean,
to the ruler of Galilee. Herod was glad for this, but not because he
intended to gain something beneficial for his soul from the sight of Jesus.
Instead, he entertained a foolish desire to see this strange man and to hear
what He had to say. For Herod suffered from a passion for novelty. He
had heard much about Jesus, and supposed Him to be a clever conjuror.
Do not many of us suffer the same passion for novelty today? Thus
Herod desired to see for himself some miracle done by Jesus, not in order
to believe, but only to feast his eyes, just as we watch tricksters in
theaters swallow illusory serpents and swords, and we are delighted and
amazed. Herod thought that Jesus was little more than one of these
performers. Herod *questioned Him with many words*, but insincerely and
with no serious intent, mocking Him all the while. Therefore Jesus
answered him nothing. For He Who made all things by His word knew
when to answer, to which David testified when he said, *He shall order
his words with judgment*.[4] What ought the Lord to have answered to this
man who was not asking in order to learn? Why should He cast the pearls
before the swine? It is in fact, as we have said above, an act of compassion to remain silent with such men as these. For the word which is
spoken and brings no benefit becomes the cause of greater condemnation
for those who do not listen. But to Pilate, whose disposition was better
than Herod's, the Lord did give an answer, but not a clear one. When

---

Ps. 111:5. The Septuagint Greek work oikonomesei, here translated *shall order*, is the same word used
by the fathers to describe the divine economy, God's providential activity in the world for man's
sake.

Pilate asked, *Thou art the King of the Jews?* what did the Lord reply? *Thou sayest it.* This has a double meaning. It can mean, "Indeed I am, and you have said what is true."[5] It can also mean, "I do not say so, you do; you have authority and you speak." But to Herod He answered nothing, for Herod was nothing but a mocker, for as Isaiah says regarding the evil seed, the lawless sons, meaning these Jews, "the exactors strip you, and mockers rule over you."[6] That Herod had just such a mocking and ridiculing intent when he desired to see Jesus and watch Him do a miracle, and that he questioned Him with the same disposition, is made clear at the end, when Herod *set Him at nought, and mocked Him,* and then dismissed Him. And it was not Herod alone, but his soldiers with him, who went beyond the limits of insult and *arrayed Him in a gorgeous robe, and sent Him again to Pilate.* But see, O reader, how everything Herod does ensnares the devil in his own devices. For when Herod performs these mockeries and insults against Christ, the truth is all the more clearly revealed. By ridiculing Him in this manner they give irrebuttable testimony that the Lord was not a leader of rebellion and sedition. Had He been, they would not have toyed with Him while so great a danger hung over them, namely, an uprising of the entire explosive nation of the Jews. The Evangelist says, *And Pilate and Herod became friends.* When Pilate sent Jesus to Herod in deference to Herod's jurisdiction, it marked the beginning of friendship between the two, because Pilate did not usurp Herod's privileges. See how the devil brings together disparate elements for the sole purpose of preparing Christ's death, forging a single conspiracy and making warring factions friends. Are we not then ashamed that the devil brings peace between enemies in order to kill Christ, while we, for the sake of our salvation, do not even preserve love towards our own friends? When Jesus was sent back to Pilate, consider how the truth shone forth. *"Ye have brought this man unto me,* says Pilate, *"as one that perverteth the people,* and I have found nothing worthy of death in Him, nor has Herod." Do you see? Surely the testimony of two men is true, especially when one is the governor and the

---

[5] Note that in Greek the form of this question is identical to the form of a statement, with only the interrogative inflection of the voice, indicated in writing by a question mark, to make the distinction.

[6] See Is. 1:4 and 3:12, but note that the text of Is. 3:12 used by Bl. Theophylact is not the same as that followed by Lancelot Brenton in his translation.

other is the king. Pilate is saying, "Neither I nor King Herod have found any fault in Him." What will the Jews say to this? The judges themselves testify that the man is guiltless, and you, the accusers, have brought forward no evidence. Who is to be believed? You, the accusers, or these judges? How Truth conquers! Jesus is silent, and His enemies bear witness on His behalf. The Jews shout and make a great noise, but there is no one to prove their accusations. Pilate is soft and unable to stand fast for the truth. He was afraid of slander, afraid that the Jews would accuse him falsely of having set free a man who had risen up against the king. Pilate had not learned to say, "Of your fear we shall not be afraid; the Lord shall be my fear."[7] Pilate says, *I will therefore chastise Him,* that is, have Him whipped with scourges, *and release Him.* The Romans were required on the feast to release one prisoner to the Jews. For when the Jews made their treaty of submission to Rome, they had been given permission to live according to their own practices and laws. It had been a Jewish practice inherited from their forefathers to demand from their rulers the release of condemned prisoners, as the people had demanded from Saul the release of Jonathan. If you do not know this story, turn to the first book of Kings and you will find it there.[8] *And they cried out all together, saying, Away with this man!* What could be worse than this? The world is stood on its head, for God's holy race is crazed for murder, while Pilate, the pagan Gentile, abhors the murder and exhorts them to show mercy. *Away with this man, and release unto us Barabbas (who for a certain sedition made in the city, and for murder, was cast into prison).* Three times Pilate releases the Lord, and three times they shout against Christ, giving triple confirmation of their own bloodthirstiness. They *denied the Holy and Righteous One,* as blessed Peter says, *and desired a murderer to be granted unto them.*[9] They loved that which was similar to themselves. Therefore, they joined Barabbas' faction, and themselves became rebels against Rome, and the cause of tens of thousands of murders and of their own destruction. The Lord also foretold these events through the mouth of the prophet Jeremiah: *I have forsaken mine house, I have left mine heritage; I have given mine heritage into the hands of*

---

[7] See Is. 8:12-13.

[8] I Kings (I Sam.) 14:42:46

[9] See Acts 3:14.

enemies. Mine inheritance has become to Me as a lion in a forest; she has uttered her voice against Me; therefore have I hated her.[10] And again, through the mouth of the prophet Hosea: *Woe to them! For they have started aside from Me: they are cowards; for they have sinned against Me: I redeemed them, but they spoke falsehoods against Me... their princes shall fall upon the edge of the sword, by reason of their unbridled tongue.*[11] Jesus then is led out to be crucified. At first they laid His Cross on Him and He went out of the city carrying it. This is because no one else would have consented to carry it, for even the wood of a cross was considered cursed.[12] Later, when they found a certain man named Simon, a Cyrenian, they laid the Cross on him, compelling the man to carry it and forcing it upon him like some odious thing from which everyone else drew back in abhorrence. This reveals a great lesson for us. The Cross is the deadening of our passions, for the Cross deprives the passions of their energy and activity, just as a crucified man is nailed down and made immobile. Therefore a teacher who follows Christ must first take up his own cross, and nail down his flesh with the fear of God,[13] and shine with passionlessness. Only then can he place the cross upon others who are obedient to him. For the name *Simon* means *obedience.* Here also are fulfilled the words of Isaiah, *Whose government is upon His shoulder.*[14] For the Lord's government, that is, His rule and kingship, is indeed the Cross. As Paul says, *He humbled Himself, and became obedient unto death, even the death of the Cross. Wherefore God also hath highly exalted Him.*[15] Therefore, because the Cross became Jesus' glory and exaltation, it is fitting that it should be called *His government,* that is, the symbol of His governing rank and power. Just as the members of the imperial Senate have their tokens of rank and dignity,

---

[10] Jer. 12:7-8

[11] Hosea 7:13,16

[12] See Deut. 21:23.

[13] From the prayer of St. Basil the Great at the end of the Sixth Hour, in which he also applies to our individual moral struggle the Lord's triumph on the Cross over the devil: *Nail down our flesh with the fear of God, and incline not our hearts unto words or thoughts of evil, but pierce our souls with longing for Thee.*

[14] Is. 9:6

[15] Phil. 2:8-9

some wearing sashes and others mantles, so too the Lord has the Cross as the symbol of His kingship. And if you consider well, you will find that Jesus does not rule over us in any other manner except by suffering and hardship. Consequently, those who feast and live in luxury are enemies of the Cross. The one who is able to be obedient to Christ and to take up his cross is the laborer for virtue, *coming in from the country.* He leaves behind this world and departs from the fields of worldly endeavor and all the works of this world, and he goes toward the heavenly Jerusalem, where there is freedom. *The great company of people, and of women,* which *followed* Christ foreshadow the great number of Jews, and the many women, who after the Cross (for this is what is meant by *follow*), would believe in Him. Read the book of Acts and you will find tens of thousands of those who believed. Do not the wailing and lamenting of the women who followed Jesus also convey a moral sense for our benefit? These women signify our weak souls when we repent. For when the soul receives contrition of heart through repentance, and mourns and laments its sins, then indeed it follows Jesus, Who was afflicted and crucified for our salvation.

28-31. But Jesus turning unto them said, Daughters of Jerusalem, weep not for Me, but weep for yourselves, and for your children. For, behold, the days are coming, in the which they shall say, Blessed are the barren, and the wombs that never bare, and the paps which never gave suck. Then shall they begin to say to the mountains, Fall on us; and to the hills, Cover us. For if they do these things in a green tree, what shall be done in the dry? The women (to whom tears come easily by nature) are weeping for the Lord as if something terrible had befallen Him, bewailing the wrong done to Him and showing their own compassion. But He does not accept their lament, and instead rebukes them. For He suffered willingly. Lamentation is not appropriate for Him Who suffers willingly for the salvation of all human nature; instead, praise and acclamations are His due. For by means of the Cross death was destroyed and hades was taken captive. Laments bring comfort, not to those who suffer willingly, but to those who suffer against their will. But when the Lord speaks to the women who are bewailing Him, is it in fact a rebuke? No, He is exhorting them to consider the catastrophes that are coming and to mourn for the people who will then suffer. For at that time, women will cook their own children for food without a tear of remorse, and the belly which had carried the child will wretchedly welcome back the thing which it had borne. "If the Romans have done these things to Me, the green tree, ever-flourishing and ever-living on account of My divinity, laden with the fruits of My teachings which nourish all men, what will the Romans not do to you, the Jewish people, the dry tree, barren of all life-creating righteousness and bearing no fruit? Had there been any amount of living sap of goodness within you, you might have been found deserving of a little bit of mercy. But now you will be like dry wood that is cast into the furnace and destroyed."

32-38. And there were also two others, malefactors, led with Him to be put to death. And when they were come to the place which is called The Skull, there they crucified Him, and the malefactors, one on the right hand, and the other on the left. Then said Jesus, Father, forgive them; for they know not what they do. And they parted His raiment, and cast lots. And the people stood beholding. And the rulers also with them derided Him, saying, He saved others; let Him save Himself, if He be Christ, the chosen of God. And the soldiers also mocked Him, coming to Him, and offering Him vinegar, and saying, If Thou be the king of the Jews, save Thyself. And a superscription also was written over Him in letters of Greek, and Latin, and Hebrew, THIS IS THE KING OF THE JEWS. The devil wanted to cast the Lord into evil repute, and so he caused two thieves to be crucified with Him. But see how the devil was deprived of one of these thieves, and how this became the cause of yet greater glory for the Lord. Of the three crosses, the two upon which the thieves were executed have always been a matter of complete indifference. But the whole world clings to the Cross upon which the Lord was hung. What could make it more clear that the Lord was not a transgressor, as were the thieves, but is instead the fountainhead of all righteousness? They lead Him to The Place of the Skull,[16] where it is said that Adam our forefather was buried, so that at the place where there had been a fall into death because of a tree, there might be an arising by means of another Tree. Jesus shows us the extreme of meekness when He prays, *Father, forgive them, for they know not what they do.* And indeed this sin would have been

---

[16] In Hebrew, *Golgotha* [see Mt. 27:33]; in Latin, *Calvaria,* or its English equivalent, Calvary.

forgiven them if they had not afterwards persisted in their unbelief. *They parted His raiment.* For what reason? Perhaps because the soldiers had need of it, and there were many of them. But it would be closer to the truth to say that they did this as an insult, for what did they see of value in His clothing? They were in fact mocking and laughing at Him. Since the rulers were also mocking Him, what could be expected of the common crowd? *He saved others; let Him save Himself, if He be Christ, the chosen of God.* It was the devil saying this through their mouths. Here the devil says to Jesus the same thing that he said to Him when he tempted Him on the pinnacle of the temple.[17] Begrudging any good [that he now feared might come] through the Cross, the devil wanted to prevent it by any possible means. The soldiers offered Him vinegar, as if they were serving a drink to a king. And there is yet another device of the devil that turns back on himself. For the devil had caused to be displayed in the letters of three languages Jesus' supposed crime of insurrection, so that every passerby would know that He had been hung on the Cross because He had made Himself a king. Yet what was intended by the devil as an accusation became instead a triumphant symbol that the most powerful of the nations, the Romans, and the most wise, the Greeks, and the most God-fearing, the Hebrews, would all be placed under the kingship of Jesus and would acclaim Him. The devil, although wise in evil-doing, did not understand. We have spoken of these things at greater length, and more profoundly, in the explanation of the Gospel according to John.

39-43. And one of the malefactors which were hanged railed at Him, saying, If Thou be Christ, save Thyself and us. But the other answering rebuked Him, saying, Dost not thou fear God, seeing thou art in the same condemnation? And we indeed justly; for we receive the due reward of our deeds: but this man hath done nothing amiss. And he said unto Jesus, Lord, remember me when Thou comest in Thy kingdom. And Jesus said unto him, Verily I say unto thee, Today shalt thou be with Me in paradise. How is it then that the other Evangelists say that the two thieves accused Him? At first both thieves did accuse Him, but then one of them, the more discerning of the two,

---

[17] See Mt. 4:5-6.

recognized in Jesus' voice His goodness and divinity, when He said on behalf of His crucifiers, *Father, forgive them.* The voice of Jesus was not only full of compassion, but it also revealed great power. He did not say, "Lord, I beseech Thee, forgive them," but instead spoke the simple and authoritative words, *Father, forgive them.* Therefore, when the former blasphemer recognized by this voice that Jesus was indeed a king, he rebuked the other thief, and said to Jesus, *Remember me in Thy kingdom.* How does the Lord reply? *Today thou shalt be with Me in paradise.* As a man, He was on the Cross, but as God, He is everywhere, both on the Cross and in paradise, filling all things, and nowhere absent. Some will ask, "How can the Lord say to the thief, *Today thou shalt be with Me in paradise,* when Paul said that none of the saints had received the promise?"[18] Some say that the Apostle was not referring to all the saints when he said that none of them had received the promise, but was speaking only of those whom he there enumerated. Though he listed many, the good thief was not among them. Listen to the words that Paul uses, *And these all...* By this he refers expressly, they say, to those whom he had just enumerated, and the thief was not one of those. Others have said that the thief has not yet attained the life in paradise, yet the Lord could still say, *Today shalt thou be with Me in paradise,* because His promise is immovable and irrevocable. For the Lord, they explain, often employs this kind of speech when He speaks of things that will be as if they had already occurred. For example, the Lord says, *He that believeth not is condemned already;*[19] and again, *He that heareth My word, and believeth...shall not come into condemnation, but hath passed from death unto life.*[20] Others have done violence to the context of these words, pausing after *today,* so that it might read, *Verily I say unto thee today, Thou shalt be with Me in paradise.*[21] Others, who appear to have hit the mark, explain it this way: the good things which are promised to us are not a life in paradise, or a return to paradise, but instead the kingdom of

---

[18] See Heb. 11:39.

[19] Jn. 3:18

[20] Jn. 5:24

[21] The reader is again reminded that ancient Greek manuscripts contained no punctuation whatsoever, not even divisions between words, and that the reader of these manuscripts must supply his own punctuation as an integral part of the act of reading and interpreting.

heaven. This is why we pray, *Thy kingdom come,* and not, "May we live in paradise." Let no one say to me that paradise and the kingdom are one and the same. For *eye hath not seen, nor ear heard, neither have ascended into the heart of man,* the good things of the kingdom.[22] But the eye of Adam saw paradise, and his ear heard the words, *Of every tree which is in paradise thou mayest eat for food.*[23] Even if you say, "Yes, but one tree was denied to him," still he could see it, and he did hear about it, and delight in it rose up in his heart. And Adam had every reason to be delighted; for was not this tree both his work and his pleasure, as husbandman of paradise? Therefore, the Lord does not contradict what Paul says. The repentant thief did obtain paradise, but he has not yet obtained the kingdom. But he will obtain the kingdom, along with all those whom Paul enumerated. In the meantime he has paradise, which is a place of spiritual rest. Many have spoken about these things. We may add that, even if the kingdom of heaven and paradise are one and the same, this does not prevent both the Lord's words and Paul's from being in agreement. For the good thief is in paradise, that is, in the kingdom, and not only he, but all those mentioned by Paul. But he does not yet enjoy the full inheritance of good things. It is not the condemned who live in kingly palaces, for these are locked in prisons where they await their appointed punishments. It is, rather, men of honor and nobility who enter palaces and pass their time within them. Then, when the time is at hand for the distribution of royal gifts, they are found worthy of them. So too with the saints: although they do not yet enjoy their reward in full, nevertheless in the meanwhile they pass their time in places of light, of fragrance, of royalty, in short, in the tabernacles of the righteous, although they are not yet entitled to the full measure of the gifts of the kingdom. Therefore the thief was in paradise, and yet did not enjoy completion, so that he *without us should not be made complete.*[24] This, I think, is the truest understanding of all. If it were the case that the gifts of the saints in paradise were as complete as the gifts they will enjoy in heaven, then [what will those who confuse paradise with heaven say when] I remind them that the saints likewise received gifts during their

---

[22] See I Cor. 2:9.

[23] Gen. 2:16

[24] Heb. 11:40

life on earth as they worked miracles? [Will they say that life on earth is the same as life in paradise?] In truth all those who were found worthy of spiritual gifts received those gifts already in this life as an earnest and pledge of the Holy Spirit. They are in paradise, although they have not yet been brought to completion and perfection and have not yet received the kingdom. As Paul says in the same Letter to the Hebrews, that *these all...have not* yet *received the promise.*[25] When he says *the promise* he means "the whole promise." These saints, therefore, have not yet received the full promise, although they are in the kingdom and in paradise. Marvel at this, O reader, that just as a victorious king returns in triumph from his conquest, bringing with him the best of his spoils, so too the Lord, having despoiled the devil of the best of the devil's own plunder, brings it with Him as He returns into man's ancient homeland, I mean, paradise. For [after His death as a man], the Lord was present in paradise not only as God, but also by reason of His human soul endowed with logos and mind. He was in paradise with His mind, and [simultaneously] He descended into hades with His soul.[26] By saving the thief, He also bound the devil, the vessel of evil, as the Lord foretold when He said that one must first bind the strong man and only then can he plunder the strong man's goods.[27]

44-49. And it was about the sixth hour, and there was a darkness over all the earth until the ninth hour. And the sun was darkened, and the veil of the temple was rent in the midst. And when Jesus had cried with a loud voice, He said, Father, into Thy hands I commit My spirit: and having said thus, He breathed His last. Now when the centurion saw what was done, he glorified God, saying, Truly this was a righteous man. And all the people that came together to that sight, beholding the things which were done, smote their breasts, and returned. And all His acquaintance, and the women that followed Him from Galilee, stood afar off, beholding these things. The Jews

---

[25] Heb. 11:39

[26] Note the first troparion (following the kontakion) in the Paschal Hours, also read by the priest at every Divine Liturgy: *In the grave bodily, but in hades with Thy soul as God; in paradise with the thief, and on the throne with the Father and the Spirit wast Thou Who fillest all things, O Christ the Uncircumscribable.*

[27] See Mt. 12:29.

once had asked to see a sign from heaven.[28] Behold, now, a sign—this strange darkness. And the veil of the temple is rent, the Lord showing through this that the Holy of Holies will no longer be inaccessible, but will be given over to the Romans for profanation. The Lord also shows that the veil which had once separated us from the holy things in heaven, the veil of enmity and sin, is now torn asunder. For this is the great barrier which separates us from that place. And the Lord also shows that He was not crucified because He was too weak to resist; He Who did such things as these had the power to shatter and destroy His crucifiers. When He had cried out with a loud voice, He gave up His breath. For He had the power to lay down His life, and to take it back again. It was the Lord's voice itself, together with the other miracles, which caused the centurion to believe. For the Lord did not die as an ordinary man, but as the Master. He named death a committal, [that is, a deposit for safe-keeping] because He intended to receive back His life. His last words, the first [such ever spoken by a man completely free of any claim by the devil], made our souls worthy of freedom, for in Christ our souls have likewise been committed to the Father and are no longer held by the devil. Before the death of Christ, the devil had a clear right to our souls. But from the moment that the Son committed His spirit, not to hades, but into the hands of the Father, our souls were freed from hades. The very thing which the Lord had said, *And I, if I be lifted up from the earth, will draw all men unto Me,*[29] is now seen to have been accomplished. For when the Lord was lifted up on the Cross, He drew both the thief and the centurion to Himself. Certain of the Jews who *smote their breasts* thereby faulted the crucifiers, and clearly justified Jesus. His disciples fled, but the women, that portion of mankind who first received the condemnation and the curse for sin, remained and beheld all these things. They were the first to enjoy the justification and the blessing [of the Cross], just as they were the first to enjoy the Resurrection. Marvel with me, O reader, at the hardheartedness of the Jews. Those who said, *Let Him now come down from the Cross, and we will believe,*[30] when they see even greater things than this they still do not believe. Was coming down from the Cross the

---

[28] Lk. 11:16

[29] Jn. 12:32

[30] Mt. 27:42

equal of darkening the sun, breaking the rocks, causing a fearful earthquake, raising the dead, tearing the veil, and altering the elements of creation? Therefore, let no one wonder why the Lord did not come down from the Cross to make them believe, but let him accept these things without idle curiosity, realizing that, even if He had come down, they would still not have believed. Moreover, had He come down from the Cross, it would have eliminated any hope of our salvation through the Cross. For the Cross, above all else, is the glory of Christ. By working greater miracles than coming down from the Cross, none of which brought the Jews to belief, He achieved two things at once: He endured and accepted the Cross until the end, making it the great trophy of victory,[31] and He showed these unbelieving Jews to be complete ingrates with no trace of good in them, who were fused to their unbelief.

50-56. And, behold, there was a man named Joseph, a councillor; and he was a good man, and righteous: the same had not consented to their counsel and deed; he was of Arimathea, a city of the Jews: who also himself waited for the kingdom of God. This man went unto Pilate, and begged the body of Jesus. And he took it down, and wrapped it in linen, and laid it in a tomb that was hewn in stone, wherein never man before was laid. And that day was the preparation, and the sabbath drew on. And the women also, who came with Him from Galilee, followed after, and beheld the tomb, and how His body was laid. And they returned, and prepared spices and myrrh oils; and rested the sabbath day according to the commandment. Although Joseph until now had hidden his faith, now he does a praiseworthy thing. Although he was a member of the council and a rich man, he dares to ask for the body of a man who had been crucified for rebellion and sedition, giving no thought to any danger to himself. Though wealth often gives rise to cowardice, Joseph begs for the body and gives it honorable burial *in a tomb that was hewn in stone, wherein never man before was laid,* so that slanderers could not say that it was a different body that rose. The women had faith in the Lord, but did not yet have a faith that befitted the Lord. It was too small and weak. For they

---

[31] A *trophy [tropaion]* in the ancient world was a monument of victory in war. It consisted of the weapons of the defeated enemy which were hung on a tree or post.

thought that He was merely a man, subject to corruption, and so they prepared myrrh oils and spices for His dead body, in accordance with the practice which prevailed among the Jews. And they *rested the sabbath day according to the commandment* of the law.

CHAPTER TWENTY-FOUR

Concerning the women who looked at the tomb.
Concerning Peter who ran to the tomb.
Concerning Cleopas.
Concerning the appearance of Jesus.
Concerning the Ascension into heaven.

1-12. Now upon the first day of the week, very early in the morning, they came unto the tomb, bringing the spices which they had prepared, and certain others with them. And they found the stone rolled away from the tomb. And they entered in, and found not the body of the Lord Jesus. And it came to pass, as they were much perplexed thereabout, behold, two men stood by them in garments shining like lightning. And as they were afraid, and bowed down their faces to the earth, they said unto them, Why seek ye the living among the dead? He is not here but is risen: remember how He spake unto you when He was yet in Galilee, saying, The Son of Man must be delivered into the hands of sinful men, and be crucified, and the third day rise again. And they remembered His words, and returned from the tomb, and told all these things unto the eleven, and to all the rest. It was Mary Magdalene, and Joanna, and Mary of James, and other women that were with them, who told these things unto the apostles. And their words seemed to them as idle tales, and they believed them not. Then arose Peter, and ran unto the tomb; and stooping down, he beheld the linen cloths lying alone, and departed, marvelling within himself at that which was come to pass.
Mian tōn sabbatōn, the first [day] of the sabbath, means "the first day of the week," which we call the Lord's Day, [Sunday], on account of the Lord's Resurrection. On this day the women came bringing aromatic spices. They came *very early in the morning,* or, as Matthew says, *after the sabbath,*[1] which amounts to the same thing. *They found the stone rolled away,* for an angel had rolled it away, as Matthew says.[2] When

---

[1] Mt. 28:1

[2] Mt. 28:2

the women entered the tomb, two men appeared to them. A single angel in Matthew's account sat upon the stone, but these *two men* appeared inside the tomb, for these are two separate appearances of angels. They appear shining white, because of the splendor of the Resurrection. They remind the women of the words spoken by Christ, that *the Son of Man must be delivered into the hands of sinful men,* namely, the Romans, who as Gentiles were an abomination, *and the third day rise again.* We have spoken sufficiently in *The Explanation* of St. Matthew's Gospel how the Resurrection is counted as being on *the third day.*[3] When the women had returned and told these things to the apostles, it seemed as if they were talking nonsense. For the miracle of the Resurrection seems incredible to men by its very nature. Yet Peter can no more remain idle than can fire. He runs to the tomb and sees only the strips of linen cloth. And now he receives this first benefit of going himself to the tomb—he marvels, instead of mocking [the women]. For it says that he *departed, marvelling within himself at that which was come to pass.* Marvelling at what? How the linen burial cloths could have been left behind when the body around which they were wound had been anointed with sticky myrrh.[4] And how a thief would have had the leisure to remove the body from the burial cloths and then rewind the burial cloths separately while soldiers were on guard outside. *Mary of James* is the Theotokos. They gave her this name as the apparent mother of James the son of Joseph, whom they also called James the Younger, that is, the Brother of God.[5] For there was also James the Elder, one of the twelve, the son of Zebedee.

13-24. And, behold, two of them went that same day to a village called Emmaus, which was from Jerusalem about threescore furlongs. And they were talking together of all these things which had happened. And it came to pass, that, while they communed together

---

[3] See Vol. 1, *The Explanation* of St. Matthew, p. 254.

[4] In Chapter 19:39-40 of his Gospel, St. John reports that Nicodemus and Joseph of Arimathea wound the body of the Lord in linen cloths together with *about an hundred pound weight* of *a mixture of myrrh and aloes. Myrrh* is a sticky and aromatic gum which exudes from a certain tree in Arabia. This substance was used to anoint the dead. See Vol. 2, *The Explanation* of St. Mark, p. 140.

[5] The author of the Epistle of St. James and the first bishop of Jerusalem, commemorated by the Church on October 23. See *The Great Collection of the Lives of the Saints*, Vol. II: October, Chrysostom Press, House Springs, Missouri, 1995, pp. 343-347.

and reasoned, Jesus Himself drew near, and went with them. But their eyes were held that they should not know Him. And He said unto them, What manner of communications are these that ye have one to another, as ye walk, and are sad? And the one of them, whose name was Cleopas, answering said unto Him, Art Thou only a stranger in Jerusalem, and hast not known the things which are come to pass there in these days? And He said unto them, What things? And they said unto Him, Concerning Jesus of Nazareth, Who was a prophet mighty in deed and word before God and all the people: and how the chief priests and our rulers delivered Him to be condemned to death, and have crucified Him. But we were hoping that it was He Who would redeem Israel: and beside all this, today is the third day since these things were done. Yea, and certain women also of our company made us astonished: they were early at the tomb; and when they found not His body, they came, saying, that they had also seen a vision of angels, who said that He was alive. And certain of them who were with us went to the tomb, and found it even so as the women had said: but Him they saw not. Some say that the other of these two walking to Emmaus was Luke himself, which is why the Evangelist did not give his name. *They were talking together of all these things which had happened,* not like men who believed, but instead like men who were bewildered and astounded by extraordinary events, unable to accept easily what was beyond belief. And *Jesus Himself drew near, and went with them.* The distance between places did not hinder Him from being with whomever He wanted, because He now had a spiritual and more divine body. For this same reason, they were not allowed to recognize Him by the features of the body in which the Saviour then appeared to them. For, as Mark says, He appeared unto two of them *in another form,*[6] and with different features. He no longer conformed the actions of His body to natural laws, but instead acted in the body in a spiritual manner that was beyond nature. This is why their eyes were prevented from recognizing Him. Why did He appear to them in another form, and why were their eyes prevented from recognizing Him? That they might reveal all of their doubting thoughts, and thus exposing the wound, be shown the medicine; that after they had been absorbed for

---

[6] Mk. 16:12

many hours in deep discussion, Christ's revealing of Himself would be rendered all the more sweet; that He might first teach them from Moses and the prophets and only then be recognized; and that they might believe all the more surely that His body is no longer a body that is clearly visible to everyone. Even though His resurrected body is the same body which suffered, He now appears only to those to whom He wills to reveal Himself. From this they gain something great—an end to doubt. Why does He no longer go about among all the people? His life after the Resurrection is different than before, no longer common everyday human life, but something divine. It is the prototype of the resurrection to come, in which we will live like angels and sons of God. For all these reasons, then, *their eyes were held that they should not know Him.* He was seen by those to whom He wished to be visible. Cleopas even reproaches their apparent fellow traveller. *Art thou only a stranger in Jerusalem?* he asks, meaning, "Are you the only inhabitant of Jerusalem who does not know what has happened?" Some have interpreted the words differently, so that his question is, "Do you live alone outside the confines of Jerusalem, taking no part in the affairs of the city, and thus do not know these things?" Do you see how little understanding they had of the Lord? They called Him *a prophet*, like Elijah, or Joshua of Nun, or Moses, *mighty in deed and word.* The deed is first, and then the word. For no word of teaching is sure and sound if the teacher has not first shown himself to be a doer of that word. First be strong in deed, and then strive to possess the word. In this way God Himself will work with you. First comes action, and then vision of the divine and enlightenment. If you do not cleanse the mirror with toil and labor, how will you see in the mirror the desired beauty? *Blessed are the pure in heart*—this comes through labor and deeds, *for they shall see God*—this is the goal and completion of vision of the divine. It is necessary to be *mighty in deed and word* first of all *before God,* and then before *all the people.* You must first please God, and then strive to be blameless before men, as far as that is possible. You must not give first consideration to pleasing man, but, rather, to revering God. You would be wrong to set out to conduct your life in such a manner as to be a stumbling block to others, but take thought about this only after you have fulfilled your duty to God. Solomon the Wise likewise instructs us to take thought about what is good first in the sight of God, and then of men.[7] Paul also says the same.[8] *But we were hoping that it was He Who would redeem Israel.* As ones whose hopes had been dashed they say, ''We hoped that He would have saved others; but, look, He did not even save Himself.'' They were so lacking in courage and faith that they, in effect, spoke the same words as did the malefactors on the cross: *He saved others; Himself He cannot save.*[9] This is why the Lord calls them *fools and slow in heart to believe.* What does this mean, to *redeem Israel?* We have said in various places that the people expected, incorrectly, that Christ would be their savior and redeemer from the temporal afflictions that beset them, and from the yoke of slavery to the Romans. And they hoped that He would rule as king over an earthly kingdom. This is why they say here, ''*We were hoping that He would redeem Israel from the Gentile Romans, yet He did not even escape from their unjust sentence against Him.*'' *And beside all this, today is the third day since these things were done. Yea, and certain women also of our company made us astonished.* They say these things as if perplexed. Yet it seems to me that they are men torn between faith and disbelief, not certain of either one. When they say, *We were hoping that it was He Who would redeem Israel,* they show their disbelief. But when they say, *Today is the third day,* they speak like men who are on the edge of recalling Christ's words to them, *On the third day I will rise again.*[10] And when they say that *the women astonished us,* this indicates that their disbelief has been shaken. Carefully examining their words, we see that they are full of human indecision and doubt; they are the words of men bewildered and confused by the miracle of the Resurrection. *And certain of them who were with us went to the tomb,* regardless whether Luke mentions just Peter, or Peter and John, as the Evangelist John says.[11] From this it is clear that what one Evangelist speaks of at greater length, another relates more briefly and in passing. So it is here, concerning the arrival of Peter and John at the tomb, that John describes it in greater detail, while Luke mentions it in a few words, even passing

---

[7] See Proverbs 3:4.

[8] Romans 12:17

[9] See Mt. 27:41-44.

[10] See Mt. 20:19.

[11] Jn. 20:3-10

over their names.

25-35. Then He said unto them, O fools, and slow of heart to believe all that the prophets have spoken: ought not the Christ to have suffered these things, and to enter into His glory? And beginning at Moses and all the prophets, He expounded unto them in all the Scriptures the things concerning Himself. And they drew nigh unto the village, whither they went: and He made as though He would have gone further. But they constrained Him, saying, Abide with us: for it is toward evening, and the day is far spent. And He went in to tarry with them. And it came to pass, as He sat at table with them, He took bread, and blessed it, and brake, and gave to them. And their eyes were opened, and they knew Him; and He vanished out of their sight. And they said one to another, Did not our heart burn within us, while He talked with us by the way, and while He opened to us the Scriptures? And they rose up the same hour, and returned to Jerusalem, and found the eleven gathered together, and them that were with them, saying, The Lord is risen indeed, and hath appeared to Simon. And they told what things were done on the way, and how He was known by them in the breaking of bread. Because they limited themselves to human thoughts and suffered from the sickness of great doubt, the Lord calls them foolish and slow to believe all that the prophets had spoken. Indeed it may happen that a man believes only in part, and not in full. For example, if a man hopes that the Christ will come for the salvation of the people, that is, for the restoration and deliverance of the Jewish nation, as opposed to the salvation of souls, such a man believes, but not as much as he should. And again, a man might believe David who says, *They have pierced My hands and My feet*,[12] and the other things which he prophesies in the person of the Lord concerning the Cross and the events on the Cross. But while accepting the prophesies concerning the Cross, he may not believe those concerning the Resurrection, such as, *Nor wilt Thou suffer Thy Holy One to see corruption*, and, *Thou wilt not abandon my soul in hades*,[13]

---

[12] Ps. 21:16

[13] Ps. 15:10

and the prophesy describing Him as *free among the dead,*[14] and *leading forth them that were shackled...them that dwell in tombs,*[15] and so forth. Such a man does not have perfect faith, but only partial faith. We must believe everything the prophets foretold concerning the Lord, both the dishonor and the glory. It was necessary that Christ suffered—this was the dishonor—but also that He enter into glory. "You are indeed foolish, for you have heard Isaiah speaking of both things, that the Lord would not only be led to the slaughter,[16] but also would be shown light.[17] The first you accept, but the second you ignore. You believe that He was bruised, but you do not consider that God is pleased to cleanse Him of His wounds. But since you are *fools,*" He says, meaning, slow-witted, because if they had been truly mindless, He would not have spoken to them, "therefore, since you are slow-witted, I will lift up your minds and make you to think more keenly." This is why He expounded to them from Moses and all the prophets, including of course the mystery of the sacrifice of Abraham, when Isaac was spared and the ram was slain. For these things prefigured Christ, as the Lord Himself explains when He says, *Your father Abraham rejoiced to see My day: and he saw and was glad.*[18] The prophecy, *thy life shall be hanging before thy eyes,*[19] also indicates the Crucifixion, when it mentions hanging, and the Resurrection, which it calls *life.* Scattered throughout the other prophetic writings, especially in the most renowned, are texts foretelling the Cross and the Resurrection and you may read them all there. You, O reader, consider how entering into glory comes by means of suffering. *He made as if He would have gone further,* just as any man might do. But then *their eyes were opened, and they knew Him,* when He, as God, permitted it. Something else is implied as well, that for those who commune of that Bread Which is truly blessed, their eyes are opened to know the Lord. For the flesh of the Lord contains a great and inexpressible power. *He vanished out of their sight,* because it was no longer fit that He, in His

---

[14] Ps. 87:4

[15] Ps. 67:7

[16] Is. 53:7

[17] See Is. 53.11.

[18] Jn. 8:56

[19] Deut. 28:66

resurrected and spiritual body, should spend much time with them in the body, as He had before. He also vanished so as to increase their fervor for Him, and indeed the Evangelist says that they were so joyful that *they rose up the same hour, and returned to Jerusalem.* They did not return to Jerusalem in *that same hour,* but instead it says that they *rose up* that same hour, and they returned to Jerusalem after as many hours as were necessary for them to walk the distance of sixty furlongs. It was during this time that the Lord also appeared to Simon. Their hearts burned within them with the fire of the Lord's words, meaning, that as He spoke to them, the conviction burned within them that what He said was true. It may also mean that as He expounded the Scriptures to them, their hearts beat with excitement as the thought formed within them, ''It is the Lord Who is teaching us.''

36-44. And as they thus spake, Jesus Himself stood in the midst of them, and saith unto them, Peace be unto you. But they were terrified and affrighted, and supposed that they had seen a spirit. And He said unto them, Why are ye troubled? And why do thoughts arise in your hearts? Behold My hands and My feet, that it is I Myself: handle Me, and see; for a spirit hath not flesh and bones, as ye see Me have. And when He had thus spoken, He showed them His hands and His feet. And while for joy they did not yet believe, and marvelled, He said unto them, Have ye here any thing to eat? And they gave Him a piece of a broiled fish, and of a honeycomb. And He took it, and did eat before them. And He said unto them, These are the words which I spake unto you, while I was yet with you, that all things must be fulfilled, which were written in the law of Moses, and in the prophets, and in the Psalms, concerning Me. The Lord, Who orders all things for our salvation, stands in the midst of His disciples, wanting to convince them of the Resurrection. First He calms their fear by the customary greeting of peace, and at the same time shows that it is He Himself, their own Teacher, Who greets them with the very same greeting with which He armed them when He sent them out to preach.[20] But because the fear within their souls was not calmed by His words, He demonstrates to them in another way that He is the Son of God, Who

---

[20] See Mt. 10:12-13.

knows the hearts of men. He says, *Why do thoughts arise in your hearts?* Most assuredly, God alone knows the heart. Then He offers additional confirmation by inviting them to touch His hands and feet. "You think that I am a spirit, that is, a phantasm, like those apparitions of the dead which often appear near the tombs. But you know that a spirit does not have flesh and bones: I have both flesh and bones, although they are more divine and spiritual." The body of the Lord is not a spirit, but it is spiritual, that is, it has no part in any coarseness, and is governed by the spirit. For the body which we have now is animate [*psychikon*], governed by the soul and made alive by natural and animate attributes and faculties. But the body after the resurrection Paul calls spiritual,[21] that is, made alive and governed by the divine spirit, and not by the soul, transformed in an ineffable and spiritual manner into incorruption and preserved incorruptible. This is how we must understand the body of the Lord after the Resurrection: it is spiritual, refined, a stranger to all coarseness. It needs nothing, not even food, although the Lord did eat to confirm the disciples' belief. He ate, not because His resurrected body by its nature needed food, but by economy, to show that His risen body was the same which suffered on the Cross. For this is the nature of the Lord's body now: to enter where the doors are shut and to pass effortlessly from one location to another. Because the disciples still did not believe and had not been convinced even by touching His hands and feet, He offers yet another proof, that of eating. But what He eats is consumed by some divine power, for all that is eaten in a natural manner passes from the mouth to the drain. But what the Lord eats here is not according to nature, as we have said, but by economy. And the very foods which He ate also convey a hidden meaning. By eating a piece of a broiled fish, He indicates that He has consumed with the fire of His divinity our human nature which had been swimming in the salty sea of this life, and He has scorched away all the damp slime our nature had taken on as it sank into the depths and was battered by the waves. Thus He made our nature food fit for God, fashioning that which before was defiled into sweet food of which God can commune. For this is suggested by the honeycomb: the sweetness, now, of our nature which before had been rejected. Another

---

[21] See I Cor. 15:44-46. English translations usually render *sōma psychikon* as *physical* or *natural body*. For the distinction between *psychē, soul* or *animating force,* and *pneuma, spirit,* see above on pp. 21, footnote 30.

meaning is suggested by the broiled fish, namely, active virtue which, aided by the coals of the asceticism of the desert and of the hesychast life, removes everything that is moist and fat. And the honeycomb suggests knowledge and divine vision, for the words of God are sweet. There is also another kind of comb, one full of wasps, which leave no honey. This signifies the wisdom of the pagan Greeks. But the honeycomb suggests the sweetness of divine wisdom[, left by Christ]. For Christ is like the bee, which is small in size (for the Word is concise and weak in worldly power—neither did Paul preach with the power of words, *lest the Cross of Christ be made of none effect.*[22]) Yet it is beloved by both kings and commoners, who apply the product of its toils for their health and healing.

45-53. Then opened He their understanding, that they might understand the Scriptures, and said unto them, Thus it is written, and it behoved Christ thus to suffer, and to rise from the dead the third day: and that repentance and remission of sins should be preached in His name among all nations, beginning at Jerusalem. And ye are witnesses of these things. And, behold, I send the promise of My Father upon you: but tarry ye in the city of Jerusalem, until ye have put on power from on high. And He led them out as far as to Bethany, and He lifted up His hands, and blessed them. And it came to pass, while He blessed them, He was parted from them, and carried up into heaven. And they worshipped Him, and returned to Jerusalem with great joy: and were continually in the temple, praising and blessing God. Amen. When He had given them peace and calmed their hearts, and confirmed the true resurrection of His body by the words which He spoke, by His hands and His feet which they touched, and by the food which He ate, then He opened their minds to understand the Scriptures. If their souls had not been still, they could not have understood; how could they come to know while they were still agitated and disquieted? For it is written, *Be still and know that I am God.*[23] Therefore He also teaches them that it was necessary for Christ *thus to suffer. Thus*—in what way? By the wood of the Cross. Because

---

[22] See I Cor. 1:17-18.

[23] Ps. 45:10

death had come through a tree, it was necessary that corruption also be destroyed through a tree. By the pain which He endured unconquered on the tree, the Lord brought to an end that pleasure which came through a tree. Likewise it was necessary that Christ *rise on the third day: and that repentance and remission of sins should be preached in His name among all nations.* Here the Lord is speaking of baptism. For in baptism repentance comes through confession and turning away from one's former wickedness and impiety. Then follows the remission of sins. How shall we understand baptism to take place in Christ's name only, when elsewhere we are taught that it is performed in the name of the Father, and of the Son, and of the Holy Spirit?[24] We answer, first of all, that when we say that baptism takes place in Christ's name, we do not mean that baptism should be performed only in Christ's name, but that the baptism of Christ, in which Christ was baptized, is spiritual, not a ritual Judaic washing. Nor is it like the baptism of John, which was for repentance only. Instead, the baptism of Christ bestows the communion of the Holy Spirit and the remission of sins, which He Himself showed when He was baptized in the Jordan for our sakes, thus allowing the Holy Spirit to be revealed in the form of a dove. Furthermore, baptism in the name of Christ means baptism in the death of Christ. For just as He died and on the third day arose, so too are we buried in the water as a type of His death, and then raised up from death incorruptible in soul and given the earnest of the incorruptibility of the body.[25] Moreover, the name *Christ* Itself indicates the Father Who chrismates, the Spirit Which is the Chrism, and the Son Who is chrismated. Likewise it is said, ''The remission of sins is in the name of the Lord.''[26] Where are the polluted tongues of those who baptize in the name of Montanus, Priscilla, and Maximilla?[27] Truly there is no remission for those who are baptized in such a manner, but only an increase of sins; for those three have perished evilly. But unto all the nations has the Word gone forth, beginning in

---

[24] Mt. 28:19

[25] See Eph. 1:13-14 and II Cor. 1:21-22.

[26] See Acts 13:38.

[27] Montanus, a prophet, and the prophetesses Priscilla and Maximilla, were the founders of a schismatic and heretical sect known as Montanists which began in Asia Minor in the second half of the second century. They prophesied when seized by an uncontrollable frenzy, and spoke in the first person as being the Father, the Son, or the Holy Spirit.

Jerusalem. For it was necessary, once Christ had united and taken to Himself all of human nature, that it no longer be divided into two parts, Jew and Gentile, but, beginning in Jerusalem, the Word rested even upon the Gentiles, making one the entire human nature. *"And ye,"* He says, *"are witnesses* of the Passion and of the Resurrection." But then the Lord anticipates the disciples' fear and agitation as they reason among themselves, "How shall we, ordinary, simple people, be sent out to bear witness to the nations, when we first must elude the men of Jerusalem who put even You to death?" Lest they have such thoughts, He says to them, "Take courage; very soon I will send upon you the promise of My Father which I spoke through the prophet Joel, that *I will pour out My Spirit upon all flesh.*[28] Sit down,[29] you who are now timid and cowardly, and stay where you are, until you have put on the power that comes not from man, but from heaven." He did not say, "until ye have received," but *"until ye have put on,"* indicating the complete protection of spiritual armor.[30] *He led them out as far as to Bethany.* We should understand that this occurred on the fortieth day after the Resurrection. You, O reader, should understand that the events which the Evangelists describe in brief actually took place over many days. Luke himself says in the Book of Acts that Jesus was *seen by them for forty days,*[31] for He appeared and vanished many times. *He blessed* the disciples, placing in them a protecting power until the coming of the Holy Spirit and at the same time teaching us, when we depart on a journey, to leave a blessing with those who are in our care, in order to protect them. He was *carried up into heaven.* It is written of Elijah that he *was carried up as it were into heaven.*[32] For Elijah only seemed as if he were carried up into heaven. But the Saviour ascended into heaven itself as the Forerunner of all men, to appear before the face of God together with His holy Flesh, and to reveal His Flesh co-enthroned with the Father. And now our nature

---

[28] Joel 2:28

[29] The Greek word *kathizō*, rendered as *tarry* in the KJV, is the simple word meaning *to sit.*

[30] The same verb *endynō* occurring here in verse 49 and rendered in the KJV "be endued with," also occurs in Ephesians 6:11 where it is translated in the KJV *"put on* the whole armour of God." In both places the verb is in the aorist tense and middle voice.

[31] Acts 1:3

[32] IV Kings (2 Kings) 2:11

in Christ is worshipped by the whole angelic host. *And they returned to Jerusalem with great joy, and were continually in the temple.* Do you see their virtue? Though the Holy Spirit has not yet come, they already are living spiritually. The same disciples who before cowered behind shut doors now go about boldly in the presence of the high priests. There is nothing worldly in them; but disdaining everything they praise God continually in the temple and bless Him. May we too become imitators of them, remaining continually in a holy life, and using this life to praise and bless God. A holy and virtuous life is the glory and blessing of God, for unto Him is due all glory unto the ages. Amen.

THE END OF THE EXPLANATION BY THEOPHYLACT OF THE HOLY GOSPEL ACCORDING TO SAINT LUKE.